Functional Programming Simplified

(Scala edition)

Alvin Alexander

*A simple, step-by-step approach
to learning functional programming*

Copyright

Functional Programming, Simplified (Scala edition)

Copyright 2017 Alvin J. Alexander[1]

All rights reserved. No part of this book may be reproduced without prior written permission from the author.

This book is presented solely for educational purposes. While best efforts have been made in its preparations, the author makes no representations or warranties of any kind and assumes no liabilities of any kind with respect to the accuracy or completeness of the contents, and specifically disclaims any implied warranties of merchantability or fitness of use for a particular purpose. The author shall not be held liable or responsible to any person or entity with respect to any loss or incidental or consequential damages caused, or alleged to have been caused, directly or indirectly, by the information or programs contained herein. Any use of this information is at your own risk.

December 7, 2017: First release
May 5, 2019: Second release (improved the text formatting of the book)

---

[1] https://alvinalexander.com

Contents

1	Introduction (or, Why I Wrote This Book)	1
2	Who This Book is For	5
3	Goals, Part 1: "Soft" Goals of This Book	9
4	Goals, Part 2: Concrete Goals	13
5	Goals, Part 3: A Disclaimer	15
6	Question Everything	17
7	Rules for Programming in this Book	23
8	One Rule for Reading this Book	27
9	What is "Functional Programming"?	29
10	What is This Lambda You Speak Of?	39
11	The Benefits of Functional Programming	43
12	Disadvantages of Functional Programming	59
13	The "Great FP Terminology Barrier"	75
14	Pure Functions	81
15	Benefits of Pure Functions	89
16	Pure Functions and I/O	97
17	Pure Function Signatures Tell All	101
18	Functional Programming as Algebra	107

CONTENTS

19	A Note About Expression-Oriented Programming	119
20	Functional Programming is Like Unix Pipelines	123
21	Functions Are Variables, Too	137
22	Using Methods As If They Were Functions	151
23	How to Write Functions That Take Functions as Input Parameters	161
24	How to Write a 'map' Function	179
25	How to Use By-Name Parameters	185
26	Functions Can Have Multiple Parameter Groups	197
27	Partially-Applied Functions (and Currying)	211
28	Recursion: Introduction	223
29	Recursion: Motivation	225
30	Recursion: Let's Look at Lists	229
31	Recursion: How to Write a 'sum' Function	235
32	Recursion: How Recursive Function Calls Work	241
33	Visualizing the Recursive sum Function	245
34	Recursion: A Conversation Between Two Developers	253
35	Recursion: Thinking Recursively	255
36	JVM Stacks and Stack Frames	261
37	A Visual Look at Stacks and Frames	269
38	Tail-Recursive Algorithms	275
39	A First Look at "State"	283
40	A Functional Game (With a Little Bit of State)	287

CONTENTS

41	A Quick Review of Case Classes	301
42	Update as You Copy, Don't Mutate	305
43	A Quick Review of for-Expressions	315
44	How to Write a Class That Can Be Used in a for-Expression	323
45	Creating a Sequence Class to be Used in a for Comprehension	325
46	Making Sequence Work In a Simple for Loop	331
47	How To Make Sequence Work as a Single Generator in a for Expression	335
48	Enabling Filtering in a for Expression	339
49	How to Enable the Use of Multiple Generators in a for Expression	345
50	A Summary of the for Expression Lessons	355
51	Pure Functions Tell No Lies	357
52	Functional Error Handling (Option, Try, Or, and Either)	363
53	Embrace The Idioms!	373
54	What to Think When You See That Opening Curly Brace	377
55	A Quick Review of How `flatMap` Works	391
56	Option Naturally Leads to `flatMap`	397
57	`flatMap` Naturally Leads to `for`	401
58	`for` Expressions are Better Than `getOrElse`	403
59	Recap: Option → flatMap → for	407
60	A Note About Things That Can Be Mapped Over	415
61	Starting to Glue Functions Together	417
62	The "Bind" Concept	421

CONTENTS

63	Getting Close to Using bind in for Expressions	427
64	Using a Wrapper Class in a for Expression	429
65	Making Wrapper More Generic	437
66	Changing "new Wrapper" to "Wrapper"	439
67	A Quick Note About Case Classes and Companion Objects	445
68	Using bind in a for Expression	447
69	How Debuggable, f, g, and h Work	459
70	A Generic Version of Debuggable	471
71	One Last Debuggable: Using List Instead of String	475
72	Key Points About Monads	481
73	Signpost: Where We're Going Next	483
74	Introduction: The IO Monad	485
75	How to Use an IO Monad	487
76	Assigning a for Expression to a Function	491
77	The IO Monad and a for Expression That Uses Recursion	493
78	Diving Deeper Into the IO Monad	495
79	I'll Come Back to the IO Monad	501
80	Functional Composition	503
81	An Introduction to Handling State	507
82	Handling State Manually	509
83	Getting State Working in a for Expression	515
84	Handling My Golfing State with a State Monad	517

CONTENTS

85	The State Monad Source Code	523
86	Signpost: Getting IO and State Working Together	527
87	Trying to Write a for Expression with IO and State	529
88	Seeing the Problem: Trying to Use State and IO Together	531
89	Solving the Problem with Monad Transformers	533
90	Beginning the Process of Understanding StateT	535
91	Getting Started: We're Going to Need a Monad Trait	539
92	Now We Can Create StateT	543
93	Using StateT in a for Expression	545
94	Trying to Combine IO and StateT in a for Expression	551
95	Fixing the IO Functions with Monadic Lifting	555
96	A First IO/StateT for-Expression	559
97	The Final IO/StateT for Expression	563
98	Summary of the StateT Lessons	567
99	Signpost: Modeling the world with Scala/FP	569
100	What is a Domain Model?	571
101	A Review of OOP Data Modeling	573
102	Modeling the "Data" Portion of the Pizza POS System with Scala/FP	581
103	First Attempts to Organize Pure Functions	585
104	Implementing FP Behavior with Modules	591
105	Implementing the Pizza POS System Using a Modular Approach	599
106	The "Functional Objects" Approach	617

107 Demonstrating the "Functional Objects" Approach	621
108 Summary of the Domain Modeling Approaches	627
109 The Problem with the IO Monad	629
110 Lenses, to Simplify "Update as You Copy"	635
111 Signpost: Concurrency	639
112 Concurrency and Mutability Don't Mix	641
113 Scala Concurrency Tools	649
114 Akka Actors	653
115 Akka Actor Examples	659
116 Scala Futures	669
117 A Second Futures Example	677
118 Key Points About Scala Futures	689
119 A Few Notes About Real World Functional Programming	691
120 Signpost: Wrapping Things Up	699
121 The Learning Path	701
122 Final Summary	703
123 Where To Go From Here	709

1

Introduction
(or, Why I Wrote This Book)

"So why do I write, torturing myself to put it down?
Because in spite of myself I've learned some things."

— Ralph Ellison

The short version of "Why I wrote this book" is that I found that trying to learn functional programming in Scala to be really hard, and I want to try to improve that situation.

The longer answer goes like this …

My programming background

My degree is in aerospace engineering, so the only programming class I took in college was a FORTRAN class I was forced to take. After college I was one of the youngest people at the aerospace company I worked at, which meant that I'd have to maintain the software applications our group used. As a result, I became interested in programming, after which I quickly became interested in (a) "How can I write code faster?", and then (b) "How can I write maintainable code?"

After that I taught myself how to program in C by reading the classic book, The C Programming Language[1] by Kernighan and Ritchie, quickly followed by learning Object-Oriented Programming (OOP) with C++ and Java. That was followed by investigating other programming languages, including Perl, PHP, Ruby, Python, and more.

Despite having exposure to all of these languages, I didn't know anything about Functional Programming (FP) until I came across Google's Guava project[2], which includes FP libraries

---
[1] http://amzn.to/2aeEAZa
[2] https://github.com/google/guava/wiki

1

for Java collections. Then, when I learned Scala[3] and came to understand the methods in the Scala collections' classes, I saw that immutable values and pure functions had some really nice benefits, so I set out to learn more about this thing called *Functional Programming*.

Trying to learn FP with Scala

As I tried to learn about FP in Scala, I found that there weren't any FP books or blogs that I liked — certainly nothing that catered to my "I've never heard of FP until recently" background. Everything I read was either (a) dry and theoretical, or (b) quickly jumped into topics I couldn't understand. It seemed like people enjoyed writing words "monad" and "functor" and then watching me break out in a cold sweat.

As I googled "scala fp" like a madman, I found a few useful blog posts here and there about functional programming in Scala — what I'll call "Scala/FP" in this book — but those were too disconnected. One article covered Topic A, another covered Topic Z, and they were written by different authors with different experiences, so it was hard to find my way from A to Z. Besides being disjointed, they were often incomplete, or maybe they just assumed that I had some piece of knowledge that I didn't really have.

Another stumbling block is that experienced FP developers use generic types *a lot*. Conversely, I only rarely used generics. They also use the word "easy" when describing their code, as though saying "easy" is some sort of Jedi mind trick. For instance, this code — which I'll break down as you go through this book — was introduced with the text, "it's very easy to access and modify state":

```
def updateHealth(delta: Int): Game[Int] =
    StateT[IO, GameState, Int] { (s: GameState) =>

    val newHealth = s.player.health + delta
    IO((s.copy(player = s.player.copy(health = newHealth)), newHealth))

}
```

I don't know about you, but the first time I saw that code, the word *easy* is not what came to mind. What came to my mind were things like, "PHP is easy. Using setter methods to modify state is easy. Whatever that is ... that's not easy."

Another problem with almost all of the Scala/FP resources is that they don't discuss functional

---

[3] http://scala-lang.org/

input/output (I/O), or how to work with user interfaces. In this book I don't shy away from those topics: I write what I know about both of them.

Learning Haskell to learn FP

In the end, the only way I could learn FP was to buy four Haskell[4] books, take a few weeks off from my regular work, and teach myself Haskell. Because Haskell is a "pure" FP language — and because most experienced Scala/FP developers spoke glowingly about Haskell — I assumed that by learning Haskell I could learn FP.

That turned out to be true. In Haskell the only way you can write code is by using FP concepts, so you can't bail out and take shortcuts when things get difficult. Because everything in Haskell is immutable, I was forced to learn about topics like recursion that I had avoided for most of my programming life. In the *beginning* this made things more difficult, but in the *end* I learned about the benefits of the new approaches I was forced to learn.

Once I understood Haskell, I went back to the Scala resources that I didn't like before and suddenly they made sense(!). But again, this only happened *after I took the time to learn Haskell*, a language I didn't plan on using in my work.

The purpose of this book

Therefore, my reasons for writing this book are:

- To save you the time of having to try to understand many different, unorganized, inconsistent Scala/FP blog posts
- To save you the time of "having to learn Haskell to learn FP" (and then having to translate that Haskell knowledge back to Scala)
- To try to make learning Scala/FP as simple as possible

> Don't get my statements about Haskell wrong: In the end, Haskell turned out to be a really interesting and even fun programming language. If I knew more about its libraries, or if it ran on the JVM and I could use the wealth of existing JVM libraries out there, I'd be interested in trying to use it.

---

[4]https://www.haskell.org

As a potential benefit of this book, if you already know Scala/OOP and are interested in learning Haskell, you can learn Scala/FP from this book, and then you'll find it much easier to understand Haskell.

2
Who This Book is For

> *"I never teach my pupils. I only attempt to provide the conditions in which they can learn."*
>
> — Albert Einstein

I kept several audiences in mind as I wrote this book:

1. Developers who want a simple introduction to functional programming in Scala
2. Developers who are interested in writing "better" code
3. Parallel/concurrent application developers
4. "Big data" application developers
5. (Possibly) Upperclass college students

Here's a quick look at why I say that I wrote this book for these people.

1) Developers who want a simple introduction to FP

First, because this book started as a series of small notes I made for myself as I learned Scala/FP, it's safe to say that I wrote it for someone like me who has worked with OOP in Java, but has only a limited FP background. Specifically, this is someone who became interested in Scala because of its clean, modern syntax, and now wants a "simple but thorough" introduction to functional programming in Scala.

Because I've also written programs in C, C++, Perl, Python, Ruby, and a few other programming languages, it's safe to say that this book is written with these programmers in mind as well.

2) Those interested in writing "better" code

At specific points in this book — such as (a) when writing about pure functions, (b) using `val` and not `var`, and (c) avoiding the use of `null` values — I also wrote this book for any developer that wants to write better code, where I define "better" as safer, easier to test, and more error-free. Even if you decide not to write 100% pure FP code, many FP techniques in this book show how you can make your functions safer from bugs.

As a personal note, an ongoing theme in my programming life is that I want to be able to write applications faster, without sacrificing quality and maintainability. A selling point of FP is that it enables you to write safe functions — *pure* functions that rely only on their inputs to produce their outputs — that you can combine together to safely create larger applications.

3) Parallel/concurrent developers

> Quiz: How many cores are in your smartphone? (This question is a tip of the cap to Derek Wyatt, who wrote about CPU cores and smartphones in his book, *Akka Concurrency*).

In addition to writing safer code, the "killer app" for FP since about 2005 is that CPUs aren't constantly doubling in speed any more. (See Herb Sutter's 2005 article, The Free Lunch is Over[1].) Because of this, CPU designers are adding more cores to CPUs to get more overall CPU cycles/second. Therefore, if you want your apps to run as fast as possible, it will help to use *concurrent programming* techniques to put all of those cores to use, and the best way we know how to do that today is to use FP.

Two of my favorite ways of writing parallel/concurrent applications involve using Scala futures and the Akka[2] messaging/actors framework. Not surprisingly, FP works extremely well with both of these approaches.

4) "Big data" app developers

More recently, Dean Wampler gave a presentation titled, "Copious Data: The 'Killer App' for Functional Programming"[3]. My experience with Big Data applications is limited to processing large Apache access log records with Spark[4], but I can confirm that the code I wrote was a lot like algebra, where I passed data into pure functions and then used only the results from those functions. My code had no dependence on "side effects," such as using mutable variables or managing state.

---

[1] http://www.gotw.ca/publications/concurrency-ddj.htm
[2] http://akka.io/
[3] https://www.infoq.com/presentations/big-data-functional-programming
[4] http://alvinalexander.com/scala/analyzing-apache-access-logs-files-spark-scala

5) Upperclass college students

As I wrote in the Scala Cookbook[5], because of its "power user" features, I don't think Scala is a good first language for a programmer to learn, and as a result of that, a book about Scala/FP is also not a good first programming book to read.

That being said, I hope this will be a good first FP book to read *after* a college student has experience with languages like C, Java, and Scala.

Caution: Not for FP experts

Finally, as a result of the people I *have* written this book for, it should come as no surprise that this book is *not* written for FP experts and theorists. I offer no new theory in this book; I just try to explain functional programming using the Scala programming language in the simplest way I can.

---

[5]http://amzn.to/24ivK4G

Goals, Part 1: "Soft" Goals of This Book

"One learns by doing the thing."

— Sophocles

Going through the thought process of "Why do I want to write a book about Scala/FP?" led me to develop my goals for this book. They are:

1. To introduce functional programming in Scala in a simple but thorough way, as though you and I are having a conversation.
2. To present the solutions in a systematic way. I want to introduce the material in the order in which I think you'll run into problems as you learn Scala/FP. In this way I can break down complex code into smaller pieces so you can see how the larger solution is built from the smaller pieces.
3. To discuss the motivation and benefits of FP features. For me it wasn't always clear *why* certain things in FP are better, so I'll keep coming back to these two points.
4. I want to save you the time and effort of having to learn Haskell (or some other language) in order to learn FP.
5. I want to help you learn to "Think in FP." (More on this shortly.)

In general, I want to help you start writing FP code without having to learn a lot of mathematics, background theory, and technical jargon like that shown in Figure 3.1.

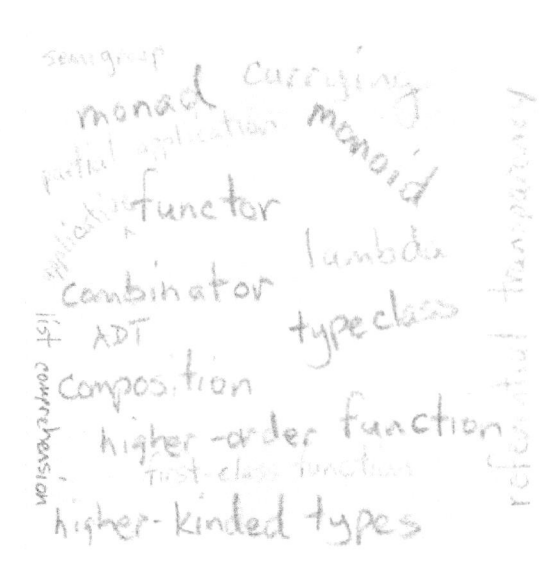

Figure 3.1: Examples of the "FP terminology barrier."

I refer to this as the "FP Terminology Barrier," and I'll discuss it more in an upcoming lesson.

A word of caution: "The Learning Cliff"

When I took a thermodynamics class in college, I learned the quote I shared at the beginning of this chapter:

> "One learns by doing the thing."

For me, this is a reminder that sometimes the only way you can learn something is to work on it with your hands. Until that first thermodynamics class I never really had to *do the thing* — work all of the exercises — to learn the material, but in that class I found out the hard way that there are times when I really have to dig in and "do the thing to learn the thing."

Aside: Working hard to learn something new

If you've read the book, Einstein: His Life and Universe[1], by Walter Isaacson, you know that Albert Einstein had to essentially go back to school and learn a *lot* of math so he could turn the Theory of Special Relativity into the Theory of General Relativity.

He published the "Einstein field equations" (shown in Figure 3.2) in 1915, and there's no way that Einstein could have developed these equations without buckling down and taking the time to learn the necessary math. (Lesson: Even one of the smartest people in the history of Earth had to work hard to learn something new, with a huge payoff in the end.)

$$R_{\mu\nu} - \tfrac{1}{2} R\, g_{\mu\nu} + \Lambda g_{\mu\nu} = \frac{8\pi G}{c^4} T_{\mu\nu}$$

Figure 3.2: The Einstein field equations

More on Point #7: "Thinking in FP"

In this book I hope to change the way you think about programming problems. As at least one functional developer has said, when you "Think in FP," you see an application as (a) data flowing into the application, (b) being transformed by a series of transformer functions, and (c) producing an output.

The first lessons in this book are aimed at helping you to "Think in FP" — to see your applications in this way, as a series of data flows and transformers.

Another important part of "Thinking in FP" is that you'll find that FP *function signatures* are very important — much more important than they are in OOP code. I cover this in depth in the lesson, "Pure Function Signatures Tell All."

---

[1] http://amzn.to/2a2DmAp

Summary

In summary, my goals for this book are:

1. To introduce functional programming in Scala in a simple, thorough way.
2. To present the solutions in a systematic way.
3. To discuss the motivation and benefits of FP features.
4. To save you the time and effort of having to learn another programming language in order to understand Scala/FP.
5. In general, to help you "Think in FP."

An important part of the learning process is having a "Question Everything" spirit, and I'll cover that next.

4

Goals, Part 2: Concrete Goals

After I released an early version of this book, I realized that I should state my goals for it more clearly; I don't want you to buy or read a book that doesn't match what you're looking for. More accurately, I don't want you to be disappointed in the book because your expectations are different than what I deliver. Therefore, I want to state some very clear and measurable goals by which you can judge whether or not you want to buy this book.

A first concrete goal is this: If you have a hard time understanding the book, Functional Programming in Scala[1], I want to provide the background material that can help make it easier to understand. That book is very good, but it's also a thin, densely-packed book, so if there are a few Scala features you don't know, you can get lost.

Second, the Introduction to Functional Game Programming[2] talk at the 2014 LambdaConf was a big influence on me. I remember going to that talk and thinking, "Wow, I thought I knew Scala and a little bit about functional programming, but I have no idea what this guy is talking about." Therefore, a second concrete goal is to make all of that talk and its associated code understandable to someone who has zero to little background in functional programming. The talk covers the IO, State, and StateT monads, and other FP features like *lenses*, so this is actually a pretty big goal.

A third, slightly-less concrete goal is that if you have no background in FP, I want to make Scala/FP libraries like Cats[3] and Scalaz[4] more understandable. That is, if you were to look at those libraries without any sort of FP background, I suspect you'd be as lost as I was at that 2014 LambdaConf talk. But if you read this book, I think you'll understand enough Scala/FP concepts that you'll be able to understand what those libraries are trying to achieve.

A fourth concrete goal is to provide you with all of the background knowledge you need — anonymous functions, type signatures, for expressions, classes that implement map and flatMap, etc. — so you can better understand the 128,000 *monad* tutorials that Google currently lists in their search results[5].

---

[1] http://amzn.to/2sbY1hE
[2] https://github.com/jdegoes/lambdaconf-2014-introgame
[3] https://github.com/typelevel/cats
[4] https://github.com/scalaz/scalaz
[5] https://www.google.com/search?q=monad+tutorial

5

Goals, Part 3: A Disclaimer

As a bit of a warning, I want to be clear that this book is *very different* than the Scala Cookbook[1]. The essence of the Cookbook is, "Here's a common problem, and here's a solution to that problem," i.e., a series of recipes.

This book is completely different.

The "reporter" metaphor

I liken this book to being a reporter who goes to a foreign country that very few people seem to know about. Out of curiosity about what he has read and seen, the intrepid reporter goes to this foreign land to learn more about it. Nobody knows how the story is going to end, but the reporter promises to report the truth as he sees and understands it.

On his journey through this new land the reporter jots down many notes, especially as he has a few "Aha!" moments when he grasps new concepts. Over time he tries to organize his notes so he can present them in a logical order, trying to translate what he has seen into English (and Scala) as simply and accurately as he can. In the end there's no promise that the reporter is going to *like* what he sees, but he promises to report everything as clearly as he can.

A reporter is not a salesman

To be clear, there's no promise of a happy ending in this story. The reporter isn't trying to sell you on moving to this new land. Instead of trying to *sell* you, the reporter aims to report what he sees as accurately as possible, hoping that — armed with this new knowledge — in the end you'll decide what's in your own best interests. Maybe you'll decide to move to this land, maybe you won't, but at least you'll be well-armed in making your decision.

---

[1] http://amzn.to/24ivK4G

A personal experience

As an example of how I think about this, many years ago I came close to moving to Santa Fe, New Mexico. As soon as I visited the town, I immediately fell in love with the plaza area, the food, and the architecture of the homes. But after thinking about the pros and cons more seriously, I decided not to move there. Instead, I decided to just vacation there from time to time, and also take home some nice souvenirs when I find them.

The same is true about this book: you may decide to move to this new land, or you may decide that you just like a few souvenirs. That choice is yours. My goal is to report what I find, as simply and accurately as I can.

6

Question Everything

"I have no special talent. I am only passionately curious."

— Albert Einstein

A Golden Rule of this book is to always ask, "*Why?*" By this I mean that you should question everything I present. Ask yourself, "Why is this FP approach better than what I do in my OOP code?" To help develop this spirit, let's take a little look at what FP is, and then see what questions you might have about it.

What is FP?

I'll describe FP more completely in the "What is Functional Programming?" lesson, but for the moment let's use the following definition of FP:

- FP applications consist of only immutable values and pure functions.
- *Pure function* means that (a) a function's output depends only on its input parameters, and (b) functions have no side effects, such as reading user input or writing output to a screen, disk, web service, etc.

While I'm intentionally keeping that definition short, it's a way that people commonly describe FP, essentially the FP elevator pitch[1].

What questions come to mind?

Given that description, what questions come to mind about FP?

Some of my first questions were:

---

[1] https://en.wikipedia.org/wiki/Elevator_pitch

- How can you possibly write an application without reading input or writing output?
- Regarding I/O:
    - How do I write database code?
    - How do I write RESTful code?
    - How do I write GUI code?
- If all variables are immutable, how do I handle changes in my code?
    - For instance, if I'm writing an order-entry system for a pizza store, what do I do when the customer wants to change their pizza crust or toppings in the middle of entering an order?

If you have a little more exposure to FP than I did, you might ask:

- Why is recursion better? Is it *really* better? Why can't I just use var fields inside my functions, as long as I don't share those vars outside the function scope?
- Is "Functional I/O" really better than "Traditional I/O"?

A little later you might ask:

- Are there certain applications where the FP approach is better? Or worse?

Decide for yourself what's better

Critical thinking is an important part of being a scientist or engineer, and I always encourage you to think that way:

> Is the approach I'm looking at better or worse than other options? If so, why?

When doing this I encourage you not to make any snap judgments. Just because you don't like something *initially* doesn't mean that thing is bad or wrong.

"The best idea wins"

With critical thinking you also need to tune out the people who yell the loudest. Just because they're loud, that doesn't mean they're right. Just focus on which ideas are the best.

In my book, A Survival Guide for New Consultants[2], I share this quote from famed physicist Richard Feynman[3]:

> "The best idea wins."

He wrote that in one of his books, where he shared an experience of how Neils Bohr would seek out a very young Feynman during the creation of the first atomic bomb. Bohr felt that the other scientists on the project were "Yes men" who would agree with anything he said, while Feynman was young, curious, and unintimidated. Because Feynman was only interested in learning and in trying to come up with the best solutions, he would tell Bohr exactly what he thought about each idea, and Bohr sought him out as a sounding board.

Feynman meant that you have to be able to have good, honest conversations with people about your ideas, and at the end of the day you have to put your ego aside, and the team should go forward with the best idea, no matter where it came from.

This goes back to my point: Don't blindly listen to people, especially the people who yell the loudest or those who can profit from selling you an idea. Put your critical thinking hat on, and make your own decisions.

A quick aside: Imperative programming

In the next sections I'll use the term "Imperative programming," so I first want to give you a definition of what it means.

With a few minor changes, Wikipedia offers this description[4]: "*Imperative programming* is a programming paradigm that uses statements that change a program's state. It consists of a series of commands for the computer to perform. It focuses on describing the details of *how* a program operates."

This Quora page[5] adds: "Imperative programming involves writing your program as a series of instructions (statements) that actively modify memory (variables, arrays). It focuses on 'how,' in the sense that you express the logic of your program based on how the computer would execute it."

If you've ever disassembled a JVM *.class* file with `javap -c` to see code like this:

---

[2] http://amzn.to/2aiZaOd
[3] http://www.feynman.com/
[4] https://en.wikipedia.org/wiki/Imperative_programming
[5] https://www.quora.com/What-is-the-difference-between-functional-and-imperative-programming

```
public void main(java.lang.String[]);
  Code:
      0: aload_0
      1: aload_1
      2: invokestatic   #60
      5: return
```

That's the extreme of what they're referring to: imperative programming at a very low level. This code tells the JVM *exactly* how it needs to solve the problem at hand.

A critical thinking exercise

To start putting your critical thinking skill to work, I'm going to show you two versions of the same algorithm. As you see the two algorithms, I want you to jot down any questions you have about the two.

First, here's an imperative version of a sum method:

```
def sum(ints: List[Int]): Int = {
    var sum = 0
    for (i <- ints) {
       sum += i
    }
    sum
}
```

This code modifies a var field within a for loop — a common pattern in imperative programming. Next, here's a Scala/FP version of that same method:

```
def sum(xs: List[Int]): Int = xs match {
    case Nil => 0
    case x :: tail => x + sum(tail)
}
```

Notice that this method uses a match expression, has no var fields, and it makes a recursive call to sum in the last line of the method body.

Given those two versions of the same algorithm, what questions come to your mind?

My questions

The questions you have will depend on your experience. If you're new to Scala/FP your first question might be, "How does that second method even work?" (Don't worry, I'll explain it more in the lessons on writing recursive functions.)

I remember that some of my first questions were:

- What's wrong with the imperative approach? Who cares if I use a `var` field in a `for` loop inside a function? How does that affect anything else?
- Will the recursive function blow the stack with large lists?
- Is one approach faster or slower than the other?
- Thinking in the long term, is one approach more maintainable than the other?
- What if I want to write a "parallel" version of a sum algorithm (to take advantage of multiple cores); is one approach better than the other?

That's the sort of thinking I want you to have when you're reading this book: Question everything. If you think something is better, be honest; *why* do you think it's better? If you think it's worse, why is it worse?

In the pragmatic world I live in, if you can't convince yourself that a feature is better than what you already know, the solution is simple: Don't use it.

As I learned FP, some of it was so different from what I was used to, I found that *questioning everything* was the only way I could come to accept it.

"We write what we want, not how to do it"

As another example of having a questioning attitude, early in my FP learning process I read quotes from experienced FP developers like this:

> "In FP we don't tell the computer *how* to do things, we just tell it *what* we want."

When I read this my first thought was pretty close to, "What does that mean? You talk to the computer?"

I couldn't figure out what they meant, so I kept questioning that statement. Were they being serious, or was this just some sort of FP koan, trying to get you interested in the topic with a mysterious statement? It felt like they were trying to sell me something, but I was open to trying to understand their point.

After digging into the subject, I finally decided that what they meant is that they don't write imperative code with `for` loops. That is, they don't write code like this:

```
def double(ints: List[Int]): List[Int] = {
    val buffer = new scala.collection.mutable.ListBuffer[Int]()
    for (i <- ints) {
        buffer += i * 2
    }
    buffer.toList
}

val newNumbers = double(oldNumbers)
```

Instead, they write code like this:

```
val newNumbers = oldNumbers.map(_ * 2)
```

With a `for` loop you tell the compiler the exact steps you want it to follow to create the new list, but with FP you say, "I don't care how `map` is implemented, I trust that it's implemented well, and what I want is a new list with the doubled value of every element in the original list."

In this example, questioning the "We write what we want" statement is a relatively minor point, but (a) I want to encourage a curious, questioning attitude, and (b) I know that you'll eventually see that statement somewhere, and I wanted to explain what it means.

> In his book Programming Erlang[a], Joe Armstrong notes that when he was first taught object-oriented programming (OOP), he felt that there was something wrong with it, but because everyone else was "Going OOP," he felt compelled to go with the crowd. Paraphrasing his words, if you're going to work as a professional programmer and put your heart and soul into your work, make sure you believe in the tools you use.
>
> [a] http://amzn.to/2aab4HF

What's next?

In the next lesson I'm going to provide a few programming *rules* that I'll follow in this book. While I'm generally not much of a "rules" person, I've found that in this case, having a few simple rules makes it easier to learning functional programming in Scala.

Rules for Programming in this Book

> *"Learn the rules like a pro, so you can break them like an artist."*
>
> — Pablo Picasso

Alright, that's enough of the "preface" material, let's get on with the book!

As I wrote earlier, I want to spare you the route I took of, "You Have to Learn Haskell to Learn Scala/FP," *but*, I need to say that I did learn a valuable lesson by taking that route:

> It's extremely helpful to completely forget about several pieces of the Scala programming language as you learn FP in Scala.

Assuming that you come from an "imperative" and OOP background as I did, your attempts to learn Scala/FP will be hindered because *it is* possible to write both imperative code and FP code in Scala. Because you *can* write in both styles, what happens is that when things in FP start to get difficult, it's easy for an OOP developer to turn back to what they already know.

To learn Scala/FP the best thing you can do is *forget* that the imperative options even exist. I promise you — Scout's Honor — this will accelerate your Scala/FP learning process.

The rules

To accelerate your Scala/FP learning process, this book uses the following programming "rules":

1. There will be no `null` values in this book. We'll intentionally forget that there is even a `null` keyword in Scala.
2. Only *pure functions* will be used in this book.
3. This book will only use immutable values (`val`) for all fields. There are no `var` fields in pure FP code, so I won't use them in this book, unless I'm trying to explain a point.

4. Whenever you use an `if`, you must always also use an `else`. Functional programming uses only *expressions*, not *statements*.
5. We won't create "classes" that encapsulate data and behavior. Instead we'll create data structures and write pure functions that operate on those data structures.

The rules are for your benefit (really)

These rules are inspired by what I learned from working with Haskell. In Haskell the only way you can *possibly* write code is by writing pure functions and using immutable values, and when those *really are your only choices*, your brain quits fighting the system. Instead of going back to things you're already comfortable with, you think, "Hmm, somehow other people have solved this problem using only immutable values, and I can, too." When your thinking gets to that point, your understanding of FP will rapidly progress.

If you're new to FP those rules may feel limiting — and you may be wondering how you can possibly get *anything* done — but if you follow these rules you'll find that they lead you to a different way of thinking about programming problems. *Because* of these rules your mind will naturally gravitate towards FP solutions to problems.

For instance, because you can't use a `var` field to initialize a mutable variable before a `for` loop, your mind will naturally think, "Hmm, what can I do here? Ah, yes, I can use recursion, or maybe a built-in collections method to solve this problem." Conversely, if you let yourself reach for that `var` field, you'll never come to this other way of thinking.

Not a rule, but a note: using ???

While I'm writing about what aspects of the Scala language I *won't* use in this book, it's also worth noting that I will often use the Scala ??? syntax when I first sketch a function's signature. For example, when I first start writing a function named `createWorldPeace`, I'll start to sketch the signature like this:

```
def createWorldPeace = ???
```

I mention this because if you haven't seen this syntax before you may wonder why I'm using it. The reason I use it is because it's perfectly legal Scala code; that line of code will compile just fine. Go ahead and paste that code into the REPL and you'll see that it compiles just like this:

```
scala> def createWorldPeace = ???
createWorldPeace: Nothing
```

However, while that code does *compile*, you'll see a long error message that begins like this if you try to *call* the createWorldPeace function:

```
scala.NotImplementedError: an implementation is missing
```

I wrote about the ??? syntax in a blog post titled, What does '???' mean in Scala?[1], but in short, Martin Odersky, creator of the Scala language, added it to Scala for teaching cases just like this. The ??? syntax just means, "The body of this function is TBD."

> If you're interested in how language designers add features to a programming language, that blog post has a link to a really interesting discussion started by Mr. Odersky. He begins the thread by stating, "If people don't hold me back I'm going to add this (???) to Predef," and then the rest of the thread is an interesting back-and-forth discussion about the pros and cons of adding this feature to the Scala language, and possibly using other names for it, such as using TODO instead of ???.

Summary

In summary, the rules we'll follow in this book are:

1. There will be no null values.
2. Only *pure functions* will be used.
3. Immutable values will be used for all fields.
4. Whenever you use an if, you must always also use an else.
5. We won't create "classes" that encapsulate data and behavior.

---

[1] http://alvinalexander.com/scala/what-does-three-question-marks-in-scala-mean

One Rule for Reading this Book

In addition to the rules for *programming* in this book, there's one rule for *reading* this book:

> If you already understand the material in a lesson, move on to the next lesson.

Because I try to thoroughly cover everything you might possible need to know leading up to advanced topics like monads, there will probably be some lessons you don't need to read. For instance, you may already know that you can use functions as variables, how to write functions that have multiple parameter groups, etc.

Therefore, there's one simple rule for reading this book: If you already understand a topic — move on! (You can always come back and read it later if you feel like there's something you missed.)

9

What is "Functional Programming"?

> *"Object-oriented programming makes code understandable by encapsulating moving parts. Functional programming makes code understandable by minimizing moving parts."*
>
> — Michael Feathers, author of Working Effectively with Legacy Code (via Twitter)

Defining "Functional Programming"

It's surprisingly hard to find a consistent definition of *functional programming*. As just one example, some people say that functional programming (FP) is about writing *pure functions* — which is a good start — but then they add something else like, "The programming language must be lazy." Really? Does a programming language really have to be lazy (non-strict) to be FP? (The correct answer is "no.")

I share links to many definitions at the end of this lesson, but I think you can define FP with just two statements:

1. FP is about writing software applications using only pure functions.
2. When writing FP code you only use immutable values — `val` fields in Scala.

And when I say "only" in those sentences, I mean *only*.

You can combine those two statements into this simple definition:

> Functional programming is a way of writing software applications using only pure functions and immutable values.

Of course that definition includes the term "pure functions," which I haven't defined yet, so let me fix that.

A working definition of "pure function"

I provide a complete description of pure functions in the "Pure Functions" lesson, but for now, I just want to provide a simple working definition of the term.

A *pure function* can be defined like this:

- The output of a pure function depends only on (a) its input parameters and (b) its internal algorithm.

    - This is unlike an OOP method, which can depend on other fields in the same class as the method.

- A pure function has no side effects, meaning that it does not read anything from the outside world or write anything to the outside world.

    - It does not read from a file, web service, UI, or database, and does not write anything either.

- As a result of those first two statements, if a pure function is called with an input parameter x an infinite number of times, it will always return the same result y.

    - For instance, any time a "string length" function is called with the string "Alvin", the result will always be 5.

As a few examples, Java and Scala functions like these are pure functions:

- `String` uppercase and lowercase methods
- `List` methods like `max`, `min`
- `Math.sin(a)`, `Math.cos(a)`

In fact, because the Java `String` class and Scala `List` class are both immutable, all of their methods act just like pure functions.

Even complex algorithms like checksums, encodings, and encryption algorithms follow these principles: given the same inputs an infinite number of times, they always return the same result.

Conversely, functions like these are *not* pure functions:

- `System.currentTimeMillis`
- `Random` class methods like `next`, `nextInt`
- I/O methods in classes like `File` and `HttpURLConnection` that read and write data

The first two examples yield different results almost every time they are called, and I/O functions are impure because they have *side effects* — they communicate with the outside world to send and receive data.

Note 1: Higher-Order Functions are a great FP language feature

If you're not familiar with the term Higher-Order Function (HOF), it basically means that (a) you can treat a function as a value (`val`) — just like you can treat a `String` as a value — and (b) you can pass that value into other functions.

In writing good FP code, you pass one function to another so often that I'm tempted to add HOFs as a requirement of my FP definition. But in the end, you can write FP code in languages that don't support HOFs, including Java. Of course that will be painful and probably very verbose, but you can do it.

Therefore, I don't include HOFs in my definition of functional programming. In the end, HOFs are a *terrific* FP language feature, and they make Scala a *much* better FP language than Java, but it's still just a *language feature*, not a part of the core definition of functional programming.

Note 2: Recursion is a by-product

Sometimes you'll see a definition of FP that states, "Recursion is a requirement of functional programming." While it's true that pure FP languages use recursion, the need for recursion is a *by-product* of the definition of FP.

Once you dig into FP, you'll see that if you only use pure functions and immutable values, the *only* way you can do things like "calculate the sum of a list" is to use recursion. Therefore, it's a result of my definition, not a part of the definition.

(I discuss this more in the recursion lessons.)

Proof: Wikipedia's FP definition

When you google "functional programming definition," the first link that currently shows up is from Wikipedia, and their definition of FP[1] backs up my statements. The first line of their definition begins like this:

> "In computer science, functional programming is a programming paradigm — a style of building the structure and elements of computer programs — that treats computation as the evaluation of mathematical functions and avoids changing-state and mutable data."

So, yes, FP is made of (a) pure functions and (b) immutable data. (Their "mathematical functions" are equivalent to my pure functions.)

As proof for another assertion I made earlier, that Wikipedia page also elaborates on features that make an FP language easier to use — such as being able to treat functions as values — where they state, "Programming in a functional style can also be accomplished in languages that are not specifically designed for functional programming." (Think Java.)

Proof: A wonderful quote from Mary Rose Cook

When I first started learning FP, I was aware that pure functions were important, but this point was really driven home when I came across an article titled A Practical Introduction to Functional Programming[2] by Mary Rose Cook[3].

Ms. Cook used to work at the Recurse Center[4] (formerly known as "Hacker School") and now works at Makers Academy[5], and in her "Practical Introduction to FP" essay, she refers to using only pure functions as a *Guide Rope* to learning FP:

> "When people talk about functional programming, they mention a dizzying number of 'functional' characteristics. They mention immutable data, first class functions, and tail call optimisation. These are *language features* that aid functional programming."

> "They mention mapping, reducing, pipelining, recursing, currying and the use of higher order functions. These are *programming techniques* used to write functional code."

---

[1] https://en.wikipedia.org/wiki/Functional_programming
[2] http://maryrosecook.com/blog/post/a-practical-introduction-to-functional-programming
[3] http://maryrosecook.com
[4] https://www.recurse.com
[5] http://www.makersacademy.com

> "They mention parallelization, lazy evaluation, and determinism. These are advantageous properties of functional programs."
>
> "Ignore all that. Functional code is characterised by one thing: *the absence of side effects*. It (a pure function) doesn't rely on data outside the current function, and it doesn't change data that exists outside the current function. Every other 'functional' thing can be derived from this property. Use it as a guide rope as you learn."

When she writes about the "absence of side effects," she's referring to building applications from pure functions.

Her guide rope statement is so good, it bears repeating:

> "Functional code is characterised by one thing: the absence of side effects."

When I first read this quote, the little light bulb went on over my head and I began focusing even more on writing *only* pure functions.

If you think about it, this statement means exactly what I wrote at the beginning of this lesson:

> Functional programming is a way of writing software applications using only pure functions and immutable values.

That's great ... but why immutable values?

At this point you might be saying, "Okay, I buy the 'pure functions' portion of your definition, but what does *immutable values* have to do with this? Why can't my variables be mutable, i.e., why can't I use *var*?"

The best FP code is like algebra

I dig into this question in the "FP is Like Algebra" lesson, but the short answer here is this:

> The best FP code is like algebra, and in algebra you never re-use variables. And not re-using variables has many benefits.

For example, in Scala/FP you write code that looks like this:

```
val a = f(x)
val b = g(a)
val c = h(b)
```

When you write simple expressions like this, both you and the compiler are free to rearrange the code. For instance, because a will always be *exactly* the same as f(x), you can replace a with f(x) at any point in your code.

The opposite of this is also true: a can always be replaced with f(x). Therefore, this equation:

```
val b = g(a)
```

is exactly the same as this equation:

```
val b = g(f(x))
```

Continuing along this line of thinking, because b is *exactly* equivalent to g(f(x)), you can also state c differently. This equation:

```
val c = h(b)
```

is exactly the same as this equation:

```
val c = h(g(f(x)))
```

From a programming perspective, knowing that you can *always* replace the immutable values a and b with their equivalent functions (and vice-versa) is extremely important. If a and b had been defined as var fields, I couldn't make the substitutions that I did. That's because with mutable variables you can't be certain that later in your program a is still f(x), and b is still g(a). However, because the fields *are* immutable, you can make these algebraic substitutions.

FP code is easier to reason about

Furthermore, because a and b can never change, the code is easier to reason about. With var fields you always have to have a background thread running in your brain, "Is a reassigned somewhere else? Keep an eye out for it." But with FP code you never have to think, "I wonder if a was reassigned anywhere?" That thought never comes to mind. a is the same as f(x), and that's all there is to it, end of story. They are completely interchangeable, just like the algebra you knew in high school.

> To put this another way, in algebra you never reassign variables, so it's obvious that the third line here is a mistake:
>
> ```
> a = f(x)
> ```

```
b = g(a)
a = h(y)      # d'oh -- `a` is reassigned!
c = i(a, b)
```

Clearly no mathematician would ever do that, and because FP code is like algebra, no FP developer would ever do that either.

Another good reason to use immutable values

Another good reason to use only immutable values is that mutable variables (var fields) don't work well with parallel/concurrent applications. Because concurrency is becoming more important as computers have more CPUs that have more cores, I discuss this in the "Benefits of Functional Programming" and "Concurrency" lessons.

As programmers gain more experience with FP, their code tends to look more like this expression:

```
val c = h(g(f(x)))
```

While that's cool — and it's also something that your brain becomes more comfortable with over time — it's also a style that makes it harder for new FP developers to understand. Therefore, in this book I write most code in the simple style first:

```
val a = f(x)
val b = g(a)
val c = h(b)
```

and then conclude with the reduced form at the end:

```
val c = h(g(f(x)))
```

As that shows, when functions are pure and variables are immutable, the code is like algebra. This is the sort of thing we did in high school, and it was all very logical. (FP developers refer to this sort of thing as "evaluation" and "substitution.")

Summary

In this lesson, I defined functional programming like this:

Functional programming is a way of writing software applications using only pure functions and immutable values.

To support that, I also defined *pure function* like this:

- The output of a pure function depends only on (a) its input parameters and (b) its internal algorithm.
- A pure function has no side effects, meaning that it does not read anything from the outside world or write anything to the outside world.
- As a result of those first two statements, if a pure function is called with an input parameter x an infinite number of times, it will always return the same result y.

I noted that higher-order functions (HOFs) are a terrific FP language feature, and also stated that recursion is a by-product of the definition of FP.

I also briefly discussed some of the benefits of immutable values (and FP in general):

- The best FP code is like algebra
- Pure functions and immutable values are easier to reason about
- Without much support (yet), I stated that immutable values make parallel/concurrent programming easier

See also

- A Postfunctional Language[6], a scala-lang.org post by Martin Odersky
- The docs.scala-lang.org definition of *functional style*[7]
- The Wikipedia definition of FP[8]
- The Clojure definition of FP[9]
- The Haskell definition of FP[10]
- The "Creative Clojure" website agrees with my definition of functional programming[11]
- Information about FP in the *Real World Haskell* book[12]

---

[6] http://www.scala-lang.org/old/node/4960
[7] http://docs.scala-lang.org/glossary/#functional-style
[8] https://en.wikipedia.org/wiki/Functional_programming
[9] http://clojure.org/about/functional_programming
[10] https://wiki.haskell.org/Functional_programming
[11] https://clojurefun.wordpress.com/2012/08/27/what-defines-a-functional-programming-language/
[12] http://book.realworldhaskell.org/read/why-functional-programming-why-haskell.html

- A practical introduction to functional programming[13]
- An intro to FP on the "Learn You a Haskell for Great Good" website[14]
- Also, see the "Benefits of Functional Programming" lesson and the concurrency lessons in this book

---

[13] http://maryrosecook.com/blog/post/a-practical-introduction-to-functional-programming
[14] http://learnyouahaskell.com/introduction

10
What is This Lambda You Speak Of?

> *"It takes a wise man to learn from his mistakes, but an even wiser man to learn from others."*
>
> — Zen Proverb

Goals

Once you get into FP, you'll quickly start hearing the terms *lambda* and *lambda calculus*. The goal of this chapter is to provide background information on where those names come from, and what they mean.

The short story

For those who don't like history, this is the shortest possible "history of functional programming" I can provide that explains where the terms lambda and lambda calculus come from.

"Lambda"

Back in the 1930s, Alonzo Church[1] was studying mathematics at Princeton University and began using the Greek symbol λ — "lambda" — to describe ideas he had about these things called *functions*. Because his work preceded the development of the first electronic, general-purpose computer[2] by at least seven years, you can imagine him writing that symbol on chalkboards to describe his concept of functions.

So, historically speaking, that's the short story of where the term "lambda" comes from: it's just a symbol that Mr. Church chose when he first defined the concept of a function.

---

[1] https://en.wikipedia.org/wiki/Alonzo_Church
[2] https://en.wikipedia.org/wiki/ENIAC

Fast-forward to today, and these days the name lambda is generally used to refer to anonymous functions. That's all it means, and it bears highlighting:

> In modern functional programming, lambda means "anonymous function."

If you're familiar with other programming languages, you may know that Python[3] and Ruby[4] use the keyword `lambda` to define anonymous functions.

The term "lambda calculus"

As an aerospace engineer, I always thought the name "calculus" referred to the form of mathematics that has to do with infinitesimal changes and derivatives, but the name calculus also has a broader meaning. The word calculus can mean "a formal system," and indeed, that's how Wikipedia defines lambda calculus[5]:

> "Lambda calculus (also written as λ-calculus) is a formal system in mathematical logic for expressing computation based on function abstraction and application using variable binding and substitution."

So we have:

- lambda means "anonymous function," and
- calculus means "a formal system"

Therefore, the term *lambda calculus* refers to "a formal way to think about functions."

That same Wikipedia link states this:

> "Lambda calculus provides a theoretical framework for describing functions and their evaluation. Although it is a mathematical abstraction rather than a programming language, it forms the basis of almost all functional programming languages today."

---

[3] http://www.secnetix.de/olli/Python/lambda_functions.hawk
[4] https://rubymonk.com/learning/books/1-ruby-primer/chapters/34-lambdas-and-blocks-in-ruby/lessons/77-lambdas-in-ruby
[5] https://en.wikipedia.org/wiki/Lambda_calculus

When I first started learning about functional programming, I found these terms to be a little intimidating, but as with most FP terms, they're just uncommon words for talking about "functions and their evaluation."

If you're interested in the deeper history of FP, including a guy named Haskell Curry, the relationship between FORTRAN and FP, and languages like Lisp, Haskell, Scala, and Martin Odersky's work that led to the creation of Scala, continue reading the next section. Otherwise feel free to move on to the next chapter.

The Longer Story (History)

For many more details about the history of functional programming, including the invention of the lambda calculus, more details about the λ symbol, several key people in the FP history, and languages like Lisp, Haskell, and Scala, see the online version of this chapter[6].

(I try to make it an interesting read, and it begins like this: Back in the 1930s — 80+ years ago — gasoline cost 17 cents a gallon, World War II hadn't started yet (not until 1939, officially), the United States was in the midst of the Great Depression (1929-1939), and a man by the name of Alonzo Church was studying mathematics at Princeton University along with other legendary figures like Alan Turing, (who finished his PhD under Church[7]) and John von Neumann.)

---

[6]https://alvinalexander.com/scala/fp-book/what-is-this-lambda-you-speak-of
[7]http://www-history.mcs.st-andrews.ac.uk/Biographies/Church.html

11

The Benefits of Functional Programming

> *"Functional programming is often regarded as the best-kept secret of scientific modelers, mathematicians, artificial intelligence researchers, financial institutions, graphic designers, CPU designers, compiler programmers, and telecommunications engineers."*
>
> — The Wikipedia F# page

As I write about the benefits of functional programming in this chapter, I need to separate my answers into two parts. First, there are the benefits of *functional programming in general*. Second, there are more specific benefits that come from using *functional programming in Scala*. I'll look at both of these in these chapter.

Benefits of functional programming in general

Experienced functional programmers make the following claims about functional programming, regardless of the language they use:

1. Pure functions are easier to reason about
2. Testing is easier, and pure functions lend themselves well to techniques like property-based testing
3. Debugging is easier
4. Programs are more bulletproof
5. Programs are written at a higher level, and are therefore easier to comprehend
6. Function signatures are more meaningful
7. Parallel/concurrent programming is easier

I'll discuss these benefits in this chapter, and then offer further proof of them as you go through this book.

Benefits of functional programming in Scala

On top of those benefits of functional programming in general, Scala/FP offers these additional benefits:

8. Being able to (a) treat functions as values and (b) use anonymous functions makes code more concise, and still readable
9. Scala syntax generally makes function signatures easy to read
10. The Scala collections' classes have a very functional API
11. Scala runs on the JVM, so you can still use the wealth of JVM-based libraries and tools with your Scala/FP applications

In the rest of this chapter I'll explore each of these benefits.

1) Pure functions are easier to reason about

The book, Real World Haskell[1], states, "Purity makes the job of understanding code easier." I've found this to be true for a variety of reasons.

First, pure functions *are* easier to reason about because you know that they can't do certain things, such as talk to the outside world, have hidden inputs, or modify hidden state. Because of this, you're guaranteed that their function signatures tell you (a) exactly what's going into each function, and (b) coming out of each function.

In his book, Clean Code[2], Robert Martin writes:

> "The ratio of time spent reading (code) versus writing is well over 10 to 1 … (therefore) making it easy to read makes it easier to write."

I suspect that this ratio is lower with FP. Because pure functions are easier to reason about:

- I spend less time "reading" them.
- I can keep fewer details in my brain for every function that I read.

This is what functional programmers refer to as "a higher level of abstraction."

---

[1] http://amzn.to/1TX9olw
[2] http://amzn.to/1UJhPQy

Because I can read pure functions faster and use less brain memory per function, I can keep more overall logic in my brain at one time.

2) Testing is easier, and pure functions lend themselves well to techniques like property-based testing

As I show in the Scala Cookbook[3], it's easier to test pure functions because you don't have to worry about them dealing with hidden state and side effects. What this means is that in imperative code you may have a method like this:

```
def doSomethingHidden(o: Order, p: Pizza): Unit ...
```

You can't tell much about what that method does by looking at its signature, but — because it returns nothing (Unit) — presumably it (a) modifies those variables, (b) changes some hidden state, or (c) interacts with the outside world.

When methods modify hidden state, you end up having to write long test code like this:

```
test("test hidden stuff that has side effects") {
    setUpPizzaState(p)
    setUpOrderState(o, p)
    doSomethingHidden(o, p)
    val result = getTheSideEffectFromThatMethod()
    assertEquals(result, expectedResult)
}
```

In FP you *can't* have code like that, so testing is simpler, like this:

```
test("test obvious stuff") {
    val result = doSomethingObvious(x, y, z)
    test(result, expectedResult)
}
```

Proofs

Beyond making unit testing easier, because functional code is like algebra it also makes it easier to use a form of testing known as *property-based testing*.

---
[3] http://amzn.to/24ivK4G

I write more about this in the lesson on using ScalaCheck[4], but the main point is that because the outputs of your functions depend only on their inputs, you can define "properties" of your functions, and then ScalaCheck "attacks" your functions with a large range of inputs.

With a few minor edits, the property-based testing page on the ScalaTest website[5] states:

> "… a *property* is a high-level specification of behavior that should hold for a range of data points. For example, a property might state, 'The size of a list returned from a method should always be greater than or equal to the size of the list passed to that method.' This property should hold no matter what list is passed."

> "The difference between a traditional unit test and a property is that unit tests traditionally verify behavior based on specific data points … for example, a unit test might pass three or four specific lists to a method that takes a list and check that the results are as expected. A property, by contrast, describes at a high level the preconditions of the method under test and specifies some aspect of the result that should hold no matter what valid list is passed."

3) Debugging is easier

Because pure functions depend only on their input parameters to produce their output, debugging applications written with pure functions is easier. Of course it's possible to still make a mistake when you write a pure function, but once you have a stack trace or debug output, all you have to do is follow the values to see what went wrong. Because the functions are pure, you don't have to worry about what's going on in the rest of the application, you just have to know the inputs that were given to the pure function that failed.

In Masterminds of Programming[6], Paul Hudak, a co-creator of the Haskell language, states, "I've always felt that the 'execution trace' method of debugging in imperative languages was broken … in all my years of Haskell programming, I have never in fact used Buddha, or GHC's debugger, or any debugger at all … I find that testing works just fine; test small pieces of code using QuickCheck[7] or a similar tool to make things more rigorous, and then — the key step — simply study the code to see why things don't work the way I expect them to. I suspect that a lot of people program similarly, otherwise there would be a lot more research on Haskell debuggers …"

---

[4] https://www.scalacheck.org/
[5] http://www.scalatest.org/user_guide/property_based_testing
[6] http://amzn.to/2bedXb4
[7] https://hackage.haskell.org/package/QuickCheck

ScalaCheck[8] is a property-based testing framework for Scala that was inspired by Haskell's QuickCheck.

4) Programs are more bulletproof

People that are smarter than I am can make the mathematical argument that *complete FP applications* are more bulletproof than other applications. Because there are fewer "moving parts" — mutable variables and hidden state — in FP applications, mathematically speaking, the overall application is less complex. This is true for simple applications, and the gap gets larger in parallel and concurrent programming (as you'll see in a later section in this chapter).

The way I can explain this is to share an example of my own bad code. A few years ago I started writing a football game for Android devices[9] (American football), and it has a lot of *state* to consider. On every play there is state like this:

- What quarter is it?
- How much time is left in the quarter?
- What is the score?
- What down is it?
- What distance is needed to make a first down?
- Much more ...

Here's a small sample of the now-embarrassing `public static` fields that I globally mutate in that application:

```
// stats for human
public static int numRunsByHuman                  = 0;
public static int numPassAttemptsByHuman          = 0;
public static int numPassCompletionsByHuman       = 0;
public static int numInterceptionsThrownByHuman   = 0;
public static int numRunningYardsByHuman          = 0;
public static int numPassingYardsByHuman          = 0;
public static int numFumblesByHuman               = 0;
public static int numFirstDownRunsByHuman         = 0;
public static int numFirstDownPassesByHuman       = 0;
```

---

[8]https://www.scalacheck.org/
[9]http://xoplay.rocks/

When I wrote this code I thought, "I've written Java Swing (GUI) code since the 1990s, and Android code for a few years. I'm working by myself on this, I don't have to worry about team communication. I know what I'm doing, what could possibly go wrong?"

In short, although a football game is pretty simple compared to a business application, it still has a lot of "state" that you have to maintain. And when you're mutating that global state from several different places, well, it turns out that sometimes the computer gets an extra play, sometimes time doesn't run off the clock, etc.

Skipping all of my imperative state-related bugs … once I learned how to handle state in FP applications, I gave up trying to fix those bugs, and I'm now rewriting the core of the application in an FP style.

> As you'll see in this book, the solution to this problem is to pass the state around as a value, such as a case class or a `Map`. In this case I might call it `GameState`, and it would have fields like `quarter`, `timeRemaining`, `down`, etc.

A second argument about FP applications being more bulletproof is that because they are built from all of these little pure functions that are known to work extraordinarily well, the overall application itself must be safer. For instance, if 80% of the application is written with well-tested pure functions, you can be very confident in that code; you know that it will never have the mutable state bugs like the ones in my football game. (And if somehow it does, the problem is easier to find and fix.)

As an analogy, one time I had a house built, and I remember that the builder was very careful about the 2x4's that were used to build the framework of the house. He'd line them up and then say, "You do *not* want that 2x4 in your house," and he would pick up a bent or cracked 2x4 and throw it off to the side. In the same way that he was trying to build the framework of the house with wood that was clearly the best, we use pure functions to build the best possible core of our applications.

> Yes, I know that programmers don't like it when I compare building a house to writing an application. But some analogies do fit.

5) Programs are written at a higher level, and are therefore easier to comprehend

In the same way that pure functions are easier to reason about, overall FP applications are also easier to reason about. For example, I find that my FP code is more concise than my imperative and OOP code, and it's also still very readable. In fact, I think it's more readable than my older code.

Some of the features that make FP code more concise and still readable are:

- The ability to treat functions as values
- The ability to pass those values into other functions
- Being able to write small snippets of code as anonymous functions
- Not having to create deep hierarchies of classes (that sometimes feel "artificial")
- Most FP languages are "low ceremony" languages, meaning that they require less boilerplate code than other languages

> If you want to see what I mean by FP languages being "low ceremony," here's a good example of OCaml[10], and this page shows examples of Haskell's syntax[11].

In my experience, when I write Scala/FP code that I'm comfortable with today, I have always been able to read it at a later time. And as I mentioned when writing about the benefits of pure functions, "concise and readable" means that I can keep more code in my head at one time.

> I emphasize that Scala/FP code is *concise and readable* because sometimes "more concise" code can create a maintenance problem. I remember that a friend who didn't like Perl once described Perl[a] code as, "Write once, read forever." Because the syntax could get so complex, he couldn't modify his own code a few weeks after writing it because he couldn't remember how each little syntactical nuance worked. I have the same problem writing complex regular expressions. If I don't document them when I create them, I can never tell how they work when I look at them later.
>
> (Personally I like the non-OO parts of Perl, and have written over 150 Perl tutorials[b].)
>
> ---
> [a]https://www.perl.org

---

[10]https://ocaml.org/learn/taste.html
[11]http://prajitr.github.io/quick-haskell-syntax/

[b] http://alvinalexander.com/perl

6) Pure function signatures are meaningful

When learning FP, another big "lightbulb going on over my head" moment came when I saw that my function signatures were suddenly much more meaningful than my imperative and OOP method signatures.

Because non-FP methods can have side effects — which are essentially *hidden* inputs and outputs of those methods — their function signatures often don't mean that much. For example, what do you think this imperative method does:

```
def doSomething(): Unit { code here ...
```

The correct answer is, *"Who knows?"* Because it takes no input parameters and returns nothing, there's no way to guess from the signature what this method does.

In contrast, because pure functions depend only on their input parameters to produce their output, their function signatures are extremely meaningful — a contract, even.

> I write more about this in the upcoming lesson, "Pure Functions Tell All."

7) Parallel programming

While writing parallel and concurrent applications is considered a "killer app" that helped spur renewed interest in FP, I have written my parallel/concurrent apps (like Sarah[12]) primarily using Akka Actors and Scala Futures, so I can only speak about them: they're awesome tools. I wrote about them in the Scala Cookbook[13] and on my website (alvinalexander.com[14]), so please search those resources for "actors" and "futures" to find examples.

Therefore, to support the claims that FP is a great tool for writing parallel/concurrent applications, I'm going to include quotes here from other resources. As you'll see, the recurring theme in these quotes is, "Because FP only has immutable values, you can't possibly have the race conditions that are so difficult to deal with in imperative code."

---

[12] http://alvinalexander.com/sarah
[13] http://amzn.to/24ivK4G
[14] http://alvinalexander.com

The first quote comes from an article titled, "Functional Programming for the Rest of Us,"[15]:

> "A functional program is ready for concurrency without any further modifications. You never have to worry about deadlocks and race conditions because you don't need to use locks. No piece of data in a functional program is modified twice by the same thread, let alone by two different threads. That means you can easily add threads without ever giving conventional problems that plague concurrency applications a second thought."

The author goes on to add the information shown in Figure 11.1.

> The concurrency story doesn't stop here. If your application is inherently single threaded the compiler can still optimize functional programs to run on multiple CPUs. Take a look at the following code fragment:
>
> ```
> String s1 = somewhatLongOperation1();
> String s2 = somewhatLongOperation2();
> String s3 = concatenate(s1, s2);
> ```
>
> In a functional language the compiler could analyze the code, classify the functions that create strings *s1* and *s2* as potentially time consuming operations, and run them concurrently. This is impossible to do in an imperative language because each function may modify state outside of its scope and the function following it may depend on it. In functional languages automatic analysis of functions and finding

Figure 11.1: A compiler can optimize functional programs to run on multiple cores.

The Clojure.org website[16] adds the statements in Figure 11.2 about how Clojure and FP help with concurrency.

Page 17 of the book, Haskell, the Craft of Functional Programming[17], states, "Haskell programs are easy to parallelize, and to run efficiently on multicore hardware, because there is no state to be shared between different threads."

In this article on the ibm.com website[18], Neal Ford states, "Immutable objects are also automatically thread-safe and have no synchronization issues. They can never exist in unknown

---

[15] http://www.defmacro.org/ramblings/fp.html
[16] http://clojure.org/about/rationale
[17] http://amzn.to/1POe1u9
[18] http://www.ibm.com/developerworks/library/j-ft4/

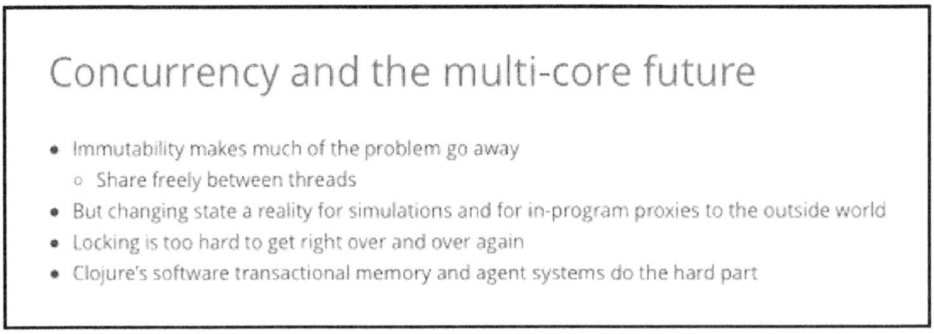

> Concurrency and the multi-core future
>
> - Immutability makes much of the problem go away
>   - Share freely between threads
> - But changing state a reality for simulations and for in-program proxies to the outside world
> - Locking is too hard to get right over and over again
> - Clojure's software transactional memory and agent systems do the hard part

Figure 11.2: Concurrency benefits from the Clojure website.

or undesirable state because of an exception."

In the pragprom.com article, Functional Programming Basics[19], Robert C. Martin extrapolates from four cores to a future with 131,072 processors when he writes:

> "Honestly, we programmers can barely get two Java threads to cooperate ... Clearly, if the value of a memory location, once initialized, does not change during the course of a program execution, then there's nothing for the 131072 processors to compete over. You don't need semaphores if you don't have side effects! You can't have concurrent update problems if you don't update! ... So that's the big deal about functional languages; and it is one big fricking deal. There is a freight train barreling down the tracks towards us, with multi-core emblazoned on it; and you'd better be ready by the time it gets here."

With a slight bit of editing, an article titled, The Downfall of Imperative Programming[20] states:

> "Did you notice that in the definition of a *data race* there's always talk of mutation? Any number of threads may *read* a memory location without synchronization, but if even one of them *mutates* it, you have a race. And that is the downfall of imperative programming: Imperative programs will always be vulnerable to data races because they contain mutable variables."

id Software[21] co-founder and technical director John Carmack states:

---

[19] https://pragprog.com/magazines/2013-01/functional-programming-basics
[20] https://www.fpcomplete.com/blog/2012/04/the-downfall-of-imperative-programming
[21] http://www.idsoftware.com/en-us

> "Programming in a functional style makes the state presented to your code explicit, which makes it much easier to reason about, and, in a completely pure system, makes thread race conditions impossible."

Writing Erlang[22] code is similar to using the Akka[23] actors library in Scala. The Erlang equivalent to an Akka actor is a "process," and in his book, Programming Erlang[24], Joe Armstrong writes:

> "Processes share no data with other processes. This is the reason why we can easily distribute Erlang programs over multicores or networks."

For a final quote, "The Trouble with Shared State" section on this medium.com article[25] states, "In fact, if you're using shared state and that state is reliant on sequences which vary depending on indeterministic factors, for all intents and purposes, the output is impossible to predict, and that means it's impossible to properly test or fully understand. As Martin Odersky puts it:"

> non-determinism = parallel processing + mutable state

The author follows that up with an understatement: "Program determinism is usually a desirable property in computing."

Deterministic algorithms and concurrency

Deterministic algorithms

If you're not familiar with the term *deterministic algorithm*, Wikipedia defines it[26] like this: "In computer science, a deterministic algorithm is an algorithm which, given a particular input, will always produce the same output, with the underlying machine always passing through the same sequence of states."

(As you'll soon see, this is basically the definition of a pure function.)

Conversely, a *nondeterministic algorithm* is like asking a user to ask the person next to them what their favorite color is: you're never guaranteed to get the same answer. If you're trying to do something like sort a list of numbers, you *really* want a deterministic solution.

---

[22] http://www.erlang.org
[23] http://akka.io
[24] http://amzn.to/2aab4HF
[25] https://medium.com/javascript-scene/master-the-javascript-interview-what-is
[26] https://en.wikipedia.org/wiki/Deterministic_algorithm

Parallel, Concurrent

Yossi Kreinin created the original version of the image[27] shown in Figure 11.3 to help explain the differences between the meanings of "concurrent" and "parallel".

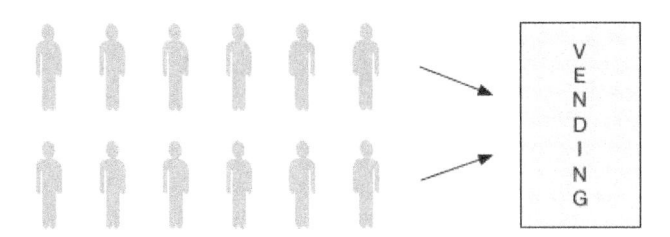

Concurrent: 2 queues, 1 vending machine

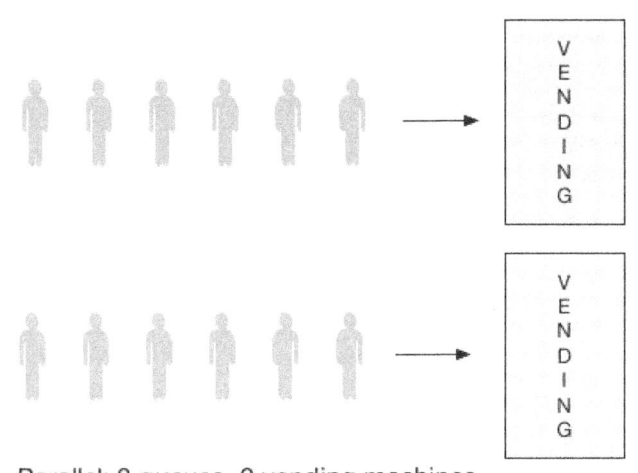

Parallel: 2 queues, 2 vending machines

Figure 11.3: The difference between concurrent and parallel.

His image is based on a diagram in this article by Erlang programmer Joe Armstrong[28]. Mr. Armstrong offers this summary in his post:

- Concurrent = Two queues and one coffee machine
- Parallel = Two queues and two coffee machines

I tend to use the two terms interchangeably, but I will be more precise with my language in

---

[27]http://yosefk.com/blog/parallelism-and-concurrency-need-different-tools.html
[28]http://joearms.github.io/2013/04/05/concurrent-and-parallel-programming.html

the "Concurrency" lessons in this book.

8) Scala/FP benefit: The ability to treat functions as values

I've already written a little about higher-order functions (HOFs), and I write more about them later in this book, so I won't belabor this point: the fact that Scala lets you (a) treat functions as values, (b) pass functions as parameters into other functions, and (c) write concise anonymous functions, are all features that make Scala a better functional programming language than another language (such as Java) that does not have these features.

9) Scala/FP benefit: Syntax makes function signatures easy to read

In my opinion, the Scala method syntax is about as simple as you can make method signatures, especially signatures that support generic types. This simplicity usually makes method signatures easy to read.

For instance, it's easy to tell that this method takes a String and returns an Int:

```
def foo(s: String): Int = ???
```

These days I prefer to use *explicit* return types on my methods, such as the Int in this example. I've found that showing the explicit type makes them easier to read later, when I'm in maintenance mode.

If you prefer methods with *implicit return types* you can write that same method like this, which is also clear and concise:

```
def foo(s: String) = ???
```

Even when you need to use generic type parameters — which make any method harder to read — Scala method signatures are still fairly easy to read:

```
def foo[A, B](a: A): B = ???
```

It's hard to make generic types much easier than that.

10) Scala/FP benefit: The collections classes have a functional API

When I first came to Scala from Java, the Scala collections API was a real surprise, and not in a pleasant way. *But*, once I had that "Aha!" moment and realized how they work, I saw what a great benefit they are. Having all of those standard functional methods eliminates almost every need for custom `for` loops.

The important benefit of this is that these standard methods make my code more consistent and concise. These days I write almost 100% fewer custom `for` loops, and that's good for me — and anyone who has to read my code.

11) Scala/FP benefit: Code runs on the JVM

Because the Scala compiler generates Java bytecode that runs on the JVM, and because Scala supports both the FP and OOP models, you can still use all of those thousands of Java/JVM libraries that have been created in the last twenty years in your Scala/FP applications. Even if those libraries aren't "Pure FP," at least you can still use them without having to "reinvent the wheel" and write a new library from scratch.

In fact, not only can you use the wealth of existing JVM libraries, you can also use all of your favorite JVM tools in general:

- Build tools like Ant, Maven, Gradle, and SBT
- Test tools like JUnit, TestNG, and mock frameworks
- Continuous integration tools
- Debugging and logging frameworks
- Profiling tools
- More …

These libraries and tools are a great strength of the JVM. If you ask experienced FP developers why they're using Scala rather than Haskell or another FP language, "libraries, tools, and JVM" is the usual answer.

One more thing …

On a personal note, a big early influence for me — before I knew about any of these benefits — was seeing people like Martin Odersky, Jonas Bonér, Bill Venners, and other leading Scala programmers use and promote an FP style. Because Scala supports both OOP and FP, it's not like they had to sell anyone on FP in order to get us to use Scala. (As a former business owner, I feel like I'm always on the lookout for people who are trying to "sell" me something.)

I don't know if they use FP 100% of the time, but what influenced me is that they started using FP and then they never said, "You know what? FP isn't that good after all. I'm going back to an imperative style."

In the 2016 version of Programming in Scala[29], Martin Odersky's biography states, "He works on programming languages and systems, more specifically on the topic of how to combine object-oriented and functional programming." Clearly FP is important to him (as is finding the best ways to merge FP and OOP concepts).

Summary

In summary, the benefits of "functional programming in general" are:

1. Pure functions are easier to reason about
2. Testing is easier, and pure functions lend themselves well to techniques like property-based testing
3. Debugging is easier
4. Programs are more bulletproof
5. Programs are written at a higher level, and are therefore easier to comprehend
6. Function signatures are more meaningful
7. Parallel/concurrent programming is easier

On top of those benefits, "functional programming in Scala" offers these additional benefits:

8. Being able to (a) treat functions as values and (b) use anonymous functions makes code more concise, and still readable
9. Scala syntax generally makes function signatures easy to read
10. The Scala collections' classes have a very functional API
11. Scala runs on the JVM, so you can still use the wealth of JVM-based libraries and tools with your Scala/FP applications

What's next

In this chapter I tried to share an honest assessment of the benefits of functional programming. In the next chapter I'll try to provide an honest assessment of the potential drawbacks and disadvantages of functional programming.

---

[29] http://amzn.to/2byNzrs

12

Disadvantages of Functional Programming

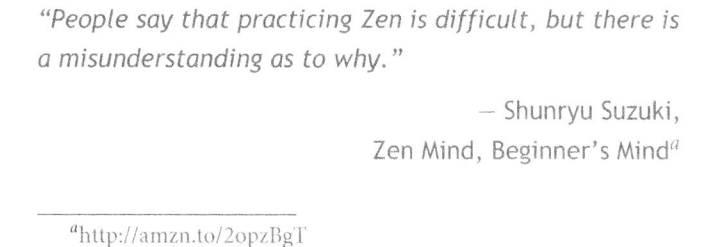

> *"People say that practicing Zen is difficult, but there is a misunderstanding as to why."*
>
> — Shunryu Suzuki,
> Zen Mind, Beginner's Mind[a]

---

[a] http://amzn.to/2opzBgT

In the last chapter I looked at the benefits of functional programming, and as I showed, there are quite a few. In this chapter I'll look at the potential drawbacks of FP.

Just as I did in the previous chapter, I'll first cover the "drawbacks of functional programming *in general*":

1. Writing pure functions is easy, but combining them into a complete application is where things get hard
2. The advanced math terminology (monad, monoid, functor, etc.) makes FP intimidating
3. For many people, recursion doesn't feel natural
4. Because you can't mutate existing data, you instead use a pattern that I call, "Update as you copy"
5. Pure functions and I/O don't really mix
6. Using only immutable values and recursion can potentially lead to performance problems, including RAM use and speed

After that I'll look at the more-specific "drawbacks of functional programming in Scala":

7. You can mix FP and OOP styles
8. Scala doesn't have a standard FP library

1) Writing pure functions is easy, but combining them into a complete application is where things get hard

Writing a pure function is generally fairly easy. Once you can define your type signature, pure functions are easier to write because of the absence of mutable variables, hidden inputs, hidden state, and I/O. For example, the `determinePossiblePlays` function in this code:

```
val possiblePlays = OffensiveCoordinator.determinePossiblePlays(gameState)
```

is a pure function, and behind it are thousands of lines of other functional code. Writing all of these pure functions took time, but it was never difficult. All of the functions follow the same pattern:

1. Data comes into the function
2. Apply an algorithm (to *transform* the data)
3. Transformed data comes out of the function

That being said, the part that *is* hard is, "How do I glue all of these pure functions together in an FP style?" That question can lead to the code I showed in the first chapter:

```
def updateHealth(delta: Int): Game[Int] =
    StateT[IO, GameState, Int] { (s: GameState) =>

    val newHealth = s.player.health + delta
        IO((s.copy(player = s.player.copy(health = newHealth)), newHealth))

}
```

As you may be aware, when you first start programming in a pure FP style, gluing pure functions together to create a complete FP application is one of the biggest stumbling blocks you'll encounter.

2) Advanced math terminology makes FP intimidating

I don't know about you, but when I first heard terms like combinator, monoid, monad, and functor, I had no idea what people were talking about. And I've been paid to write software since the 1990s.

As I discuss in the next chapter, terms like this are intimidating, and that "fear factor" becomes a barrier to learning FP.

> Because I cover this topic in the next chapter, I won't write any more about it here.

3) For many people, recursion doesn't feel natural

One reason I may not have known about those mathematical terms is because my degree is in aerospace engineering, not computer science. Possibly for the same reason, I *knew* about recursion, but never had to use it. That is, until I became serious about writing pure FP code.

As I wrote in the "What is FP?" chapter, the thing that happens when you use only pure functions and immutable values is that you *have* to use recursion. In pure FP code you no longer use var fields with for loops, so the only way to loop over elements in a collection is to use recursion.

Fortunately, you can learn how to write recursive code. If there's a secret to the process, it's in learning how to "think in recursion." Once you gain that mindset and see that there are patterns to recursive algorithms, you'll find that recursion gets much easier, even natural.

Two paragraphs ago I wrote, "the only way to loop over elements in a collection is to use recursion," but that isn't 100% true. In addition to gaining a "recursive thinking" mindset, here's another Scala/FP secret: once you understand the Scala collections' methods, you won't need to use recursion as often as you think. In the same way that collections' methods are replacements for custom for loops, they're also replacements for many custom recursive algorithms. Once you're comfortable with the collections' methods, you'll find that you reach for them before you reach for recursion.

4) Because you can't mutate existing data, you instead use a pattern that I call, "Update as you copy"

For over 20 years I've written imperative code where it was easy — and extraordinarily common — to mutate existing data. For instance, once upon a time I had a niece named "Emily Means":

```
val emily = Person("Emily", "Means")
```

Then one day she got married and her last name became "Walls", so it seemed logical to update her last name, like this:

```
emily.setLastName("Walls")
```

In FP you don't do this. You don't mutate existing objects.

Instead, what you do is (a) you copy an existing object to a new object, and then as a copy of the data is flowing from the old object to the new object, you (b) update any fields you want to change by providing new values for those fields, such as the `lastName` field in Figure 12.1.

```
    Old Object          (copy process)         New Object
                       
firstName: "Emily"     - - - - - - - ▶    firstName: "Emily"
lastName: "Means"      - - -"Walls"- - ▶   lastName: "Walls"
```

Figure 12.1: Results of the "update as you copy" concept.

The way you "update as you copy" in Scala/FP is with the copy method that comes with *case classes*. First, you start with a case class:

```
case class Person (firstName: String, lastName: String)
```

Then, when your niece is born, you write code like this:

```
val emily1 = Person("Emily", "Means")
```

Later, when she gets married and changes her last name, you write this:

```
val emily2 = emily1.copy(lastName = "Walls")
```

After that line of code, `emily2.lastName` has the value `"Walls"`.

Note: I intentionally use the variable names `emily1` and `emily2` in this example to make it clear that you never change the original variable. In FP you constantly create intermediate variables like `name1` and `name2` during the "update as you copy" process, but there are FP techniques that make those intermediate variables transparent. I show those techniques in lessons later in this book.

"Update as you copy" gets worse with nested objects

The "Update as you copy" technique isn't too hard when you're working with this simple `Person` object, but think about this: What happens when you have nested objects, such as a `Family` that has a `Person` who has a `Seq[CreditCard]`, and that person wants to add a new credit card, or update an existing one? (This is like an Amazon Prime member who adds a family member to their account, and that person has one or more credit cards.) Or what if the nesting of objects is even deeper?

In short, this is a real problem that results in some nasty-looking code, and it gets uglier with each nested layer. Fortunately, other FP developers ran into this problem long before I did, and they came up with ways to make this process easier. I cover this problem and its solution in the "Lens" lesson later in this book.

5) Pure functions and I/O don't really mix

As I wrote in the "What is Functional Programming" lesson, a *pure function* is a function (a) whose output depends only on its input, and (b) has no side effects. Therefore, by definition, any function that deals with these things is *impure*:

- File I/O
- Database I/O
- Internet I/O
- Any sort of UI/GUI input
- Any function that mutates variables
- Any function that uses "hidden" variables

Given this situation, a great question is, "How can an FP application possibly work without these things?"

The short answer is what I wrote in the Scala Cookbook: you write as much of your application's code in an FP style as you can, and then you write a thin I/O layer around the outside of the FP code, like putting "I/O icing" around an "FP cake," as shown in Figure 12.2.

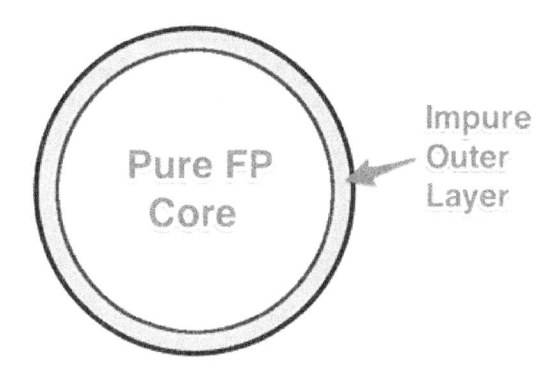

Figure 12.2: A thin, impure I/O layer around a pure core.

Pure and impure functions

In reality, no programming language is really "pure," at least not by my definition. (Several FP experts say the same thing.) Wikipedia lists Haskell as a "pure" FP language[1], and the way Haskell handles I/O equates to this Scala code:

```
def getCurrentTime(): IO[String] = ???
```

The short explanation of this code is that Haskell has an IO type that you *must* use as a wrapper when writing I/O functions. This is enforced by the Haskell compiler.

For example, getLine is a Haskell function that reads a line from STDIN, and returns a type that equates to IO[String] in Scala. Any time a Haskell function returns something wrapped in an IO, like IO[String], that function can only be used in certain places within a Haskell application.

> If that sounds hard core and limiting, it is. But it turns out to be a good thing.

Some people imply that this IO wrapper makes those functions pure, but in my opinion, this isn't true. At first I thought I was confused about this — that I didn't understand something — and then I read this quote from Martin Odersky on scala-lang.org[2]:

> "The IO monad does not make a function pure. It just makes it obvious that it's impure."

For the moment you can think of an IO instance as being like a Scala Option. More accurately, you can think of it as being an Option that always returns a Some[YourDataTypeHere], such as a Some[Person] or a Some[String].

As you can imagine, just because you wrap a String that you get from the outside world inside of a Some, that doesn't mean the String won't vary. For instance, if you prompt me for my name, I might reply "Al" or "Alvin," and if you prompt my niece for her name, she'll reply "Emily," and so on. I think you'll agree that Some["Al"], Some["Alvin"], and Some["Emily"] are different values.

Therefore, even though (a) the return type of Haskell I/O functions must be wrapped in the IO type, and (b) the Haskell compiler only permits IO types to be in certain places, they are *impure* functions: they can return a different value each time they are called.

---

[1] https://en.wikipedia.org/wiki/List_of_programming_languages_by_type#Functional_languages
[2] http://www.scala-lang.org/old/node/11194.html

6) Using only immutable values and recursion can lead to performance problems, including RAM use and speed

An author can get himself into trouble for stating that one programming paradigm can use more memory or be slower than other approaches, so let me begin this section by being very clear:

> *When you first write a simple ("naive") FP algorithm*, it is possible — just possible — that the immutable values and data-copying I mentioned earlier can create a performance problem.

I demonstrate an example of this problem in a blog post on Scala Quicksort algorithms[3]. In that article I show that the basic ("naive") recursive `quickSort` algorithm found in the "Scala By Example" PDF uses about 660 MB of RAM while sorting an array of ten million integers, and is four times slower than using the `scala.util.Sorting.quickSort` method.

Having said that, it's important to note how `scala.util.Sorting.quickSort` works. In Scala 2.12, it passes an `Array[Int]` directly to `java.util.Arrays.sort(int[])`. The way that sort method works varies by Java version, but Java 8 calls a `sort` method in `java.util.DualPivotQuicksort`. The code in that method (and one other method it calls) is at least 300 lines long, and is *much* more complex than the simple/naive `quickSort` algorithm I show.

Therefore, while it's true that the "simple, naive" `quickSort` algorithm in the "Scala By Example" PDF has those performance problems, I need to be clear that I'm comparing (a) a very simple algorithm that you might initially write, to (b) a much larger, performance-optimized algorithm.

7) Scala/FP drawback: You can mix FP and OOP styles

If you're an FP purist, a drawback to using *functional programming in Scala* is that Scala supports both OOP and FP, and therefore it's possible to mix the two coding styles in the same code base.

While that is a *potential* drawback, many years ago when I worked with a technology known as Function Point Analysis[4] — totally unrelated to functional programming — I learned of a philosophy called "House Rules" that eliminates this problem. With House Rules, the developers get together and agree on a programming style. Once a consensus is reached, that's the

---

[3] http://alvinalexander.com/scala/scala-quicksort-algorithms-fp-recursive-imperative-performance
[4] http://alvinalexander.com/fpa/

style that you use. Period.

As a simple example of this, when I owned a computer programming consulting company, the first developers I hired wanted a Java coding style that looks like this:

```
public void doSomething()
{
    doX();
    doY();
}
```

As shown, they wanted curly braces on their own lines, and the code was indented four spaces. I doubt that everyone on the team loved that style, but once we agreed on it, that was it.

I think you can use the House Rules philosophy to state what parts of the Scala language your organization will use in your applications. For instance, if you want to use a strict "Pure FP" style, use the rules I set forth in this book. You can always change the rules later, but it's important to start with something.

> There are two ways to look at the fact that Scala supports both OOP and FP. As mentioned, in the first view, FP purists see this as a drawback.
>
> But in a second view, people interested in using both paradigms within one language see this as a benefit. For example, Joe Armstrong has written that Erlang processes — which are the equivalent of Akka actors — can be written in an imperative style. Messages between processes are immutable, but the code within each process is single-threaded and can therefore be imperative. If a language only supports FP, the code in each process (actor) would have to be pure functional code, when that isn't strictly necessary.
>
> In the 2016 version of **Programming in Scala**[a], Martin Odersky's biography states, "He works on programming languages and systems, more specifically on the topic of how to combine object-oriented and functional programming." Trying to merge the two styles appears to be an important goal for Mr. Odersky.
>
> Personally, I like Scala's support of both the OOP and FP paradigms because it lets me use whatever style best fits the problem at hand. (In a terrific addition to
>
> this, adding Akka to the equation lets me use Scala the way other programmers use Erlang.)
>
> ---
> [a]http://amzn.to/2byNzrs

8) Scala/FP drawback: Scala doesn't have a standard FP library

Another potential drawback to *functional programming in Scala* is that there isn't a built-in library to support certain FP techniques. For instance, if you want to use an IO data type as a wrapper around your impure Scala/FP functions, there isn't one built into the standard Scala libraries.

To deal with this problem, independent libraries like Scalaz[5], Cats[6], and others have been created. But, while these solutions are built into a language like Haskell, they're third-party libraries in Scala.

"Should I use FP *everywhere*?"

After I listed all of the benefits of functional programming in the previous chapter, I asked the question, "Should I write *all* of my code in an FP style?" At that time you might have thought, "Of course! This FP stuff sounds great!"

Now that you've seen some of the drawbacks of FP, I think I can provide a better answer.

---

[5] https://github.com/scalaz/scalaz
[6] https://github.com/typelevel/cats

1a) GUIs and Pure FP are not a good fit

The first part of my answer is that I like to write Android apps, and I also enjoy writing Java Swing and JavaFX code, and the interface between (a) those frameworks and (b) your custom code isn't a great fit for FP.

As one example of what I mean, in an Android football game[7] I work on in my spare time, the OOP game framework I use provides an `update` method that I'm supposed to override to update the screen:

```
@Override
public void update(GameView gameView) {
    // my custom code here ...
}
```

Inside that method I have a lot of imperative GUI-drawing code that currently creates the UI shown in Figure 12.3.

There isn't a place for FP code at this point. The framework expects me to update the pixels on the screen within this method, and if you've ever written anything like a video game, you know that to achieve the best performance — and avoid screen flickering — it's generally best to update only the pixels that need to be changed. So this really is an "update" method, as opposed to a "completely redraw the screen" method.

Other "thick client," GUI frameworks like Swing and JavaFX have similar interfaces, where they are OOP and imperative by design. Figure 12.4 shows an example of a little text editor I wrote and named "AlPad[8]," and its major feature is that it lets me easily add and remove tabs to keep little notes organized.

The way you write Swing code like this is that you first create a `JTabbedPane`:

```
JTabbedPane tabbedPane = new JTabbedPane();
```

Once created, you keep that tabbed pane alive for the entire life of the application. Then when you later want to add a new tab, you *mutate* the `JTabbedPane` instance like this:

---

[7] http://xoplay.rocks/
[8] http://alvinalexander.com/apps/alpad

Figure 12.3: The UI for my "XO Play" application.

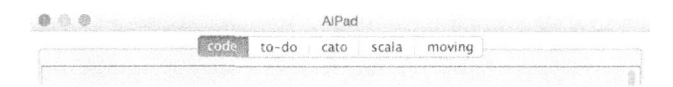

Figure 12.4: A few tabs in my "AlPad" application.

```
tabbedPane.addTab(
    "to-do",
    null,
    newPanel,
    "to-do");
```

That's the way GUI code usually works: you create components and then mutate them during the life of the application to create the desired user interface. The same is true for other Swing components, like `JFrame`, `JList`, `JTable`, etc.

Because these frameworks are OOP and imperative by nature, this interface point is where FP typically doesn't fit.

When you're working with these frameworks you have to conform to their styles at this interface point, but there's nothing to keep you from writing the rest of your code in an FP style. In my Android football game I have a function call that looks like this:

```
val possiblePlays = OffensiveCoordinator.determinePossiblePlays(gameState)
```

In that code, `determinePossiblePlays` is a pure function, and behind it are several thousand lines of other pure functions. So while the GUI code has to conform to the Android game framework I'm using, the decision-making portion of my app — the "business logic" — is written in an FP style.

1b) Caveats to what I just wrote

Having stated that, let me add a few caveats.

First, *Web* applications are completely different than *thick client* (Swing, JavaFX) applications. In a thick client project, the entire application is typically written in one large codebase that results in a binary executable that users install on their computers. Eclipse, IntelliJ IDEA, and NetBeans are examples of this.

Conversely, the web applications I've written in the last few years use (a) one of many JavaScript-based technologies for the UI, and (b) the Play Framework[9] on the server side. With Web applications like this, you have impure data coming into your Scala/Play application through data mappings and REST functions, and you probably also interact with impure database calls and impure network/internet I/O, but just like my football game, the "logic" portion of your application can be written with pure functions.

---

[9] https://www.playframework.com/

Second, the concept of Functional-Reactive Programming[10] (FRP) combines FP techniques with GUI programming. The RxJava[11] project includes this description:

> "RxJava is a Java VM implementation of Reactive Extensions[12]: a library for composing asynchronous and event-based programs by using observable sequences ... It extends the Observer Pattern to support sequences of data/events and adds operators that allow you to compose sequences together *declaratively* while abstracting away concerns about things like low-level threading, synchronization, thread-safety and concurrent data structures."

(Note that declarative programming[13] is the opposite of imperative programming[14].)

The ReactiveX.io website[15] states:

> "ReactiveX is a combination of the best ideas from the Observer pattern, the Iterator pattern, and functional programming."

This short RxScala example from the RxScala website[16] gives you a taste of the concept:

```
object Transforming extends App {

    /**
     * Asynchronously calls 'customObservableNonBlocking'
     * and defines a chain of operators to apply to the
     * callback sequence.
     */
    def simpleComposition()
    {
        AsyncObservable.customObservableNonBlocking()
            .drop(10)
```

---

[10] https://en.wikipedia.org/wiki/Functional_reactive_programming
[11] https://github.com/ReactiveX/RxJava
[12] http://reactivex.io/
[13] https://en.wikipedia.org/wiki/Declarative_programming
[14] https://en.wikipedia.org/wiki/Imperative_programming
[15] http://reactivex.io/
[16] https://github.com/ReactiveX/RxScala/blob/0.x/examples/src/main/scala/Transforming.scala

```
            .take(5)
            .map(stringValue => stringValue + "_xform")
            .subscribe(s => println("onNext => " + s))
    }

    simpleComposition()

}
```

This code does the following:

1. Using an "observable," it receives a stream of `String` values. Given that stream of values, it ...
2. Drops the first ten values
3. "Takes" the next five values
4. Appends the string `"_xform"` to the end of each of those five values
5. Outputs those resulting values with `println`

As this example shows, the code that receives the stream of values is written in a functional style, using methods like `drop`, `take`, and `map`, combining them into a chain of calls, one after the other.

> If you'd like to learn more about this topic, the RxScala project is located here[17], and Netflix's "Reactive Programming in the Netflix API with RxJava" blog post[18] is a good start.

2) Pragmatism (the best tool for the job)

I tend to be a pragmatist more than a purist, so when I need to get something done, I want to use the best tool for the job.

For instance, when I first started working with Scala and needed a way to stub out new SBT projects, I wrote a Unix shell script. Because this was for my personal use and I only work on Mac and Unix systems, creating a shell script was *by far* the simplest way to create a standard set of subdirectories and a *build.sbt* file.

---

[17] https://github.com/ReactiveX/RxScala
[18] http://techblog.netflix.com/2013/02/rxjava-netflix-api.html

Conversely, if I also programmed on Microsoft Windows or Linux systems, or if I had been interested in creating a more robust solution like the Lightbend Activator[19], I might have written a Scala/FP application, but I didn't have those motivating factors. For my needs, writing that shell script was the most pragmatic solution to the problem.

> Another way to think about this is instead of asking, "Is FP the right tool for every application I need to write?," go ahead and ask that question with a different technology. For instance, you can ask, "Should I use *Akka actors* to write every application?" If you're familiar with Akka, I think you'll agree that writing an Akka application to create a few subdirectories and a *build.sbt* file would be overkill — even though Akka is a terrific tool for other applications.

Summary

In summary, potential drawbacks of *functional programming in general* are:

1. Writing pure functions is easy, but combining them into a complete application is where things get hard.
2. The advanced math terminology (monad, monoid, functor, etc.) makes FP intimidating.
3. For many people, recursion doesn't feel natural.
4. Because you can't mutate existing data, you instead use a pattern that I call, "Update as you copy."
5. Pure functions and I/O don't really mix.
6. Using only immutable values and recursion can potentially lead to performance problems, including RAM use and speed.

Potential drawbacks of *functional programming in Scala* are:

7. You can mix FP and OOP styles.
8. Scala doesn't have a standard FP library.

What's next

Having covered the benefits and drawbacks of functional programming, in the next chapter I want to help "free your mind," as Morpheus might say. That chapter is on something I call, "The Great FP Terminology Barrier," and how to break through that barrier.

---

[19]https://www.lightbend.com/activator/download

13

The "Great FP Terminology Barrier"

> *"They say no ship can survive this."*
>
> — Hikaru Sulu, talking about "The Great Barrier" in *Star Trek V: The Final Frontier*

A short excursion to ... The Twilight Zone

Hello, Rod Serling of The Twilight Zone[1] here. Al will be back shortly, but for now, let me take you to another place and time ... an alternate universe ...

In this alternate universe you are born a few years earlier, and one day you find yourself writing some code. One week, you create a `List` class, and then a few days after that you find yourself writing the same `for` loops over and over again to iterate over list elements. Recognizing a pattern and also wanting to be DRY ("Don't Repeat Yourself"), you create a cool new method on the `List` class to replace those repetitive `for` loops:

```
val xs = List(1, 2, 3).applyAFunctionToEveryElement(_ * 2)
```

You originally named this method, "apply a function to every element *and return a value for each element*," but after deciding that was way too long for a function name, you shortened it to `applyAFunctionToEveryElement`.

But the problem with this shorter name is that it's not technically accurate. Because you are applying a function to each element and then returning the corresponding result for each element, you need a better name. But what name is accurate — and concise?

Pulling out your handy thesaurus, you come up with possible method names like these:

- apply

---

[1] http://www.imdb.com/title/tt0052520/

- convert
- evolve
- transform
- transmute
- metamorphose

As you try to settle on which of these names is best, your mathematics buddy peers over your shoulder and asks, "What are you doing?" After you explain what you're working on, he says, "Oh, cool. In mathematics we call that sort of thing 'map.'" Then he pats you on the back, wishes you luck, and goes back to doing whatever it is that mathematicians do.

While some of the names you've come up with are good, this brief talk with your friend makes you think that it might be good to be consistent with mathematics. After all, you want mathematicians and scientists to use your programming language, so you decide to name your new method map:

```
val xs = List(1, 2, 3).map(_ * 2)
```

"Whoa," you think to yourself, "that looks cool. I'll bet there are zillions of functions that people can pass into map to achieve all kinds of cool things. And then I can use phrases like 'map over a list.'" Things are taking shape.

map as a general concept

As you think about your invention, it occurs to you that there are at least a few different data types in the world that can be mapped over ... not just lists, but hashmaps, too. Shoot, you can even think of a String as a Seq[Char], and then even that can be mapped over. In time you realize that *any* collection whose elements can be iterated over can implement your new map function.

As this thought hits you, you realize that a logical thing to do is to create a trait that declares a map method. Then all of these other collections can extend that trait and implement their own map methods. With this thought, you begin sketching a new trait:

```
trait ThingsThatCanBeMappedOver {

    // extending classes need to implement this
    def map[A, B](f: A => B): TODO[B]

}
```

You realize that the map function signature isn't quite right — you're going to have to invent some other things to make this work — but never mind those details for now, you're on a roll.

With that trait, you can now implement your List class like this:

```
class List extends ThingsThatCanBeMappedOver {
    ...
}
```

As you write that first line of code you realize that the trait name ThingsThatCanBeMappedOver isn't quite right. It's accurate, but a little long and perhaps unprofessional. You start to pull out your thesaurus again, but that act makes you think of your math buddy; what would he call this trait? It occurs to you that he would be comfortable writing code like this:

```
class List extends Map {
    ...
}
```

and as a result, you decide to call your new trait Map:

```
trait Map {

    // extending classes need to implement this
    def map[A, B](f: A => B): TODO[B]

}
```

There, that looks professional, and math-y like, too. Now you just have to figure out the correct function signature, and possibly implement a default method body.

Sadly, just at that moment, Rod Serling returns you to this version of planet Earth ...

And the moral is ...

In this version of Earth's history, someone beat you to the invention of "things that can be mapped over," and for some reason — possibly because they had a mathematics background — they made this declaration:

> "Things that can be mapped over shall be called ... *Functor*."

Huh?

History did not record whether the Ballmer Peak[2], caffeine, or other chemicals were involved in that decision.

In this book, when I use the phrase, "Functional Programming Terminology Barrier," this is the sort of thing I'm referring to. If a normal human being had discovered this technique, they might have come up with a name like `ThingsThatCanBeMappedOver`, but a mathematician discovered it and came up with the name, "Functor."

> Moral: A lot of FP terminology comes from mathematics. Don't let it get you down.

A few more FP terms

As a few more examples of the *terminology barrier* I'm referring to, here are some other terms you'll run into as you try to learn functional programming:

Term	Definition
combinator	Per the *Haskell wiki*, this has two meanings, but the common meaning is, "a style of organizing libraries centered around the idea of combining things." This refers to being able to combine functions together like a Unix command pipeline, i.e., `ps aux	grep root	wc -l`.
higher-order function	A function that takes other functions as parameters, or whose result is a function.
lambda	Another word for "anonymous function."

As these examples show, when you get into FP you'll start seeing new terminology, and oftentimes they aren't terms that you need to know for other forms of programming. For instance, I taught Java and OOP classes for five years, and I didn't know these words at that time.

A common theme is that these terms generally come from mathematics fields like category theory[3]. Personally, I like math, so this is good for me. When someone uses a term like

---
[2] https://xkcd.com/323/
[3] https://en.wikipedia.org/wiki/Category_theory

"Combinatory Logic[4]," I think, "Oh, cool, what's that? Is it something that can make me a better programmer?"

However, a bad thing about it is that it's easy to get lost in the terminology. If you've ever been lost in a forest, the feeling is just like that.

> As I write later in this book, I personally wasted a lot of time wondering, "What is *currying*? Why does everyone write about it so much?" That was a real waste of time.

I'll say this more than once in this book: the best thing you can do to learn FP is to write code using only pure functions and immutable values, and see where that leads you. If you place those restrictions on yourself, you'll eventually come up with the same inventions that mathematicians have come up with — and you might have simpler names for all of the terms.

> "Mathematicians have big, scary words like 'identity' and 'associativity' and 'commutativity' to talk about this stuff — it's their shorthand."
>
> ~ From the book, *Coders at Work*

More terms coming …

The key point of this lesson is that there's generally no need to worry about a lot of mathematical and FP jargon, especially when you're first getting started. As I found out through my own experience, all this terminology does is create a learning barrier.

That being said, one *good* thing about terminology is that it lets us know that we're all talking about the same thing. Therefore, I'll introduce new terms as they naturally come up in the learning process.

---

[4] https://wiki.haskell.org/Combinatory_logic

14

Pure Functions

> *"When a function is pure, we say that 'output depends (only) on input.'"*
>
> — From the book, *Becoming Functional*
> (with the word "only" added by me)

Goals

This lesson has two main goals:

1. Properly define the term "pure function."
2. Show a few examples of pure functions.

It also tries to simplify the pure function definition, and shares a tip on how to easily identify many impure functions.

Introduction

As I mentioned in the "What is Functional Programming?" chapter, I define functional programming (FP) like this:

> *Functional programming* is a way of writing software applications using only pure functions and immutable values.

Because that definition uses the term "pure functions," it's important to understand what a pure function is. I gave a partial definition of pure functions in that chapter, and now I'll provide a more complete definition.

Definition of "pure function"

Just like the term *functional programming*, different people will give you different definitions of a pure function. I provide links to some of those at the end of this lesson, but skipping those for now, Wikipedia defines a pure function[1] like this:

1. The function always evaluates to the same result value given the same argument value(s). It cannot depend on any hidden state or value, and it cannot depend on any I/O.
2. Evaluation of the result does not cause any semantically observable side effect or output, such as mutation of mutable objects or output to I/O devices.

That's good, but I prefer to reorganize those statements like this:

1. A pure function depends only on (a) its declared input parameters and (b) its algorithm to produce its result. A pure function has no "back doors," which means:

    1. Its result can't depend on *reading* any hidden value outside of the function scope, such as another field in the same class or global variables.
    2. It cannot *modify* any hidden fields outside of the function scope, such as other mutable fields in the same class or global variables.
    3. It cannot depend on any external I/O. It can't rely on input from files, databases, web services, UIs, etc; it can't produce output, such as writing to a file, database, or web service, writing to a screen, etc.

2. A pure function does not modify its input parameters.

This can be summed up concisely with this definition:

> A *pure function* is a function that depends *only* on its declared input parameters and its algorithm to produce its output. It does not read any other values from "the outside world" — the world outside of the function's scope — and it does not modify any values in the outside world.

A mantra for writing pure functions

Once you've seen a formal pure function definition like that, I prefer this short mantra:

---
[1] https://en.wikipedia.org/wiki/Pure_function

Output depends only on input.

Even though that isn't 100% accurate (because it doesn't address side effects), I prefer it because it's short and easy to remember. In this book I'll generally just write, "Output depends only on input" when referring to pure functions.

The universe of a pure function

Another way to state this is that the universe of a pure function is only the input it receives, and the output it produces, as shown in Figure 14.1.

Figure 14.1: The entire universe of a pure function

If it seems like I'm emphasizing this point a lot, it's because I am(!). One of the most important concepts of functional programming is that FP applications are built almost entirely with pure functions, and pure functions are very different than what I used to write in my OOP career.

A great benefit of pure functions is that when you're writing them you don't have to think about anything else; all you have to think about is the universe of this function, which is what's coming into the function body from the outside world; what happens inside the function body; and what information you send back into the outside world.

Examples of pure and impure functions

Given the definition of pure functions and these simpler mantras, let's look at some examples of *pure* and *impure* functions.

Examples of pure functions

Mathematical functions are great examples of pure functions because it's pretty obvious that "output depends only on input." Methods like these in scala.math._[2] are all pure functions:

---
[2]http://www.scala-lang.org/api/current/#scala.math.package

- abs
- ceil
- max
- min

I refer to these as "methods" because they are defined using def in the package object math. However, these methods work just like functions, so I also refer to them as pure functions.

Because a Scala String is immutable, every method available to a String is a pure function, including:

- charAt
- isEmpty
- length
- substring

Many methods that are available on Scala's collections' classes fit the definition of a pure function, including the common ones:

- drop
- filter
- map
- reduce

Examples of impure functions

Conversely, the following functions are *impure*.

Going right back to the collections' classes, the foreach method is impure. foreach is used only for its side effects, which you can tell by looking at its signature on the Seq class[3]:

```
def foreach(f: (A) => Unit): Unit
```

Date and time related methods like getDayOfWeek, getHour, and getMinute are all impure because their output depends on something other than their inputs. Their results rely on some form of hidden I/O.

---

[3] http://www.scala-lang.org/api/current/#scala.collection.immutable.Seq

Methods on the `scala.util.Random` class like `nextInt` are also impure because their output depends on something other than their inputs.

In general, impure functions do one or more of these things:

- Read hidden inputs (variables not explicitly passed in as function input parameters)
- Write hidden outputs
- Mutate the parameters they are given
- Perform some sort of I/O with the outside world

Tip: Telltale signs of impure functions

By looking at function signatures *only*, there are two ways you can identify many impure functions:

- They don't have any input parameters
- They don't return anything (or they return `Unit` in Scala, which is the same thing)

For example, here's the signature for the `println` method of the Scala Predef object[4]:

```
def println(x: Any): Unit
```

Because `println` is such a commonly-used method, you already know that it writes information to the outside world, but if you didn't know that, its `Unit` return type would be a terrific hint of that behavior. It doesn't return anything, so it *must* be mutating something or interacting with the outside world.

Similarly when you look at Scala's "read*" methods you'll see that a method like `readLine` takes no input parameters, which is also a giveaway that it is impure:

```
def readLine(): String
```

Because it takes no input parameters, the mantra, "Output depends only on input" clearly can't apply to it.

Simply stated:

---

[4] http://www.scala-lang.org/api/current/#scala.Predef$

- *If a function has no input parameters*, how can its output depend on its input?
- *If a function has no result*, it must have side effects: mutating variables, or performing some sort of I/O.

While this is an easy way to spot many impure functions, other impure methods can have both (a) input parameters and (b) a non-Unit return type, but still be impure because they read variables outside of their scope, mutate variables outside of their scope, or perform I/O.

Summary

As you saw in this lesson, this is my formal definition of a pure function:

> A *pure function* is a function that depends *only* on its declared inputs and its internal algorithm to produce its output. It does not read any other values from "the outside world" — the world outside of the function's scope — and it does not modify any values in the outside world.

Once you understand the complete definition, I prefer the short mantra:

> Output depends *only* on input.

or this more accurate statement:

1. Output depends only on input
2. No side effects

See also

- The Wikipedia definition of a pure function[5]
- **Wikipedia has** a good discussion on "pure functions" on their Functional Programming page[6]
- The wolfram.com definition of a pure function[7]
- The schoolofhaskell.com definition of a pure function[8]
- The ocaml.org definition of a pure function[9]

---

[5] https://en.wikipedia.org/wiki/Pure_function
[6] https://en.wikipedia.org/wiki/Functional_programming#Pure_functions
[7] https://reference.wolfram.com/language/tutorial/PureFunctions.html
[8] https://www.schoolofhaskell.com/school/starting-with-haskell/basics-of-haskell/3-pure-functions-laziness-io
[9] https://ocaml.org/learn/tutorials/functional_programming.html#Pureandimpurefunctionalprogramming

Benefits of Pure Functions

The goal of this lesson is simple: to list and explain the benefits of writing pure functions.

Benefits of pure functions

My favorite benefits of pure functions are:

- They're easier to reason about
- They're easier to combine
- They're easier to test
- They're easier to debug
- They're easier to parallelize

FP developers talk about other benefits of writing pure functions. For instance, Venkat Subramaniam[1] adds these benefits:

- They are idempotent
- They offer referential transparency
- They are memoizable
- They can be lazy

In this lesson I'll examine each of these benefits.

Pure functions are easier to reason about

Pure functions are easier to reason about than impure functions, and I cover this in detail in the lesson, "Pure Function Signatures Tell All." The key point is that because a pure function has no side effects or hidden I/O, you can get a terrific idea of what it does just by looking at its signature.

---

[1] http://blog.agiledeveloper.com/2015/12/benefits-of-pure-functions.html

Pure functions are easier to combine

Because "output depends only on input," pure functions are easy to combine together into simple solutions. For example, you'll often see FP code written as a chain of function calls, like this:

```
val x = doThis(a).thenThis(b)
               .andThenThis(c)
               .doThisToo(d)
               .andFinallyThis(e)
```

This capability is referred to as *functional composition*. I'll demonstrate more examples of it throughout this book.

As you'll see in the "FP is Like Unix Pipelines" lesson, Unix pipelines are easy to create because most Unix commands are like pure functions: they read input and produce transformed output based only on the inputs and the algorithm you supply.

Pure functions are easier to test

As I showed in the "Benefits of Functional Programming" chapter, pure functions are easier to test than impure functions. I expand on this in several other lessons in this book, including the lessons on property-based testing.

Pure functions are easier to debug

In the "Benefits of Functional Programming" chapter I wrote that on a large scale, FP *applications* are easier to debug. In the small scale, pure functions are also easier to debug than their impure counterparts. Because the output of a pure function depends only on the function's input parameters and your algorithm, you don't need to look outside the function's scope to debug it.

Pure functions are easier to parallelize

I wrote in the "Benefits of Functional Programming" chapter that it's easier to write parallel/concurrent applications with FP. Because all of those same reasons apply here I won't repeat them, but I will show one example of how a compiler can optimize code within a pure function.

I'm not a compiler writer, so I'll begin with this statement from the "pure functions" section of the Wikipedia functional programming page[2]:

> "If there is no data dependency between two pure expressions, then their order can be reversed, or they can be performed in parallel and they cannot interfere with one another (in other terms, the evaluation of any pure expression is thread-safe)."

As an example of what that means, in this code:

```
val x = f(a)
val y = g(b)
val z = h(c)
val result = x + y + z
```

there are no data dependencies between the first three expressions, so they can be executed in any order. The only thing that matters is that they are executed before the assignment to `result`. If the compiler/interpreter wants to run those expressions in parallel, it can do that and then merge their values in the final expression. This can happen because (a) the functions are pure, and (b) there are no dependencies between the expressions.

That same Wikipedia page also states:

> "If the entire language does not allow side-effects, then any evaluation strategy can be used; this gives the compiler freedom to reorder or combine the evaluation of expressions in a program (for example, using deforestation)."

The 2006 article, Functional Programming for the Rest Of Us[a], includes a quote similar to these Wikipedia quotes. It states, "An interesting property of functional languages is that they can be reasoned about mathematically. Since a functional language is simply an implementation of a formal system, all mathematical operations that could be done on paper still apply to the programs written in that language. The compiler could, for example, convert pieces of code into equivalent but more efficient pieces with a mathematical proof that two pieces of code are equivalent. Relational databases have been performing these optimizations for years. There is

---

[2]https://en.wikipedia.org/wiki/Functional_programming#Pure_functions

no reason the same techniques can't apply to regular software."

[a]http://www.defmacro.org/ramblings/fp.html

Pure functions are idempotent

I don't use the word "idempotent" too often, so I'll quote from Venkat Subramaniam's explanation of the benefit of idempotence in regards to pure functions[3] (with a few minor edits by me):

> The word *idempotent* has a few different meanings ... a function or operation is idempotent if the result of executing it multiple times for a given input is the same as executing it only once for the same input. If we know that an operation is idempotent, we can run it as many times as we like ... it's safe to retry.

In a related definition, in A practical introduction to functional programming[4], Mary Rose Cook states:

> A process is *deterministic* if repetitions yield the same result every time.

The terms *idempotent* and *deterministic* are similar to a favorite phrase of mine: if you call a pure function with the same input(s) an infinite number of times, you will always get the same result.

> Honestly, with these definitions it feels like I'm writing, "A benefit of pure functions is that they are pure functions." My only reason for keeping this section is so that you have some exposure to the terms *idempotent* and *deterministic*.
>
> This demonstrates that like many other uncommon phrases in functional programming, you can understand a *concept* long before you know that someone created a label for that concept.

Pure functions offer referential transparency

Referential transparency (RT) is another technical term that you'll hear in the FP world. It's similar to idempotency, and refers to what you (and a compiler) can do because your func-

---

[3]http://blog.agiledeveloper.com/2015/12/benefits-of-pure-functions-idempotent.html
[4]https://maryrosecook.com/blog/post/a-practical-introduction-to-functional-programming

tions are pure.

If you like algebra, you'll like RT. It's said that an expression is *referentially transparent* if it can be replaced by its resulting value without changing the behavior of the program.

For instance, assume that x and y are immutable values within some scope of an application, and within that scope they're used to form this expression:

```
x + y
```

Then you can assign this expression to a third variable z:

```
val z = x + y
```

Now, throughout the given scope of your program, anywhere the expression x + y is used, it can be replaced by z without affecting the result of the program (and vice-versa).

Note that although I state that x and y are immutable values, they can also be the result of pure functions. For instance, "hello".length + "world".length will always be 10. This result could be assigned to z, and then z could be used everywhere instead of this expression. In Scala this looks like this:

```
val x = "hello".length    // 5
val y = "world".length    // 5
val z = x + y             // 10
```

Because all of those values are immutable, you can use z anywhere you might use x+y, and in fact, in this example you can replace z with 10 anywhere, and your program will run exactly the same.

> In FP we say things like, "10 cannot be reduced any more." (More on this later.)

Conversely, if x or y was an impure function, such as a "get the current time" function, z could not be a reliable replacement for x + y at different points in the application.

Pure functions are memoizable

Because a pure function always returns the same result when given the same inputs, a compiler (or your application) can also use caching optimizations, such as *memoization*.

Wikipedia defines memoization like this[5]:

> "Memoization is an optimization technique used primarily to speed up computer programs by storing the results of expensive function calls and returning the cached result when the same inputs occur again."

For example, I previously noted that my Android football game has this function call:

```
val possiblePlays = OffensiveCoordinator.determinePossiblePlays(gameState)
```

The `determinePossiblePlays` function currently has several thousand lines of pure functions behind it, and over time it's only going to get more complicated. Although this function doesn't currently use memoization, it would be fairly simple to create a cache for it, so that each time it received the same `gameState` it would return the same result.

The cache could be implemented as a `Map`, with a type of `Map[GameState, Seq[OffensivePlay]]`. Then when `determinePossiblePlays` receives a `GameState` instance, it could perform a fast lookup in this cache.

> While those statements are true, I don't want to oversimplify this too much. `determinePossiblePlays` makes decisions based on many `GameState` factors, including two important (a) game score and (b) time remaining. Those two variables would have to be factors in any cache.

Pure functions can be lazy

Laziness is a major feature of the Haskell language, where everything is lazy (lazily evaluated). In Scala I primarily use laziness with large data sets and streams — i.e., impure functions — so I haven't personally taken advantage of this benefit yet.

---

[5]https://en.wikipedia.org/wiki/Memoization

A quote from a Haskell co-creator

As a final note, here's a quote from the book, Masterminds of Programming[6], which discusses some of the benefits I just described:

> When asked, "What are the advantages of writing in a language without side effects?," Simon Peyton Jones, co-creator of Haskell, replied, "You only have to reason about values and not about state. If you give a function the same input, it'll give you the same output, every time. This has implications for reasoning, for compiling, for parallelism."

Summary

In this lesson I wrote about the benefits of pure functions. My favorite benefits are:

- They're easier to reason about
- They're easier to combine
- They're easier to test
- They're easier to debug
- They're easier to parallelize

Other FP developers write about these benefits of pure functions:

- They are idempotent
- They offer referential transparency
- They are memoizable
- They can be lazy

See also

- **Wikipedia has** a good discussion on the benefits of "pure functions" on their Functional Programming page[7]
- The Haskell.org definition of referential transparency[8]
- **Stack Exchange provides** a definition of referential transparency[9]

---

[6] http://amzn.to/2bedXb4
[7] https://en.wikipedia.org/wiki/Functional_programming#Pure_functions
[8] https://wiki.haskell.org/Referential_transparency
[9] http://programmers.stackexchange.com/questions/254304/what-is-referential-transparency

- Stack Overflow says, Don't worry about the term RT, it's for pointy-headed purists[10]
- If you like debates on the precise meaning of technical terms, reddit.com has a thread titled, Purity and referential transparency are different[11]

---

[10] http://stackoverflow.com/questions/4865616/purity-vs-referential-transparency
[11] https://www.reddit.com/r/haskell/comments/21y560/purity_and_referential_transparency_are_different/

16

Pure Functions and I/O

"The ancient Greeks have a knack of wrapping truths in myths."

George Lloyd

Goal

The goal of this lesson is to answer the question, "Because pure functions can't have I/O, how can an FP application possibly get anything done if all of its functions are pure functions?"

So how do you do anything with functional programming?

Given my pure function mantra, "Output depends only on input," a logical question at this point is:

> "How do I get anything done if I can't read any inputs or write any outputs?"

Great question!

The answer is that you violate the "Write Only Pure Functions" rule! It seems like many other resources go through great lengths to avoid answering that question, but I just gave you that answer fairly early in this book. (You're welcome.)

The general idea is that you write as much of your application as possible in an FP style, and then handle the UI and all forms of input/output (I/O) (such as Database I/O, Web Service I/O, File I/O, etc.) in the best way possible for your current programming language and tools.

In Scala the percentage of your code that's considered impure I/O will vary, depending on the application type, but will probably be in this range:

- On the low end, it will be about the same as a language like Java. So if you were to write an application in Java and 20% of it was going to be impure I/O code and 80% of it would be other stuff, in FP that "other stuff" will be pure functions. This assumes that you treat your UI, File I/O, Database I/O, Web Services I/O, and any other conceivable I/O the same way that you would in Java, without trying to "wrap" that I/O code in "functional wrappers." (More on this shortly.)

- On the high end, it will approach 100%, where that percentage relies on two things. First, you wrap all of your I/O code in functional wrappers. Second, your definition of "pure function" is looser than my definition.

I/O wrapper's code

I don't mean to make a joke or be facetious in that second statement. It's just that some people may try to tell you that by putting a wrapper layer around I/O code, the *impure* I/O function somehow becomes *pure*. Maybe somewhere in some mathematical sense that is correct, I don't know. Personally, I don't buy that.

Let me explain what I'm referring to.

Imagine that in Scala you have a function that looks like this:

```
def promptUserForUsername: String = ???
```

Clearly this function is intended to reach out into the outside world and prompt a user for a username. You can't tell *how* it does that, but the function name and the fact that it returns a String gives us that impression.

Now, as you might expect, every user of an application (like Facebook or Twitter) should have a unique username. Therefore, any time this function is called, it will return a different result. By stating that (a) the function gets input from a user, and (b) it can return a different result every time it's called, this is clearly not a *pure* function. It is *impure*.

However, now imagine that this same function returns a String that is wrapped in another type that I'll name IO:

```
def promptUserForUsername: IO[String] = ???
```

Notice that this a little like using the Option/Some/None pattern in Scala.

What's the benefit?

That's interesting, but what does this do for us?

Personally, I think it has one main benefit: I can glance at this function signature, and know that it deals with I/O, and therefore it's an impure function. In this particular example I can also infer that from the function name, but what if the function was named differently?:

```
def getUsername: IO[String] = ???
```

In this case `getUsername` is a little more ambiguous, so if it just returned String, I wouldn't know exactly how it got that String. But when I see that a String is wrapped with IO, I know that this function interacts with the outside world to get that String. That's pretty cool.

Does using IO make a function pure?

But this is where it gets interesting: some people state that wrapping promptUserForUsername's return type with IO makes it a pure function.

I am not that person.

The way I look at it, the first version of promptUserForUsername returned String values like these:

```
"alvin"
"kim"
"xena"
```

and now the second version of promptUserForUsername returns that same infinite number of different strings, but they're wrapped in the IO type:

```
IO("alvin")
IO("kim")
IO("xena")
```

Does that somehow make promptUserForUsername a pure function? I sure don't think so. It still interacts with the outside world, and it can still return a different value every time it's called, so by definition it's still an impure function.

I emphasize this point because you may read that Haskell's IO monad makes I/O pure. However, as Martin Odersky states in this Google Groups Scala debate[1]:

> "The IO monad does not make a function pure. It just makes it obvious that it's impure."

---

[1] https://groups.google.com/forum/#!topic/scala-debate/xYlUlQAnkmE%5B251-275%5D

Summary

As I showed in this lesson, when you need to write I/O code in functional programming languages, the solution is to violate the "Only Write Pure Functions" rule. The general idea is that you write as much of your application as possible in an FP style, and then handle the UI, Database I/O, Web Service I/O, and File I/O in the best way possible for your current programming language and tools.

I also showed that wrapping your I/O functions in an IO type doesn't make a function pure, but it is a great way to add something to your function's type signature to let every know, "This function deals with I/O." When a function returns a type like IO[String] you can be very sure that it reached into the outside world to get that String, and when it returns IO[Unit], you can be sure that it wrote something to the outside world.

What's next

So far I've covered a lot of background material about pure functions, and in the next lesson I share something that was an important discovery for me: The signatures of pure functions are much more meaningful than the signatures of impure functions.

See also

- The this Google Groups Scala debate[2] where Martin Odersky states, "The IO monad does not make a function pure. It just makes it obvious that it's impure."
- For more details about the IO monad in Haskell, see the "I/O in Haskell" section in the longer, online version of this lesson[3].

---

[2]https://groups.google.com/forum/#!topic/scala-debate/xYlUlQAnkmE%5B251-275%5D
[3]https://alvinalexander.com/scala/fp-book/pure-functions-and-io-input-output

17

Pure Function Signatures Tell All

> *"In Haskell, a function's type declaration tells you a whole lot about the function, due to the very strong type system."*
>
> From the book,
> *Learn You a Haskell for Great Good!*

One thing you'll find in FP is that the signatures of pure functions tell you a lot about what those functions do. In fact, it turns out that the signatures of functions in FP applications are *much* more important than they are in OOP applications. As you'll see in this lesson:

> Because pure functions have no side effects, their outputs depend only on their inputs, and all FP values are immutable, pure function signatures tell you exactly what the function does.

OOP function signatures

When writing OOP applications I never gave much thought to method signatures. When working on development teams I always thought, "Meh, let me see the method source code so I can figure out what it *really* does." I remember one time a junior developer wrote what should have been a simple Java "setter" method named `setFoo`, and its source code looked something like this:

```
public void setFoo(int foo) {
    this.foo = foo;
    makeAMeal(foo);
    foo++;
    washTheDishes(foo);
    takeOutTheTrash();
}
```

In reality I don't remember everything that setter method did, but I clearly remember the foo++ part, and then saw that it used the foo and foo++ values in other method calls. A method that —according to its signature — appeared to be a simple setter method was in fact much, much more than that.

I hope you see the problem here: there's no way to know what's *really* happening inside an impure function without looking at its source code.

Therefore, the first moral of this story is that because OOP methods *can* have side effects, I grew to only trust methods from certain people.

The second moral is that this situation can't happen with pure functions (certainly not as blatantly as this example).

Signatures of pure functions

The signatures of pure functions in Scala/FP have much more meaning than OOP functions because:

- They have no side effects
- Their output depends only on their inputs
- All values are immutable

To understand this, let's play a simple game.

A game called, "What can this pure function possible do?"

As an example of this — and as a first thought exercise — look at this function signature and ask yourself, "If FOO is a pure function, what can it possibly do?":

```
def FOO(s: String): Int = ???
```

Ignore the name FOO; I gave the function a meaningless name so you'd focus only on the rest of the type signature to figure out what this function can possibly do.

To solve this problem, let's walk through some preliminary questions:

- Can this function read user input? It can't have side effects, so, no.
- Can it write output to a screen? It can't have side effects, so, no.
- Can it write (or read) information to (or from) a file, database, web service, or any other external data source? No, no, no, and no.

So what can it do?

If you said that there's an excellent chance that this function does one of the following things, pat yourself on the back:

- Converts a `String` to an `Int`
- Determines the length of the input string
- Calculates a hashcode or checksum for the string

Because of the rules of pure functions, those are the only types of things this function can do. The `Int` result *must* depend on the `String` input. Output depends only on input.

A second game example

Here's a second example that shows how the signatures of pure functions tell you a lot about what a function does. Given this simple class:

```
case class Person[name: String]
```

What can a pure function with this signature possibly do?:

```
def FOO(people: Seq[Person], n: Int): Person = ???
```

I'll pause to let you think about it …

By looking only at the function signature, you can guess that the function probably returns the Nth element of the given `List[Person]`.

That's pretty cool. Because it's a pure function you know that the `Person` value that's returned must be coming from the `Seq[Person]` that was passed in.

As an additional exercise, if I remove the n input parameter from the function:

```
def FOO(people: Seq[Person]): Person = ???
```

Can you guess what this function can do?

(Pause to let you think …)

My best guesses are:

- It's a `head` function

- It's a `tail` function (that returns only the last element)

- It's a Frankenstein's Monster function that builds one `Person` from many `Persons`

A third game example

Here's a different variation of the "What can this pure function possibly do?" game. Imagine that you have the beginning of a function signature, where the input parameters are defined, but the return type is undefined:

```
def foo(s: String, i: Int) ...
```

Given only this information, can you answer the "What can this function possibly do?" question? That is, can you answer that question if you don't know what the function's return type is?

(Another pause to let you think ...)

The answer is "no." Even though `foo` is a pure function, you can't tell what it does until you see its return type. But ...

Even though you can't tell *exactly* what it does, you can guess a little bit. For example, because output depends only on input, these return types are all allowed by the definition of a pure function:

```
def foo1(s: String, i: Int): Char = ???
def foo2(s: String, i: Int): String = ???
def foo3(s: String, i: Int): Int = ???
def foo4(s: String, i: Int): Seq[String] = ???
```

Even though you can't tell what this function does without seeing its return type, I find this game fascinating. Where OOP method signatures had no meaning to me, I can make some really good guesses about what FP method signatures are trying to tell me — even when the function name is meaningless.

Trying to play the game with an impure method

Let's look at one last example. What can this method possibly do?:

```
def foo(p: Person): Unit = ...
```

Because it returns `Unit` (nothing), it *must* have a side effect of some sort. You can't know what those side effects are, but you can guess that it may do any or all of these things:

- Write to STDOUT
- Write to a file
- Write to a database
- Write to a web service
- Update some other variable(s) with the data in p
- Mutate the data in p
- Ignore p and do something totally unexpected

As you can see, trying to understand what an impure method can possibly do is much more complicated than trying to understand what a pure function can possibly do. As a result of this, I came to understand this phrase:

> Pure function signatures tell all.

Summary

As shown in this lesson, when a method has side effects there's no telling what it does, but when a function is pure its signature lets you make very strong guesses at what it does — even when you can't see the function name.

The features that make this possible are:

- The output of a pure function depends only on its inputs
- Pure functions have no side effects
- All values are immutable

What's next

Now that I've written several small lessons about pure functions, the next two lessons will show how combining pure functions into applications feels both like (a) algebra and (b) Unix pipelines.

18

Functional Programming as Algebra

Introduction

I like to start most lessons with a relevant quote, and this one comes from the book, Land of Lisp[1]:

> "Some advanced Lispers will cringe when someone says that a function 'returns a value.' This is because Lisp derives from something called lambda calculus, which is a fundamental programming-like algebra developed by Alonzo Church. In the lambda calculus you 'run' a program by performing substitution rules on the starting program to determine the result of a function. Hence, the result of a set of functions just sort of magically appears by performing substitutions; never does a function consciously 'decide' to return a value. Because of this, Lisp purists prefer to say that a function 'evaluates to a result.'"

Here's another quote, from the book, Thinking Functionally with Haskell[2]:

> "FP has a simple mathematical basis that supports equational reasoning about the properties of programs."

Because of functional programming's main features — pure functions and immutable values — writing FP code is like writing algebraic equations. Because I always liked algebra and thought it was simple, this made FP appealing to me.

I'll demonstrate what I mean in this lesson.

---

[1] http://amzn.to/1PjyUeL
[2] http://amzn.to/1PAJZtK

Goals

The first goal of this lesson is to give some examples of how FP code is like algebra.

A second goal of this lesson is to keep building an "FP way of thinking" about programming problems. The mindset of this lesson is that each pure function you write is like writing an algebraic equation, and then gluing those functions together to create a program is like combining a series of algebraic equations together to solve a math problem.

As the first quote I shared states, when you begin to think about your functions as "evaluating to a result," you'll be in a state of mind where you're thinking about solving problems and writing your code as being like writing algebraic equations, and that's a good thing.

Background: Algebra as a reason for "Going FP"

Hopefully you'll find your own reasons for "Going FP," but for me the lightbulb went on over my head when I realized that FP let me look at my code this way. Gluing pure functions together felt like combining a series of algebraic equations together — i.e., algebraic substitution — and because I like algebra, this was a good thing.

Before learning FP, my background was in OOP. I first learned and then taught Java and OOP in the 1990s and early 2000s, and with that background I always looked at problems from the eyes of an OOP developer. OOP never made me see writing code as being like writing mathematical expressions. I always thought, "Okay, these things here are my objects (`Pizza`, `Topping`, `Order`), these are their behaviors (`addTopping`), and they hide their internal workings from other objects."

But since learning FP I now see my code as being more like algebra, and it's a very different perspective. I clearly remember my first thought when I saw the connection between FP and algebra:

> "Whoa ... if my function's output depends solely on its input, well, shoot, I can always write *one* pure function. If I can write one pure function, then I can write another, and then another. And then once they're all working I can glue them together to form a complete solution, like a series of equations. And since they're all pure functions

> they can't really fail — especially not because of hidden state issues — at least not if I test them properly."

Sometimes programming can get a little overwhelming when you think about writing an entire application, but when I realized that I can always write one pure function, that gave me a tremendous sense of confidence.

As a programming tip, when you're writing a pure function, think of that function as your world, your only concern in the entire world. Because "output depends only on input," all you have to think about is that some inputs are coming into your function (your world), and all you need to do is create an algorithm to transform those inputs into the desired result.

Background: Defining algebra

It's important to understand what "algebra" is so you can really internalize this lesson. Unfortunately, trying to find a good definition of algebra is difficult because many people go right from the word "algebra" to "mathematics," and that's not what I have in mind. This informal definition of algebra by Daniel Eklund[3] fits my way of thinking a little better:

> For purposes of simplicity, let us define algebra to be two things: 1) a SET of objects (not "objects" as in object-oriented), and 2) the
> OPERATIONS used on those objects to create new objects from that set.

As emphasized, the key words in that sentence are *set* and *operations*. Mr. Eklund goes on to define "numeric algebra":

> In the case of *numeric* algebra — informally known as high-school algebra — the SET is the set of numbers (whether they be natural, rational, real, or complex) and the OPERATIONS used on these objects can be (but definitely not limited to be) addition or multiplication. The *algebra of numbers* is therefore the study of this set, and the laws by which these operators generate (or don't generate) new members from this set.

As an example, a *set* of natural numbers[4] is [0,1,2 ... infinity]. *Operations* on that set can be add, subtract, and multiply, and new members are generated using these operators, such as 1 + 2 yielding 3.

---
[3]http://merrigrove.blogspot.com/2011/12/another-introduction-to-algebraic-data.html
[4]https://en.wikipedia.org/wiki/Natural_number

Mr. Eklund goes on to define other types of algebras, but for our purposes I'll just share one more sentence:

> The key thing to realize here is that an algebra lets us talk about the objects and the operations abstractly, and to consider the laws that these operations obey as they operate on the underlying set.

In Scala/FP, the "objects" Mr. Eklund refers to can be thought of as the built-in Scala types and the custom types you create, and the "operations" can be thought of as the pure functions you write that work with those types.

For instance, in a pizza store application, the "set" might include types like Pizza, Topping, Customer, and Order. To find the operations that work with that set, you have to think about the problem domain. In a pizza store you add toppings to a pizza that a customer wants, and then you can add one or more pizzas to an order for that customer. The types are your set (the nouns), and the functions you create define the only possible operations (verbs) that can manipulate that set.

Given that discussion, a Scala trait for a Pizza type might look like this:

```
trait Pizza {
    def setCrustSize(s: CrustSize): Pizza
    def setCrustType(t: CrustType): Pizza
    def addTopping(t: Topping): Pizza
    def removeTopping(t: Topping): Pizza
    def getToppings(): Seq[Topping]
}
```

In the same way that 1 is a natural number and can work with operations like *add* and *subtract*, Pizza is a type and can work with the operations (methods) it defines.

From algebra to FP

If you haven't worked with algebra in a while, it may help to see a few algebraic functions as a refresher:

```
f(x) = x + 1
f(x,y) = x + y
f(a,b,c,x) = a * x^2 + b*x + c
```

It's easy to write those algebraic equations as pure functions in Scala/FP. Assuming that all the values are integers, they can be written as these functions in Scala:

```
def f(x: Int) = x + 1
def f(x: Int, y: Int) = x + y
def f(a: Int, b: Int, c: Int, x: Int) = a*x*x + b*x + c
```

These are pure functions ("output depends only on input") that use only immutable values. This shows one way that FP is like algebra, by starting with algebraic functions and then writing the Scala/FP versions of those functions.

From FP to algebra

Similarly I can start with Scala/FP code and show how it looks like algebraic equations. For example, take a look at these Scala expressions:

```
val emailDoc = getEmailFromServer(src)
val emailAddr = getAddr(emailDoc)
val domainName = getDomainName(emailAddr)
```

You can see how that code is like algebra if I add comments to it:

```
val emailDoc = getEmailFromServer(src)       // val b = f(a)
val emailAddr = getAddr(emailDoc)            // val c = g(b)
val domainName = getDomainName(emailAddr)    // val d = h(c)
```

No matter what these functions do behind the scenes, they are essentially algebraic expressions, so you can reduce them just like you reduce mathematical expressions. Using simple substitution, the first two expressions can be combined to yield this:

```
val emailAddr = getAddr(getEmailFromServer(src))
val domainName = getDomainName(emailAddr)
```

Then those two expressions can be reduced to this:

```
val domainName = getDomainName(getAddr(getEmailFromServer(src)))
```

If you look at the comments I added to the code, you'll see that I started with this:

```
val b = f(a)
val c = g(b)
val d = h(c)
```

and reduced it to this:

```
val d = h(g(f(a)))
```

I can make these substitutions because the code is written as a series of expressions that use pure functions.

You can write the code in the three lines, or perform the substitutions to end up with just one line. Either approach is valid, and equal. What makes this possible is that other than `getEmailFromServer(src)`, which is presumably an impure function, the code:

- Only uses pure functions (no side effects)
- Only uses immutable values

When your code is written like that, it really is just a series of algebraic equations.

Benefit: Algebra is predictable

A great thing about algebra is that the results of algebraic equations are incredibly predictable. For example, if you have a `double` function like this:

```
def double(i: Int) = i * 2
```

you can then call it with the number 1 an infinite number of times and it will always return 2. That may seem obvious, but hey, it's how algebra works.

Because of this, you know that these things will *always* happen:

```
println(double(1))   // prints 2
println(double(2))   //   "    4
println(double(3))   //   "    6
```

And you also know that this can *never* happen:

```
println(double(1))   // prints 5   (can never happen)
println(double(1))   // prints 17  (can never happen)
```

With pure functions you can never have two different return values for the same input value(s). This can't happen with pure functions, and it can't happen with algebra, either.

A game: What can possibly go wrong?

A great thing about thinking about your code as algebra is that you can look at one of your pure functions and ask, "What can possibly go wrong with this function?" When you do so, I hope that trying to find any problems with it will be very difficult. After thinking about it long and hard I hope you get to the point of saying, "Well, I guess the JVM could run out of RAM (but that doesn't have anything directly to do with my function)."

My point is that because it's isolated from the rest of the world, it should be a real struggle to think about how your pure function can possibly fail. When you're writing OOP code you have to concern yourself that "output *does not* only depend on input," which means that you have to think about everything else in the application that can fail or be a problem — i.e., things like (a) state of the application outside the function's scope, and (b) variables being mutated while you're trying to use them — but with FP code you don't have those concerns.

For example, imagine that you're writing a multi-threaded imperative application, you've been given a list of users, and the purpose of your function is to sort that list of users. There are a lot of ways to sort lists, so that isn't hard, but what happens to your code if that list of users is mutated by another thread while your function is trying to sort the list? For instance, imagine that 20 users are removed from the list while you're trying to sort it; what will happen to your function?

You can demonstrate this problem for yourself. Remembering that Scala Array elements can be mutated, imagine that you have an Array[String] like this:

```
// 1 - a mutable sequence to work with
val arr = Array("one", "two", "three", "four", "five")
```

Then imagine that you begin printing the length of each string in a different thread, like this:

```
// 2 - start printing the numbers in a different thread
val thread = new Thread {
    override def run {
        printStringLength(arr)
    }
}
thread.start
```

If you now mutate the array like this:

```
// 3 - mutate the sequence to see how that other thread works
Thread.sleep(100)
arr(3) = null
```

you can easily generate a `NullPointerException` if your `printStringLength` method looks like this:

```
def printStringLength(xs: Seq[String]) {
    for (x <- xs) {
        println(x.length)
        Thread.sleep(200)
    }
}
```

Conversely, it's impossible to replicate this example if you use a Scala `Vector` or `List`. Because these sequences are immutable, you can't accidentally mutate a sequence in one thread while it's being used in another.

Transform as you copy, don't mutate

In my previous Java/OOP life I mutated variables all the time. That's how I did almost everything, and frankly, I didn't know there was another way. I knew that a Java `String` was immutable, but based on my OOP thinking, I thought this was more of a pain than anything that was actually helpful to me.

But when you think of your code as algebra, you realize that mutating a variable has nothing to do with algebra. For instance, I never had a math instructor who said, "Okay, x is currently 10, but let's go ahead and add 1 to it so x is now 11." Instead what they said is, "Okay, we have x, which is 10, and what we'll do is add 1 to it to get a new value y":

```
x = 10
y = x + 1
```

In FP code you do the same thing. You never mutate x, but instead you use it as a foundation to create a new value. In Scala, you typically do this using the case class `copy` method.

The case class `copy` method

When you use a Scala *case class* you automatically get a `copy` method that supports this "transform as you copy" algebraic philosophy.

A simple way to demonstrate this is to show what happens when a person changes their name. I'll demonstrate this with two variations of a `Person` class, first showing an OOP/imperative approach, and then showing an FP/algebraic approach.

With OOP code, when Jonathan Stuart Leibowitz changes his name to Jon Stewart, you write code like this:

```
// oop design
class Person(var name: String)

// create an instance with the original name
var p = new Person("Jonathan Stuart Leibowitz")

// change the name by mutating the instance
p.name = "Jon Stewart"
```

In my OOP life I wrote code like that all the time and never gave it a second thought. But you just don't do that sort of thing in algebra. Instead, what you do in FP/algebraic code is this:

```
// fp design
case class Person(name: String)

// create an instance with the original name
val p = Person("Jonathan Stuart Leibowitz")

// create a new instance with the "update as you copy" approach
val p2 = p.copy(name = "Jon Stewart")
```

The FP approach uses the `copy` method to create a new value `p2` from the original `p`, resulting in `p2.name` being "Jon Stewart."

Mathematically, the last two lines of the FP approach are similar to this:

```
val p  = a
val p2 = p + b
```

It's good to see the case class `copy` approach now, because (a) it's a Scala/FP idiom, and (b) we're going to use it a lot in this book.

> As I mentioned earlier, I *never* thought of my OOP code as having the slightest thing to do with algebra. Now I think of it that way all the time, and that thought process is the result of writing pure functions and using only immutable

variables.

Later in this book: Algebraic Data Types

Another way that FP relates to algebra is with a concept known as Algebraic Data Types, or ADTs. Don't worry about that name, ADT is a simple concept. For example, this code is an ADT:

```
sealed trait Bool
case object True extends Bool
case object False extends Bool
```

This code from the book, Beginning Scala[5], is also an ADT:

```
sealed trait Shape
case class Circle(radius: Double) extends Shape
case class Square(length: Double) extends Shape
case class Rectangle(h: Double, w: Double) extends Shape
```

I don't want to get into this in much detail right now, I just want to let you know that there's more algebra later in this book. The "algebra" in ADTs is described on the Haskell wiki[6] like this:

> "Algebraic" refers to the property that an Algebraic Data Type is created by "algebraic" operations. The "algebra" here is "sums" and "products" (of types).

Again, don't fear the term; it's another complicated-sounding term for a simple concept, as shown in these examples.

Summary

In this lesson I tried to show a few ways that functional programming is like algebra. I showed how simple algebraic functions can be written as pure functions in Scala, and I showed how a series of Scala expressions looks just like a series of algebraic functions. I also demonstrated how a series of expressions can be reduced using simple algebraic substitution. I also noted that in the future you'll learn about a term named Algebraic Data Types.

---

[5] http://amzn.to/1MRH8tp
[6] https://wiki.haskell.org/Algebraic_data_type

The intent of this lesson is to help you keep building an "FP way of thinking" about programming problems. If you write your code using only pure functions and immutable variables, your code will natural migrate towards this algebraic way of thinking:

> Pure Functions + Immutable Values == Algebra

Who knows, you may even start saying that your functions "evaluate to a result."

19

A Note About Expression-Oriented Programming

> *"Statements do not return results and are executed solely for their side effects, while expressions always return a result and often do not have side effects at all."*
>
> From the Wikipedia page on Expression-Oriented Programming[a]

[a] https://en.wikipedia.org/wiki/Expression-oriented_programming_language

Goals

This chapter isn't a *lesson* so much as it as an observation — a short note that the FP code I'm writing in this book also falls into a category known as *Expression-Oriented Programming*, or EOP.

In fact, because Pure FP code is more strict than EOP, FP is a superset of EOP. As a result, we just happen to be writing EOP code while we're writing Scala/FP code.

Therefore, my goals for this lesson are:

- To show the difference between *statements* and *expressions*
- To briefly explain and demonstrate EOP
- To note that all "Pure FP" code is also EOP code

(I wrote about EOP in the Scala Cookbook[1], so I'll keep this discussion short.)

Statements and expressions

When you write pure functional code, you write a series of expressions that combine pure functions. In addition to this code conforming to an FP style, the style also fits the definition of "Expression-Oriented Programming," or EOP. This means that every line of code returns a result ("evaluates to a result"), and is therefore an *expression* rather than a *statement*.

> As noted in the quote at the beginning of this chapter, statements do not return results, and are executed solely for their side effects.

An *expression* has the form:

```
val resultingValue = somePureFunction(someImmutableValues)
```

Contrast that with the OOP "statement-oriented code" I used to write:

```
order.calculateTaxes()
order.updatePrices()
```

Those two lines of code are *statements* because they don't have a return value; they're just executed for their side effects.

In FP and EOP you write those same statements as expressions, like this:

```
val tax = calculateTax(order)
val price = calculatePrice(order)
```

While that may seem like a minor change, the effect on your overall coding style is huge. Writing code in an EOP style is essentially a gateway to writing in an FP style.

A key point

A key point of this lesson is that when you see statements like this:

---

[1] http://amzn.to/24ivK4G

```
order.calculateTaxes()
order.updatePrices()
```

you should think, "Ah, these are *statements* that are called for their side effects. This is imperative code, not FP code."

Scala supports EOP (and FP)

Scala provides strong support for FP code, and therefore, EOP code. As I noted in the Scala Cookbook[2], these are obviously *expressions*:

```
val x = 2 + 2
val doubles = List(1,2,3,4,5).map(_ * 2)
```

But it's a little less obvious that the if/then construct can also be used to write expressions:

```
val greater = if (a > b) a else b
```

The match construct also evaluates to a result, and is used to write expressions:

```
val evenOrOdd = i match {
    case 1 | 3 | 5 | 7 | 9 => println("odd")
    case 2 | 4 | 6 | 8 | 10 => println("even")
}
```

And try/catch blocks are also used to write expressions:

```
def toInt(s: String): Int = {
    try {
        s.toInt
    } catch {
        case _ : Throwable => 0
    }
}
```

---

[2]http://amzn.to/24ivK4G

Summary

When every line of code has a return value, it's said that you are writing *expressions*, and using an EOP style. In contrast, *statements* are lines of code that do not have return values, and are executed for their side effects. When you see statements in code you should think, "This is imperative code, not FP code."

As noted in this lesson, because EOP is a subset of an FP style, when you write Scala/FP code you are also writing EOP code.

What's next

Given this background, the next lesson shows how writing Unix pipeline commands also fits an EOP style, and in fact, an FP style.

20

Functional Programming is Like Unix Pipelines

> *"Pipes facilitated function composition on the command line. You could take an input, perform some transformation on it, and then pipe the output into another program. This provided a very powerful way of quickly creating new functionality with simple composition of programs. People started thinking how to solve problems along these lines."*
>
> Alfred Aho, one of the creators of the AWK programming language, in the book, Masterminds of Programming[a]

---

[a] http://amzn.to/2bedXb4

Goals

The primary goal of this lesson is to show that you can think of writing functional programs as being like writing Unix pipeline commands. Stated another way, if you've written Unix pipeline commands before, you have probably written code in a functional style, whether you knew it or not.

As a second, smaller goal, I want to demonstrate a few ways that you can look at your code visually to help you "Think in FP."

> Note: This section is written for Unix and Linux users. If you don't know Unix, (a) I highly recommend learning it, and (b) you may want to (sadly) skip this section, as it may not make much sense unless you know the Unix commands that I show.

Discussion

One way to think about FP is that it's like writing Unix/Linux pipeline commands, i.e., a series of two or more commands that you combine at the Unix command line to get a desired result.

For example, imagine that your boss comes to you and says, "I need a script that will tell me how many unique users are logged into a Unix system at any given time." How would you solve this problem?

Knowing Unix, you know that the who command shows the users that are currently logged in. So you know that you want to start with who — that's your data source. To make things interesting, let's assume that who doesn't support any command-line arguments, so all you can do is run who without arguments to generate a list of users logged into your system, like this:

```
$ who
al         console   Oct 10 10:01
joe        ttys000   Oct 10 10:44
tallman    ttys001   Oct 10 11:05
joe        ttys002   Oct 10 11:47
```

who's output is well structured and consistent. It shows the username in the first column, the "console" they're logged in on in the second column, and the date and time they logged in on in the last columns.

> Some Unix systems may show the IP address the user is logged in from. I left that column off of these examples to keep things simple.

If you didn't have to automate this solution, you could solve the problem by looking at the unique usernames in the first column. In this case there are four lines of output, but only three of the usernames are unique — al, joe, and tallman — so the answer to your boss's question is that there are three unique users logged into the system at the moment.

Now that you know how to solve the problem manually, the question becomes, how do you automate this solution?

An algorithm

The solution's algorithm appears to be:

- Run the who command
- Create a list of usernames from the first column

- Get only the unique usernames from that list
- Count the size of that list

In Unix that algorithm translates to chaining these commands together:

- Start with who as the data source
- Use a command like cut to create the list of usernames
- Use uniq to get only the unique usernames from that list
- Use wc -l to count those unique usernames

Implementing the algorithm

A solution for the first two steps is to create this simple Unix pipeline:

```
who | cut -d' ' -f1
```

That cut command can be read as, "Using a blank space as the field separator (-d' '), print the first field (-f1) of every row of the data stream from STDIN to STDOUT." That pipeline command results in this output:

```
al
joe
tallman
joe
```

Notice what I did here: I combined two Unix commands to get a desired result. If you think of the who command as providing a list of strings, you can think of the cut command as being a pure function: it takes a list of strings as an input parameter, runs a transformation algorithm on that incoming data, and produces an output list of strings. It doesn't use anything but the incoming data and its algorithm to produce its result.

As a quick aside, the signature for a Scala cut function that works like the Unix cut command might be written like this:

```
def cut(strings: Seq[String],
        delimiter: String,
        field: Int): Seq[String] = ???
```

Getting back to the problem at hand, my current pipeline command generates this output:

```
al
```

```
joe
tallman
joe
```

and I need to transform that data into a "number of unique users."

To finish solving the problem, all I need to do is to keep combining more pure functions — er, Unix commands — to get the desired answer. That is, I need to keep transforming the data to get it into the format I want.

The next thing I need to do is reduce that list of *all users* down to a list of *unique users*. I do that by adding the `uniq` command to the end of the current pipeline:

```
who | cut -d' ' -f1 | uniq
```

`uniq` transforms its STDIN to this STDOUT:

```
al
joe
tallman
```

Now all I have to do to get the number of unique users is count the number of lines that are in the stream with `wc -l`:

```
who | cut -d' ' -f1 | uniq | wc -l
```

That produces this output:

```
      3
```

Whoops. What's that 3 doing way over there to the right? I want to think of my result as being an `Int` value, but this is more like a `String` with a bunch of leading spaces. What to do?

Well, it's Unix, so all I have to do is add another command to the pipeline to transform this string-ish result to something that works more like an integer.

There are many ways to handle this, but I know that the Unix `tr` command is a nice way to remove blank spaces, so I add it to the end of the current pipeline:

```
who | cut -d' ' -f1 | uniq | wc -l | tr -d ' '
```

That gives me the final, desired answer:

3

That looks more like an integer, and it won't cause any problem if I want to use this result as an input to some other command that expects an integer value (with no leading blank spaces).

The solution as a shell script

Now that I have a solution as a Unix pipeline, I can convert it into a little shell script. For the purposes of this lesson, I'll write it in a verbose manner rather than as a pipeline:

```
WHO=`who`
RES1=`echo $WHO  | cut -d' ' -f1`
RES2=`echo $RES1 | uniq`
RES3=`echo $RES2 | wc -l`
RES4=`echo $RES3 | tr -d ' '`
echo $RES4
```

Hmm, that looks suspiciously like a series of *expressions*, followed by a print statement, doesn't it? Some equivalent Scala code might look like this:

```
val who: Seq[String] = getUsers    // an impure function
val res1 = cut(who, " ", 1)
val res2 = uniq(res1)
val res3 = countLines(res2)
val res4 = trim(res3)
println(res4)                      // a statement
```

Combining simple expressions

I usually write "one expression at a time" code like this when I first start solving a problem, and eventually see that I can combine the expressions. For example, because the first and last lines of code are impure functions I might want to leave them alone, but what about these remaining lines?:

```
val res1 = cut(who, " ", 1)
val res2 = uniq(res1)
val res3 = countLines(res2)
val res4 = trim(res3)
```

In the first line, because cut is a pure function, res1 and cut(who, " ", 1) will always be equivalent, so I can eliminate res1 as an intermediate value:

```
val res2 = uniq(cut(who, " ", 1))
val res3 = countLines(res2)
val res4 = trim(res3)
```

Next, because res2 is always equivalent to the right side of its expression, I can eliminate res2 as an intermediate value:

```
val res3 = countLines(uniq(cut(who, " ", 1)))
val res4 = trim(res3)
```

Then I eliminate res3 for the same reason:

```
val res4 = trim(countLines(uniq(cut(who, " ", 1))))
```

Because there are no more intermediate values, it makes sense to rename res4:

```
val result = trim(countLines(uniq(cut(who, " ", 1))))
```

If you want, you can write the entire original series of expressions and statements — including getUsers and the println statement — like this:

```
println(trim(countLines(uniq(cut(getUsers, " ", 1)))))
```

As a recap, I started with this:

```
val who: Seq[String] = getUsers
val res1 = cut(who, " ", 1)
val res2 = uniq(res1)
val res3 = countLines(res2)
val res4 = trim(res3)
println(res4)
```

and ended up with this:

```
println(trim(countLines(uniq(cut(getUsers, " ", 1)))))
```

The thing that enables this transformation is that all of those expressions in the middle of the original code are pure function calls.

That code shows the Scala equivalent of the Unix pipeline solution:

```
who | cut -d' ' -f1 | uniq | wc -l | tr -d ' '
```

> I find solutions like this amusing, because condensed Scala code like this tends to look like Lisp code. To read the code, you start at the inside (with getUsers), and work your way out (to cut, then uniq, etc.).

As a final note, you don't have to use this condensed style. Use whatever style you're comfortable with.

How is this like functional programming?

"That's great," you say, "but how is this like functional programming?"

Well, when you think of the who command as generating a list of strings (Seq[String]), you can then think of cut, uniq, wc, and tr as being a series of transformer functions, because they transform the input they're given into a different type of output, as shown in Figure 20.1.

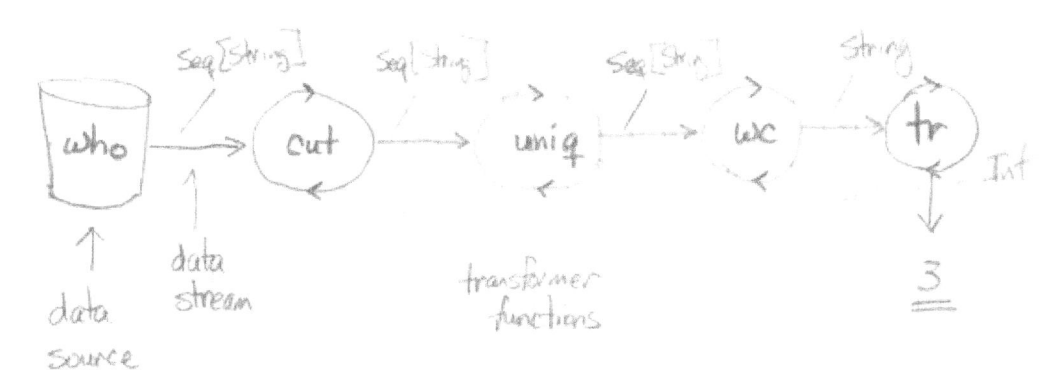

Figure 20.1: Unix commands transform their input into their output

Looking at just the wc command — and thinking of it as a pure function — you can think of it as taking a Seq[String] as its first input parameter, and when it's given the -l argument, it returns the number of lines that it counts in that Seq.

In these ways the wc command is a pure function:

- It takes a Seq[String] as input
- It does not rely on any other state or hidden values
- It does not read or write to any files
- It does not alter the state of anything else in the universe
- Its output depends only on its input

- Given the same input at various points in time, it always returns the same value

The one thing that wc did that I didn't like is that it left-pads its output with blank spaces, so I used the `tr` command just like the wc command to fix that problem: as a pure function.

A nice way to think of this code is like this:

```
Input -> Transformer -> Transformer ... Transformer-> Output
```

With that thought, this example looks as shown in Figure 20.2.

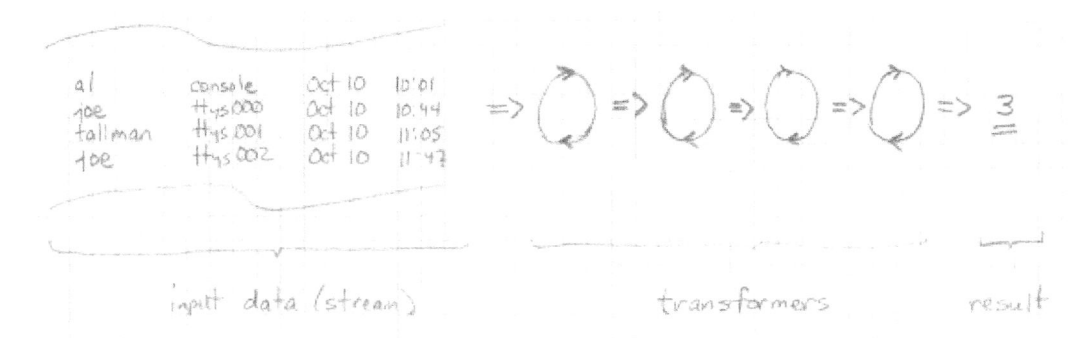

Figure 20.2: Using a series of transformers in a pipeline to solve a problem

Note a few key properties in all of this. First, data flows in only one direction, as shown in Figure 20.3.

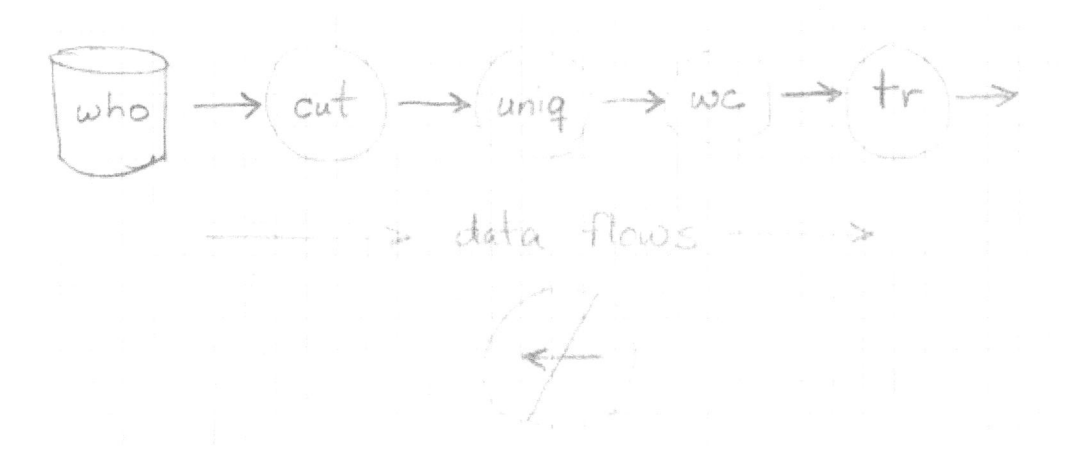

Figure 20.3: Pipeline data flows in only one direction

Second, Figure 20.4 shows that the input data a function is given is never modified.

Finally, as shown in Figure 20.5, you can think of functions as having an *entrance* and an *exit*,

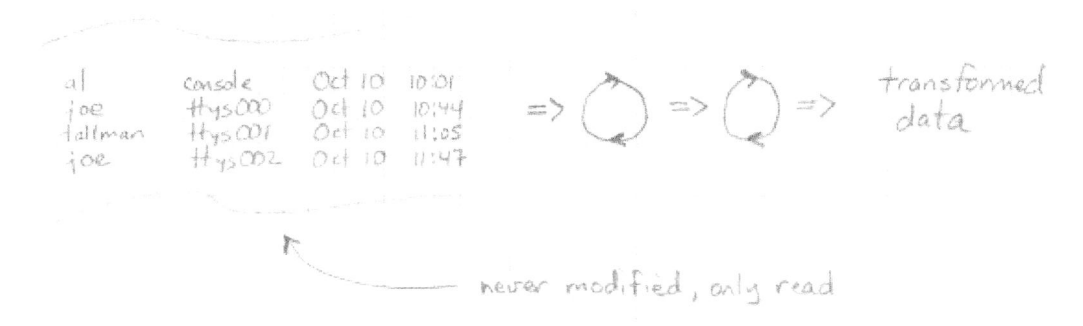

Figure 20.4: Data is never modified

but there are no side doors or windows for data to slip in or out.

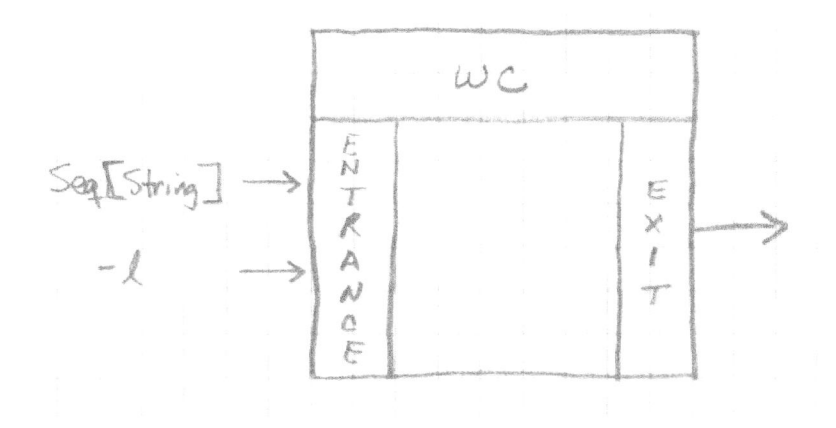

Figure 20.5: Pure functions have one entrance and one exit

These are all important properties of pure functions (and Unix commands).

Pipelines as combinators

There's another interesting point about this example in regards to FP. When I combine these commands together like this:

```
who | cut -d' ' -f1 | uniq | wc -l | tr -d ' '
```

I create what's called in Unix a *pipeline* or *command pipeline*. In FP we call that same thing a *combinator*. That is, I combined the three commands — pure functions — together to get the data I wanted.

If I had structured my Scala code differently I could have made it look like this:

```
who.cut(delimiter=" ", field=1)
   .uniq
   .wc(lines = true)
   .tr(find=" ", replace="")
```

I'll add a more formal definition of "combinator" later in this book, but in general, when you see code like this — a chain of functions applied to some initial data — this is what most people think when they use the term "combinator." This is another case where an FP term sounds scary, but remember that whenever you hear the term "combinator" you can think "Unix pipeline."

Look back at how you thought about that problem

At this point it's worth taking a moment to think about the thought process involved in solving this problem. If you look back at how it was solved, our thinking followed these steps:

- We started with the problem statement: wanting to know how many users are logged into the system.
- We thought about what data source had the information we needed, in this case the output of the who command.
- At this point I should note that implicit in my own thinking is that I knew the *structure* of the data I'd get from the who command. That is, as an experienced Unix user I knew that who returns a list of users, with each user login session printed on a new line.
- Depending on your thought process you may have thought of the who output as a multiline String or as a List (or more generally as a Seq in Scala). Either thought is fine.
- Because you knew the structure of the who data, and you know your Unix commands, you knew that you could apply a sequence of standard commands to the who data to get the number of unique users.
- You may or may not have known beforehand that the wc -l output is padded with blank spaces. I did not.

The functional programming thought process

The reason I mention this thought process is because that's what the functional programming thought process is like:

- You start with a problem to solve.
- You either know where the data source is, or you figure it out.
- Likewise, the data is either in a known format, or in a format you need to learn.

- You clearly define the output you want in the problem statement.
- You apply a series of pure functions to the input data source(s) to transform the data into a new structure.
- If all of the functions that you need already exist, you use them; otherwise you write new pure functions to transform the data as needed.

> Note the use of the word *apply* in this discussion. Functional programmers like to say that they *apply* functions to input data to get a desired output. As you saw, using the word "apply" in the previous discussion was quite natural.

More exercises

If you'd like to test that process with some more examples, here are a few more exercises you can work with to get the hang of an FP style of problem-solving:

- Write a pipeline to show the number of processes owned by the root user.
- Write a pipeline to show the number of open network connections. (Tip: I use `netstat` as the data source.)
- Use the `lsof` command to show what computers your computer is currently connected to.
- Write a pipeline command to show which processes are consuming the most RAM on your computer.
- Write a command to find the most recent *.gitignore* file on your computer.

Data flow diagrams

Besides demonstrating how writing Unix pipeline commands are like writing FP code (and vice-versa), I'm also trying to demonstrate "The FP Thought Process." Because "output depends only on input," FP lends itself to something that used to be called "Data Flow Diagrams" — or DFDs — back in the old days.

There's a formal notation for DFDs, but I don't care for it. (There are actually several formal notations.) If I was going to sketch out the solution to the last problem, I'd draw it like the image in Figure 20.6.

Because I'm using my own graphical drawing language here, I'll note that at the moment:

- I prefer to draw *data flows* as streams (simple tables).
- I like to annotate streams with their data types.

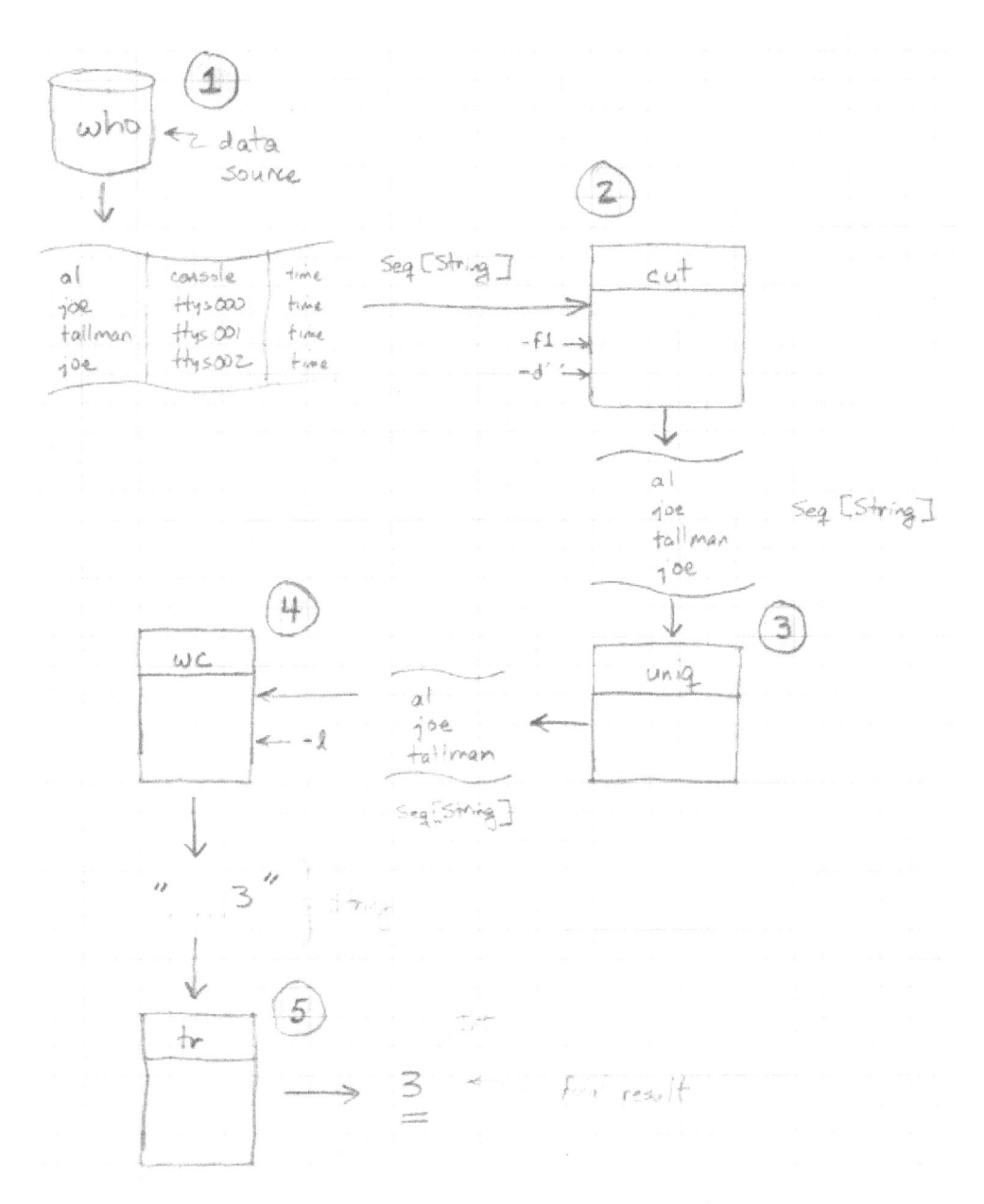

Figure 20.6: A DFD-like sketch of the pipeline solution

- I like to draw functions as rectangles (because of the whole front-door/back-door, entrance/exit concept).

I'm not suggesting that you have to draw out every problem and solution like this, but if you're working on a hard problem, this can be helpful.

"Conservation of data"

If I'm working on a difficult problem, or trying to explain a solution to other people, I like to draw visual diagrams like that. The book, Complete Systems Analysis[1], by Robertson and Robertson, defines something else that they call a "Rule of Data Conservation," which they state like this:

> "Each process (function) in the data flow diagram must be able to produce the output *data flows* from its input."

Using their diagramming process, the data that flows from the who command would be described like this:

```
Who = Username + Terminal + Date + Time
```

If you take the time to draw the data flows like this, it's possible to make sure that the "Rule of Data Conservation" is satisfied — at least assuming that you know each function's algorithm.

"Black holes and miracles"

A set of Power Point slides I found at DePaul.edu makes the following interesting observations about data flows:

- Data stays at rest unless moved by a process
- Processes cannot consume or create data
    - Must have at least 1 input data flow (to avoid miracles)
    - Must have at least 1 output data flow (to avoid black holes)

Just substitute "function" for "process" in their statements, and I really like those last two lines — avoiding *black holes* and *miracles* — as they apply to writing pure functions.

---

[1] http://amzn.to/1Q45ZLy

One caveat about this lesson

In this lesson I tried to show how writing Unix pipeline commands is like writing FP code. One part I didn't show is a program that runs continuously until the user selects a "Quit" option. But fear not, I'll show this in an upcoming lesson, I just need to provide a little more background information, including covering topics like recursive programming.

Summary

As I mentioned at the beginning, my main goal for this lesson is to demonstrate that writing Unix pipeline commands is like writing functional code. Just like functional programming, when you write Unix pipeline commands:

- You have data sources, or inputs, that bring external data into your application.
- Unix commands such as `cut`, `uniq`, etc., are like pure functions. They take in immutable inputs, and generate output based only on those inputs and their algorithms.
- You combine Unix commands with pipelines in the same way that you use FP functions as "combinators."

21

Functions Are Variables, Too

> *"A variable is a named entity that refers to an object. A variable is either a val or a var. Both vals and vars must be initialized when defined, but only vars can be later reassigned to refer to a different object."*
>
> — The Scala Glossary

Goals

The goal of this lesson is to show that in a good FP language like Scala[1], you can use functions as values. In the same way that you create and use String and Int values, you can use a function:

```
val name = "Al"                  // string value
val weight = 222                 // int value
val double = (i: Int) => i * 2   // function value
```

To support this goal, this lesson shows:

- How to define a function as a `val`
- The "implicit" form of the `val` function syntax
- How to pass a function to another function
- Other ways to treat functions as values

---

[1] http://scala-lang.org/

Scala's `val` function syntax

Understanding Scala's `val` function syntax is important because you'll see function signatures in a variety of places, including:

- When you define `val` functions
- When you define function input parameters (i.e., when one function takes another function as an input parameter)
- When you're reading the Scaladoc for almost every method in the Scala collections classes
- In the REPL output

You'll see examples of most of these in this lesson.

Formalizing some definitions

Before getting into this lesson, it will help to make sure that I'm formal about how I use certain terminology. For instance, given this expression:

```
val x = 42
```

it's important to be clear about these things:

1) Technically, x is a *variable*, a specific type of variable known as an *immutable variable*. Informally, I prefer to refer to x as a "value," as in saying, "x is an integer value." I prefer this because x is declared as a `val` field; it's bound to the `Int` value 42, and that can never change. But to be consistent with (a) other programming resources as well as (b) algebraic terminology, I'll refer to x as a *variable* in this lesson.

    Wikipedia states[2] that in algebra, "a variable is an alphabetic character representing a number, called the value of the variable, which is either arbitrary or not fully specified or unknown." So in this way, referring to x as a variable is consistent with algebraic terms.

2) x has a *type*. In this case the type isn't shown explicitly, but we know that the type is an `Int`. I could have also defined it like this:

    ```
    val x: Int = 42
    ```

    But because programmers and the Scala compiler know that 42 is an `Int`, it's convenient to use the shorter form.

---
[2] https://en.wikipedia.org/wiki/Variable_%28mathematics%29

3) Variables themselves have *values*, and in this example the variable x has the value 42. (As you can imagine, it might be confusing if I wrote, "The value x has the value 42.)"

I'm formalizing these definitions now because as you're about to see, these terms also apply to creating functions: functions also have variable names, types, and values.

Function literals

If you haven't heard of the term "function literal" before, it's important to know that in this example:

```
xs.map(x => x * 2)
```

this part of the code is a *function literal*:

```
x => x * 2
```

It's just like saying that this is a *string literal*:

```
"hello, world"
```

I mention this because …

Function literals can be assigned to variables

In functional programming languages, function literals can be assigned to variable names. In Scala this means:

- You can define a function literal and assign it to a `val` field, which creates an immutable variable
- You give that variable a name, just like any other `val` field
- A function variable has a value, which is the code in its function body
- A function variable has a *type* — more on this shortly
- You can pass a function around to other functions, just like any other `val`
- You can store a function in a collection, such as a `Map`
- In general, you use a function variable just like any other variable

The `val` function syntax

In my blog post, Explaining Scala's `val` Function Syntax[3], I show two different ways to define functions using `val`s in Scala. In this lesson I'll use only the following approach, which shows the "*implicit* return type" syntax:

```
val isEven = (i: Int) => i % 2 == 0
```

In this case "implicit" means that this function doesn't *explicitly* state that it returns a `Boolean` value; both you and the compiler can infer that by looking at the function body.

I discuss the implicit syntax in detail in that blog post, but Figure 21.1 shows a quick look at what each of those fields means.

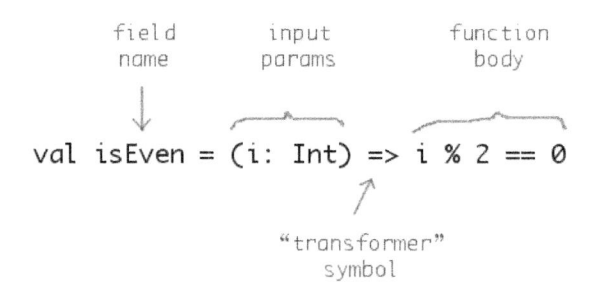

```
       field          input         function
       name           params         body
         ↓              ⌒              ⌒
    val isEven = (i: Int) => i % 2 == 0
                         ↗
                   "transformer"
                      symbol
```

Figure 21.1: Scala's implicit return type syntax for functions.

If that syntax looks a little unusual, fear not, I show more examples of it in this lesson.

Other ways to write this function

This function body is a short way of saying that it returns `true` if the `Int` it is given is an even number, otherwise it returns `false`. If you don't like the way that code reads, it may help to put curly braces around the function body:

```
val isEven = (i: Int) => { i % 2 == 0 }
```

Or you can make the if/else condition more obvious:

```
val isEven = (i: Int) => if (i % 2 == 0) true else false
```

---

[3]https://goo.gl/3ARUU8

You can also put curly braces around that function body:

```
val isEven = (i: Int) => { if (i % 2 == 0) true else false }
```

Finally, if you prefer a *really* long form, you can write isEven like this:

```
val isEven = (i: Int) => {
    if (i % 2 == 0) {
        true
    } else {
        false
    }
}
```

Note: I only show this last version to show an example of a multi-line function body. I don't recommend writing short functions like this.

If you were going to explain any of these functions to another person, a good explanation would be like this:

> "The function isEven transforms the input Int into a Boolean value based on its algorithm, which in this case is i % 2 == 0."

When you read that sentence, it becomes clear that the Boolean return value is implied (implicit). I know that when I look at the code I have to pause for a moment before thinking, "Ah, it has a Boolean return type," because it takes a moment for my brain to
evaluate the function body to determine its return type. Therefore, even though it's more verbose, I generally prefer to write functions that explicitly specify their return type, because then I don't have to read the function body to determine the return type.

In my opinion, if (a) you have to read a function's body to determine its return type while (b) what you're really trying to do is understand some other block of code — such as when you're debugging a problem — then (c) this forces you to think about low-level details that aren't important to the problem at hand. That's just my opinion, but it's what I've come to believe; I'd rather just glance at the function's type signature.

Stated another way, it's often easier to *write* functions that don't declare their return types, but it's harder to *maintain* them.

The general implicit `val` function syntax

You can come to understand the implicit `val` function syntax by pasting a few functions into the Scala REPL. For instance, when you paste this function into the REPL:

```
val isEven = (i: Int) => i % 2 == 0
```

you'll see that the REPL responds by showing that `isEven` is an instance of something called `<function1>`:

```
scala> val isEven = (i: Int) => i % 2 == 0
isEven: Int => Boolean = <function1>
```

And when you paste a function that takes two input parameters into the REPL:

```
val sum = (a: Int, b: Int) => a + b
```

you'll see that it's an instance of `<function2>`:

```
scala> val sum = (a: Int, b: Int) => a + b
sum: (Int, Int) => Int = <function2>
```

When I line up the REPL output for those two examples, like this:

```
isEven:    Int          => Boolean   = <function1>
sum:       (Int, Int)   => Int       = <function2>
```

you can begin to see that the general form for the way the REPL displays function variables is this:

```
variableName: type = value
```

You can see this more clearly when I highlight the function types and values. This is the REPL output for `isEven`:

```
isEven: Int => Boolean = <function1>
------  --------------   -----------
name         type           value
```

and this is the output for the sum function:

```
sum:    (Int, Int) => Int    =   <function2>
----    -----------------        -----------
name         type                   value
```

The type of the `isEven` function can be read as, "Transforms an `Int` value into a `Boolean` value," and the `sum` function can be read as, "Takes two `Int` input parameters and transforms them into an `Int`."

> Cool FP developers generally don't say, "a function returns a result." They say things like, "a function transforms its inputs into an output value." Or, as it's stated in the Land of Lisp[4] book, Lisp purists prefer to say that "a function *evaluates* to a result." This may seem like a minor point, but I find that using phrases like this helps my brain to think of my code as being a combination of algebraic functions (or equations) — and that's a good way to think.

What `<function1>` and `<function2>` mean

In the "Explaining Scala's `val` Function Syntax" blog post I write more about this topic, but in short, the output `<function1>` indicates that `isEven` is an instance of the Function1 trait[5] (meaning that it has one input parameter), and `<function2>` means that `sum` is an instance of the Function2 trait[6] (meaning that it has two input parameters). The actual "value" of a function is the full body of the function, but rather than show all of that, the REPL uses `<function1>` and `<function2>` to show that `isEven` and `sum` are instances of these types.

As I discuss in that blog post, behind the scenes the Scala compiler converts this function:

```
val sum = (a: Int, b: Int) => a + b
```

into code that looks a lot like this:

```
val sum = new Function2[Int, Int, Int] {
    def apply(a: Int, b: Int): Int = a + b
}
```

I don't want to get too hung up on these details right now, but this is where the Function2

---

[4]http://amzn.to/1PjyUeL
[5]http://www.scala-lang.org/api/current/scala/Function1.html
[6]http://www.scala-lang.org/api/current/scala/Function2.html

reference comes from. For more information on this topic, see my "Explaining Scala's `val` Function Syntax" blog post.

Passing functions into other functions

A great thing about functional programming is that you can pass functions around just like other variables, and the most obvious thing this means is that you can pass one function into another. A good way to demonstrate this is with the methods in the Scala collections classes.

For example, given this list of integers (`List[Int]`):

```
val ints = List(1,2,3,4)
```

and these two functions that take `Int` parameters:

```
val isEven = (i: Int) => i % 2 == 0
val double = (i: Int) => i * 2
```

you can see that `isEven` works great with the `List` class `filter` method:

```
scala> ints.filter(isEven)
res0: List[Int] = List(2, 4)
```

and the `double` function works great with the `map` method:

```
scala> ints.map(double)
res1: List[Int] = List(2, 4, 6, 8)
```

Passing functions into other functions like this is what functional programming is all about.

How this works (the short answer)

In the upcoming lessons on Higher-Order Functions (HOFs) I show how to *write* methods like `map` and `filter`, but here's a short discussion of how the process of passing one function into another function (or method) works.

Technically `filter` is written as a method that takes a function as an input parameter. Any function it accepts must (a) take an element of the *type* contained in the collection, and (b) return a `Boolean` value. Because in this example `filter` is invoked on `ints` — which is a `List[Int]` — it expects a function that takes an `Int` and returns a `Boolean`. Because `isEven` transforms an `Int` to a `Boolean`, it works great with `filter` for this collection.

A look at the Scaladoc

The `filter` method Scaladoc is shown in Figure 21.2. Notice how it takes a predicate which has the generic type A as its input parameter, and it returns a List of the same generic type A. It's defined this way because `filter` doesn't *transform* the list elements, it just filters out the ones you don't want.

```
def filter(p: (A) => Boolean): List[A]
    Selects all elements of this traversable collection which satisfy a predicate.

    p          the predicate used to test elements.
    returns    a new traversable collection consisting of all elements of this traversable collection
               that satisfy the given predicate p. The order of the elements is preserved.
```

Figure 21.2: The `filter` method of Scala's List class

As shown in Figure 21.3, map also takes a function that works with generic types. In my example, because ints is a List[Int], you can think of the generic type A in the image as an Int. Because map is intended to let you *transform* data, the generic type B can be any type. In my example, double is a function that takes an Int and returns an Int, so it works great with map.

```
def map[B](f: (A) => B): List[B]
    [use case]
    Builds a new collection by applying a function to all elements of this list.

    B          the element type of the returned collection.
    f          the function to apply to each element.
    returns    a new list resulting from applying the given function f to each element of this list
               and collecting the results.
```

Figure 21.3: The map method of Scala's List class

I explain this in more detail in upcoming lessons, but the important point for this lesson is that you *can* pass a function variable into another function.

Because functions are variables ...

Because functions are variables, you can do all sorts of things with them. For instance, if you define two functions like this:

```
val double = (i: Int) => i * 2
val triple = (i: Int) => i * 3
```

you can have fun and store them in a Map:

```
val functions = Map(
    "2x" -> double,
    "3x" -> triple
)
```

If you put that code into the REPL, you'll have two functions stored as values inside a Map.

Now that they're in there, you can pass the Map around as desired, and then later on get references to the functions using the usual Map approach, i.e., by supplying their key values. For example, this is how you get a reference to the double function that's stored in the Map:

```
scala> val dub = functions("2x")
d: Int => Int = <function1>
```

This is just like getting a String or an Int or any other reference out of a Map — you specify the key that corresponds to the value.

Now that you have a reference to the original double function, you can invoke it:

```
scala> dub(2)
res0: Int = 4
```

You can do the same things with the other function I put in the Map:

```
scala> val trip = functions("3x")
t: Int => Int = <function1>

scala> trip(2)
res1: Int = 6
```

These examples show how to create functions as variables, store them in a Map, get them out of the Map, and then use them.

The point of this example

Besides showing how to put function variables into Maps, a key point of this example is: in Scala you can use a function variable just like a String variable or an Int variable. The sooner you begin treating functions as variables in your own code, the further you'll be down the path of becoming a great functional programmer.

Exercise

Given what I've shown so far, this request may be a bit of an advanced exercise, but ... here's that Map example again:

```
val functions = Map(
    "2x" -> double,
    "3x" -> triple
)
```

Given that Map, sketch its data type here:

As an example of what I'm looking for, this Map:

```
val m = Map("age" -> 42)
```

has a data type of:

`Map[String, Int]`

That's what I'm looking for in this exercise: the *type* of the Map named `functions`.

Solution to the exercise

If you pasted the Map code into the REPL, you saw its output:

`Map[String, Int => Int] = Map(2x -> <function1>, 3x -> <function1>)`

The first part of that output shows the Map's data type:

`Map[String, Int => Int]`

The data type for the Map's *key* is `String`, and the type for its *value* is shown as `Int => Int`. That's how you write the *type* for a function that transforms a single `Int` input parameter to a resulting `Int` value. As you know from the previous discussion, this means that it's an instance of the `Function1` trait.

As a second example, if the Map was holding a function that took two Int's as input parameters and returns an Int — such as the earlier sum function — its type would be shown like this:

```
Map[(Int, Int) => Int]
```

That would be a Function2 instance, because it takes two input parameters.

Examples of val functions

To help you get comfortable with the "implicit return type" version of the val function syntax, here are the functions I showed in this lesson:

```
val isEven = (i: Int) => i % 2 == 0
val sum = (a: Int, b: Int) => a + b
val double = (i: Int) => i * 2
val triple = (i: Int) => i * 3
```

And here are a few more functions that show different input parameter types:

```
val strlen = (s: String) => s.length
val concat = (a: String, b: String) => a + b

case class Person(firstName: String, lastName: String)
val fullName = (p: Person) => s"${p.firstName} ${p.lastName}"
```

Summary

Here's a summary of what I showed in this lesson:

- Function literals can be assigned to `val` fields to create function variables
- To be consistent with algebra and other FP resources, I refer to these fields are *variables* rather than *values*
- Examples of the `val` function syntax
- A function is an instance of a `FunctionN` trait, such as `Function1` or `Function2`
- What various function type signatures look like in the REPL
- How to pass a function into another function
- How to treat a function as a variable by putting it in a `Map`
- That, in general, you can use a function variable just like any other variable

In regards to `val` function signatures, understanding them is important because you'll see them in many places, including function literals, the Scaladoc, REPL output, and other developer's code. You'll also need to know this syntax so you can write your own functions that take other functions as input parameters.

What's next

The next lesson shows that you can use `def` methods just like `val` functions. That's important because most developers prefer to use the `def` method syntax to define their algorithms.

See also

- Scala's Function1 trait[7]
- The online version of Explaining the `val` Function Syntax[8]

---

[7] http://www.scala-lang.org/api/current/scala/Function1.html
[8] https://alvinalexander.com/scala/fpbook/explaining-scala-val

22

Using Methods As If They Were Functions

"The owls are not what they seem."

From the television series, *Twin Peaks*

Goals

As shown in Figure 22.1, have you noticed that the Scaladoc for the List class map method clearly shows that it takes a *function*?

```
def map[B](f: (A) ⇒ B): List[B]
    [use case]
    Builds a new collection by applying a function to all elements of this list.

    B         the element type of the returned collection.
    f         the function to apply to each element.
    returns   a new list resulting from applying the given function f to each element of this list and collecting the results.
```

Figure 22.1: The map *method of Scala's* List *class*

But despite that, you can somehow pass it a *method* and it still works, as shown in this code:

```
// [1] create a method
scala> def doubleMethod(i: Int) = i * 2
doubleMethod: (i: Int)Int

// [2] supply the method where a function is expected
scala> List(1,2,3).map(doubleMethod)
res0: List[Int] = List(2, 4, 6)
```

The intent of this lesson is to provide an explanation of how this works, and because it works, how it affects your Scala/FP code.

151

Motivation

I think it's safe to say that most Scala/FP developers prefer to define their "functions" using the `def` keyword. But because the result isn't 100% exactly the same as writing a `val` function, it can be important to understand the differences between the two approaches, which I do in this lesson.

A `def` method is not a `val` (Part 1)

From the previous lessons, you know that this example creates an instance of the `Function1` trait:

```
scala> val isEven = (i: Int) => i % 2 == 0
isEven: Int => Boolean = <function1>
```

However, when you write the same algorithm using `def`, the REPL output shows that you create something else:

```
scala> def isEven(i: Int) = i % 2 == 0
isEven: (i: Int)Boolean
```

The REPL output for the two examples is clearly different. This is because a `val` function is an instance of a `Function0` to `Function22` trait, but a `def` method is ... well ... when you're not working in the REPL — when you're writing a real application — it's a method that needs to be defined inside of a `class`, `object`, or `trait`.

A deeper look

You can see the differences between `def` methods and `val` functions even more clearly by working with the Scala compiler at the command line. First, create a file named *Methods.scala* and put this code in it:

```
class Methods {
    def sum(a: Int, b: Int) = a + b
}
```

When you compile that code with `scalac`:

```
$ scalac Methods.scala
```

and then run `javap` on the resulting *Methods.class* file you'll see this output:

```
$ javap Methods
Compiled from "Methods.scala"
public class Methods {
    public int sum(int, int);
    public Methods();
}
```

`sum` is clearly a method in the class named `Methods`. Conversely, if you create a sum2 *function* in that same class, like this:

```
class Methods {
    def sum(a: Int, b: Int) = a + b
    val sum2 = (a: Int, b: Int) => a + b
}
```

and then compile it with `scalac` and examine the bytecode again with `javap`, you'll see that a `val` function creates something completely different:

```
public Function2<Object, Object, Object> sum2();
```

(I edited that output slightly to make it more clear.)

This lesson explores these differences, particularly from the point of view of using `def` methods just as though they are real `val` functions.

A def method is not a variable (Part 2)

In addition to showing that `def` methods are different than `val` functions, the REPL also shows that a method is not a variable that you can pass around. That is, you know that you can assign an `Int` to a variable name:

```
scala> val x = 1
x: Int = 1
```

and then show information about that variable:

```
scala> x
res0: Int = 1
```

You can also define a *function* and assign it to a variable:

```
scala> val double = (i: Int) => i * 2
```

```
double: Int => Int = <function1>
```

and then show information about it:

```
scala> double
res1: Int => Int = <function1>
```

But if you define a method using `def`:

```
scala> def triple(i: Int) = i * 3
triple: (i: Int)Int
```

and then try to show that method's "variable," what you'll actually get is an error:

```
scala> triple
<console>:12: error: missing arguments for method triple;
follow this method with `_' if you want to treat it as a partially applied function
       triple
       ^
```

The REPL shows this error because the `triple` method is not a variable in the same way that an `Int` or a function is a variable.

> Not yet, anyway. Very shortly I'll demonstrate how you can *manually* create a variable from a method.

Recap

The reason I show these examples is to demonstrate that until you do something like passing a method into a function, a `def` method is not the same as a `val` function. Despite that, we know that somehow you *can* later treat a method as a function.

Which leads to the next question ...

How is it that I can use a method like a function?

The answer of why you can use a method like a function is hinted at in Version 2.9 of *The Scala Language Specification*:

> "*Eta-expansion* converts an expression of *method* type to an equivalent expression of *function* type."

What that means is that when the Scala compiler is given these two lines of code:

```
def isEven(i: Int) = i % 2 == 0    // define a method
val evens = nums.filter(isEven)    // pass the method into a function
```

it uses this "Eta Expansion" capability to automatically convert the *method* isEven into a *function* — a true Function1 instance — so it can be passed into filter.

This happens automatically during the compilation process, so you generally don't even have to think about. In fact, I used Scala for almost a year before I thought, "Hey, how is this even working?"

How to manually convert a method to a function

To give you an idea of how Eta Expansion works, let's use the earlier triple example. I first defined this method:

```
scala> def triple(i: Int) = i * 3
triple: (i: Int)Int
```

and then when I tried to show its value in the REPL, I got this error:

```
scala> triple
<console>:12: error: missing arguments for method triple;
follow this method with `_' if you want to treat it as a
partially applied function
       triple
       ^
```

The error message states that you can follow this method with an underscore to treat the method as a *partially applied function*. That's true, and I demonstrate it in the next lesson. But for this lesson, the important thing to know is that *when you do this, you create a function from your method*.

To demonstrate this, go ahead and do what the error message says. Follow the method name with an underscore, and also assign that result to a variable name:

```
scala> val tripleFn = triple _
tripleFn: Int => Int = <function1>
```

Notice that the signature of this result is Int => Int. This means that tripleFn is a function that takes one Int as an input parameter, and returns an Int result. The REPL output also shows that tripleFn has a value <function1>, which means that it's an instance of the Function1 trait. Because it's now a real function, you can display its value in the REPL:

```
scala> tripleFn
res0: Int => Int = <function1>
```

This new function works just like the method works, taking an Int input parameter and returning an Int result:

```
scala> tripleFn(1)
res0: Int = 3
```

As you'd expect, this manually-created function works just fine with the map method of a List[Int]:

```
// create a List[Int]
scala> val x = List(1,2,3)
x: List[Int] = List(1, 2, 3)

// pass in the `tripleFn` function
scala> x.map(tripleFn)
res1: List[Int] = List(3, 6, 9)
```

This is a short example of what Eta Expansion does for you behind the scenes, during the compilation process.

The key point of these examples is (a) this is how things work behind the scenes, and (b) this process happens automatically when you pass a def method into a function that expects a *function* input parameter. Eta Expansion also lets you use def methods just like they are functions in many other situations.

> It's hard to really "prove" in the REPL that this is what happens because I don't know of any way to disable Eta Expansion. While you can't prove it in the REPL, you can show what happens behind the scenes with the Scala compiler at the command line. If you start with this class:
>
> ```
> class EtaExpansionTest {
>
>     def double(i: Int) = i * 2
> ```

```
    def foo = {
        val xs = List(1,2,3)
        xs.map(double)    // pass the `double` method into `map`
    }
}
```

and then compile it with this command:

```
$ scalac -Xprint:all Methods.scala
```

you'll see a *lot* of output, and if you take the time to dig through that output, you'll be amazed at what the compiler does to the xs.map(double) code by the time it's done with it. I won't go into all of that here, but if you're interested in how this process works, I encourage you to dig into that output.

In some places it doesn't happen automatically

In the previous lesson I showed that you can define functions and then store them in a Map. Can you do the same thing with methods?

Well, if you define two methods like this:

```
def double(i: Int) = i * 2
def triple(i: Int) = i * 3
```

and then try to store them in a Map, like this:

```
val functions = Map(
    "2x" -> double,
    "3x" -> triple
)
```

you'll get the following error messages:

```
<console>:13: error: missing arguments for method double;
follow this method with `_' if you want to treat it as a
partially applied function
           "2x" -> double,
                   ^
<console>:14: error: missing arguments for method triple;
```

```
follow this method with `_' if you want to treat it as a
partially applied function
          "3x" -> triple
                    ^
```

Prior to this lesson those errors might have been a head-scratcher, but now you know how to solve this problem — how to manually convert the methods into functions by following the *method* invocations with an underscore:

```
val functions = Map(
    "2x" -> double _,
    "3x" -> triple _
)
```

As before, that syntax converts the double and triple *methods* into *functions*, and then everything works as shown in the previous lesson. In this case that means that you can get a function back out of the Map and use it:

```
scala> val dub = functions("2x")
dub: Int => Int = <function1>

scala> dub(3)
res0: Int = 6
```

Why this lesson is important

The reason I showed everything in this lesson is because most developers prefer the def method syntax over the val function syntax. Given the choice to write an algorithm using either approach, developers seem to prefer the def approach, and I believe that's because the def syntax is easier to read.

Because of this, in the rest of this book I'll often write def methods and refer to them as functions. Technically this isn't accurate, but because (a) methods can be used just like functions, and (b) I don't want to have to keep writing, "*A method that acts like a function*," I will now start using this terminology.

Summary

Here's a summary of what I showed in this lesson:

- The Scaladoc for collections methods like `map` and `filter` show that they take *functions* as input parameters.
- Despite that, somehow you can pass *methods* into them.
- The reason that works is called "Eta Expansion."
- I showed how to manually convert a method to a function (using the partially-applied function approach).
- As a result of Eta Expansion, you can use `def` to define methods, and then generally treat them in the same way that you use `val` functions.

What's next

In this lesson I showed that you can generally treat a `def` method just like a `val` function, and not have to worry about the differences between the two. I also showed that if the compiler doesn't take care of that process for you automatically, you can handle it manually.

In the next lesson you'll see how to write functions that take other functions as input parameters. With this background, you know that this also means that those functions will be able to take methods as input parameters as well.

23

How to Write Functions That Take Functions as Input Parameters

> *"Haskell functions can take functions as parameters and return functions as return values. A function that does either of those is called a higher order function. Higher order functions aren't just a part of the Haskell experience, they pretty much are the Haskell experience."*
>
> From Learn You a Haskell for Great Good![a]
>
> ---
> [a] http://amzn.to/1POaUCv

Motivation and Goals

The topic I'm about to cover is a big part of functional programming: *power programming* that's made possible by passing functions to other functions to get work done.

So far I've shown I've shown how to be a *consumer* of functions that take other functions as input parameters, that is, a consumer of *Higher Order Functions* (HOFs) like map and filter. In this lesson I'm going to show how to be the *producer* of HOFs, i.e., the writer of HOF APIs.

Therefore, the primary goal of this lesson is to show how to write functions that take other functions as input parameters. To do that I'll show:

- The syntax you use to define function input parameters
- Many examples of that syntax
- How to execute a function once you have a reference to it

As a beneficial side effect of this lesson, you'll be able to read the source code and Scaladoc for other HOFs, and you'll be able to understand the function signatures they're looking for.

Terminology

Before we start, here are a few notes about the terminology I'll use in this lesson.

1) I use the acronym "FIP" to stand for "function input parameter." This isn't an industry standard, but because I use the term so often, I think the acronym makes the text easier to read.
2) As shown already, I'll use "HOF" to refer to "Higher Order Function."
3) As discussed in the previous lesson, because def methods are easier to read than val functions, from now on I'll write def methods and refer to them as "functions," even though that terminology isn't 100% accurate.

Introduction

In the previous lesson I showed this function:

```
def isEven(i: Int) = i % 2 == 0
```

I then showed that isEven works great when you pass it into the List class filter method:

```
scala> val list = List.range(0, 10)
list: List[Int] = List(0, 1, 2, 3, 4, 5, 6, 7, 8, 9)

scala> val evens = list.filter(isEven)
evens: List[Int] = List(0, 2, 4, 6, 8)
```

The key points of this are:

- The filter method accepts a function as an input parameter.
- The functions you pass into filter must match the type signature that filter expects, i.e., the FIP you pass in must accept an input parameter of the type stored in the list and return a Boolean.

Understanding filter's Scaladoc

The Scaladoc shows the type of functions filter accepts, which you can see in Figure 23.1.

The Scaladoc text shows that filter takes a *predicate*, which is just a function that returns a Boolean value.

This part of the Scaladoc:

```
def filter(p: (A) => Boolean): List[A]
    Selects all elements of this traversable collection which satisfy a predicate.
        p           the predicate used to test elements.
        returns     a new traversable collection consisting of all elements of this traversable collection that
                    satisfy the given predicate p. The order of the elements is preserved.
```

Figure 23.1: The Scaladoc shows the type of functions `filter` *accepts*

```
p: (A) => Boolean
```

means that `filter` takes a function input parameter which it names p, and p must transform a generic input A to a resulting Boolean value. In my example, where list has the type List[Int], you can replace the generic type A with Int, and read that signature like this:

```
p: (Int) => Boolean
```

Because isEven has this type — it transforms an input Int into a resulting Boolean — it can be used with `filter`.

A lot of functionality with a little code

The `filter` example shows that with HOFs you can accomplish a lot of work with a little bit of code. If List didn't have the `filter` method, you'd have to write a custom method like this to do the same work:

```
// what you'd have to do if `filter` didn't exist
def getEvens(list: List[Int]): List[Int] = {
    val tmpArray = ArrayBuffer[Int]()
    for (elem <- list) {
        if (elem % 2 == 0) tmpArray += elem
    }
    tmpArray.toList
}

val result = getEvens(list)
```

Compare all of that imperative code to this equivalent functional code:

```
val result = list.filter(_ % 2 == 0)
```

As you can see, this is a great advantage of functional programming. The code is much more concise, and it's also easier to comprehend.

> As FP developers like to say, you don't tell the computer specifically "how" to do something — you don't specify the nitty-gritty details inside a custom for loop. Instead, in your FP code you express a thought like, "I want to create a filtered version of this list with this little algorithm." When you do that, and you have good FP language to work with, you write your code at a much higher programming level.

"Common control patterns"

In many situations Scala/FP code can be easier to understand than imperative code. That's because a great benefit of Scala/FP is that methods like `filter`, `map`, `head`, `tail`, etc., are all standard, built-in functions, so once you learn them you don't have to write custom `for` loops any more. As an added benefit, you also don't have to read other developers' custom `for` loops.

> I say this a lot, but we humans can only keep so much in our brains at one time. Concise, readable code is simpler for your brain and better for your productivity.

I know that when you first come to Scala all of these methods on the collections classes don't feel like a benefit, they feel overwhelming. But once you realize that almost *every* `for` loop you've ever written falls into neat categories like `map`, `filter`, `reduce`, etc., you also realize what a great benefit these methods are. (And you'll reduce the amount of custom `for` loops you write by at least 90%.)

Here's what Martin Odersky wrote about this in his book, Programming in Scala[1]:

> "You can use functions within your code to factor out common control patterns, and you can take advantage of higher-order functions in the Scala library to reuse control patterns that are common across all programmers' code."

Given this background and these advantages, let's see how to write functions that take other functions as input parameters.

---

[1] http://amzn.to/2fiqDBh

Defining functions that take functions as parameters

To define a function that takes another function as an input parameter, all you have to do is define the signature of the function you want to accept.

To demonstrate this, I'll define a function named `sayHello` that takes a function as an input parameter. I'll name the input parameter `callback`, and also say that `callback` must have no input parameters and must return nothing. This is the Scala syntax that matches those requirements:

```
def sayHello(callback: () => Unit) {
    callback()
}
```

In this code, `callback` is an input parameter, and more specifically it is a *function input parameter* (or FIP). Notice how it's defined with this syntax:

```
callback: () => Unit
```

Here's how this works:

- `callback` is the name I give to the input parameter. In this case `callback` is a function I want to accept.
- The `callback` signature specifies the *type* of function I want to accept.
- The `()` portion of `callback`'s signature (on the left side of the => symbol) states that it takes no input parameters.
- The `Unit` portion of the signature (on the right side of the => symbol) indicates that the `callback` function should return nothing.
- When `sayHello` is called, its function body is executed, and the `callback()` line inside the body invokes the function that is passed in.

Figure 23.2 reiterates those points.

Now that I've defined `sayHello`, I'll create a function to match `callback`'s signature so I can test it. The following function takes no input parameters and returns nothing, so it matches `callback`'s type signature:

```
def helloAl(): Unit = { println("Hello, Al") }
```

Because the signatures match, I can pass `helloAl` into `sayHello`, like this:

```
sayHello(helloAl)
```

```
                    ┌── input parameter name
                    │    ┌── callback's input types
                    │    │    ┌── callback's return type
                    ▼    ▼    ▼
        def sayHello(callback:() => Unit) {
            callback()              ◄─── the function that
        }                                is passed in is
                                         invoked here
```

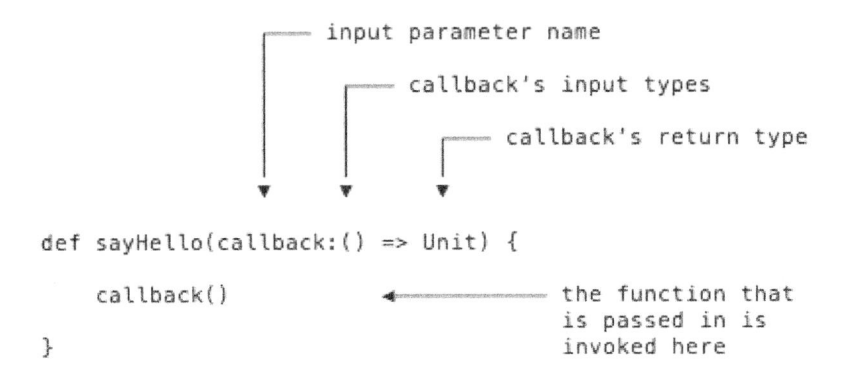

Figure 23.2: How sayHello *and* callback *work.*

The REPL demonstrates how all of this works:

```
scala> def sayHello(callback:() => Unit) {
     |     callback()
     | }
sayHello: (callback: () => Unit)Unit

scala> def helloAl(): Unit = { println("Hello, Al") }
helloAl: ()Unit

scala> sayHello(helloAl)
Hello, Al
```

If you've never done this before, congratulations. You just defined a function named say-Hello that takes another function as an input parameter, and then invokes that function when it's called.

It's important to know that the beauty of this approach is not that sayHello can take *one* function as an input parameter; the beauty is that it can take *any* function that matches callback's signature. For instance, because this next function takes no input parameters and returns nothing, it also works with sayHello:

```
def holaLorenzo(): Unit = { println("Hola, Lorenzo") }
```

Here it is in the REPL:

```
scala> sayHello(holaLorenzo)
Hola, Lorenzo
```

This is a good start. Let's build on it by defining functions that can take more complicated functions as input parameters.

The general syntax for defining function input parameters

I defined `sayHello` like this:

```
def sayHello(callback: () => Unit)
```

Inside of that, the `callback` function signature looks like this:

```
callback: () => Unit
```

I can explain this syntax by showing a few more examples. Imagine that we're defining a new version of `callback`, and this new version takes a `String` and returns an `Int`. That signature looks like this:

```
callback: (String) => Int
```

Next, imagine that you want to create a different version of `callback`, and this one should take two `Int` parameters and return an `Int`. Its signature looks like this:

```
callback: (Int, Int) => Int
```

As you can infer from these examples, the general syntax for defining function input parameter type signatures is:

```
variableName: (parameterTypes ...) => returnType
```

With `sayHello`, this is how the values line up:

General	sayHello	Notes
variableName	callback	The name you give the FIP
parameterTypes	()	The FIP takes no input parameters
returnType	Unit	The FIP returns nothing

Naming your function input parameters

I find that the parameter name `callback` is good when you first start writing HOFs. Of course you can name it anything you want, and other interesting names at first are `aFunction`, `theFunction`, `theExpectedFunction`, or maybe even `fip`. But from now on I'll make this name shorter and generally refer to the FIPs in my examples as just `f`, like this:

```
sayHello(f: () => Unit)
foo(f:(String) => Int)
bar(f:(Int, Int) => Int)
```

Looking at some function signatures

Using this as a starting point, let's look at signatures for some more FIPs so you can see the differences. To get started, here are two signatures that define a FIP that takes a String and returns an Int:

```
sampleFunction(f: (String) => Int)
sampleFunction(f: String => Int)
```

The second line shows that when you define a function that takes only one input parameter, you can leave off the parentheses.

Next, here's the signature for a function that takes two Int parameters and returns an Int:

```
sampleFunction(f: (Int, Int) => Int)
```

As a little quiz, can you imagine what sort of function matches that signature?

(A brief pause here so you can think about that.)

Any function that takes two Int input parameters and returns an Int matches that signature, so all of these functions fit:

```
def sum(a: Int, b: Int): Int = a + b
def product(a: Int, b: Int): Int = a * b
def subtract(a: Int, b: Int): Int = a - b
```

You can see how `sum` matches up with the FIP signature in Figure 23.3.

```
sampleFunction(f:(Int, Int) => Int)


    def sum(a: Int, b: Int): Int = a + b
```

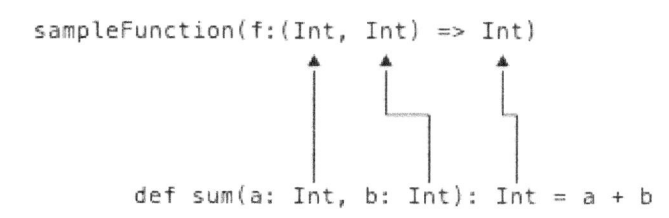

Figure 23.3: How sum *matches up with the parameters in the FIP signature.*

An important part of this is that no matter how complicated the type signatures get, they always follow this same general syntax:

```
variableName: (parameterTypes ...) => returnType
```

For example, all of these FIP signatures follow the same pattern:

```
f: () => Unit
f: String => Int
f: (String) => Int
f: (Int, Int) => Int
f: (Person) => String
f: (Person) => (String, String)
f: (String, Int, Double) => Seq[String]
f: List[Person] => Person
```

A note about "type signatures"

I'm being a little loose with my verbiage here, so let me tighten it up for a moment. When I say that this is a "type signature":

```
f: String => Int
```

that isn't 100% accurate. The *type signature* of the function is really just this part:

```
String => Int
```

Therefore, being 100% accurate, these are the type signatures I just showed:

```
() => Unit
String => Int
(String) => Int
(Int, Int) => Int
(Person) => String
(Person) => (String, String)
(String, Int, Double) => Seq[String]
List[Person] => Person
```

This may seem like a picky point, but because FP developers talk about type signatures all the time, I wanted to show the precise definition.

> It's common in FP to think about types a *lot* in your code. You might say that you "think in types."

A function that takes an Int parameter

Now let's look at a few more FIPs, with each example building on the one before it. First, here's a function named runAFunction that defines a FIP whose signature states that it takes an Int and returns nothing:

```
def runAFunction(f: Int => Unit): Unit = {
    f(42)
}
```

The function body says, "Whatever function you give to me, I'm going to pass the Int value 42 into it." This isn't terribly useful or functional, but it's a start.

Next, let's define a function that matches f's type signature. The following printIntPlus1 function takes an Int parameter and returns nothing, so it matches:

```
def printIntPlus1 (i: Int): Unit = { println(i+1) }
```

Now you can pass printIntPlus1 into runAFunction:

```
runAFunction(printIntPlus1)
```

Because printIntPlus1 is invoked inside runAFunction with the value 42, this prints 43. Here's what it all looks like in the REPL:

```
scala> def runAFunction(f: Int => Unit): Unit = {
     |     f(42)
     | }
runAFunction: (f: Int => Unit)Unit

scala> def printIntPlus1 (i: Int): Unit = { println(i+1) }
printIntPlus1: (i: Int)Unit

scala> runAFunction(printIntPlus1)
43
```

Here's a second function that takes an Int and returns nothing:

```
def printIntPlus10(i: Int) { println(i+10) }
```

When you pass printIntPlus10 into runAFunction, you'll see that it also works, printing 52:

```
runAFunction(printIntPlus10)    // prints 52
```

The power of the technique

Although these examples don't do too much yet, you can see the power of HOFs:

> You can easily swap in interchangeable algorithms.

As long as the signature of the function you pass in matches the signature that's expected, your algorithms can do anything you want. This is comparable to swapping out algorithms in the OOP Strategy design pattern[2].

Let's keep building on this...

Taking a function parameter along with other parameters

Here's a function named executeNTimes that has two input parameters: a function, and an Int:

---

[2]http://alvinalexander.com/java/java-strategy-design-pattern-in-java

```
def executeNTimes(f: () => Unit, n: Int) {
    for (i <- 1 to n) f()
}
```

As the code shows, executeNTimes executes the f function n times. To test this, define a function that matches f's signature:

```
def helloWorld(): Unit = { println("Hello, world") }
```

and then pass this function into executeNTimes along with an Int:

```
scala> executeNTimes(helloWorld, 3)
Hello, world
Hello, world
Hello, world
```

As expected, executeNTimes executes the helloWorld function three times. Cool.

More parameters, everywhere

Next, here's a function named executeAndPrint that takes a function and two Int parameters, and returns nothing. It defines the FIP f as a function that takes two Int values and returns an Int:

```
def executeAndPrint(f: (Int, Int) => Int, x: Int, y: Int): Unit = {
    val result = f(x, y)
    println(result)
}
```

executeAndPrint passes the two Int parameters it's given into the FIP it's given in this line of code:

```
val result = f(x, y)
```

Except for the fact that this function doesn't have a return value, this example shows a common FP technique:

- Your function takes a FIP.
- It takes other parameters that work with that FIP.
- You apply the FIP (f) to the parameters as needed, and return a value. (Or, in this example of a function with a side effect, you print something.)

To demonstrate `executeAndPrint`, let's create some functions that match f's signature. Here are a couple of functions take two `Int` parameters and return an `Int`:

```
def sum(x: Int, y: Int) = x + y
def multiply(x: Int, y: Int) = x * y
```

Now you can call `executeAndPrint` with these functions as the first parameter and whatever `Int` values you want to supply as the second and third parameters:

```
executeAndPrint(sum, 3, 11)       // prints 14
executeAndPrint(multiply, 3, 9)   // prints 27
```

Let's keep building on this…

Taking multiple functions as input parameters

Now let's define a function that takes (a) multiple FIPs and (b) other parameters to feed those FIPs. Let's define a function like this:

- It takes one function parameter that expects two `Int`s, and returns an `Int`
- It takes a second function parameter with the same signature
- It takes two other `Int` parameters
- The `Int`s will be passed to the two FIPs
- It will return the results from the first two functions as a tuple — a `Tuple2`, to be specific

Since I learned FP, I like to think in terms of "Function signatures first," so here's a function signature that matches those bullet points:

```
def execTwoFunctions(f1:(Int, Int) => Int,
                     f2:(Int, Int) => Int,
                     a: Int,
                     b: Int): Tuple2[Int, Int] = ???
```

Given that signature, can you imagine what the function body looks like?

(I'll pause for a moment to let you think about that.)

Here's what the complete function looks like:

```
def execTwoFunctions(f1: (Int, Int) => Int,
                     f2: (Int, Int) => Int,
                     a: Int,
                     b: Int): Tuple2[Int, Int] = {
    val result1 = f1(a, b)
    val result2 = f2(a, b)
    (result1, result2)
}
```

That's a verbose (clear) solution to the problem. You can shorten that three-line function body to just this, if you prefer:

```
(f1(a,b), f2(a,b))
```

Now you can test this new function with the trusty sum and multiply functions:

```
def sum(x: Int, y: Int) = x + y
def multiply(x: Int, y: Int) = x * y
```

Using these functions as input parameters, you can test execTwoFunctions:

```
val results = execTwoFunctions(sum, multiply, 2, 10)
```

The REPL shows the results:

```
scala> val results = execTwoFunctions(sum, multiply, 2, 10)
results: (Int, Int) = (12,20)
```

I hope these examples give you a taste for not only how to write HOFs, but the power of using them in your own code.

Okay, that's enough examples for now. I'll cover two more topics before finishing this lesson, and then in the next lesson you can see how to write a map function with everything I've shown so far.

The FIP syntax is just like the val function syntax

A nice thing about Scala is that once you know how things work, you can see the consistency of the language. For example, the syntax that you use to define FIPs is the same as the "explicit return type" (ERT) syntax that you use to define functions.

I show the ERT syntax in detail in a blog post titled, "Explaining Scala's val Function Syntax[3]."

What I mean by this is that when I define this function:

```
sampleFunction(f: (Int, Int) => Int)
```

the part of this code that defines the FIP signature is exactly the same as the ERT signature for the sum function that I define in that blog post:

```
val sum: (Int, Int) => Int = (a, b) => a + b
```

You can see what I mean if you line the two functions up, as shown in Figure 23.4.

```
sampleFunction(f: (Int, Int) => Int)

         val sum: (Int, Int) => Int = (a, b) => a + b
```

Figure 23.4: The FIP signature is exactly the same as the ERT signature for the sum function.

Once you understand the FIP type signature syntax, it becomes easier to read things like (a) the ERT function syntax and (b) the Scaladoc for HOFs.

The general thought process of designing HOFs

Personally, I'm rarely smart enough to see exactly what I want to do with all of my code beforehand. Usually I *think* I know what I want to do, and then as I start coding I realize that I really want something else. Because of this, my usual thought process when it comes to writing HOFs looks like this:

1. I write some code
2. I write more code
3. I realize that I'm starting to duplicate code
4. Knowing that duplicating code is bad, I start to refactor the code

Actually, I have this same thought process whether I'm writing OOP code or FP code, but the difference is in *what I do next.*

---

[3]https://alvinalexander.com/scala/fpbook/explaining-scala-val-function

With OOP, what I might do at this point is to start creating class hierarchies. For instance, if I was working on some sort of tax calculator in the United States, I might create a class hierarchy like this:

```
trait StateTaxCalculator
class AlabamaStateTaxCalculator extends StateTaxCalculator ...
class AlaskaStateTaxCalculator extends StateTaxCalculator ...
class ArizonaStateTaxCalculator extends StateTaxCalculator ...
```

Conversely, in FP my approach is to first define an HOF like this:

```
def calculateStateTax(f: Double => Double, personsIncome: Double): Double = ...
```

Then I define a series of functions I can pass into that HOF, like this:

```
def calculateAlabamaStateTax(income: Double): Double = ...
def calculateAlaskaStateTax(income: Double): Double = ...
def calculateArizonaStateTax(income: Double): Double = ...
```

As you can see, that's a very different implementation process.

> Note: I have no idea whether I'd approach these problems *exactly* as shown. I just want to demonstrate the difference in the general thought process between the two approaches, and in that regard — creating a class hierarchy versus a series of functions with a main HOF — I think this example shows that.

To summarize this, the thought process, "I need to refactor this code to keep it DRY," is the same in both OOP and FP, but the way you refactor the code is very different.

Summary

A function that takes another function as an input parameter is called a "Higher Order Function," or HOF. This lesson showed how to write HOFs in Scala, including showing the syntax for function input parameters (FIPs) and how to execute a function that is received as an input parameter.

As the lesson showed, the general syntax for defining a function as an input parameter is:

```
variableName: (parameterTypes ...) => returnType
```

Here are some examples of the syntax for FIPs that have different types and numbers of arguments:

```
def exec(f:() => Unit) = ???    // note: i don't show the function body
                                // for any of these examples

def exec(f: (String) => Int)
def exec(f: String => Int)      // parentheses not needed
def exec(f: (Int) => Int)
def exec(f: (Double) => Double)
def exec(f: (Person) => String)
def exec(f: (Int) => Int, a: Int, b: Int)
def exec(f: (Pizza, Order) => Double)
def exec(f: (Pizza, Order, Customer, Discounts) => Currency)
def exec(f1: (Int) => Int, f2:(Double) => Unit, s: String)
```

24

How to Write a 'map' Function

"He lunged for the maps. I grabbed the chair and hit him with it. He went down. I hit him again to make sure he stayed that way ..."

— Ilona Andrews, *Magic Burns*

In the previous lesson you saw how to write higher-order functions (HOFs). In this lesson you'll use that knowledge to write a map function that takes a FIP and a List.

Writing a map function

Imagine a world in which you know of the concept of "mapping," but sadly a map method isn't built into Scala's List class. Further imagine that you're not worried about *all* lists, you just want a map function for a List[Int].

Knowing that life is better with map, you sit down to write your own map method.

First steps

As I got better at FP, I came to learn that my first actions in writing most functions are:

1. Accurately state the problem as a sentence
2. Sketch the function signature

I'll follow that approach to solve this problem.

Accurately state the problem

For the first step, I'll state the problem like this:

I want to write a map function that can be used to apply other functions to each element in a List[Int] that it's given.

Sketch the function signature

My second step is to sketch a function signature that matches that statement. A blank canvas is always hard to look at, so I start with the obvious; I want a map function:

```
def map
```

Looking back at the problem statement, what do I know? Well, first, I know that map is going to take a function as an input parameter, and it's also going to take a List[Int]. Without thinking too much about the input parameters just yet, I can sketch this:

```
def map(f: (?) => ?, list: List[Int]): ???
```

Knowing how map works, I know that it should return a List that contains the same number of elements that are in the input List. For the moment, the important part about this is that this means that map will return a List of some sort:

```
def map(f: (?) => ?, list: List[Int]): List...
                                       ----
```

Given how map works — it applies a function to every element in the input list — the *type* of the output List can be anything: a List[Double], List[Float], List[Foo], etc. This tells me that the List that map returns needs to be a generic type, so I add that at the end of the function declaration:

```
def map(f: (?) => ?, list: List[Int]): List[A]
                                       -------
```

Because of Scala's syntax, I need to add the generic type before the function signature as well:

```
def map[A](f: (?) => ?, list: List[Int]): List[A]
        ---
```

A great thing about going through that thought process is that it tells me everything I need to know about the signature for the function input parameter f:

- Because f's input parameter will come from the List[Int], the parameter type must be Int

- Because the overall map function returns a List of the generic type A, f must also return the generic type A

The first statement lets me make this change to the definition of f:

```
def map[A](f: (Int) => ?, list: List[Int]): List[A]
                         ---
```

and the second statement lets me make this change:

```
def map[A](f: (Int) => A, list: List[Int]): List[A]
                       -
```

When I define a FIP that has only one input parameter I can leave the parentheses off, so if you prefer that syntax, the finished function signature looks like this:

```
def map[A](f: Int => A, list: List[Int]): List[A]
```

Cool. That seems right. Now let's work on the function body.

The map function body

A map function works on every element in a list, and because I haven't covered recursion yet, this means that we're going to need a for loop to loop over every element in the input list.

Because I know that map returns a list that has one element for each element in the input list, I further know that this loop is going to be a for/yield loop without any filters:

```
def map[A](f: (Int) => A, list: List[Int]): List[A] = {
    for {
        x <- list
    } yield ???
}
```

The only question now is, what exactly should the loop *yield*?

(I'll pause for a moment here to let you think about that.)

The answer is that the for loop should yield the result of applying the input function f to the current element in the loop. Therefore, I can finish the yield expression like this:

```
def map[A](f: (Int) => A, list: List[Int]): List[A] = {
    for {
```

```
        x <- list
    } yield f(x)    //<-- apply 'f' to each element 'x'
}
```

And that is the solution for the problem that was stated.

You can use the REPL to confirm that this solution works as desired. First, paste the map function into the REPL. Then create a list of integers:

```
scala> val nums = List(1,2,3)
nums: List[Int] = List(1, 2, 3)
```

Next, write a function that matches the signature map expects:

```
scala> def double(i: Int): Int = i * 2
double: (i: Int)Int
```

Then you can use map to apply double to each element in nums:

```
scala> map(double, nums)
res0: List[Int] = List(2, 4, 6)
```

The map function works.

Bonus: Make it generic

I started off by making map work only for a List[Int], but at this point it's easy to make it work for any List. This is because there's nothing inside the map function body that depends on the given List being a List[Int]:

```
// nothing here that's specific to an Int
for {
    x <- list
} yield f(x)
```

That's as "generic" as code gets; there are no Int references in there. Therefore, you can make map work with generic types by replacing each Int reference in the function signature with a generic type. Because this type appears before the other generic type in the function signature, I'll first convert the old A's to B's:

```
def map[B](f: (Int) => B, list: List[Int]): List[B] = ...
```

Then I replace the Int references with A, and put an A in the opening brackets, resulting in this signature:

```
def map[A,B](f: (A) => B, list: List[A]): List[B] = {
           -         -                -
```

If you want to take this even further, there's also nothing in this code that depends on the input "list" being a List. Because map works its way from the first element in the list to the last element, it doesn't matter if the Seq is an IndexedSeq or a LinearSeq, so you can use the parent Seq class here instead of List:

```
def map[A,B](f: (A) => B, list: Seq[A]): Seq[B] = {
                                 ---     ---
```

With this new signature, the complete, generic map function looks like this:

```
def map[A,B](f: (A) => B, list: Seq[A]): Seq[B] = {
    for {
        x <- list
    } yield f(x)
}
```

I hope you enjoyed that process. It's a good example of how I design functions these days, starting with the signature first, then implementing the function body, then adding generic types where it makes sense.

Exercise: Write a `filter` function

Now that you've seen how to write a map function, I encourage you to take the time to write a filter function. Because filter doesn't return a sequence that's the same size as the input sequence, its algorithm will be a little different, but it still needs to return a sequence in the end.

What's next

Where this lesson provides a detailed example of how to write a function that takes other functions as an input parameter, the next lesson will show how to write functions that take "blocks of code" as input parameters. That technique and syntax is similar to what I just showed, but the "use case" for this other technique — known as "by-name parameters" — is a little different.

After that lesson, I'll demonstrate how to combine these techniques with a Scala feature that lets a function have multiple input parameter groups.

How to Use By-Name Parameters

Introduction

In previous lessons I showed how to pass a function into another function. I showed *how* to do that (the syntax), and I also showed *why* to do that (to easily pass in new algorithms).

While that's a great feature, sometimes you just want to write a function that takes a more general "block of code." I typically do this when I'm writing a custom control structure, and as it turns out, it's also common technique in FP.

In Scala we say that a function that defines an input parameter like this is a "by-name" parameter, which is also referred to as a "call by-name" parameter.

Goals

My goals for this lesson are to show:

- The differences between by-value and by-name parameters
- The by-name syntax
- How to use by-name parameters
- Examples of when they are appropriate
- A comparison of by-name parameters and higher-order functions

Background: By-value parameters

If you define a `Person` class like this:

```
case class Person(var name: String)
```

and then pass it into a Scala function, it's said to be a "call by-value" argument. You can read more about this on Wikipedia's "evaluation strategy" page[1], but in short, the way I think of

---

[1] https://en.wikipedia.org/wiki/Evaluation_strategy

this is that the function receives a pointer to the object that's passed in.

This has a few repercussions. First, it means that there's no copy of the object. Under the covers, the function essentially receives a pointer that says, "You can find this Person instance at so-and-so memory address in the computer's RAM."

Second, if the object has mutable fields, the function can mutate those fields. When a function receives a Person instance and the name field is a var, the function can change the name:

```
def changeName(p: Person) = {
    p.name = "Al"
}
```

This change affects the Person instance that was passed in.

In regards to the name "by-value," the book, Programming Scala[2], makes this statement:

> "Typically, parameters to functions are by-value parameters; that is, the value of the parameter is determined before it is passed to the function."

In Scala the term "call by-value" means that the value is either:

- A primitive value (like an Int) that can't be changed
- A pointer to an object (like Person)

Background: By-name parameters

"By-name" parameters are quite different than by-value parameters. Rob Norris, (aka, "tpolecat") makes the observation[3] that you can think about the two types of parameters like this:

- A *by-value* parameter is like receiving a val field; its body is evaluated once, when the parameter is bound to the function.
- A *by-name* parameter is like receiving a def method; its body is evaluated whenever it is used inside the function.

Those statements aren't 100% accurate, but they are decent analogies to start with.

---

[2] https://www.safaribooksonline.com/library/view/programming-scala/9780596801908/ch08s12.html
[3] https://tpolecat.github.io/2014/06/26/call-by-name.html

A little more accurately, the book Scala Puzzlers[4] says that by-name parameters are "evaluated only when they are referenced inside the function." The Scala Language Specification adds this:

> This (by-name) indicates that the argument is not evaluated at the point of function application, but instead is evaluated at each use within the function.

According to Wikipedia[5] these terms date back to a language named ALGOL 60[6] (yes, the year 1960). But for me, the term "by-name" isn't very helpful. When you look at those quotes from the Puzzlers book and the Language Specification, you see that they both say, "a by-name parameter is only evaluated when it's accessed inside a function." Therefore, I find that the following names are more accurate and meaningful than "by-name":

- Call on access
- Evaluate on access
- Evaluate on use
- Evaluate when accessed
- Evaluate when referenced

However, because I can't change the universe, I'll continue to use the terms "by-name" and "call by-name" in this lesson, but I wanted to share those alternate names, which I think are more meaningful.

Example: Creating a timer

That's enough background about the names. Let's look at some code that shows how to create a by-name parameter, and what it gives you.

On Unix systems you can run a `time` command (`timex` on some systems) to see how long commands take to execute:

```
$ time find . -name "*.scala"
```

That command returns the results of the `find` command it was given, along with the time it took to run. The `time` portion of the output looks like this:

---

[4]http://amzn.to/21ScXJc
[5]https://en.wikipedia.org/wiki/Evaluation_strategy
[6]https://en.wikipedia.org/wiki/ALGOL_60

```
real    0m4.351s
user    0m0.491s
sys     0m1.341s
```

This is cool, and it can be a helpful way to troubleshoot performance problems. Seeing how cool it is, you decide that you'd like to create a similar "timer" method in Scala.

Designing a Scala timer

Thinking in advance about how your new `timer` function should work, you decide that a nice API will let you write code like this:

```
val (result, time) = timer(someLongRunningAlgorithm)
```

and this:

```
val (result, time) = timer {
    ...
    ...
}
```

As shown, a `timer` like this gives you both the result of the algorithm and the time it took to run.

Trying to define a function signature

Having seen how to define signatures for function input parameters (FIPs) in the previous lessons, you realize that you know how to write a `timer` ... or at least you think you can.

The problem you run into right away is, "Just what is that algorithm that's being passed in?" It could look like this:

```
def timer(f:(Int) => Int) ...
```

or this:

```
def timer(f:(Double) => Double) ...
```

or anything else:

```
def timer(f:() => Unit) ...
```

```
def timer(f:(Person) => String) ...
def timer(f:(Pizza, Order) => Double) ...
def timer(f:(Pizza, Order, Customer, Discounts) => Currency) ...
```

"Hmm," you begin thinking, "this is quite a problem …" in fact, I can't use generic types to solve this problem.

Fortunately the Scala creators gave us a nice solution for problems like these.

By-name syntax

The solution for situations like this is to use Scala's by-name syntax. It's similar to defining FIPs, but it also makes it possible to solve problems like this. The general syntax for defining a by-name parameter looks like this:

```
def timer(blockOfCode: => theReturnType) ...
```

If you look back at the function input parameter examples, you'll see that the by-name syntax is similar to this example:

```
def timer(f:() => Unit) ...
```

The main difference is that with the by-name syntax, you leave off the () after the input parameter.

Therefore, to create a `timer` that can accept a block of code that returns any type, you make the return type generic. I can sketch the `timer` signature like this:

```
def timer[A](blockOfCode: => A) = ???
```

With that signature in hand, I can then complete the `timer` function like this:

```
def timer[A](blockOfCode: => A) = {
    val startTime = System.nanoTime
    val result = blockOfCode
    val stopTime = System.nanoTime
    val delta = stopTime - startTime
    (result, delta/1000000d)
}
```

As shown, the `timer` method uses the by-name syntax to accept a block of code as an input parameter. Inside the `timer` function there are three lines of code that deal with determining how long the `blockOfCode` takes to run, with this line sandwiched in between those time-related expressions:

```
val result = blockOfCode
```

That line (a) executes `blockOfCode` and (b) assigns its return value to `result`. Because `blockOfCode` is defined to return a generic type (`A`), it may return `Unit`, an `Int`, a `Seq[Person]`, a `Map[Person, Seq[Person]]`, whatever.

Now you can use the `timer` function for all sorts of things. It can be used for something that isn't terribly useful, like this:

```
scala> val (result, time) = timer(println("Hello"))
Hello
result: Unit = ()
time: Double = 0.160
```

It can be used for an algorithm that reads a file and returns an iterator:

```
scala> def readFile(filename: String) = io.Source.fromFile(filename).getLines
readFile: (filename: String)Iterator[String]

scala> val (result, time) = timer(readFile("/etc/passwd"))
result: Iterator[String] = non-empty iterator
time: Double = 32.119
```

Or it can be used for just about anything else:

```
val (result, time) = timer{ aLongRunningAlgorithmThatReturnsSomething }
```

"When is my code block run?"

A great question right now is, "When are my by-name parameters executed?"

In the case of the `timer` function, it executes the `blockOfCode` when the second line of the function is reached. But if that doesn't satisfy your curious mind, you can create another example like this:

```
def test[A](codeBlock: => A) = {
    println("before 1st codeBlock")
    val a = codeBlock
```

```
    println(a)
    Thread.sleep(10)

    println("before 2nd codeBlock")
    val b = codeBlock
    println(b)
    Thread.sleep(10)

    println("before 3rd codeBlock")
    val c = codeBlock
    println(c)
}
```

After you paste that code into the Scala REPL, you can then test it like this:

```
scala> test( System.currentTimeMillis )
```

That line of code will produce output like this:

```
before 1st codeBlock
1480206447942
before 2nd codeBlock
1480206447954
before 3rd codeBlock
1480206447966
```

As that output shows, the block of code that's passed in is executed each time it's referenced inside the function.

Another example: A Swing utility

As another example of how I use this technique, when I was writing a lot of Swing (GUI) code with Scala, I wrote this `invokeLater` function to accept blocks of code that should be run on the JVM's Event Dispatch Thread (EDT):

```
def invokeLater(codeBlock: => Unit) {
    SwingUtilities.invokeLater(new Runnable() {
        def run() {
            codeBlock
        }
    })
}
```

If you haven't used Swing before, it's important to make sure that any code that updates the UI is run on the EDT, and this function simplifies that process.

invokeLater defines codeBlock as a by-name input parameter, and codeBlock is expected to return Unit (nothing). I define it like that because every block of code it accepts is intended to update the Swing GUI, which means that each code block is used to achieve that side effect.

As an example, here are two calls I make to invokeLater from my Sarah application[7]:

```
invokeLater(mainFrame.setSarahIsSleeping())
invokeLater(mainFrame.setSarahIsListening())
```

In these examples, mainFrame.setSarahIsSleeping() and mainFrame.setSarahIsListening() are both function calls, and those functions update Sarah's Swing GUI.

In those examples I pass functions into invokeLater, but I can pass a block of code into it as well:

```
invokeLater {
    val controller = mainController.getMainFrameController()
    controller.setBackground(SARAH_IS_SLEEPING_COLOR)
}
```

Either approach — passing in a function, or passing in a block of code — is valid.

Why have by-name parameters?

Programming in Scala[8], written by Martin Odersky and Bill Venners, provides a great exam-

---
[7] http://alvinalexander.com/sarah
[8] http://amzn.to/2fiqDBh

ple of why by-name parameters were added to Scala. Their example goes like this:

1. Imagine that Scala does not have an `assert` function, and you want one.
2. You attempt to write one using function input parameters, like this:

```
def myAssert(predicate: () => Boolean) =
    if (assertionsEnabled && !predicate())
        throw new AssertionError
```

That code uses the FIP techniques I showed in previous lessons, and assuming that the variable `assertionsEnabled` is in scope, it will compile just fine. The problem is that when you go to use it, you have to write code like this:

```
myAssert(() => 5 > 3)
```

Because `myAssert` states that `predicate` is a function that takes no input parameters and returns a `Boolean`, that's how you have to write this line of code. It works, but it's not pleasing to the eye.

The solution is to change `predicate` to be a by-name parameter:

```
def byNameAssert(predicate: => Boolean) =
    if (assertionsEnabled && !predicate)
        throw new AssertionError
```

With that simple change, you can now write assertions like this:

```
byNameAssert(5 > 3)
```

That's much more pleasing to look at than this:

```
myAssert(() => 5 > 3)
```

Programming in Scala[9] states that this is the primary use case for by-name parameters:

> The result is that using `byNameAssert` looks exactly like using a built-in control structure.

If you want to experiment with this code, here's the source code for a small but complete test

---
[9] http://amzn.to/2fiqDBh

class I created from their example:

```
object ByNameTests extends App {

    var assertionsEnabled = true

    def myAssert(p: () => Boolean) =
        if (assertionsEnabled && !p())
            throw new AssertionError

    myAssert(() => 5 > 3)

    def byNameAssert(p: => Boolean) =
        if (assertionsEnabled && !p)
            throw new AssertionError

    byNameAssert(5 > 3)

}
```

As you can see from that code, there's only a small syntactical difference between (a) defining a FIP that takes no input parameters and (b) a by-name parameter:

```
p: () => Boolean    // a function input parameter
p: => Boolean       // a by-name parameter
```

As you can also tell from these two lines:

```
myAssert(() => 5 > 3)
byNameAssert(5 > 3)
```

you need to call them differently.

Summary

This lesson showed:

- The differences between by-value and by-name parameters
- Examples of the by-name syntax
- How to use by-name parameters in your functions
- Examples of when by-name parameters are appropriate
- Some comparisons of by-name parameters and higher-order functions

26

Functions Can Have Multiple Parameter Groups

"Logic clearly dictates that the needs of the many outweigh the needs of the few."

Spock in *Star Trek II: The Wrath of Khan*

Introduction

Scala lets you create functions that have multiple input parameter groups, like this:

```
def foo(a: Int, b: String)(c: Double) ...
```

Because I knew very little about FP when I first started working with Scala, I originally thought this was just some sort of syntactic nicety. But then I learned that one cool thing this does is that it enables you to write your own control structures. For instance, you can write your own `while` loop, and I show how to do that in this lesson.

Beyond that, the book Scala Puzzlers[1] states that being able to declare multiple parameter groups gives you these additional benefits (some of which are advanced and I rarely use):

- They let you have both implicit and non-implicit parameters
- They facilitate type inference
- A parameter in one group can use a parameter from a previous group as a default value

I demonstrate each of these features in this lesson, and show how multiple parameter groups are used to create partially-applied functions in the next lesson.

---

[1] http://amzn.to/21ScXJc

Goals

The goals of this lesson are:

- Show how to write and use functions that have multiple input parameter groups
- Demonstrate how this helps you create your own control structures, which in turn can help you write your own DSLs
- Show some other potential benefits of using multiple input parameter groups

First example

Defining a function with multiple parameter groups is one of the easier things in this book. Instead of writing a "normal" *add* function with one parameter group like this:

```
def add(a: Int, b: Int, c: Int) = a + b + c
```

just put your function's input parameters in different groups, with each group surrounded by parentheses:

```
def sum(a: Int)(b: Int)(c: Int) = a + b + c
```

After that, you can call sum like this:

```
scala> sum(1)(2)(3)
res0: Int = 6
```

That's all there is to the basic technique. The rest of this lesson shows the advantages that come from using this approach.

A few notes about this technique

When you write sum with three input parameter groups like this, you can't call it with three parameters in one group:

```
scala> sum(1,2,3)
<console>:12: error: too many arguments for method
sum: (a: Int)(b: Int)(c: Int)Int
       sum(1,2,3)
           ^
```

You must supply the input parameters in three separate input lists.

Another thing to note is that each parameter group can have multiple input parameters:

```
def doFoo(firstName: String, lastName: String)(age: Int) = ???
```

How to write your own control structures

To show the kind of things you can do with multiple parameter groups, let's build a control structure of our own. To do this, imagine for a moment that you don't like the built-in Scala `while` loop — or maybe you want to add some functionality to it — so you want to create your own `whilst` loop, which you can use like this:

```
var i = 0
whilst (i < 5) {
    println(i)
    i += 1
}
```

A thing that your eyes will soon learn to see when looking at code like this is that `whilst` *must* be defined to have two parameter groups. The first parameter group contains `i < 5`. Note that this expression yields a `Boolean` value. This tells you that `whilst` must be defined so that its first parameter group expects a `Boolean` parameter.

The second parameter group is the block of code enclosed in curly braces immediately after that. These two groups are highlighted in Figure 26.1.

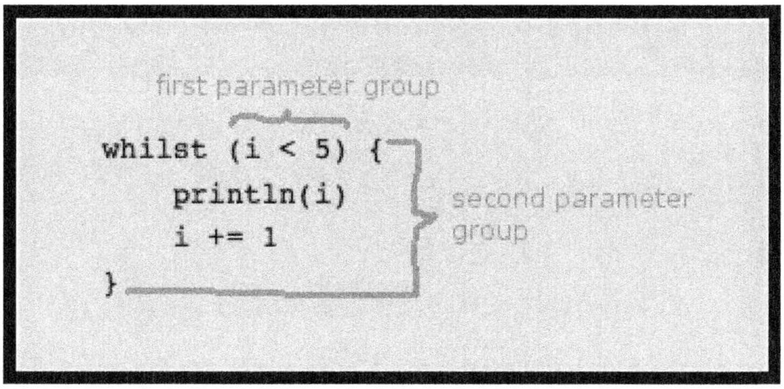

Figure 26.1: The second parameter group is enclosed in the curly braces.

You'll see this pattern *a lot* in Scala/FP code, so it helps to get used to it. I demonstrate more examples in this chapter, but the lesson for the moment is that when you see code like this, you should think:

- I see a function named whilst that has two parameter groups.
- The first parameter group must evaluate to a Boolean value.
- The second parameter group is probably defined as a by-name parameter. This specific block of code returns nothing (Unit), because the last expression in the code block (i += 1) returns nothing.

How to create whilst

To create the whilst control structure, define it as a function that takes two parameter groups. As mentioned, the first parameter group must evaluate to a Boolean value, and the second group takes a block of code that evaluates to Unit; the user wants to run this block of code in a loop as long as the first parameter group evaluates to true.

When I write functions the first thing I like to do is sketch the function's signature, and the previous paragraph tells me that whilst's signature should look like this:

```
def whilst(testCondition: => Boolean)(codeBlock: => Unit) = ???
```

The two parameters groups are highlighted in Figure 26.2.

```
                first parameter group      second parameter group
def whilst(testCondition: => Boolean)(codeBlock: => Unit) {
```

Figure 26.2: The two parameter groups in whilst's function signature.

Using by-name parameters

Notice that both parameter groups use *by-name* parameters. The first parameter (testCondition) needs to be a by-name parameter because it specifies a test condition that will repeatedly be tested inside the function. If this *wasn't* a by-name parameter, the i < 5 code shown here:

```
var i = 0
whilst (i < 5) ...
```

would immediately be translated by the compiler into this:

```
whilst (0 < 5) ...
```

and then that code would be further "optimized" into this:

```
whilst (true) ...
```

If this happens, the whilst function would receive true for its first parameter, and the loop will run forever. This would be bad.

But when testCondition is defined as a by-name parameter, the i < 5 code block is passed into whilst without being evaluated, which is what we desire.

Using a by-name parameter in the *last* parameter group when creating control structures is a common pattern in Scala/FP. This is because (as I just showed) a by-name parameter lets the consumer of your control structure pass in a block of code to solve their problem, typically enclosed in curly braces, like this:

```
customControlStructure(...) {
    // custom code block here
    ...
    ...
}
```

The final code

So far, I showed that the whilst signature begins like this:

```
def whilst(testCondition: => Boolean)(codeBlock: => Unit) = ???
```

In FP, the proper way to implement whilst's body is with recursion, but because I haven't covered that yet, I'm going to cheat here and implement whilst with an inner while loop. Admittedly that's some serious cheating, but for the purposes of this lesson I'm not really interested in whilst's body; I'm interested in its signature, along with what this general approach lets you accomplish.

Therefore, having defined whilst's signature, this is what whilst looks like as a wrapper around a while loop:

```
def whilst(testCondition: => Boolean)(codeBlock: => Unit) {
    while (testCondition) {
        codeBlock
    }
```

}

Note that whilst doesn't return anything. That's *implied* by the current function signature, and you can make it more explicit by adding a Unit return type to the function signature:

```
def whilst(testCondition: => Boolean)(codeBlock: => Unit): Unit = {
                                                         --------
```

I prefer this style of coding, and with that change, the final whilst function looks like this:

```
def whilst(testCondition: => Boolean)(codeBlock: => Unit): Unit = {
    while (testCondition) {
        codeBlock
    }
}
```

Using whilst

Because I cheated with the function body, that's all there is to writing whilst. Now you can use it anywhere you would use while. This is one possible example:

```
var i = 1
whilst(i < 5) {
    println(i)
    i += 1
}
```

Exercise: Write a control structure using three parameter groups

The whilst example shows how to write a custom control structure using two parameter groups. It also shows a common pattern:

- Use one or more parameter groups to break the input parameters into different "compartments"
- Specifically define the parameter in the last parameter group as a by-name parameter so the function can accept a custom block of code

Control structures can have more than two parameter lists. As an exercise, imagine that you want to create a control structure that makes it easy to execute a condition if two test conditions are both true. Imagine the control structure is named ifBothTrue, and it will be used like this:

```
ifBothTrue(age > 18)(numAccidents == 0) {
    println("Discount!")
}
```

Just by looking at that code, you should be able to answer these questions:

- How many input parameter groups does ifBothTrue have?
- What is the type of the first group?
- What is the type of the second group?
- What is the type of the third group?

Sketch the signature of the ifBothTrue function. Start by sketching *only* the function signature, as I did with the whilst example:

Once you're confident that you have the correct function signature, sketch the function body here:

Solution

In this case, because ifBothTrue takes two test conditions followed by a block of code, and it doesn't return anything, its signature looks like this:

```
def ifBothTrue(test1: => Boolean)
              (test2: => Boolean)
              (codeBlock: => Unit): Unit = ???
```

Because the code block should only be run if both test conditions are true, the complete function should be written like this:

```
def ifBothTrue(test1: => Boolean)
```

```
                (test2: => Boolean)
                (codeBlock: => Unit): Unit = {
    if (test1 && test2) {
        codeBlock
    }
}
```

You can test ifBothTrue with code like this:

```
val age = 19
val numAccidents = 0
ifBothTrue(age > 18)(numAccidents == 0) { println("Discount!") }
```

Benefit: Using implicit values

A nice benefit of multiple input parameter groups comes when you use them with *implicit* parameters. This can help to simplify code when a resource is needed, but passing that resource explicitly to a function makes the code harder to read.

To demonstrate how this works, here's a function that uses multiple input parameter groups:

```
def printIntIfTrue(a: Int)(implicit b: Boolean) = if (b) println(a)
```

Notice that the Boolean in the second parameter group is tagged as an implicit value — but don't worry about that just yet. For the moment, just note that if you paste this function into the REPL and then call it with an Int and a Boolean, it does what it looks like it should do, printing the Int when the Boolean is true:

```
scala> printIntIfTrue(42)(true)
42
```

Given that background, let's see what that implicit keyword on the second parameter does for us.

Using implicit values

Because b is defined as an *implicit* value in the *last* parameter group, if there is an implicit Boolean value in scope when printIntIfTrue is invoked, printIntIfTrue will use that Boolean without you having to explicitly provide it.

You can see how this works in the REPL. First, as an intentional error, try to call printIntIfTrue without a second parameter:

```
scala> printIntIfTrue(1)
<console>:12: error: could not find implicit value for parameter b: Boolean
       printIntIfTrue(1)
                     ^
```

Of course that fails because printIntIfTrue requires a Boolean value in its second parameter group. Next, let's see what happens if we define a regular Boolean in the current scope:

```
scala> val boo = true
boo: Boolean = true

scala> printIntIfTrue(1)
<console>:12: error: could not find implicit value for parameter b: Boolean
       printIntIfTrue(1)
                     ^
```

Calling printIntIfTrue still fails, as expected. Now notice what happens when boo is defined as an implicit Boolean value:

```
scala> implicit val boo = true
boo: Boolean = true

scala> printIntIfTrue(33)
33
```

printIntIfTrue works with only one parameter!

This works because:

1. The Boolean parameter in printIntIfTrue's last parameter group is tagged with the implicit keyword
2. boo is declared to be an implicit Boolean value

The way this works is like this:

1. The Scala compiler knows that printIntIfTrue is defined to have two parameter groups.
2. It also knows that the second parameter group declares an implicit Boolean parameter.
3. When printIntIfTrue(33) is called, only one parameter group is supplied.

4. At this point Scala knows that one of two things must now be true. Either (a) there better be an implicit `Boolean` value in the current scope, in which case Scala will use it as the second parameter, or (b) Scala will throw the compiler error shown earlier.

Because `boo` is an implicit `Boolean` value and it's in the current scope, the Scala compiler reaches out and automatically uses it as the input parameter for the second parameter group. That is, `boo` is used just as though it had been passed in explicitly.

The benefit

If that code looks too "magical," I'll say two things about this technique:

- It works really well in certain situations
- Don't overuse it, because when it's used wrongly it makes code hard to understand and maintain (which is pretty much an anti-pattern)

An area where this technique works really well is when you need to refer to a shared resource several times, and you want to keep your code clean. For instance, if you need to reference a database connection several times in your code, using an implicit connection can clean up your code. It tends to be obvious that an implicit connection is hanging around, and of course database access code isn't going to work without a connection.

An implicit execution context

A similar "shared resource" example is when you need an *execution context* in scope when you're writing multi-threaded code with the Akka library. For example, with Akka you usually create an implicit `ActorSystem` like this early in your code:

```
implicit val actorSystem = ActorSystem("FutureSystem")
```

Then, at one or more places later in your code you can create a `Future` like this, and the `Future` "just works":

```
val future = Future {
    1 + 1
}
```

The reason this `Future` works is because it's written with an implicit input parameter in its last parameter group, like the `printIntIfTrue` function. If you dig through the Akka source code you'll see that `Future`'s `apply` method is written like this:

```
def apply [T] (body: => T)(implicit executor: ExecutionContext) ...
         --------
```

As that shows, the executor parameter in the last parameter group is an `implicit` value of the `ExecutionContext` type. Because an `ActorSystem` is an instance of an `ExecutionContext`, when you define the `ActorSystem` as being `implicit`, like this:

```
implicit val actorSystem = ActorSystem("FutureSystem")
--------
```

`Future`'s `apply` method can find it and "pull it in" automatically. This makes the `Future` code more readable. If `Future` didn't use an `implicit` value, each invocation of a new `Future` would have to look something like this:

```
val future = Future(actorSystem) {
    code to run here ...
}
```

That's not too bad with just one `Future`, but more complicated code is definitely cleaner without it repeatedly referencing the `actorSystem`.

> If you're new to Akka Actors, my article, A simple working Akka Futures example[2], explains everything I just wrote about actors, futures, execution contexts, and actor systems.

Limits on implicit parameters

The Scala language specification[3] tells us these things about implicit parameters:

- A method or constructor can have only one implicit parameter list, and it must be the last parameter list given
- If there are several eligible arguments which match the implicit parameter's type, a most specific one will be chosen using the rules of static overloading resolution

I'll show some of what this means in the following "implicit parameter FAQs".

---

[2]http://alvinalexander.com/scala/scala-akka-futures-example-simple-working
[3]http://www.scala-lang.org/files/archive/spec/2.11/07-implicit-parameters-and-views.html#implicit-parameters

FAQ: Can you use `implicit` *more than once in your parameter lists?*

No, you can't. This code will not compile:

```
def printIntIfTrue(implicit a: Int)(implicit b: Boolean) = if (b) println(a)
```

FAQ: Does the `implicit` *have to be in the last parameter list?*

Yes. This code, with an `implicit` in the first list, won't compile:

```
def printIntIfTrue(implicit b: Boolean)(a: Int) = if (b) println(a)
```

Using default values

As the Scala Puzzlers[4] book notes, you can supply default values for input parameters when using multiple parameter groups, in a manner similar to using one parameter group. Here I specify default values for the parameters a and b:

```
scala> def f2(a: Int = 1)(b: Int = 2) = { a + b }
f2: (a: Int)(b: Int)Int
```

That part is easy, but the "magic" in this recipe is knowing that you need to supply empty parentheses when you want to use the default values:

```
scala> f2
<console>:13: error: missing argument list for method f2
Unapplied methods are only converted to functions when a
function type is expected. You can make this conversion explicit
by writing `f2 _` or `f2(_)(_)` instead of `f2`.
       f2
       ^

scala> f2()()
res0: Int = 3

scala> f2(10)()
```

---

[4] http://amzn.to/21ScXJc

```
res1: Int = 12

scala> f2()(10)
res2: Int = 11
```

As the Puzzlers book also notes, a parameter in the second parameter group can use a parameter from the first parameter group as a default value. In this next example I assign *a* to be the default value for the parameter *b*:

```
def f2(a: Int = 1)(b: Int = a) = { a + b }
```

The REPL shows that this works as expected:

```
scala> def f2(a: Int = 1)(b: Int = a) = { a + b }
f2: (a: Int)(b: Int)Int

scala> f2()()
res0: Int = 2

scala> f2(10)()
res1: Int = 20
```

I haven't had a need for these techniques yet, but in case you ever need them, there you go.

Summary

In this lesson I covered the following:

- I showed how to write functions that have multiple input parameter groups.
- I showed how to call functions that have multiple input parameter groups.
- I showed to write your own control structures, such as `whilst` and `ifBothTrue`. The keys to this are (a) using multiple parameter groups and (b) accepting a block of code as a by-name parameter in the last parameter group.
- I showed how to use `implicit` parameters, and possible pitfalls of using them.
- I showed how to use default values with multiple parameter groups.

What's next

The next lesson expands on this lesson by showing what "Currying" is, and by showing how multiple parameter groups work with partially-applied functions.

See Also

- My article, How to use the using control structure from Beginning Scala[5]
- Joshua Suereth's scala-arm project[6] is similar to the using control structure
- The Scala "Breaks" control structure is created using the techniques shown in this lesson, and I describe it in my article, How to use break and continue in Scala[7]

---

[5] http://alvinalexander.com/scala/using-control-structure-beginning-scala-david-pollak
[6] https://github.com/jsuereth/scala-arm
[7] http://alvinalexander.com/scala/break-continue-for-while-loops-in-scala-examples-how-to

27

Partially-Applied Functions (and Currying)

Motivation

My motivations for writing this lesson are a little different than usual. Typically I think, "You'll want to know this feature so you can use it like ___," but the first motivation for this lesson goes like this: You'll want to know about the concept of "currying" because experienced FP developers mention it quite a bit, especially if they have Haskell programming experience. (I did mention that Haskell was named after Haskell *Curry*, didn't I?)

A second motivation is that the concept of currying is related to the multiple parameter groups I showed in the previous lesson come from.

That being said, the *primary motivation* for writing this lesson is that having multiple parameter groups make it a little easier to create *partially-applied functions*, and these can be useful in your FP code.

I'll cover all of these topics in this lesson.

Goals

Given that introduction, the goals of this lesson are:

- Provide a definition of *currying*
- Show how to create partially-applied functions from functions that have (a) multiple parameter groups or (b) single parameter groups

I'll also show how to create "curried" functions from regular functions, and show how Scala gets these features to work with the JVM.

Currying

When I first got started in FP, I got lost in some of its nomenclature, and "currying" was a particularly deep rabbit's hole of "Time in My Life I Wish I Had Spent Differently."

All that the theory of *currying* means is that a function that takes *multiple* arguments can be translated into a series of function calls that each take a *single* argument. In pseudocode, this means that an expression like this:

```
result = f(x)(y)(z)
```

is mathematically the same as something like this:

```
f1 = f(x)
f2 = f1(y)
result = f2(z)
```

That's all it means. The Wikipedia page on Currying[1] describes currying like this:

> In mathematics and computer science, currying is the technique of translating the evaluation of a function that takes multiple arguments into evaluating a sequence of functions, each with a single argument.

They later state:

> There are analytical techniques that can only be applied to functions with a single argument. Practical functions frequently take more arguments than this.

What this means

In my daily working life, this theory usually isn't important. It's one of those things that's "nice to know," but the important things are (a) how this impacted the design of the Scala language, and (b) what you can do because of this theory.

In Scala this seems to fit most naturally with functions that have multiple input parameters groups, and I'll demonstrate that in this lesson.

> Terminology note: In the remainder of this lesson I'll occasionally use the acronym "PAF" to mean "partially-applied function."

Partially-applied functions

To understand PAFs, I'll start with two definitions from this online JavaScript course[2]:

---
[1] https://en.wikipedia.org/wiki/Currying
[2] https://github.com/learn-javascript-courses/javascript-questions/issues/7

1) *Application*: The process of applying a function to its arguments in order to produce a return value.

As in algebra, in FP you say that "a function is applied to its arguments," so "Application" in this context can also be called "Full Application," or "Complete Application."

2) *Partial Application*: This is the process of applying a function to *some* of its arguments. A partially-applied function gets returned for later use. In other words, a PAF is a function that takes a function with multiple parameters and returns a function with fewer parameters.

The best way to explain PAFs is with examples, so let's look at a few.

Example 1 (partially-applied functions)

The following example shows how PAFs work. In the first step, you define a function with multiple parameter groups:

```
scala> def plus(a: Int)(b: Int) = a + b
plus: (a: Int)(b: Int)Int
```

Next, rather than giving the function all of the parameters in the two parameter groups it specifies, you give it (a) the parameter for the first group (a), and (b) a placeholder for the parameter in the second list, the ubiquitous underscore character:

```
scala> def plus2 = plus(2)(_)
plus2: Int => Int
```

The REPL output shows that this creates a new function named plus2 which has the type Int => Int. This means that plus2 takes an Int as input, and returns an Int as a result.

At this point you can think of plus2 as looking like this:

```
def plus(b: Int) = 2 + b
```

What's happened is that plus2 has been "seeded" with the initial Int value 2, and now it's just sitting there, waiting for another Int value that it can add to it. Let's give it another 2:

```
scala> plus2(2)
res0: Int = 4
```

Here's what it looks like when you give it a 3:

```
scala> plus2(3)
res1: Int = 5
```

As this shows, `plus2` gladly adds 2 to any `Int` it is given.

Before I move on to the next example, notice that you can create `plus2` in either of these ways:

```
def plus2 = plus(2)(_)
def plus2 = plus(2)_
```

I prefer the first syntax, but some people prefer the second approach.

Example 2 (partially-applied functions)

The general benefit that this approach gives you is that it's a way to create specialized methods from more general methods. I demonstrate this in the Scala Cookbook[3], and I'll share a variation of that example here.

When you're emitting HTML from Scala code, a `wrap` function that adds a prefix and a suffix to an HTML snippet can be really useful:

```
def wrap(prefix: String)(html: String)(suffix: String) = {
    prefix + html + suffix
}
```

You can use that function to do something like this, where I wrap a string in opening and closing `<div>` tags:

---

[3] http://amzn.to/24ivK4G

```
val hello = "Hello, world"
val result = wrap("<div>")(hello)("</div>")
```

Of course that <div> tag can be more complicated, such as specifying a CSS class or id, but I'm keeping this simple.

It turns out that wrap is a really nice, *general* function, so you can wrap text in DIV tags, P tags, SPAN tags, etc. But if you're going to be wrapping a lot of strings with DIV tags, what you probably want is a more specific wrapWithDiv function. This is a great time to use a partially-applied function, because that's what they do: they let you create a *specific* function from a *general* function:

```
val wrapWithDiv = wrap("<div>")(_: String)("</div>")
```

Now you can call wrapWithDiv, just passing it the HTML you want to wrap:

```
scala> wrapWithDiv("<p>Hello, world</p>")
res0: String = <div><p>Hello, world</p></div>


scala> wrapWithDiv("<img src=\"/images/foo.png\" />")
res1: String = <div><img src="/images/foo.png" /></div>
```

Of course you can still call the original wrap function:

```
wrap("<pre>", "val x = 1", "</pre>")
```

You can also create other, more-specific functions:

```
val wrapWithPre = wrap("<pre>")(_: String)("</pre>")
```

Besides the unique syntax, the important point is that you make a more specific function by "seeding" the more general function with one or more initial parameters. That is, you *partially apply* parameters to the general function to create the specific function.

Handling the missing parameter

As I showed in that example, it's necessary to specify the *type* of the missing parameter, as I did in this code:

```
val wrapWithDiv = wrap("<div>")(_: String)("</div>")
```

If you don't specify the type, you'll get a compiler error that looks like this:

```
scala> val wrapWithDiv = wrap("<div>")(_)("</div>")
<console>:11: error: missing parameter type for
expanded function ((x$1) => wrap("<div>")(x$1)("</div>"))
       val wrapWithDiv = wrap("<div>")(_)("</div>")
                                        ^
```

Summary: Partially-applied functions

As a summary, PAFs give you this capability:

- You write a general function
- You create a specific function from the general function
- You still have access to both functions, and you kept your code "DRY" — you didn't copy and paste code to make the new function

Creating curried functions from regular functions

As a fun example of some things you can do with PAFs, the "partially-applied functions" section of the *Scala Exercises* website[4] demonstrates that you can create curried functions from "normal" Scala functions. For instance, you can start with a normal, one-parameter group function like this:

```
def add(x: Int, y: Int) = x + y
```

Then they show that you can create a Function2 instance from add by adding an underscore after it, like this:

```
scala> val addFunction = add _
addFunction: (Int, Int) => Int = <function2>
```

After that, they prove that it's a Function2 instance like this:

```
(add _).isInstanceOf[Function2[_, _, _]]
```

Finally, they create a "curried" function from that Function2 instance:

---

[4]http://scala-exercises.47deg.com/koans#partiallyappliedfunctions

```
val addCurried = (add _).curried
```

Now you can use the new curried function like this:

```
addCurried(1)(2)
```

As this shows, calling the `curried` method on the `add` function instance creates a new function that has two parameter groups. (So, a curried function can be thought of as a function with multiple parameter groups.)

You can also create a partially-applied function from the curried function, like this:

```
val addCurriedTwo = addCurried(2)    // create a PAF
addCurriedTwo(10)                    // use the PAF
```

> The technique of converting a `def` method into a true function uses a Scala technology known as "Eta Expansion," which I discuss in the *Using Methods As If They Were Functions* lesson.

See it in the REPL

You can see how all of those steps work by pasting the code into the REPL:

```
scala> def add(x: Int, y: Int) = x + y
add: (x: Int, y: Int)Int

scala> (add _).isInstanceOf[Function2[_, _, _]]
res0: Boolean = true

scala> val addCurried = (add _).curried
addCurried: Int => (Int => Int) = <function1>

scala> addCurried(1)(2)
res1: Int = 3

scala> val addCurriedTwo = addCurried(2)
addCurriedTwo: Int => Int = <function1>

scala> addCurriedTwo(10)
```

```
res2: Int = 12
```

Personally, I mostly use curried functions to create control structures, as I demonstrated with `whilst` and `ifBothTrue` in the previous lesson. (So, at the moment, this is a technique I know about, but have not used.)

Partially-applied functions without multiple parameter groups

So far I've shown that you can create a partially-applied function with functions that have multiple parameter groups, but because Scala is really convenient, you can create PAFs with single parameter group functions as well.

To demonstrate this, first define a function as usual, with one parameter group:

```
def wrap(prefix: String, html: String, suffix: String) = {
    prefix + html + suffix
}
```

Then create a PAF by applying the first and third parameters, but not the second:

```
val wrapWithDiv = wrap("<div>", _: String, "</div>")
```

The `wrapWithDiv` function you create in this manner works the same as the `wrapWithDiv` function created in the previous example:

```
scala> val wrapWithDiv = wrap("<div>", _: String, "</div>")
wrapWithDiv: String => String = <function1>

scala> wrapWithDiv("Hello, world")
res1: String = <div>Hello, world</div>
```

Extra credit: How can all of this work with the JVM?

If you're interested in how things work under the covers, a good question at this point is, "How can this stuff possibly work with the JVM?" The JVM certainly wasn't written to account for things like currying and PAFs, so how does any of this work?

A short answer is that (a) the Scala compiler "uncurries" your code, and (b) you can see this during the compilation process. For example, write a little Scala class like this:

```
class Currying {
```

```
    def f1(a: Int, b: Int) = { a + b }     // 1 param group
    def f2(a: Int)(b: Int) = { a + b }     // 2 param groups
}
```

Then compile that class with this command:

```
$ scalac -Xprint:all Currying.scala
```

if you dig through the end of that output, you'll see that the Scala compiler has an "uncurry" phase. A short version of the tail end of the compiler output looks like this:

```
[[syntax trees at end of typer]] // Currying.scala
package <empty> {
  class Currying extends scala.AnyRef {
    def <init>(): Currying = {
      Currying.super.<init>();
      ()
    };
    def f1(a: Int, b: Int): Int = a.+(b);
    def f2(a: Int)(b: Int): Int = a.+(b)
  }
}

.
.
.


[[syntax trees at end of uncurry]] // Currying.scala
package <empty> {
  class Currying extends Object {
    def <init>(): Currying = {
      Currying.super.<init>();
      ()
    };
    def f1(a: Int, b: Int): Int = a.+(b);
    def f2(a: Int, b: Int): Int = a.+(b)
  }
}
```

As that output shows, I wrote the two functions f1 and f2 differently, but after the compiler's "uncurry" phase they end up looking the same.

> Things might look more interesting in the output if I had created a partially-applied function, but I'll leave that as an exercise for the reader.

Currying vs partially-applied functions

The concepts of currying and partially-applied functions are related, but they aren't exactly the same. As I wrote at the beginning, currying is defined like this:

> A function that takes multiple arguments can be translated into a series of function calls that each take a single argument.

This is particularly important in a language like Haskell, where all functions are technically curried functions. In Scala this is generally a theoretical thing that's good to know about, and it's good to know that you can create a curried function from a normal function, but these aren't "core" features you absolutely need to know to write code in Scala.

A partially-applied function on the other hand is a function that you manually create by supplying fewer parameters than the initial function defines. As I showed in this lesson, you can create the PAF plus2 like this:

```
def plus(a: Int)(b: Int) = a + b
def plus2 = plus(2)(_)
```

So, both concepts are related to multiple parameter groups, but in general, I use PAFs more often than I concern myself with curried functions.

Don't get bogged down in terminology

As I mentioned at the beginning of this lesson, don't get bogged down in the precise meaning of things like "curried functions." It is good to know how multiple input parameter groups work because it's a technique that is used a lot in Scala/FP, but don't get lost in worrying about the exact meaning of currying like I did. Understanding how multiple parameter groups work is the important thing.

Summary

This lesson covered the following topics:

- It provides a definition of *currying*
- It shows how to create partially-applied functions from functions that have (a) multiple parameter groups or (b) single parameter groups

It also shows how to create "curried" functions from regular functions, and provided a little look at how Scala gets these features to work with the JVM.

What's next

I've covered a lot of Scala/FP background material so far, but occasionally I had to mix in a few *var* fields in my examples because that's the only way to solve certain problems with the tools I've shown so far.

Well, no more of that.

In the next few lessons things are going to be fun, as I get to cover *recursion*. Once you understand recursive calls, I think you'll find that they're a natural way to think about writing iterative algorithms.

Once I cover recursion you'll then be very close to handling many more FP concepts, the first of which will be how to handle "state" in FP applications. But to handle state in an FP manner, you'll need to know how to write recursive functions ...

Recursion: Introduction

As you may have noticed from this book's index, you're about to jump into a series of lessons on recursive programming. I separated this text into a series of small lessons to make the content easier to read initially, and then easier to refer to later.

Please note that some of these lessons may be overkill for some people. Many people find recursive programming to be difficult, so I demonstrate it in several different ways. I start by reviewing the List class, then show a straightforward, "Here's how to write a recursive function" lesson. After that I add a few more lessons to explain recursion in different ways.

If at any point you feel like you understand how to write recursive functions, feel free to skip any or all of these lessons. You can always come back to them later if you need to.

29

Recursion: Motivation

"To iterate is human, to recurse divine."

L. Peter Deutsch

What is recursion?

Before getting into the motivation to use recursion, a great question is, "What is recursion?"

Simply stated, a *recursive function* is a function that calls itself. That's it.

As you'll see in this lesson, a common use of recursive functions is to iterate over the elements in a list.

Why do I need to write recursive functions?

The next question that usually comes up right about now is, "Why do I need to write recursive functions? Why can't I use for loops to iterate over lists?"

The short answer is that algorithms that use for loops require the use of var fields, and as you know from our rules[1], functional programmers don't use var fields.

(Read on for the longer answer.)

If you had var fields

Of course if you *could* use mutable variables in your programming language, you might write a "sum the integers in a list" algorithm like this:

```
def sum(xs: List[Int]): Int = {
```

---

[1] /book/scala-fp-rules-for-programming-in-book.html

```
    var sum = 0
    for (x <- xs) {
        sum += x
    }
    sum
}
```

That algorithm uses a `var` field named `sum` and a `for` loop to iterate through every element in the given list to calculate the sum of those integers. From an imperative programming standpoint, there's nothing wrong with this code. I wrote imperative code like this in Java for more than fifteen years.

But from a functional programmer's point of view, there are several problems with this code.

Problem 1: We can only keep so much in our brains

One problem is that reading a lot of custom `for` loops dulls your brain.

As an OOP/imperative programmer I never noticed it, but if you *think about the way you thought* when you read that function, one of the first things you thought is, "Hmm, here's a `var` field named `sum`, so Al is probably going to modify that field in the rest of the algorithm." Then you thought, "Okay, here's a `for` loop ... he's looping over `xs` ... ah, yes, he's using `+=`, so this really is a 'sum' loop, so that variable name makes sense." Once you learn FP — or even if you just learn the methods available on Scala collections classes — you realize *that's a lot of thinking* about a little custom `for` loop.

If you're like me a few years ago, you may be thinking that what I just wrote is overkill. You probably look at mutable variables and `for` loops all the time. But studies show that we can only keep *just so much* information in our brains at one time, therefore:

- The less information we *have* to keep in there is a win, and
- Boilerplate `for` loop code is a waste of our brain's RAM

Maybe this seems like a small win at the moment, but speaking from my own experience, anything I can do to keep my brain's RAM free for important things is a win.

Problem #2: It's not algebraic

Another problem is that this code doesn't look or feel like algebra. I discussed this in the "Functional Programming is Like Algebra" lesson, so I won't repeat that discussion here.

Problem #3: There are no `var` *fields in FP*

Of course from our perspective as functional programmers, the *huge* problem with this code is that it requires a `var` field, and Scala/FP developers don't use those. A `var` field is a crutch, and the best thing you can do to expedite your FP education is to completely forget that they exist.

In my own FP experience, I learned that there's a different way to solve iterative problems once I let go of `var` fields and `for` loops.

What to do?

Because we can't use `var` fields, we need to look at a different tool to solve problems like this. That tool is *recursion*.

If you're like me, at first you'll *need* to write recursive functions (because that's all you can do), but after a while you'll *want* to write recursive functions.

30
Recursion: Let's Look at Lists

> *"In computer science, a linked list is a linear collection of data elements, called nodes, each pointing to the next node by means of a pointer."*
>
> Wikipedia's Linked List entry[a]

---

[a]https://en.wikipedia.org/wiki/Linked_list

Visualizing lists

Because the `List` data structure — and the *head* and *tail* components of a `List` — are so important to recursion, it helps to visualize what a list and its head and tail components look like. Figure 30.1 shows one way to visualize a `List`.

Figure 30.1: One way to visualize the head and tail elements of a list.

This creative imagery comes from the online version of "Learn You a Haskell for Great Good"[1], and it does a great job of imprinting the concept of head and tail components of a list into your brain. As shown, the "head" component is simply the first element in the list, and the "tail" is the rest of the list.

A slightly more technical way to visualize the head and tail of a list is shown in Figure 30.2.

---

[1]http://learnyouahaskell.com/starting-out

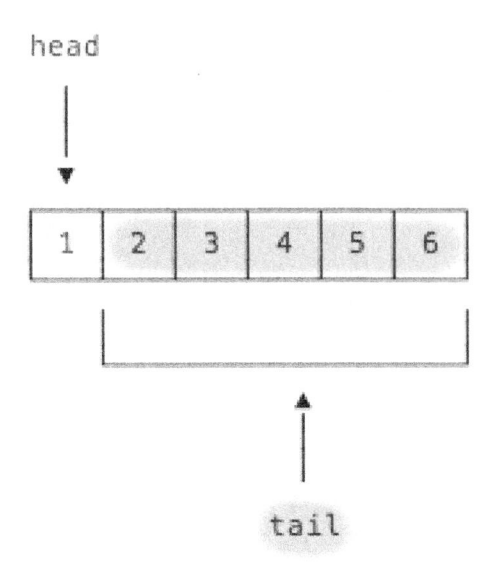

Figure 30.2: A slightly more technical way to visualize a list.

An even more accurate way to show this is with a `Nil` value in the very last position, as shown in Figure 30.3, because that's what it really looks like.

Linked lists and "cons" cells

To be clear, the `List` that I'm talking about is a *linked list* — scala.collection.immutable.List[2], which is the default list you get if you type `List` in your IDE or the REPL. This `List` is a series of cells, where each cell contains two things: (a) a value, and (b) a pointer to the next cell. This is shown in Figure 30.4.

As shown, the last cell in a linked list contains the `Nil` value. The `Nil` in the last cell is *very* important: it's how your recursive Scala code will know when it has reached the end of a `List`.

When drawing a list like this, Figure 30.5 clearly shows the head element.

Figure 30.6 shows the tail elements of a list.

Just like Haskell — and Lisp before it — the default Scala `List` works with these head and tail components, and I'll use them extensively in the examples that follow.

---

[2]http://www.scala-lang.org/api/current/#scala.collection.immutable.List

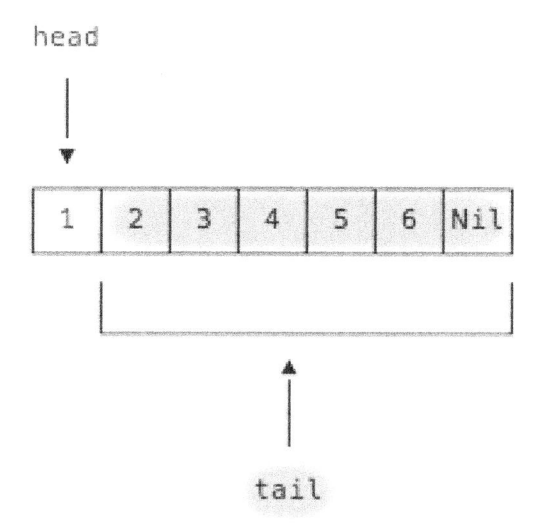

Figure 30.3: An even more accurate way to visualize a list.

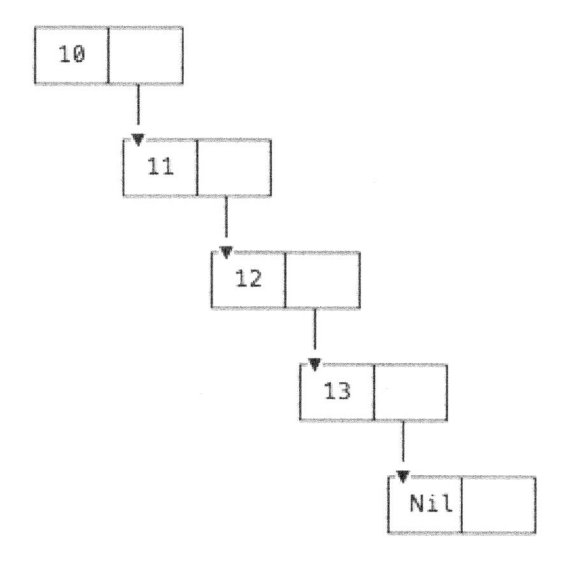

Figure 30.4: A linked list contains a value and a pointer to the next cell.

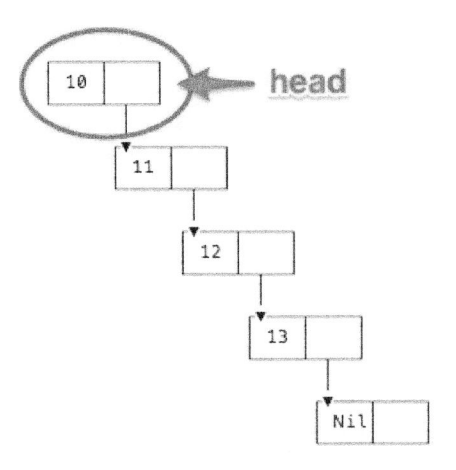

Figure 30.5: The head element of a list.

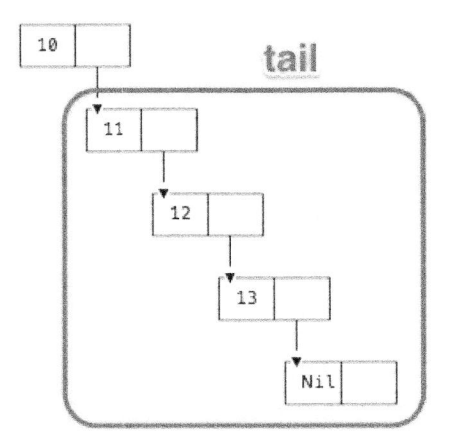

Figure 30.6: The tail elements of a list.

For historical reasons these cells are known as "cons cells." That name comes from Lisp, and if you like history, you can read more about it on Wikipedia[3].

Note 1: The empty `List`

As a first note about `List`s, a `List` with no elements in it is an *empty list*. An empty `List` contains only one cell, and that cell contains a `Nil` element, as shown in Figure 30.7.

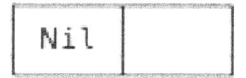

Figure 30.7: A list with no elements contains only one cell, which contains a `Nil` element.

You can create an empty `List[Int]` in Scala in two ways:

```
scala> val empty1: List[Int] = List()
empty: List[Int] = List()

scala> val empty2: List[Int] = Nil
empty: List[Int] = List()

scala> empty1 == empty2
res0: Boolean = true
```

As those examples show:

```
List() == Nil
```

Note 2: Several ways to create `List`s

There are several ways to create *non-empty* `List`s in Scala, but for the most part I'll use two approaches. First, here's a technique you're probably already familiar with:

```
val list = List(1,2,3)
```

Second, this is an approach you may not have seen yet:

---

[3]https://en.wikipedia.org/wiki/Cons

```
val list = 1 :: 2 :: 3 :: Nil
```

These two techniques result in the exact same List[Int], which you can see in the REPL:

```
scala> val list1 = List(1,2,3)
list: List[Int] = List(1, 2, 3)

scala> val list2 = 1 :: 2 :: 3 :: Nil
list: List[Int] = List(1, 2, 3)

scala> list1 == list2
res1: Boolean = true
```

The second approach is known as using "cons cells." As you can see, it's a very literal approach to creating a List, where you specify each element in the List, including the Nil element in the last position. If you forget the Nil element at the end, the Scala compiler will bark at you:

```
scala> val list = 1 :: 2 :: 3
<console>:10: error: value :: is not a member of Int
       val list = 1 :: 2 :: 3
                       ^
```

I show this because it's important — very important — to know that the last element in a List *must* be the Nil element. (I like to say that the Nil element is to a List as a caboose is to a train.) We're going to take advantage of this knowledge as we write our first recursive function.

31

Recursion: How to Write a 'sum' Function

With all of the images of the previous lesson firmly ingrained in your brain, let's write a sum function using recursion!

Source code

The source code for this lesson is at this Github URL:

- github.com/alvinj/RecursiveSum

Sketching the sum function signature

Given a List of integers, such as this one:

```
val list = List(1, 2, 3, 4)
```

let's start tackling the problem in the usual way, by thinking, "Write the function signature first."

What do we know about the sum function we want to write? Well, we know a couple of things:

- It will take a list of integers as input
- Because it returns a sum of those integers, the function will return a single value, an Int

Armed with only those two pieces of information, I can sketch the function signature like this:

```
def sum(list: List[Int]): Int = ???
```

The sum function body

When thinking about the function body, a functional programmer will think of a "sum" algorithm as follows:

1. If the sum function is given an empty list of integers, it should return 0. (Because the sum of nothing is zero.)
2. Otherwise, if the list is *not* empty, the result of the function is the combination of (a) the value of its head element (1, in this case), and (b) the sum of the remaining elements in the list (2,3,4).

A slight restatement of that second sentence is:

> "The sum of a list of integers is the sum of the *head* element, plus the sum of the *tail* elements."

Thinking about a List in terms of its head and tail elements is a standard way of thinking when writing recursive functions.

Now that we have a little idea of how to *think* about the problem recursively, let's see how to implement those sentences in Scala code.

Implementing the first sentence in code

The first sentence above states:

> If the sum function is given an empty list of integers,
> it should return 0.

Recursive Scala functions are often implemented using match expressions. Using (a) that information, and (b) remembering that an empty list contains only the Nil element, you can start writing the body of the sum function like this:

```
def sum(list: List[Int]): Int = list match {
    case Nil => 0
```

This is a Scala way of saying, "If the List is empty, return 0." If you're comfortable with match expressions and the List class, I think you'll agree that this makes sense.

Note 1: Using return

If you prefer using return statements at this point in your Scala career, you can write that code like this:

```
def sum(list: List[Int]): Int = list match {
    case Nil => return 0
```

Because a pure function doesn't "return" a value as much as it "evaluates" to a result, you'll want to quickly drop `return` from your vocabulary, but ... I also understand that using `return` can help when you first start writing recursive functions.

Note 2: Using if/then instead

You can also write this function using an if/then expression, but because you'll often use *pattern matching* with recursive algorithms, I use a `match` expression here.

Note 3: Can also use `List()`

Because `Nil` is equivalent to `List()`, you can also write that `case` expression like this:

```
case List() => 0
```

However, most functional programmers use `Nil`, and I'll continue to use `Nil` in this lesson.

Implementing the second sentence in code

That `case` expression is a Scala/FP implementation of the first sentence, so let's move on to the second sentence.

The second sentence says, "If the list is *not* empty, the result of the algorithm is the combination of (a) the value of its head element, and (b) the sum of its tail elements."

To split the list into head and tail components, I write the second case expression like this:

```
case head :: tail => ???
```

If you know your case expressions, you know that if sum is given a list like List(1,2,3,4), this pattern has the result of assigning head to the value 1, and assigning tail the value List(2,3,4):

```
head = 1
tail = List(2,3,4)
```

This case expression is a start, but how do I finish it? I go back to the second sentence:

> If the list is *not* empty, the result of the algorithm is the combination of (a) the value of its head element, and (b) the sum of the tail elements.

The "value of its head element" is easy to add to the case expression:

```
case head :: tail => head ...
```

But then what? As the sentence says, "the value of its head element, and the sum of the tail elements," which tells us we'll be adding *something* to head:

```
case head :: tail => head + ???
```

What are we adding to head? *The sum of the list's tail elements.* Hmm, now how can we get the sum of a list of tail elements? How about this:

```
case head :: tail => head + sum(tail)
```

Whoa. That code is a straightforward implementation of the sentence, isn't it? (I'll pause here to let that sink in.) If you combine this new case expression with the existing code, you get the following sum function:

```
def sum(list: List[Int]): Int = list match {
    case Nil => 0
    case head :: tail => head + sum(tail)
}
```

And that is a recursive "sum the integers in a List" function in Scala/FP. No var's, no for loop.

A note on those names

If you're new to case expressions, it's important to note that the head and tail variable names in the second case expression can be anything you want. I wrote this:

```
case head :: tail => head + sum(tail)
```

but I could have written this:

```
case h :: t => h + sum(t)
```

or this:

```
case x :: xs => x + sum(xs)
```

This last example uses variable names that are commonly used with FP, lists, and recursive programming. When working with a list, a single element is often referred to as x, and multiple elements are referred to as xs. It's a way of indicating that x is singular and xs is plural, like referring to a single "pizza" or multiple "pizzas." With lists, the head element is definitely singular, while the tail can contain one or more elements. I'll generally use this naming convention in this book.

Proof that sum works

To demonstrate that sum works, you can clone my RecursiveSum project on Github[1] — which uses ScalaTest[2] to test sum — or you can copy the following source code that extends a Scala App to test sum:

---

[1] https://github.com/alvinj/RecursiveSum
[2] http://www.scalatest.org/

```
object RecursiveSum extends App {

    def sum(list: List[Int]): Int = list match {
        case Nil => 0
        case x :: xs => x + sum(xs)
    }

    val list = List(1, 2, 3, 4)
    val sum = sum(list)
    println(sum)

}
```

When you run this application you should see the output, 10. If so, congratulations on your first recursive function!

"That's great," you say, "but how exactly did that end up printing 10?"

To which I say, "Excellent question. Let's dig into that!"

> As I've noted before, I tend to write verbose code that's hopefully easy to understand, especially in books, but you can shrink the last three lines of code to this, if you prefer:
>
> ```
> println(sum(List(1,2,3,4)))
> ```

32

Recursion: How Recursive Function Calls Work

An important point to understand about recursive function calls is that just as they "wind up" as they are called repeatedly, they "unwind" rapidly when the function's end condition is reached.

In the case of the sum function, the end condition is reached when the Nil element in a List is reached. When sum gets to the Nil element, this pattern of the match expression is matched:

```
case Nil => 0
```

Because this line simply returns 0, there are no more recursive calls to sum. This is a typical way of ending the recursion when operating on all elements of a List in recursive algorithms.

Lists end with Nil

As I wrote in the earlier List lesson, a literal way to create a List is like this:

```
1 :: 2 :: 3 :: 4 :: Nil
```

This is a reminder that with any Scala List you are guaranteed that the last List element is Nil. Therefore, if your algorithm is going to operate on the entire list, you should use:

```
case Nil => ???
```

as your function's end condition.

This is the first clue about how the unfolding process works.

> Note 1: This is a feature of the Scala List class. You'll have to change the approach if you work with other sequential collection classes like Vector, ArrayBuffer, etc. (More on this later in the book.)

> Note 2: Examples of functions that work on every element in a list are map, filter, foreach, sum, product, and many more. Examples of functions that *don't*

operate on every list element are `take` and `takeWhile`.

Understanding how the sum example ran

A good way to understand how the `sum` function example ran is to add `println` statements inside the `case` expressions.

First, change the `sum` function to look like this:

```
def sum(list: List[Int]): Int = list match {
    case Nil => {
        println("case1: Nil was matched")
        0
    }
    case head :: tail => {
        println(s"case2: head = $head, tail = $tail")
        head + sum(tail)
    }
}
```

Now when you run it again with a `List(1,2,3,4)` as its input parameter, you'll see this output:

```
case2: head = 1, tail = List(2, 3, 4)
case2: head = 2, tail = List(3, 4)
case2: head = 3, tail = List(4)
case2: head = 4, tail = List()
case1: Nil was matched
```

That output shows that `sum` is called repeatedly until the list is reduced to `List()` (which is the same as `Nil`). When `List()` is passed to `sum`, the first `case` is matched and the recursive calls to `sum` come to an end. (I'll demonstrate this visually in the next lesson.)

The book, Land of Lisp[1] states, "recursive functions are list eaters," and this output shows why that statement is true.

---

[1] http://amzn.to/1PjyUeL

How the recursion works ("going down")

Keeping in mind that `List(1,2,3,4)` is the same as `1::2::3::4::Nil`, you can read the output like this:

1. The first time `sum` is called, the `match` expression sees that the given `List` doesn't match the `Nil` element, so control flows to the second `case` statement.
2. The second `case` statement matches the `List` pattern, then splits the incoming list of `1::2::3::4::Nil` into (a) a head element of 1 and

    (b) the remainder of the list, `2::3::4::Nil`. The remainder — the tail — is then passed into another `sum` function call.

3. A new instance of `sum` receives the list `2::3::4::Nil`. It sees that this list does not match the `Nil` element, so control flows to the second `case` statement.
4. That statement matches the `List` pattern, then splits the list into a head element of 2 and a tail of `3::4::Nil`. The tail is passed as an input parameter to another `sum` call.
5. A new instance of `sum` receives the list `3::4::Nil`. This list does not match the `Nil` element, so control passes to the second `case` statement.
6. The list matches the pattern of the second `case` statement, which splits the list into a head element of 3 and a tail of `4::Nil`. The tail is passed as an input parameter to another `sum` call.
7. A new instance of `sum` receives the list `4::Nil`, sees that it does not match `Nil`, and passes control to the second `case` statement.
8. The list matches the pattern of the second `case` statement. The list is split into a head element of 4 a tail of `Nil`. The tail is passed to another `sum` function call.
9. The new instance of `sum` receives `Nil` as an input parameter, and sees that it *does* match the `Nil` pattern in the first `case` expression. At this point the first `case` expression is evaluated.
10. The first `case` expression returns the value 0. This marks the end of the recursive calls.

At this point — when the first case expression of this `sum` instance returns 0 — all of the recursive calls "unwind" until the very first `sum` instance returns its answer to the code that called it.

How the unwinding works ("coming back up")

That description gives you an idea of how the recursive `sum` function calls work until they reach the end condition. Here's a description of what happens *after* the end condition is reached:

1. The last sum instance — the one that received List() — returns 0. This happens because List() matches Nil in the first case expression.
2. This returns control to the previous sum instance. The second case expression of that sum function has return 4 + sum(Nil) as its return value. This is reduced to return 4 + 0, so this instance returns 4. (I didn't use a return statement in the code, but it's easier to read this now if I say "return.")
3. Again, this returns control to the previous sum instance. That sum instance has return 3 + sum(List(4)) as the result of its second case expression. You just saw that sum(List(4)) returns 4, so this case expression evaluates to return 3 + 4, or 7.
4. Control is returned to the previous sum instance. Its second case expression has return 2 + sum(List(3,4)) as its result. You just saw that sum(List(3,4)) returns 7, so this expression evaluates to return 2 + 7, or 9.
5. Finally, control is returned to the original sum function call. Its second case expression is return 1 + sum(List(2,3,4)). You just saw that sum(List(2,3,4)) returns 9, so this call is reduced to return 1 + 9, or 10. This value is returned to whatever code called the first sum instance.

Initial visuals of how the recursion works

One way to visualize how the recursive sum function calls work — the "going down" part — is shown in Figure 32.1.

```
sum(List(1,2,3,4))
    -> sum(List(2,3,4))
        -> sum(List(3,4))
            -> sum(List(4))
                -> sum(List())
```

Figure 32.1: How the original sum call leads to another, then to another ...

After that, when the end condition is reached, the "coming back up" part — what I call the unwinding process — is shown in Figure 32.2.

```
                    -> sum(Nil)        // return 0
                -> sum(List(4))        // return 4 + sum(List())       => return 4 + 0 => 4
            -> sum(List(3,4))          // return 3 + sum(List(4))      => return 3 + 4 => 7
        -> sum(List(2,3,4))            // return 2 + sum(List(3, 4))   => return 2 + 7 => 9
sum(List(1,2,3,4))                     // return 1 + sum(List(2, 3, 4)) => return 1 + 9 => 10
```

Figure 32.2: How sum function calls unwind, starting with the last sum call

If this isn't clear, fear not, in the next lesson I'll show a few more visual examples of how this works.

33

Visualizing the Recursive sum Function

Another way to view recursion is with visual diagrams. To demonstrate this, I'll use the rectangular symbol shown in Figure 33.1 to represent a function.

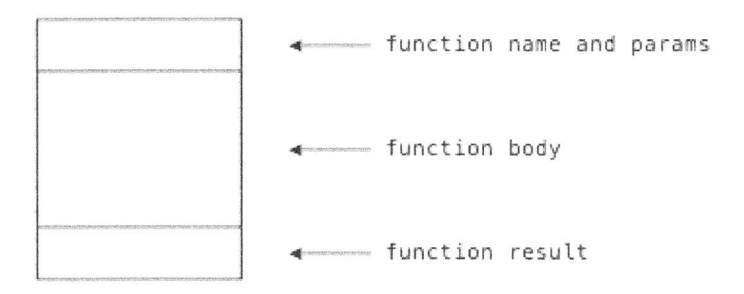

Figure 33.1: This rectangular symbol will be used to represent functions in this lesson

The first step

Using that symbol and a list with only three elements, Figure 33.2 shows a representation of the first sum function call.

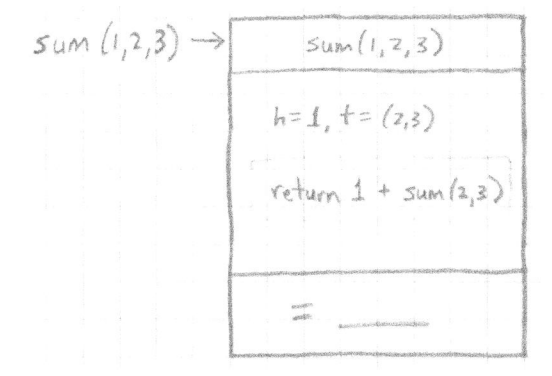

Figure 33.2: A visual representation of the first sum call

The top cell in the rectangle indicates that this first instance of sum is called with the parameters 1,2,3. Note that I'm leaving the "List" name off of these diagrams to make them more readable.

245

The body of the function is shown in the middle region of the symbol, and it's shown as `return 1 + sum(2,3)`. As I mentioned before, you don't normally use the `return` keyword with Scala/FP functions, but in this case it makes the diagram more clear.

In the bottom region of the symbol I've left room for the final return value of the function. At this time we don't know what the function will return, so for now I just leave that spot empty.

The next steps

For the next step of the diagram, assume that the first `sum` function call receives the parameter list `(1,2,3)`, and its body now calls a new instance of `sum` with the input parameter `sum(2,3)` (or `sum(List(2,3))`, if you prefer). You can imagine the second `case` expression separating the `List` into head and tail elements, as shown in Figure 33.3.

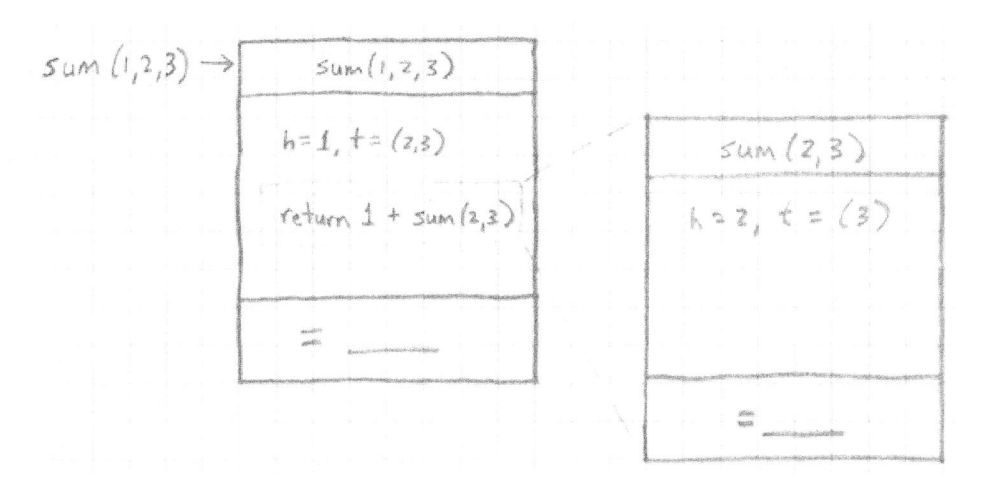

Figure 33.3: The first `sum` function invokes a second `sum` function call

Then this `sum` instance makes a recursive call to another `sum` instance, as shown in Figure 33.4. Again I leave the return value of this function empty because I don't know what it will be until its `sum` call returns.

It's important to be clear that these two function calls are completely different instances of `sum`. They have their own input parameter lists, local variables, and return values. It's just as if you had two different functions, one named `sum3elements` and one named `sum2elements`, as shown in Figure 33.5.

Just as the variables inside of `sum3elements` and `sum2elements` have completely different scope, the variables in two different instances of `sum` also have completely different scope.

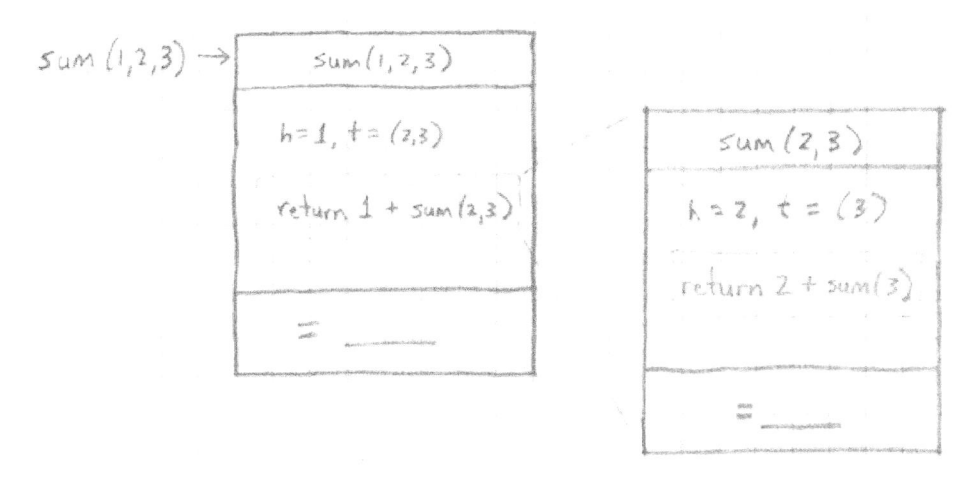

Figure 33.4: The second sum *function call begins to invoke the third* sum *instance*

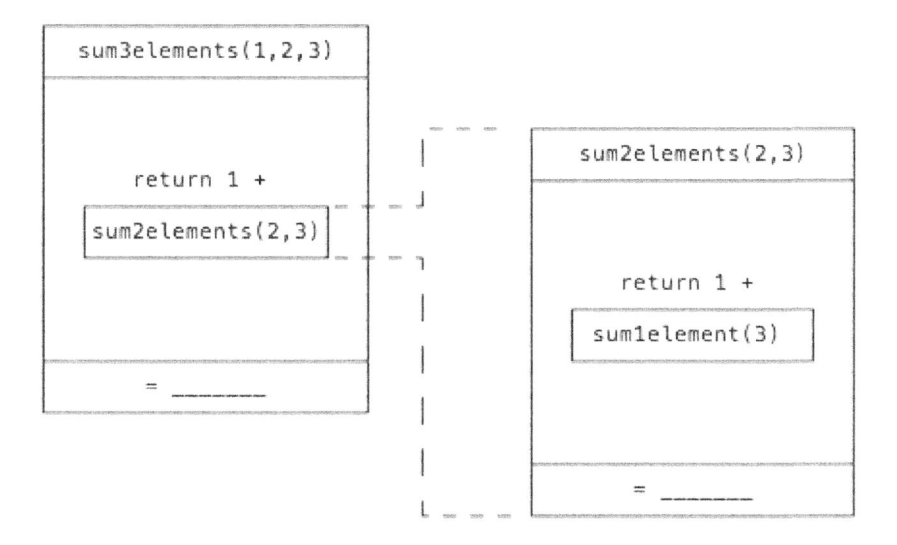

Figure 33.5: One sum *function calling another* sum *instance is just like calling a different function*

248   *Visualizing the Recursive sum Function*

Getting back to the sum example, you can now imagine that the next step will proceed just like the previous one, as shown in Figure 33.6.

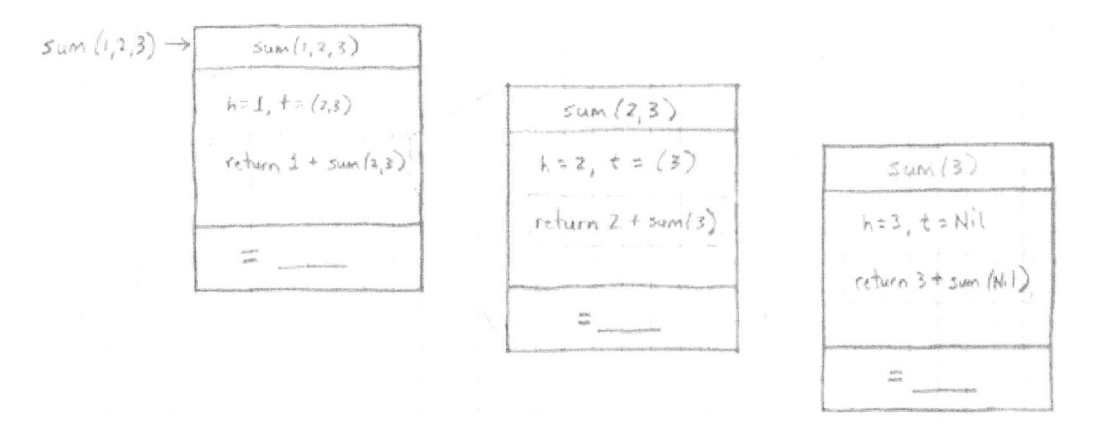

Figure 33.6: The third sum function has now been called

The last recursive sum call

Now we're at the point where we make the last recursive call to sum. In this case, because 3 was the last integer in the list, a new instance of sum is called with the Nil value. This is shown in Figure 33.7.

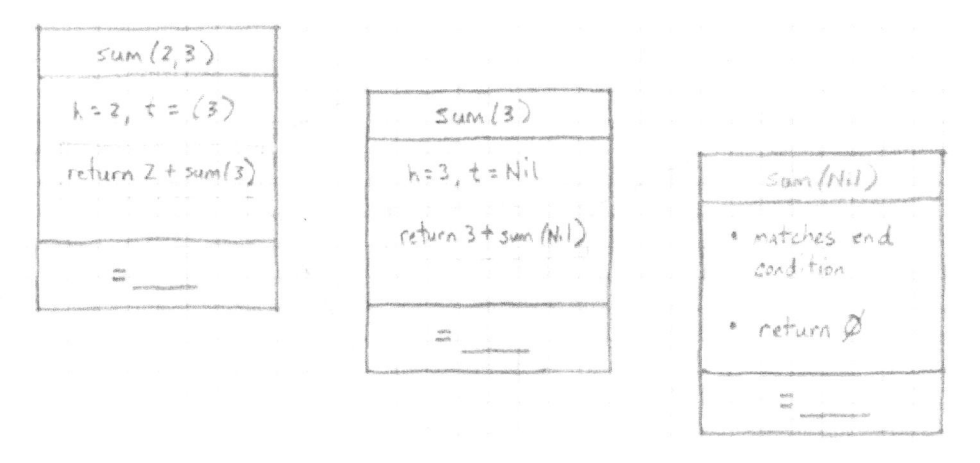

Figure 33.7: Nil is passed into the final sum function call

With this last sum call, the Nil input parameter matches the first case expression, and that expression simply returns 0. So now we can fill in the return value for this function, as shown in Figure 33.8.

Now this sum instance returns 0 back to the previous sum instance (Figure 33.9).

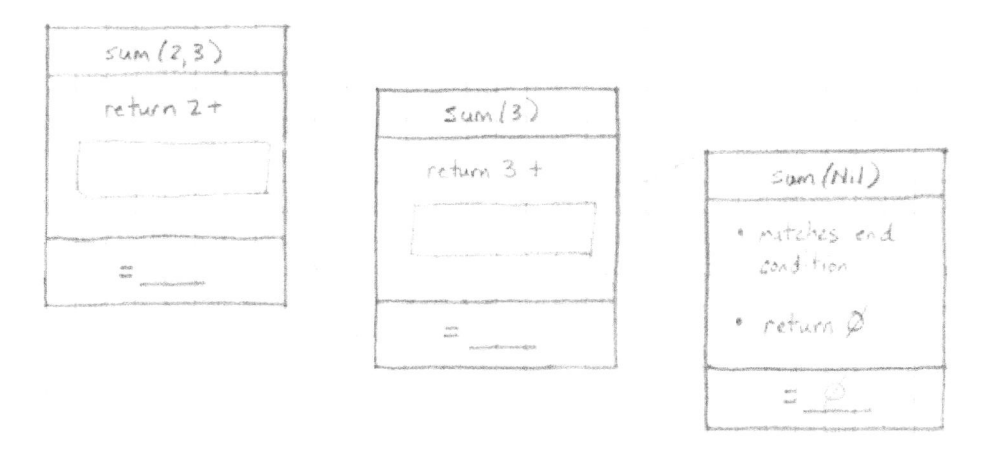

Figure 33.8: The return value of the last sum *call is* 0

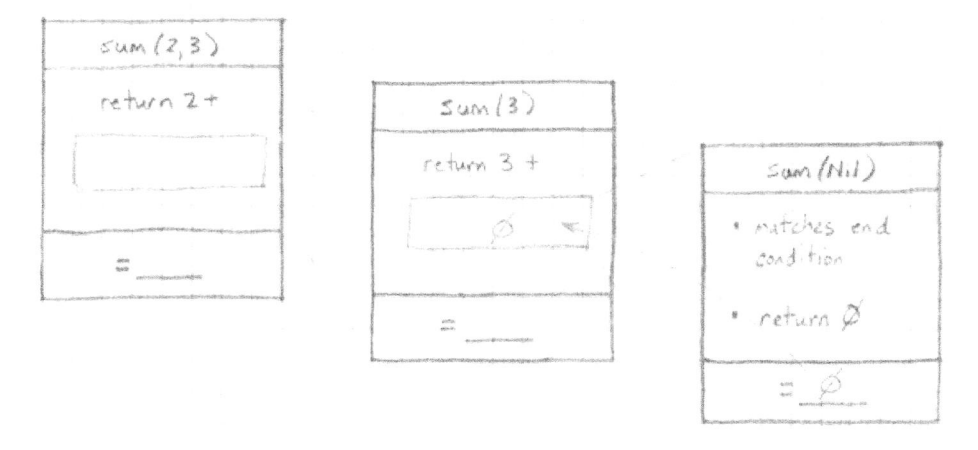

Figure 33.9: 0 *is returned back to the previous* sum *call*

The result of this function call is 3 + 0 (which is 3), so you can fill in its return value, and then flow it back to the previous sum call. This is shown in Figure 33.10.

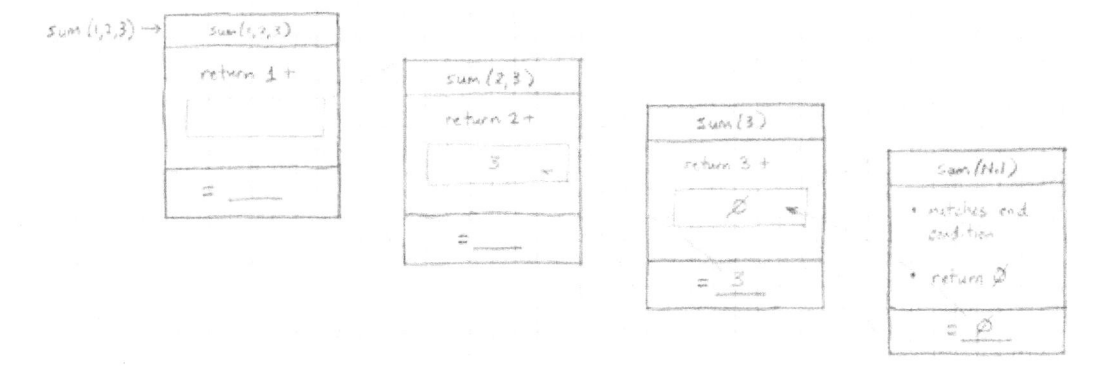

Figure 33.10: The third sum call returns to the second

The result of this function call is 2 + 3 (5), so that result can flow back to the previous function call, as shown in Figure 33.11.

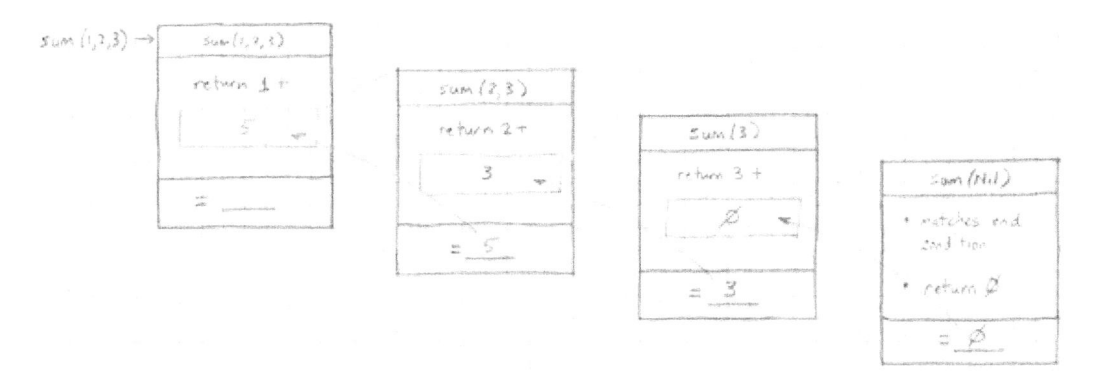

Figure 33.11: The second sum call returns to the first

Finally, the result of this sum instance is 1 + 5 (6). This was the first sum function call, so it returns the value 6 back to whoever called it, as shown in Figure 33.12.

Other visualizations

There are other ways to draw recursive function calls. Another nice approach is to use a modified version of a UML "Sequence Diagram[1]," as shown in Figure 33.13. Note that in this diagram "time" flows from the top to the bottom.

---

[1] https://en.wikipedia.org/wiki/Sequence_diagram

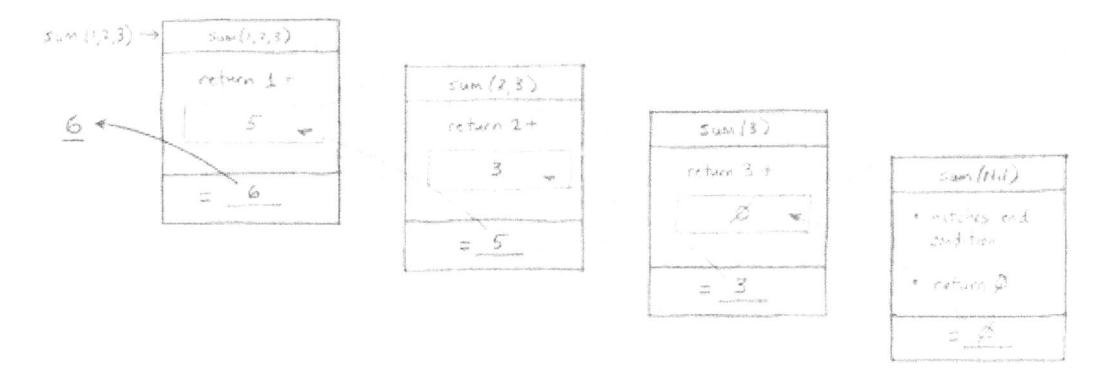

Figure 33.12: The first sum *call returns to the final result*

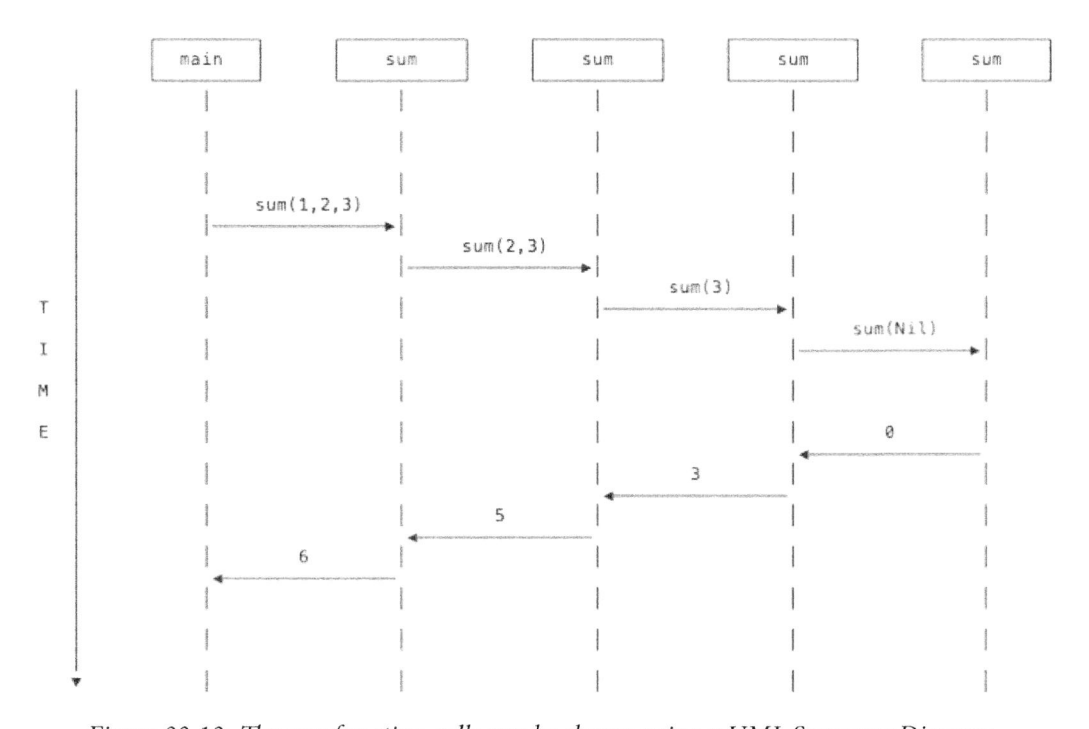

Figure 33.13: The sum *function calls can be shown using a UML Sequence Diagram*

This diagram shows that the main method calls sum with the parameter List(1,2,3), where I again leave off the List part; it calls sum(2,3), and so on, until the Nil case is reached, at which point the return values flow back from right to left, eventually returning 6 back to the main method.

You can write the return values like that, or with some form of the function's equation, as shown in Figure 33.14. Personally, I use whatever diagram seems to help the most.

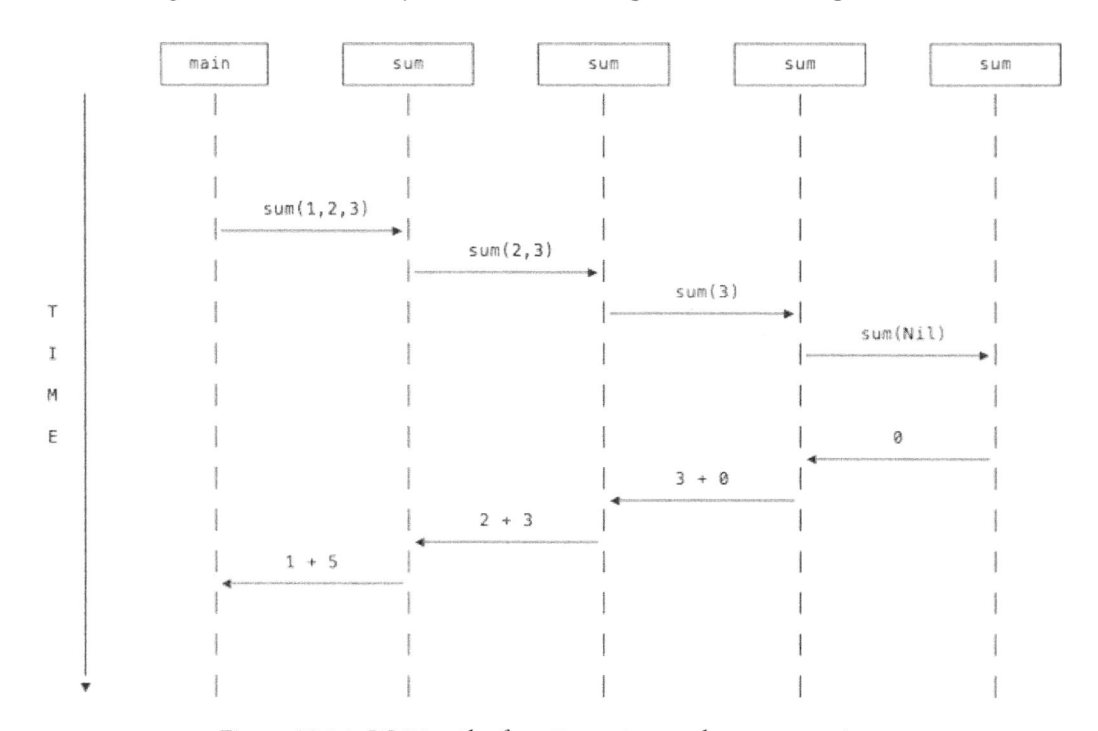

```
main         sum          sum          sum          sum
 |            |            |            |            |
 |            |            |            |            |
 | sum(1,2,3) |            |            |            |
 |----------->|            |            |            |
 |            | sum(2,3)   |            |            |
 |            |----------->|            |            |
 |            |            | sum(3)     |            |
T|            |            |----------->|            |
 |            |            |            | sum(Nil)   |
I|            |            |            |----------->|
 |            |            |            |            |
M|            |            |            |            |
 |            |            |            |     0      |
E|            |            |            |<-----------|
 |            |            |    3 + 0   |            |
 |            |            |<-----------|            |
 |            |   2 + 3    |            |            |
 |            |<-----------|            |            |
 |   1 + 5    |            |            |            |
 |<-----------|            |            |            |
 |            |            |            |            |
 |            |            |            |            |
 ▼
```

Figure 33.14: Writing the function return values as equations

Summary

Those are some visual examples of how recursive function calls work. If you find yourself struggling to understand how recursion works, I hope these diagrams are helpful.

34

Recursion: A Conversation Between Two Developers

As an homage to one of my favorite Lisp books — an early version of what is now *The Little Schemer* — this lesson shows a little question and answer interaction that you can imagine happening between two Scala programmers.

Given this sum function:

```
def sum(list: List[Int]): Int = list match {
    case Nil => 0
    case x :: xs => x + sum(xs)
}
```

I hope this "conversation" will help drive home some of the points about how recursion works:

Person 1	Person 2
What is this? `val x = List(1,2,3,4)`	An expression that defines a `List[Int]`, which in this case contains the integers 1 through 4. The expression binds that list to the variable x.
And what is this? `x.head`	The first element of the list x, which is 1.
How about this? `x.tail`	That's the remaining elements in the list x, which is `List(2,3,4)`.
How about this: `x.tail.head`	It is the number 2.
How did you come up with that?	`x.tail` is `List(2,3,4)`, and `List(2,3,4).head` is the first element of that list, or 2.
How about this: `x.tail.tail`	That's `List(3,4)`.
Explain, please.	`x.tail` is `List(2,3,4)`, and then `List(2,3,4).tail` is `List(3,4)`.
Are you ready for more?	Yes, please.

Person 1	Person 2
Given the definition of our `sum` function, explain the first step in: `sum(List(1,2,3))`.	The `sum` function receives `List(1,2,3)`. This does not match the `Nil` case, but does match the second case, where x is assigned to 1 and xs is `List(2,3)`.
Then what happens?	A new instance of `sum` is called with the parameter `List(2,3)`.
And then?	A new instance of `sum` receives the input parameter `List(2,3)`. This does not match the `Nil` case, but does match the second case, where x is assigned to 2 and xs is `List(3)`.
Please continue.	`sum` is called with the parameter `List(3)`.
Go on.	A new instance of `sum` receives `List(3)`. This does not match the `Nil` case, but does match the second case, where x is assigned to 3 and xs is `List()`.
Don't stop now.	`sum` is called with the parameter `List()`.
What happens inside this instance of `sum`?	It receives `List()`. This is the same as `Nil`, so it matches the first case.
Cool. Something different. Now what happens?	That case returns 0.
Ah, finally a return value!	You're telling me.
Okay, so now what happens?	This ends the recursion, and then the recursive calls unwind, as described in the previous lesson.

35

Recursion: Thinking Recursively

> *"To understand recursion, one must first understand recursion."*
>
> Stephen Hawking

Goal

This lesson has one primary goal: to show that the thought process followed in writing the sum function follows a common recursive programming "pattern." Indeed, when you write recursive functions you'll generally follow the three-step process shown in this lesson.

I don't want to make this too formulaic, but the reality is that if you follow these three steps in your thinking, it will make it easier to write recursive functions, especially when you first start.

The general recursive thought process (the "three steps")

As I mentioned in the previous lessons, when I sit down to write a recursive function, I think of three things:

- What is the function signature?
- What is the end condition for this algorithm?
- What is the actual algorithm? For example, if I'm processing all of the elements in a List, what does my algorithm do when the function receives a non-empty List?

Let's take a deep dive into each step in the process to make more sense of these descriptions.

Step 1: What is the function signature?

Once I know that I'm going to write a recursive function, the first thing I ask myself is, "What is the signature of this function?"

If you can describe the function verbally, you should find that you know (a) the parameters that will be passed into the function and (b) what the function will return. In fact, if you *don't* know these things, you're probably not ready to write the function yet.

The sum function

In the sum function the algorithm is to add all of the integers in a given list together to return a single integer result. Therefore, because I know the function takes a list of integers as its input, I can start sketching the function signature like this:

```
def sum(list: List[Int]) ...
```

Because the description also tells me that the function returns an Int result, I add the function's return type:

```
def sum(list: List[Int]): Int = ???
```

This is the Scala way to say that "the sum function takes a list of integers and returns an integer result," which is what I want. In FP, sketching the function signature is often half of the battle, so this is actually a big step.

Step 2: How will this algorithm end?

The next thing I usually think about is, "How will this algorithm end? What is its end condition?"

Because a recursive function like sum keeps calling itself over and over, it's of the utmost importance that there is an end case. If a recursive algorithm doesn't have an end condition, it will keep calling itself as fast as possible until either (a) your program crashes with a StackOverflowError, or (b) your computer's CPU gets extraordinarily hot. Therefore, I offer this tip:

> Always have an end condition, and write it as soon as possible.

In the sum algorithm you know that you have a List, and you want to march through the entire List to add up the values of all of its elements. You may not know it at this point in your recursive programming career, but right away this statement is a big hint about the end condition. Because (a) you know that you're working with a List, (b) you want to operate on the entire List, and (c) a List ends with the Nil element, (d) you can begin to write the end condition case expression like this:

```
case Nil => ???
```

To be clear, this end condition is correct because you're working with a List, and you know that the algorithm will operate on the entire List. Because the Nil element is to a List as a caboose is to a train, you're guaranteed that it's always the last element of the List.

> Note: If your algorithm will not work on the entire List, the end condition will be different than this.

Now the next question is, "What should this end condition return?"

A key here is that the function signature states that it returns an Int. Therefore, you know that this end condition must return an Int of some sort. But what Int? Because this is a "sum" algorithm, you also know that you don't want to return anything that will affect the sum. Hmmm ... what Int can you return when the Nil element is reached that won't affect the sum?

The answer is 0.

(More on this shortly.)

Given that answer, I can update the first case condition:

```
def sum(list: List[Int]): Int = list match {
    case Nil => 0
    case ???
}
```

That condition states that if the function receives an empty List — denoted by Nil — the function will return 0.

Now we're ready for the third step.

> I'll expand more on the point of returning 0 in this algorithm in the coming lessons, but for now it may help to know that there's a mathematical theory involved in this decision. What's happening here is that you're returning something known as an "identity" element for the current data set and algorithm. As a quick demonstration of what I'm talking about, here are a few other *identity* elements for different data sets and algorithms:
>
> 1) Imagine that you want to write a "product" algorithm for a list of integers. What would you

return for the end condition in this case? The correct answer is 1. This is because the product involves multiplying all elements of the list, and multiplying any number by 1 gives you the original number, so this doesn't affect the final result in any way.

2) Imagine that you're writing a concatenation algorithm for a List[String]. What would you return for the end condition in this case? The correct answer is ``''`, an empty String (because once again, it does not affect the final result).

Step 3: What is the algorithm?

Now that you've defined the function signature and the end condition, the final question is, "What is the algorithm at hand?"

When your algorithm will operate on all of the elements in a List and the first case condition handles the "empty list" case, this question becomes, "What should my function do when it receives a *non-empty* List?"

The answer for a "sum" function is that it should add all of the elements in the list. (Similarly, the answer for a "product" algorithm is that it should multiply all of the list elements.)

The sum algorithm

At this point I go back to the original statement of the sum algorithm:

> "The sum of a list of integers is the sum of the *head* element, plus the sum of the *tail* elements."

Because the first case expression handles the "empty list" case, you know that the second case condition should handle the case of the non-empty list. A common way to write the *pattern* for this case expression is this:

```
case head :: tail => ???
```

This pattern says, "head will be bound to the value of the first element in the List, and tail will contain all of the remaining elements in the List."

Because my description of the algorithm states that the sum is "the sum of the *head* element, plus the sum of the *tail* elements," I start to write a case expression, starting by adding the head element:

```
case head :: tail => head + ???
```

and then I write this code to represent "the sum of the tail elements":

```
case head :: tail => head + sum(tail)
```

That is a Scala/FP recursive way of expressing the thought, "The sum of a list of integers is the sum of the *head* element, plus the sum of the *tail* elements."

(I described that thought process in detail in the previous lessons, so I won't repeat all of that thought process here.)

Now that we have the function signature, the end condition, and the main algorithm, we have the completed function:

```
def sum(list: List[Int]): Int = list match {
    case Nil => 0
    case head :: tail => head + sum(tail)
}
```

Naming conventions

As I noted in the previous lessons, when FP developers work with lists, they often prefer to use the variable name x to refer to a single element and xs to refer to multiple elements, so this function is more commonly written with these variable names:

```
def sum(list: List[Int]): Int = list match {
    case Nil => 0
    case x :: xs => x + sum(xs)
}
```

(But you don't have to use those names; use whatever is easiest for you to read.)

The last two steps are iterative

In practice, the first step — sketching the function signature — is almost always the first step in the process. As I mentioned, it's hard to write a function if you don't know what the inputs and output will be.

But the last two steps — defining the end condition, and writing the algorithm — are interchangeable, and even iterative. For instance, if you're working on a List and you want to do something for *every* element in the list, you know the end condition will occur when you reach the Nil element. But if you're not going to operate on the entire list, or if you're working with something other than a List, it can help to bounce back and forth between the end case and the main algorithm until you come to the solution.

> Note that the sum algorithm I've shown specifically works on a Scala List, which ends with a Nil element. It will not work with other sequences like Vector, ArrayBuffer, ListBuffer, or other sequences that do not have a Nil value as the last element in the sequence. I discuss the handling of those other sequences later in the book.

Summary

When I sit down to write a recursive function, I generally think of three things:

- What is the function signature?
- What is the end condition for this algorithm?
- What is the main algorithm?

To solve the problem I almost always write the function signature first, and after that I usually write the end condition next, though the last two steps can also be an iterative process.

What's next

Now that you've seen this "general pattern" of writing recursive functions, the next two lessons are exercises that give you a taste of how to use the patterns to write your own recursive functions.

First, I'll have you write another recursive function to operate on all of the elements in a List, and then you'll work on a recursive algorithm that operates on only a subset of a List.

36

JVM Stacks and Stack Frames

For functions without deep levels of recursion, there's nothing wrong with the algorithms shown in the previous lessons. I use this simple, basic form of recursion when I know that I'm working with limited data sets. But in applications where you don't know how much data you might be processing, it's important that your recursive algorithms are *tail-recursive*, otherwise you'll get a nasty `StackOverflowError`.

For instance, if you run the `sum` function from the previous lessons with a larger list, like this:

```
object RecursiveSum extends App {

    def sum(list: List[Int]): Int = list match {
        case Nil => 0
        case x :: xs => x + sum(xs)
    }

    val list = List.range(1, 10000)   // MUCH MORE DATA
    val x = sum(list)
    println(x)

}
```

you'll get a `StackOverflowError`, which is *really* counter to our desire to write great, bullet-proof, functional programs.

> The actual number of integers in a list needed to produce a `StackOverflowError` with this function will depend on the `java` command-line settings you use, but the last time I checked[1] the default Java stack size it was 1,024 kb — yes, 1,024 *kilobytes* — just over one million *bytes*. That's not much RAM to work with. I write more about this at the end of this lesson, including how to change the default stack size with the `java` command's `-Xss` parameter.

---

[1] http://www.oracle.com/technetwork/java/hotspotfaq-138619.html

I'll cover tail recursion in an upcoming lesson, but in this lesson I want to discuss the JVM stack and stack frames. If you're not already familiar with these concepts, this discussion will help you understand what's happening here. It can also help you debug "stack traces" in general.

What is a "Stack"?

To understand the potential "stack overflow" problem of recursive algorithms, you need to understand what happens when you write recursive algorithms.

The first thing to know is that in all computer programming languages there is this thing called "the stack," also known as the "call stack."

Official Java/JVM "stack" definition

Oracle provides the following description of the stack and stack frames[2] as they relate to the JVM:

> "Each JVM thread has a private Java virtual machine stack, created at the same time as the thread. A JVM stack stores frames, also called "stack frames". A JVM stack is analogous to the stack of a conventional language such as C — it holds local variables and partial results, and plays a part in method invocation and return."

Therefore, you can visualize that a single stack has a pile of stack frames that look like Figure 36.1.

As that quote mentions, each thread has its own stack, so in a multi-threaded application there are multiple stacks, and each stack has its own stack of frames, as shown in Figure 36.2.

The Java stack

To explain the stack a little more, all of the following quoted text comes from the free, online version of a book titled, Inside the Java Virtual Machine[3], by Bill Venners. (I edited the text slightly to include only the portions relevant to stacks and stack frames.)

---

[2] https://docs.oracle.com/javase/specs/jvms/se7/html/jvms-2.html
[3] http://www.artima.com/insidejvm/ed2/jvm8.html

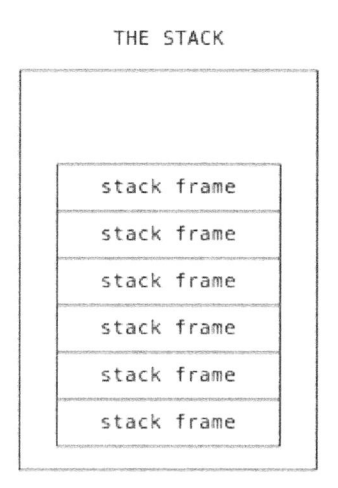

Figure 36.1: A single stack has a pile of stack frames.

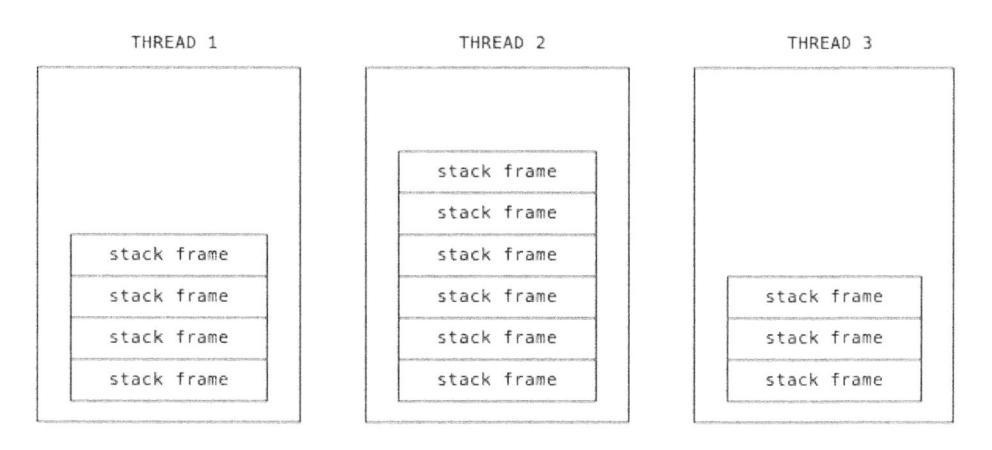

Figure 36.2: Each thread has its own stack.

"When a new thread is launched, the JVM creates a new stack for the thread. A Java stack stores a thread's state in discrete frames. *The JVM only performs two operations directly on Java stacks: it pushes and pops frames.*"

"The method that is currently being executed by a thread is the thread's current method. The stack frame for the current method is the current frame. The class in which the current method is defined is called the current class, and the current class's constant pool is the current constant pool. As it executes a method, the JVM keeps track of the current class and current constant pool. When the JVM encounters instructions that operate on data stored in the stack frame, it performs those operations on the current frame."

"*When a thread invokes a Java method, the JVM creates and pushes a new frame onto the thread's stack.* This new frame then becomes the current frame. As the method executes, it uses the frame to store parameters, local variables, intermediate computations, and other data."

> As the previous paragraph implies, each instance of a method has its own stack frame. Therefore, when you see the term "stack frame," you can think, "all of the stuff a method instance needs."

What is a "Stack Frame"?

The same chapter in that book[4] describes the "stack frame" as follows: "The stack frame has three parts: local variables, operand stack, and frame data."

You can visualize that as shown in Figure 36.3.

The book continues:

"The sizes of the local variables and operand stack, which are measured in *words*, depend upon the needs of each individual method. These sizes are determined at compile time and included in the class file data for each method."

That's important: *the size of a stack frame varies depending on the local variables and operand stack.* The book describes that size like this:

"When the JVM invokes a method, it checks the class data to determine the number of words required by the method in the local variables and operand stack. It creates a stack frame of the proper size for the method and pushes it onto the stack."

---

[4] http://www.artima.com/insidejvm/ed2/jvm8.html

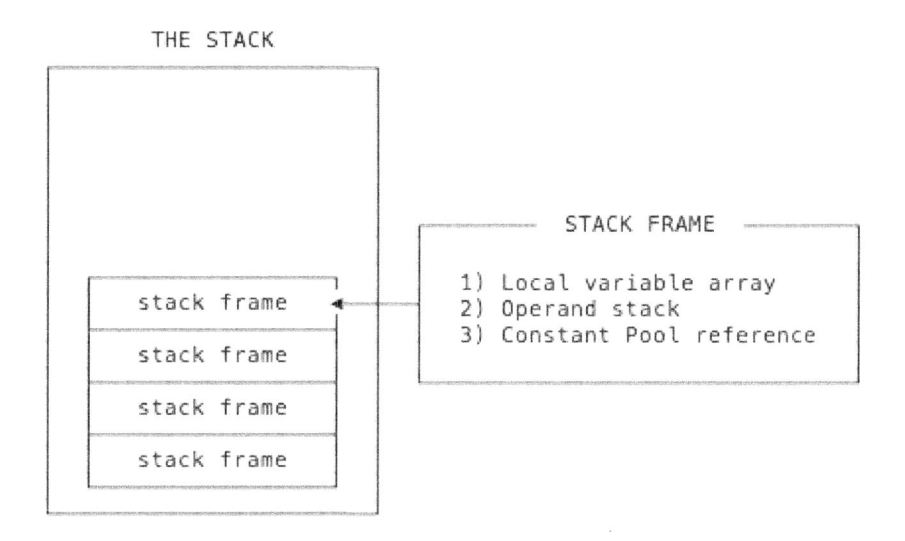

```
                    THE STACK
┌─────────────────────────────────┐
│                                 │      ┌──── STACK FRAME ────────────┐
│                                 │      │                             │
│                                 │      │  1) Local variable array    │
│         ┌──────────────┐        │      │  2) Operand stack           │
│         │ stack frame  │◄───────┼──────┤  3) Constant Pool reference │
│         ├──────────────┤        │      │                             │
│         │ stack frame  │        │      └─────────────────────────────┘
│         ├──────────────┤        │
│         │ stack frame  │        │
│         ├──────────────┤        │
│         │ stack frame  │        │
│         └──────────────┘        │
└─────────────────────────────────┘
```

Figure 36.3: Each stack frame has three parts.

Word size, operand stack, and constant pool

These descriptions introduce the phrases word size, operand stack, and constant pool. Here are definitions of those terms:

First, *word size* is a unit of measure. From Chapter 5 of the same book[5], the word size can vary in JVM implementations, but it must be at least 32 bits so it can hold a value of type long or double.

Next, the *operand stack* is defined here on oracle.com[6], but as a word of warning, that definition gets into machine code very quickly. For instance, it shows how two integers are added together with the iadd instruction. You are welcome to dig into those details, but for our purposes, a simple way to think about the operand stack is that it's memory (RAM) that is used as a working area inside a stack frame.

The Java *Run-Time Constant Pool* is defined at this oracle.com page[7], which states, "A run-time constant pool ... contains several kinds of constants, ranging from numeric literals known at compile-time, to method and field references that must be resolved at run-time. The run-time constant pool serves a function similar to that of a symbol table for a conventional programming language, although it contains a wider range of data than a typical symbol table."

---

[5]http://www.artima.com/insidejvm/ed2/jvm3.html
[6]https://docs.oracle.com/javase/specs/jvms/se7/html/jvms-2.html#jvms-2.6.2
[7]https://docs.oracle.com/javase/specs/jvms/se7/html/jvms-2.html#jvms-2.5.5

Summary to this point

I can summarize what we've learned about stacks and stack frames like this:

- Each JVM thread has a private stack, created at the same time as the thread.
- A stack stores frames, also called "stack frames."
- A stack frame is created every time a new method is called.

We can also say this about what happens when a Java/Scala/JVM method is invoked:

- When a method is invoked, a new stack frame is created to contain information about that method.
- Stack frames can have different sizes, depending on the method's parameters, local variables, and algorithm.
- As the method is executed, the code can only access the values in the current stack frame, which you can visualize as being the top-most stack frame.

As it relates to recursion, that last point is important. As a function like our sum function works on a list, such as List(1,2,3), information about that instance of sum is in the top-most stack frame, and that instance of sum can't see the data of other instances of the sum function. This is how what appears to be a single, local variable — like the values head and tail inside of sum — can seemingly have many different values at the same time.

One last resource on the stack and recursion

Not to belabor the point, but I want to share one last description of the stack (and the heap) that has specific comments about recursion. The discussion in Figure 36.4 comes from a book named Algorithms[8], by Sedgewick and Wayne.

There are two important lines in this description that relate to recursive algorithms:

- "When the method returns, that information is popped off the stack, so the program can resume execution just after the point where it called the method."
- "recursive algorithms can sometimes create extremely deep call stacks and exhaust the stack space."

---

[8]http://amzn.to/1WSRnEY

> **SERIOUS STACK SPACE**
>
> Normally a computer allocates two areas of memory for a program: the stack and the heap.
>
> The stack is used to store information about method calls. When a piece of code calls a method, information about the call is placed on the stack. When the method returns, that information is popped off the stack, so the program can resume execution just after the point where it called the method. (The stack is the same kind of stack described in Chapter 5.) The list of methods that were called to get to a particular point of execution is called the *call stack*.
>
> The heap is another piece of memory that the program can use to create variables and perform calculations.
>
> Typically the stack is much smaller than the heap. The stack usually is large enough for normal programs because your code typically doesn't include methods calling other methods to a very great depth. However, recursive algorithms can sometimes create extremely deep call stacks and exhaust the stack space, causing the program to crash.
>
> For this reason, it's important to evaluate the maximum depth of recursion that a recursive algorithm requires in addition to studying its run time and memory requirements.

Figure 36.4: A discussion of the JVM stack and heap.

Analysis

From all of these discussions I hope you can see the potential problem of recursive algorithms:

- When a recursive function calls itself, information for the new instance of the function is pushed onto the stack.
- Each time the function calls itself, another copy of the function information is pushed onto the stack. Because of this, a new stack frame is needed for each level in the recursion.
- As a result, more and more memory that is allocated to the stack is consumed as the function recurses. If the sum function calls itself a million times, a million stack frames are created.

37

A Visual Look at Stacks and Frames

Given the background information of the previous lesson, let's take a visual look at how the JVM stack and stack frames work by going back to our recursive sum function from the previous lesson.

Before the sum function is initially called, the only thing on the call stack is the application's main method, as shown in Figure 37.1.

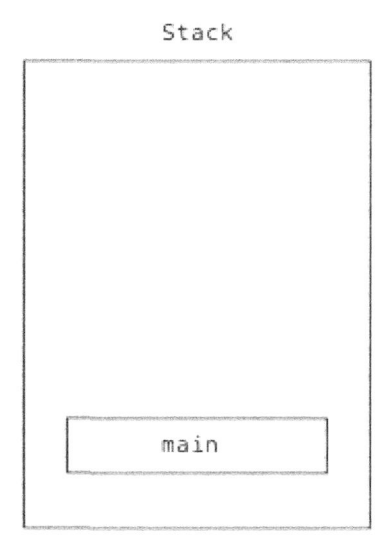

```
          Stack
    ┌─────────────────┐
    │                 │
    │                 │
    │                 │
    │                 │
    │  ┌───────────┐  │
    │  │   main    │  │
    │  └───────────┘  │
    └─────────────────┘
```

Figure 37.1: main *is the only thing on the call stack before* sum *is called.*

Then main calls sum with List(1,2,3), which I show in Figure 37.2 without the "List" to keep things simple.

The data that's given to sum matches its second case expression, and in my pseudocode, that expression evaluates to this:

```
return 1 + sum(2,3)
```

Next, when a new instance of sum is called with List(2,3), the stack looks as shown in Figure 37.3.

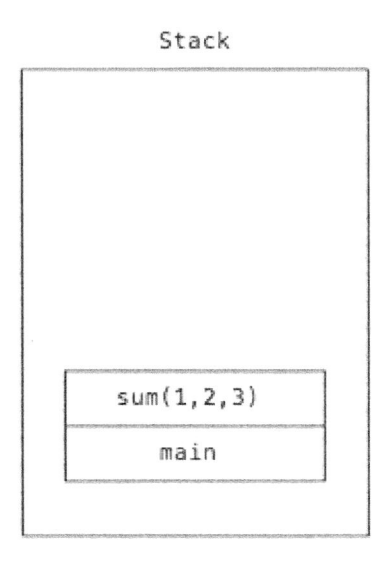

Figure 37.2: The first sum *call is added to the stack.*

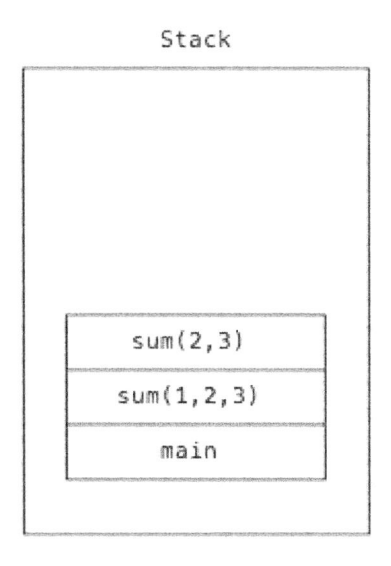

Figure 37.3: The second sum *call is added to the stack.*

Again the second case expression is matched inside of sum, and it evaluates to this:

```
return 2 + sum(3)
```

When a new instance of sum is called with the input parameter List(3), the stack looks like Figure 37.4.

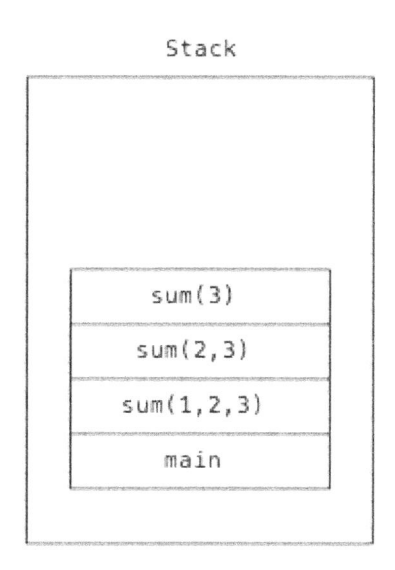

```
                        Stack

                    ┌─────────────┐
                    │   sum(3)    │
                    ├─────────────┤
                    │  sum(2,3)   │
                    ├─────────────┤
                    │ sum(1,2,3)  │
                    ├─────────────┤
                    │    main     │
                    └─────────────┘
```

Figure 37.4: The third sum call is added to the stack.

Again the second case expression is matched, and that code evaluates to this:

```
return 3 + sum(Nil)
```

Finally, another instance of sum is called with the input parameter List() — also known as Nil — and the stack now looks like Figure 37.5.

A Visual Look at Stacks and Frames

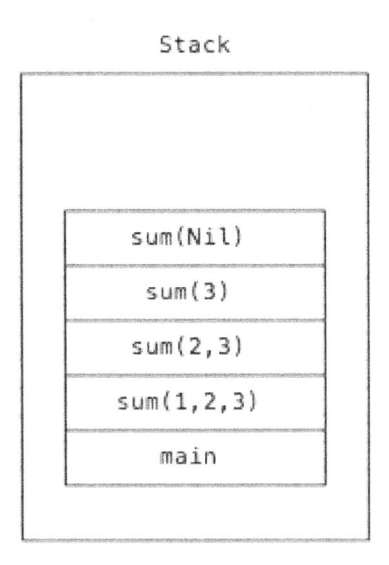

```
                Stack
    ┌─────────────────────────┐
    │                         │
    │                         │
    │    ┌───────────────┐    │
    │    │   sum(Nil)    │    │
    │    ├───────────────┤    │
    │    │    sum(3)     │    │
    │    ├───────────────┤    │
    │    │   sum(2,3)    │    │
    │    ├───────────────┤    │
    │    │  sum(1,2,3)   │    │
    │    ├───────────────┤    │
    │    │     main      │    │
    │    └───────────────┘    │
    │                         │
    └─────────────────────────┘
```

Figure 37.5: The final sum call is added to the stack.

This time, when sum(Nil) is called, the first case expression is matched:

```
case Nil => 0
```

That pattern match causes this sum instance to return 0, and when it does, the call stack unwinds and the stack frames are popped off of the stack, as shown in the series of images in Figure 37.6.

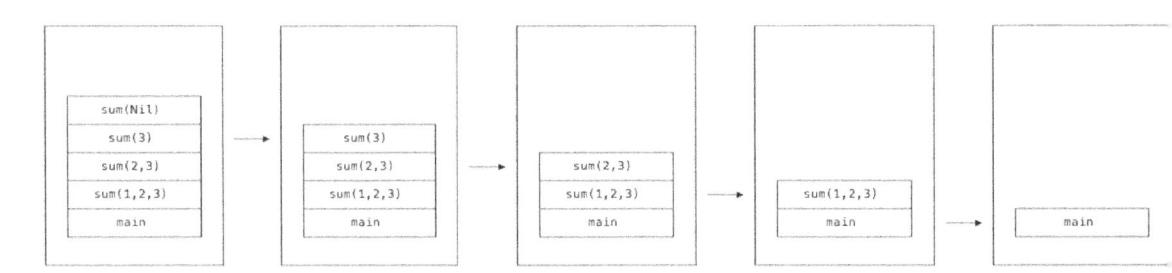

Figure 37.6: The unwinding of the call stack.

In this process, as each sum call returns, its frame is popped off of the stack, and when the recursion completely ends, the main method is the only frame left on the call stack. (The value 6 is also returned by the first sum invocation to the place where it was called in the main method.)

I hope that gives you a good idea of how recursive function calls are pushed-on and popped-off the JVM call stack.

Manually dumping the stack with the sum example

If you want to explore this in code, you can also see the series of sum stack calls by modifying the sum function. To do this, add a couple of lines of code to the Nil case to print out stack trace information when that case is reached:

```
def sum(list: List[Int]): Int = list match {
    case Nil => {
        // this manually creates a stack trace
        val stackTraceAsArray = Thread.currentThread.getStackTrace
        stackTraceAsArray.foreach(println)
        // return 0 as before
        0
    }
    case x :: xs => x + sum(xs)
}
```

Now, if you call sum with a list that goes from 1 to 5:

```
val list = List.range(1, 5)
sum(list)
```

you'll get this output when the Nil case is reached:

```
java.lang.Thread.getStackTrace(Thread.java:1588)
recursion.SumWithStackDump$.sum(SumWithStackDump.scala:19)
recursion.SumWithStackDump$.sum(SumWithStackDump.scala:19)
recursion.SumWithStackDump$.sum(SumWithStackDump.scala:19)
recursion.SumWithStackDump$.sum(SumWithStackDump.scala:19)
recursion.SumWithStackDump$.sum(SumWithStackDump.scala:19)
```

While that output isn't too exciting, it shows that when the stack dump is manually triggered when the Nil case is reached, the sum function is on the stack five times. You can verify that this is correct by repeating the test with a List that has three elements, in which case you'll see the sum function referenced only three times in the output:

```
java.lang.Thread.getStackTrace(Thread.java:1588)
recursion.SumWithStackDump$.sum(SumWithStackDump.scala:13)
recursion.SumWithStackDump$.sum(SumWithStackDump.scala:19)
recursion.SumWithStackDump$.sum(SumWithStackDump.scala:19)
```

Clearly the sum function is being added to the stack over and over again, once for each call.

> I encourage you to try this on your own to become comfortable with what's happening.

Summary: Our current problem with "basic recursion"

I hope this little dive into the JVM stack and stack frames helps to explain our current problem with "basic recursion." As mentioned, if I try to pass a List with 10,000 elements into the current recursive sum function, it will generate a StackOverflowError. Because we're trying to write bulletproof programs, this isn't good.

What's next

Now that we looked at (a) basic recursion with the sum function, (b) how that works with stacks and stack frames in the last two lessons, and (c) how basic recursion can throw a StackOverflowError with large data sets, the next lesson shows how to fix these problems with something called "tail recursion."

38

Tail-Recursive Algorithms

"Tail recursion is its own reward."

From the "Functional" cartoon on xkcd.com (https://xkcd.com/1270/).

Goals

The main goal of this lesson is to solve the problem shown in the previous lessons: Simple recursion creates a series of stack frames, and for algorithms that require deep levels of recursion, this creates a `StackOverflowError` (and crashes your program).

"Tail recursion" to the rescue

Although the previous lesson showed that algorithms with deep levels of recursion can crash with a `StackOverflowError`, all is not lost. With Scala you can work around this problem by making sure that your recursive functions are written in a tail-recursive style.

A *tail-recursive function* is just a function whose *very last action* is a call to itself. When you write your recursive function in this way, the Scala compiler can optimize the resulting JVM bytecode so that the function requires only one stack frame — as opposed to one stack frame for each level of recursion!

On Stack Overflow[1], Martin Odersky explains tail-recursion in Scala:

> "Functions which call themselves as their last action are called tail-recursive. The Scala compiler detects tail recursion and replaces it with a jump back to the beginning of the function, after updating the function parameters with the new values ... as long as the last thing you do is calling yourself, it's automatically tail-recursive (i.e., optimized)."

---
[1] from%20http://stackoverflow.com/questions/12496959/summing-values-in-a-list

But that sum function looks tail-recursive to me ...

"Hmm," you might say, "if I understand Mr. Odersky's quote, the sum function you wrote at the end of the last lesson (shown in Figure 38.1) sure looks tail-recursive to me."

```
// note: this code won't compile yet
@tailrec
private def sumWithAccumulator(list: List[Int], accumulator: Int): Int = list match {
    case Nil => 0
    case x :: xs => x + sum(xs)
}
```

Figure 38.1: The call to sum *appears to be the last action.*

"Isn't the 'last action' a call to itself, making it tail-recursive?"

If that's what you're thinking, fear not, that's an easy mistake to make. But the answer is no, this function is not tail-recursive. Although sum(tail) is at the end of the second case expression, you have to think like a compiler here, and when you do that you'll see that the last two actions of this function are:

1. Call sum(xs)

2. When that function call returns, add its value to x and return that result

When I make that code more explicit and write it as a series of one-line statements, you see that it looks like this:

```
val s = sum(xs)
val result = x + s
return result
```

As shown, the last calculation that happens before the return statement is that the sum of x and s is calculated. If you're not 100% sure that you believe that, there are a few ways you can prove it to yourself.

1) Proving it with the previous "stack trace" example

One way to "prove" that the sum algorithm is not tail-recursive is with the "stack trace" output from the previous lesson. The JVM output shows the sum method is called once for each step in the recursion, so it's clear that the JVM feels the need to create a new instance of sum for each element in the collection.

2) Proving it with the @tailrec annotation

A second way to prove that sum isn't tail-recursive is to attempt to tag the function with a Scala annotation named @tailrec. This annotation won't compile unless the function is tail-recursive. (More on this later in this lesson.)

If you attempt to add the @tailrec annotation to sum:

```
// need to import tailrec before using it
import scala.annotation.tailrec

@tailrec
def sum(list: List[Int]): Int = list match {
    case Nil => 0
    case x :: xs => x + sum(xs)
}
```

the scalac compiler (or your IDE) will show an error message like this:

```
Sum.scala:10: error: could not optimize @tailrec annotated method sum:
it contains a recursive call not in tail position
def sum(list: List[Int]): Int = list match {
                                ^
```

This is another way to "prove" that the Scala compiler doesn't think sum is tail-recursive.

So, how do I write a tail-recursive function?

Now that you know the current approach isn't tail-recursive, the question becomes, "How do I make it tail-recursive?"

A common pattern used to make a recursive function that "accumulates a result" into a tail-recursive function is to follow these steps:

1. Keep the original function signature the same (i.e., sum's signature).
2. Create a second function by (a) copying the original function, (b) giving it a new name, (c) making it private, (d) giving it a new "accumulator" input parameter, and (e) adding the @tailrec annotation to it.
3. Modify the second function's algorithm so it uses the new accumulator. (More on this shortly.)
4. Call the second function from inside the first function. When you do this you give the

second function's accumulator parameter a "seed" value (a little like the *identity* value I wrote about in the previous lessons).

Let's jump into an example to see how this works.

Example: How to make sum tail-recursive

1) Leave the original function signature the same

To begin the process of converting the recursive sum function into a *tail-recursive* sum algorithm, leave the external signature of sum the same as it was before:

```
def sum(list: List[Int]): Int = ...
```

2) Create a second function

Now create the second function by copying the first function, giving it a new name, marking it private, giving it a new "accumulator" parameter, and adding the @tailrec annotation to it. The highlights in Figure 38.2 show the changes.

```
// note: this code won't compile yet
@tailrec
private def sumWithAccumulator(list: List[Int], accumulator: Int): Int = list match {
    case Nil => 0
    case x :: xs => x + sum(xs)
}
```

Figure 38.2: Starting to create the second function.

This code won't compile as shown, so I'll fix that next.

> Before moving on, notice that the data type for the accumulator (Int) is the same as the data type held in the List that we're iterating over.

3) Modify the second function's algorithm

The third step is to modify the algorithm of the newly-created function to use the accumulator parameter. The easiest way to explain this is to show the code for the solution, and then explain the changes. Here's the source code:

```
@tailrec
private def sumWithAccumulator(list: List[Int], accumulator: Int): Int = {
    list match {
        case Nil => accumulator
        case x :: xs => sumWithAccumulator(xs, accumulator + x)
    }
}
```

Here's a description of how that code works:

- I marked it with `@tailrec` so the compiler can help me by verifying that my code truly is tail-recursive.
- `sumWithAccumulator` takes two parameters, `list: List[Int]`, and `accumulator: Int`.
- The first parameter is the same list that the `sum` function receives.
- The second parameter is new. It's the "accumulator" that I mentioned earlier.
- The inside of the `sumWithAccumulator` function looks similar. It uses the same match/case approach that the original `sum` method used.
- Rather than returning 0, the first `case` statement returns the `accumulator` value when the `Nil` pattern is matched. (More on this shortly.)
- The second `case` expression is tail-recursive. When this case is matched it immediately calls `sumWithAccumulator`, passing in the `xs` (tail) portion of `list`. What's different here is that the second parameter is the sum of the `accumulator` and the head of the current list, `x`.
- Where the original `sum` method passed itself the tail of `xs` and then later added that result to `x`, this new approach keeps track of the accumulator (total sum) value as each recursive call is made.

The result of this approach is that the "last action" of the `sumWithAccumulator` function is this call:

```
sumWithAccumulator(xs, accumulator + x)
```

Because this last action really is a call back to the same function, the JVM can optimize this code as Mr. Odersky described earlier.

4) Call the second function from the first function

The fourth step in the process is to modify the original function to call the new function. Here's the source code for the new version of `sum`:

```
def sum(list: List[Int]): Int = sumWithAccumulator(list, 0)
```

Here's a description of how it works:

- The sum function signature is the same as before. It accepts a List[Int] and returns an Int value.
- The body of sum is just a call to the sumWithAccumulator function. It passes the original list to that function, and also gives its accumulator parameter an initial seed value of 0.

Note that this "seed" value is the same as the *identity* value I wrote about in the previous recursion lessons. In those lessons I noted:

- The identity value for a sum algorithm is 0.
- The identity value for a product algorithm is 1.
- The identity value for a string concatenation algorithm is "".

A few notes about sum

Looking at sum again:

```
def sum(list: List[Int]): Int = sumWithAccumulator(list, 0)
```

a few key points about it are:

- Other programmers will call sum. It's the "Public API" portion of the solution.
- It has the same function signature as the previous version of sum. The benefit of this is that other programmers won't have to provide the initial seed value. In fact, they won't know that the internal algorithm uses a seed value. All they'll see is sum's signature:

    ```
    def sum(list: List{[}Int{]}): Int
    ```

A slightly better way to write sum

Tail-recursive algorithms that use accumulators are typically written in the manner shown, with one exception: Rather than mark the new accumulator function as private, most Scala/FP developers like to put that function *inside* the original function as a way to limit its scope.

When doing this, the thought process is, "Don't expose the scope of sumWith-Accumulator unless you want other functions to call it."

When you make this change, the final code looks like this:

```
// tail-recursive solution
def sum(list: List[Int]): Int = {
    @tailrec
    def sumWithAccumulator(list: List[Int], currentSum: Int): Int = {
        list match {
            case Nil => currentSum
            case x :: xs => sumWithAccumulator(xs, currentSum + x)
        }
    }
    sumWithAccumulator(list, 0)
}
```

Feel free to use either approach. (Don't tell anyone, but I prefer the first approach; I think it reads more easily.)

A note on variable names

If you don't like the name accumulator for the new parameter, it may help to see the function with a different name. For a "sum" algorithm a name like runningTotal or currentSum may be more meaningful:

```
// tail-recursive solution
def sum(list: List[Int]): Int = {
    @tailrec
    def sumWithAccumulator(list: List[Int], currentSum: Int): Int = {
        list match {
            case Nil => currentSum
            case x :: xs => sumWithAccumulator(xs, currentSum + x)
        }
    }
    sumWithAccumulator(list, 0)
}
```

I encourage you to use whatever name makes sense to you. I prefer currentSum for this algorithm, but you'll often hear this approach referred to as using an "accumulator," which is why I used that name first.

Proving that this is tail-recursive

You can follow my earlier efforts to demonstrate that this function really is tail-recursive, but at this point I'm satisfied with one proof: When you compile this code with the `@tailrec` annotation, the compiler doesn't give you an error message like it did before.

Summary

In this lesson I:

- Defined tail recursion
- Introduced the `@tailrec` annotation
- Showed how to write a tail-recursive function
- Showed a formula you can use to convert a simple recursive function to a tail-recursive function

What's next

This lesson covered the basics of converting a simple recursive function into a tail-recursive function. I'm usually not smart enough to write a tail-recursive function right away, so I usually write my algorithms using simple recursion, then convert them to use tail-recursion.

To help in your efforts, the next lesson will show more examples of tail-recursion for different types of algorithms.

See also

- My list of Scala recursion examples[2]
- Martin Odersky explaining tail recursion on Stack Overflow[3]

---

[2]http://alvinalexander.com/scala/scala-recursion-examples-recursive-programming
[3]http://stackoverflow.com/questions/12496959/summing-values-in-a-list

39

A First Look at "State"

In the next lesson I'm going to start writing a command-line game, but before I get into that I want to discuss the concept of handling "state" in software applications.

Every non-trivial application maintains some sort of *state*. For instance, the state of a word processing application is the current document, along with whether the document has been saved or not (whether the document is "clean" or "dirty"). Similarly, the state of a spreadsheet application is the spreadsheet and its clean/dirty state. Web versions of these applications have additional state, such as who the current user is, when they logged in, what their IP address is, etc.

Even voice applications like Siri and Amazon Echo have state. As I learned in writing *SARAH* (https://alvinalexander.com/sarah), one thing you need to do is to maintain speaking/listening state, otherwise the computer will hear itself talking, then respond to itself, eventually kicking off an endless loop.

Siri and others are also gaining a concept that I call *context*, or the "context of a conversation," which also requires state management. Imagine asking Siri to order a pizza. It will respond by asking what toppings you want, where you want to order the pizza from, how you want to pay, etc. This is "conversational state."

Handling state in a game

In my spare time I work on developing an Android football game where I play against a computer opponent. If you know American Football (as opposed to what we Americans call "soccer"), in between each play you can think of the state of a football game as having these attributes:

- Which team has the ball (you are on offense or defense)
- Current field position
- Down and distance (such as "1st and 10")
- Current score
- Time remaining

(There are more state variables than this, but I'm keeping this example simple.)

In Scala you might model this game state like this:

```
case class GameState (
    iHaveTheBall: Boolean,
    fieldPosition: Int,
    down: Int,
    distance: Int,
    myScore: Int,
    computerScore: Int,
    timeRemaining: Int
)
```

On the first play of the game the initial state might look like this:

```
GameState (
    iHaveTheBall: true,
    fieldPosition: 25,
    down: 1,
    distance: 10,
    myScore: 0,
    computerScore: 0,
    timeRemaining: 3600
)
```

Then, after the next play the state might look like this:

```
GameState (
    iHaveTheBall: true,
    fieldPosition: 29,
    down: 2,
    distance: 6,
    myScore: 0,
    computerScore: 0,
    timeRemaining: 3536
)
```

A football game typically has about 150 plays, so in my game there is a `GameState` instance for each of those plays.

Why state is important

State is important for many reasons, not the least of which is to know when the game is over and who won. An important part about state in my football game is that I use it to help the computer make decisions about what plays it calls.

When the computer is playing on offense is uses a function that looks like this:

```
val possiblePlays: List[OffensivePlay] =
    OffensiveCoordinator.determinePossiblePlays(gameState)
```

The `determinePossiblePlays` function is a pure function. I pass `GameState` into it, and with thousands of lines of purely functional code behind it, it returns a list of all the possible plays that the algorithms believe make sense for the state that was passed in.

For instance, if it's fourth down and goal at the opponent's one-yard line with five seconds left in the game and the computer is down 21-17, it's smart enough to know that it needs to try to score a touchdown rather than kick a field goal. This is what I mean by "state" in the context of a football game.

> As the game gets smarter I also maintain a history of all previously-called plays, so the computer can adjust its play calls based on the player's tendencies.

More state

As you can imagine, a point of sales application for a pizza store will have state that includes:

- The number and types of pizzas ordered
- Customer contact information
- Customer payment information
- The date and time of the order
- Who took the order
- More ...

Once you begin to think about it this way, you'll see that every application maintains state of some sort.

State and functional programming

As I mentioned, my football game has about 150 `GameState` instances for every game. In the context of functional programming, this raises an interesting question: In Scala/FP I can only have `val` instances, so how can I possibly create 150 new variables for each game? Put another way, if you assume that I keep all of the plays in a `List`, the question becomes, "How do I append `GameState` values to an immutable `List`?"

Questions like this bring you to a key point I got to when I was learning FP:

- How am I supposed to handle I/O, which by its very nature is impure?
- How am I supposed to handle state?

In the next lesson I'll show one way to handle state in a simple game by building on what you just learned in the previous lessons: recursion.

40

A Functional Game
(With a Little Bit of State)

"In theory, theory and practice are the same. In practice, they're not."

— Yogi Berra

Introduction

Now that I've given you a little background about "state", let's build a simple game that requires us to use state. I'll build the game using recursion, and also *immutable state* — something I had never heard of when I first starting writing the Scala Cookbook[1].

Goals

Here are my goals for this lesson:

- To write our first functional application
- Show a first example of how to handle "state" in a Scala/FP application

Source code

The best way to understand this lesson is to have its source code open in an IDE as you read it. The source code is available at this URL:

- github.com/alvinj/FPCoinFlipGame[2]

---

[1] http://amzn.to/24ivK4G
[2] https://github.com/alvinj/FPCoinFlipGame

Some of this project's code contains some wide lines that are hard to read in a book. You'll really want to check the code out of Github to see it properly.

Coin Flip: A simple FP game

To get started using state in a Scala application, I'll build a little game you can play at the command line. The application will flip a coin (a virtual coin), and as the player, your goal is to guess whether the result is heads or tails. The computer will keep track of the total number of flips and the number of correct guesses.

When you start the game, you'll see this command-line prompt:

```
(h)eads, (t)ails, or (q)uit: _
```

This is how the application prompts you for your guess. Enter h for heads, t for tails, or q to quit the game. If you enter h or t, the application will flip a virtual coin, then let you know if your guess was correct or not.

As an example of how it works, I just played the game and made four guesses, and the input/output of that session looks like this:

```
(h)eads, (t)ails, or (q)uit: h
Flip was Heads. #Flips: 1, #Correct: 1

(h)eads, (t)ails, or (q)uit: h
Flip was Tails. #Flips: 2, #Correct: 1

(h)eads, (t)ails, or (q)uit: h
Flip was Heads. #Flips: 3, #Correct: 2

(h)eads, (t)ails, or (q)uit: t
Flip was Tails. #Flips: 4, #Correct: 3

(h)eads, (t)ails, or (q)uit: q

=== GAME OVER ===
#Flips: 4, #Correct: 3
```

Admittedly this isn't the most exciting game in the world, but it turns out to be a nice way to learn how to handle immutable state in a Scala/FP application.

One note before proceeding: The input/output in this game will *not* be handled in a functional way. I'll cover that in a future lesson.

On to the game!

Coin Flip game state

Let's analyze how this game works:

- The computer is going to flip a virtual coin.
- You're going to guess whether that result is heads or tails.
- You can play the game for as many flips as you want.
- After each flip the output will look like this:
  Flip was Tails. #Flips: 4, #Correct: 2

These statements tell us a few things about the game state:

- We need to track how many coin flips there are.
- We need to track how many guesses the player made correctly.

I could track more information, such as the history of the guess for each coin flip and the actual value, but to keep it simple, all I want to do at this time is to track (a) the number of flips, and (b) the number of correct guesses. As a result, a first stab at modeling the game state looks like this:

```
case class GameState (
    numFlips: Int,
    numCorrectGuesses: Int
)
```

Game pseudocode

Next, let's start working on the game code.

You know you're going to need some sort of main loop, and in the imperative world, pseudocode for that loop looks like this:

```
var input = ""
while (input != "q") {
    // prompt the player to select heads, tails, or quit
    // get the player's input
    if (input == "q") {
        print the game summary
        quit
    }
    // flip the coin
    // see if the player guessed correctly
    // print the #flips and #correct
}
```

I/O functions

That's not how I'll write the loop, but it does give me an idea of some I/O functions I'm going to need. From that pseudocode it looks like I'm going to need these functions:

- A "show prompt" function
- A "get user input" function
- A function to print the number of flips and correct answers

These functions have nothing to do with FP — they're impure I/O functions that connect our application to the outside world — so I'll write them in the "usual way". Here's the "show prompt" function:

```
def showPrompt: Unit = { print("\n(h)eads, (t)ails, or (q)uit: ") }
```

Next, here's the "get user input" function:

```
def getUserInput = readLine.trim.toUpperCase
```

> Prior to Scala 2.11.0, `readLine` was made available to you without an import statement via Scala's `Predef` object, but since then it's available at *scala.io.StdIn.readLine*. Also, notice that I convert all input to uppercase to make it easier to work with later.

Next, while the game is being played I want to print output like this:

```
Flip was Tails. #Flips: 4, #Correct: 3
```

and when the game is over I want to print this output:

```
=== GAME OVER ===
#Flips: 4, #Correct: 3
```

To accommodate these needs I create these functions:

```
def printableFlipResult(flip: String) = flip match {
    case "H" => "Heads"
    case "T" => "Tails"
}

def printGameState(printableResult: String, gameState: GameState): Unit = {
    print(s"Flip was $printableResult. ")
    printGameState(gameState)
}

def printGameState(gameState: GameState): Unit = {
    println(s"#Flips: ${gameState.numFlips}, #Correct: ${gameState.numCorrect}")
}

def printGameOver: Unit = println("\n=== GAME OVER ===")
```

Note that the `printGameState` functions take the `GameState` as an input parameter, and use its fields to print the output. The assumption is that these functions always receive the latest, up-to-date `GameState` instance.

If you know Scala, that's all fairly standard "print this out" and "read this in" code.

Writing a coin toss function

When you look back at this piece of the original pseudocode:

```
// flip the coin
```

you'll see that one more thing I can get out of the way before writing the main loop is a function to simulate a coin toss.

A simple way to simulate a coin toss is to use a random number generator and limit the generator to return values of 0 and 1, where 0 means "heads" and 1 mean "tails." This is how you limit Scala's `Random.nextInt` method to yield only 0 or 1:

```
val r = new scala.util.Random
r.nextInt(2)
```

The `r.nextInt(2)` code tells `nextInt` to return integer values that are less than 2, i.e., 0 and 1.

Knowing that, I can write a coin flip function like this:

```
// returns "H" for heads, "T" for tails
def tossCoin(r: Random) = {
    val i = r.nextInt(2)
    i match {
        case 0 => "H"
        case 1 => "T"
    }
}
```

With these functions out of the way, let's get to the main part of the lesson: how to write the main loop of the program with an immutable game state.

Writing the main loop in FP style

So now we need a "loop" ... how can we write one in an FP style? Using the tools we know so far, the best way to handle this is with our new friend, recursion. Because you may have never done this before, let me add a few important notes:

- With recursion the main loop is going to call itself repeatedly (recursively)
- Because the game state needs to be updated as the game goes along, a `GameState` instance needs to be passed into each recursive call
- Because each instance of the loop will simulate the flip of a coin, and because the `tossCoin` function requires a `scala.util.Random` instance, it's also best to pass a `Random` instance into each recursive call as well

Given that background, I can start writing some code. First, here's the `GameState` I showed earlier:

```
case class GameState (
    numFlips: Int,
    numCorrectGuesses: Int
)
```

Next, I know I'm going to need (a) a Scala `App`, (b) initial `GameState` and `Random` instances, and (c) some sort of `mainLoop` call to get things started. I also know that `mainLoop` will take the `GameState` and `Random` instances, which leads me to this code:

```
object CoinFlip extends App {
    val s = GameState(0, 0)
    val r = new Random
    mainLoop(s, r)
}
```

Next, I can sketch the `mainLoop` function like this:

```
@tailrec
def mainLoop(gameState: GameState, random: Random) {
    // a) prompt the user for input
    // b) get the user's input
    // c) flip the coin
    // d) compare the flip result to the user's input
    // e) write the output
    // f) if the user didn't type 'h', loop again:
    mainLoop(newGameState, random)
}
```

If you feel like you understand what I've sketched in this `mainLoop` code, I encourage you to set this book aside and work on filling out `mainLoop`'s body on your own, using (a) the I/O functions I showed earlier and (b) any other code you might need. That's all that needs to be done now: fill out the body, and figure out where the recursive `mainLoop` call (or calls) need to be made.

Writing the skeleton code

The next thing I did to solve this problem was to stub out the following skeleton code:

```
object CoinFlip extends App {

    val r = Random
    val s = GameState(0, 0)
    mainLoop(s, r)

    @tailrec
```

```
def mainLoop(gameState: GameState, random: Random) {

    // a) prompt the user for input
    showPrompt()

    // b) get the user's input
    val userInput = getUserInput()

    userInput match {
        case "H" | "T" => {
            // c) flip the coin
            val coinTossResult = tossCoin(random)
            val newNumFlips = gameState.numFlips + 1

            // d) compare the flip result to the user's input
            if (userInput == coinTossResult) {
                // they guessed right
                // e) write the output
                // f) if the user didn't type 'h', loop again:
                mainLoop(newGameState, random)
            } else {
                // they guessed wrong
                // e) write the output
                // f) if the user didn't type 'h', loop again:
                mainLoop(newGameState, random)
            }
        }
        case _  => {
            // assume they type 'Q'
            println("\n=== GAME OVER ===")
            printGameState(gameState)
            // we return out of the recursion here
        }
    }
}

}
```

That code is slightly different than my pseudocode, but it's in the ballpark.

Now all I need to do is finish off the 'e' and 'f' portions of the algorithm. I'll show those sections in the completed code that follows.

The complete source code

The following source code shows the first cut of my solution for this application.

First, I put all of my "utility" functions in a separate object named `CoinFlipUtils`, in a file named *CoinFlipUtils.scala*:

```
package com.alvinalexander.coinflip.v1

import scala.util.Random
import scala.io.StdIn.readLine

object CoinFlipUtils {

    def showPrompt(): Unit = { print("\n(h)eads, (t)ails, or (q)uit: ") }

    def getUserInput(): String = readLine.trim.toUpperCase

    def printableFlipResult(flip: String): String = flip match {
        case "H" => "Heads"
        case "T" => "Tails"
    }

    def printGameState(
        printableFlipResult: String,
        gameState: GameState): Unit =
    {
        print(s"Flip was $printableFlipResult. ")
        printGameState(gameState)
    }

    def printGameState(gameState: GameState): Unit = {
        println(s"#Flips: ${gameState.numFlips}, #Correct:
            ${gameState.numCorrect}")
    }
```

```
    def printGameOver(): Unit = println("\n=== GAME OVER ===")

    // returns "H" for heads, "T" for tails
    def tossCoin(r: Random): String = {
        val i = r.nextInt(2)
        i match {
            case 0 => "H"
            case 1 => "T"
        }
    }

}
```

I did that to keep the code organized, and also to keep my next file smaller. Here's the source code for *CoinFlip.scala*, which primarily consists of the `mainLoop`:

```
package com.alvinalexander.coinflip.v1

import CoinFlipUtils._
import scala.annotation.tailrec
import scala.util.Random

case class GameState(numFlips: Int, numCorrect: Int)

object CoinFlip extends App {

    val r = Random
    val s = GameState(0, 0)
    mainLoop(s, r)

    @tailrec
    def mainLoop(gameState: GameState, random: Random) {

        showPrompt()
        val userInput = getUserInput()

        // handle the result
        userInput match {
            case "H" | "T" => {
```

```
            val coinTossResult = tossCoin(random)
            val newNumFlips = gameState.numFlips + 1
            if (userInput == coinTossResult) {
                val newNumCorrect = gameState.numCorrect + 1
                val newGameState = gameState.copy(
                    numFlips = newNumFlips,
                    numCorrect = newNumCorrect
                )
                printGameState(
                    printableFlipResult(coinTossResult), newGameState
                )
                mainLoop(newGameState, random)
            } else {
                val newGameState = gameState.copy(numFlips = newNumFlips)
                printGameState(
                    printableFlipResult(coinTossResult), newGameState
                )
                mainLoop(newGameState, random)
            }
        }
        case _ => {
            printGameOver()
            printGameState(gameState)
            // return out of the recursion here
        }
    }
  }

}
```

There are a few ways to shorten and refactor that code, but it gives you an idea of what needs to be done for this game.

When the user's guess is correct

Note that when the user's guess matches the coin flip, I use this code:

```
val newNumCorrect = gameState.numCorrect + 1
val newGameState = gameState.copy(
    numFlips = newNumFlips,
    numCorrect = newNumCorrect
)
printGameState(printableFlipResult(coinTossResult), newGameState)
mainLoop(newGameState, random)
```

The key here is that when the user's guess is correct I need to create a new `GameState` and pass that new instance into the next `mainLoop` call. I show that code in a long form, but I can remove the `newNumCorrect` temporary variable:

```
val newGameState = gameState.copy(
    numFlips = newNumFlips,
    numCorrect = gameState.numCorrect + 1
)
printGameState(printableFlipResult(coinTossResult), newGameState)
mainLoop(newGameState, random)
```

When the user's guess is incorrect

In the case where the user's guess is incorrect, I only need to update `numFlips` when creating a new `GameState` instance, so that block of code looks like this:

```
val newGameState = gameState.copy(numFlips = newNumFlips)
printGameState(printableFlipResult(coinTossResult), newGameState)
mainLoop(newGameState, random)
```

When the user wants to quit the game

In the case where the user enters anything other than H or T, I assume they want to quit the game, so I call these procedures:

```
printGameOver()
printGameState(gameState)
```

At this point I don't call `mainLoop` any more, so the recursion ends, all of the recursive calls unwind, and the game ends.

Summary

At the beginning of this lesson I noted that the goals for this lesson were:

- To write our first functional application
- Show a first example of how to handle "state" in an FP application

A few important parts about this lesson that you may not have seen before in traditional imperative code are:

- The use of an explicit `GameState` variable
- Using recursion as a way of looping
- The recursion let us define the `GameState` instance as an immutable `val` field

A Functional Game (With a Little Bit of State)

41

A Quick Review of Case Classes

"The biggest advantage of case classes is that they support pattern matching."

Programming in Scala
(Odersky, Spoon, and Venners)[a]

---

[a]http://amzn.to/2fiqDBh

Goals

In this book I generally assume that you know the basics of the Scala programming language, but because `case` classes are so important to *functional programming in Scala* it's worth a quick review of what case classes are — the features they provide, and the benefits of those features.

Discussion

As opposed to a "regular" Scala `class`, a `case` class generates a lot of code for you, with the following benefits:

- An `apply` method is generated, so you don't need to use the `new` keyword to create a new instance of the class.

- *Accessor* methods are generated for each constructor parameter, because `case` class constructor parameters are public `val` fields by default.

- (You won't use `var` fields in this book, but if you did, *mutator* methods would also be generated for constructor parameters declared as `var`.)

- An `unapply` method is generated, which makes it easy to use `case` classes in `match` expressions. This is huge for Scala/FP.

- As you'll see in the next lesson, a `copy` method is generated. I never use this in Scala/OOP code, you'll use it all the time in Scala/FP.

- `equals` and `hashCode` methods are generated, which lets you compare objects and easily use them as keys in maps (and sets).

- A default `toString` method is generated, which is helpful for debugging.

A quick demo

To demonstrate how case classes work, here are a few examples that show each of these features and benefits in action.

No need for new

When you define a class as a `case` class, you don't have to use the `new` keyword to create a new instance:

```
scala> case class Person(name: String, relation: String)
defined class Person

// "new" not needed before Person
scala> val christina = Person("Christina", "niece")
christina: Person = Person(Christina,niece)
```

This is a nice convenience when writing Scala/OOP code, but it's a *terrific* feature when writing Scala/FP code, as you'll see throughout this book.

No mutator methods

Case class constructor parameters are `val` by default, so an *accessor* method is generated for each parameter, but mutator methods are not generated:

```
scala> christina.name
res0: String = Christina

// can't mutate the `name` field
scala> christina.name = "Fred"
<console>:10: error: reassignment to val
       christina.name = "Fred"
                 ^
```

unapply *method*

Because an `unapply` method is automatically created for a `case` class, it works well when you need to extract information in `match` expressions, as shown here:

```
scala> christina match { case Person(n, r) => println(n, r) }
(Christina,niece)
```

Conversely, if you try to use a regular Scala class in a `match` expression like this, you'll quickly see that it won't compile. You'll see many more uses of case classes with `match` expressions in this book because *pattern matching* is a BIG feature of Scala/FP.

> A class that defines an `unapply` method is called an *extractor*, and `unapply` methods enable match/case expressions.

copy *method*

A `case` class also has a built-in `copy` method that is extremely helpful when you need to clone an object and change one or more of the fields during the cloning process:

```
scala> case class BaseballTeam(name: String, lastWorldSeriesWin: Int)
defined class BaseballTeam

scala> val cubs1908 = BaseballTeam("Chicago Cubs", 1908)
cubs1908: BaseballTeam = BaseballTeam(Chicago Cubs,1908)

scala> val cubs2016 = cubs1908.copy(lastWorldSeriesWin = 2016)
cubs2016: BaseballTeam = BaseballTeam(Chicago Cubs,2016)
```

I refer to this process as "update as you copy," and this is such a big Scala/FP feature that I cover it in depth in the next lesson.

equals *and* hashCode *methods*

Case classes also have generated `equals` and `hashCode` methods, so instances can be compared:

```
scala> val hannah = Person("Hannah", "niece")
hannah: Person = Person(Hannah,niece)
```

```
scala> christina == hannah
res1: Boolean = false
```

These methods also let you easily use your objects in collections like sets and maps.

`toString` methods

Finally, `case` classes also have a default `toString` method implementation, which at the very least is helpful when debugging code:

```
scala> christina
res0: Person = Person(Christina,niece)
```

> For more details on case classes, see the "Generating Boilerplate Code with Case Classes" chapter in the Scala Cookbook[1].

Summary

In this lesson I showed that the following methods are automatically created when you declare a class as a `case class`:

- `apply`
- `unapply`
- accessor methods are created for each constructor parameter
- `copy`
- `equals` and `hashCode`
- `toString`

These built-in methods make case classes easier to use in a functional programming style.

What's next

I thought it was worth this quick review of Scala `case` classes because the next thing we're going to do is dive into the `case` class `copy` method. Because you don't mutate objects in FP, you need to do something else to create updated instances of objects when things change, and the way you do this in Scala/FP is with the `copy` method.

---

[1] http://amzn.to/24ivK4G

42

Update as You Copy, Don't Mutate

> *"I've been imitated so well I've heard people copy my mistakes."*
>
> Jimi Hendrix

Goals

In functional programming you don't modify (mutate) existing objects, you create new objects with updated fields based on existing objects. For instance, last year my niece's name was "Emily Means," so I could have created a `Person` instance to represent her, like this:

```
val emily = Person("Emily", "Means")
```

Then she got married, and her last name became "Walls." In an imperative programming language you would just change her last name, like this:

```
emily.setLastName("Walls")
```

But in FP you don't do this, you don't mutate existing objects. Instead, what you do is (a) you copy the existing object to a new object, and (b) during the copy process you update any fields you want to change by supplying their new values.

The way you do this in Scala/FP is with the copy method that comes with the Scala *case class*. This lesson shows a few examples of how to use copy, including how to use it with nested objects.

Source code

So you can follow along, the source code for this lesson is available at github.com/alvinj/FpUpdateAsYouCopy[1]

Basic copy

When you're working with a simple object it's easy to use copy. Given a case class like this:

```
case class Person (firstName: String, lastName: String)
```

if you want to update a person's last name, you just "update as you copy," like this:

```
val emily1 = Person("Emily", "Means")
val emily2 = emily1.copy(lastName = "Walls")
```

As shown, in simple situations like this all you have to do to use copy is:

- Make sure your class is a case class.
- Create an initial object (emily1), as usual.
- When a field in that object needs to be updated, use copy to create a new object (emily2) from the original object, and specify the name of the field to be changed, along with its new value.

When you're updating one field, that's all you have to do. (That's also all you have to do to update multiple fields, as I'll show shortly.)

The original instance is unchanged

An important point to note about this is that the first instance remains unchanged. You can verify that by running a little App like this:

```
object CopyTest1 extends App {

    println("--- Before Copy ---")
    val emily1 = Person("Emily", "Means")
    println(s"emily1 = $emily1")
```

---

[1] https://github.com/alvinj/FpUpdateAsYouCopy

```
    // emily got married
    println("\n--- After Copy ---")
    val emily2 = emily1.copy(lastName = "Walls")
    println(s"emily1 = $emily1")
    println(s"emily2 = $emily2")

}
```

The output of `CopyTest1` looks as follows, showing that the original `emily1` instance is unchanged after the copy:

```
--- Before Copy ---
emily1 = Person(Emily,Means)

--- After Copy ---
emily1 = Person(Emily,Means)
emily2 = Person(Emily,Walls)
```

What happens in practice is that you discard the original object, so thinking about the old instance isn't typically an issue; I just want to mention it. (You'll see more examples of how this works as we go along.)

> In practice you also won't use intermediate variables with names like `emily1`, `emily2`, etc. We just need to do that now, until we learn a few more things.

Updating several attributes at once

It's also easy to update multiple fields at one time using `copy`. For instance, had `Person` been defined like this:

```
case class Person (
    firstName: String,
    lastName: String,
    age: Int
)
```

you could create an instance like this:

```
val emily1 = Person("Emily", "Means", 25)
```

and then create a new instance by updating several parameters at once, like this:

```
// emily is married, and a year older
val emily2 = emily1.copy(lastName = "Walls", age = 26)
```

That's all you have to do to update two or more fields in a simple `case` class.

Copying nested objects

As shown, using `copy` with simple `case` classes is straightforward. But when a `case` class contains other `case` classes, and those contain more `case` classes, things get more complicated and the required code gets more verbose.

For instance, let's say that you have a `case` class hierarchy like this:

```
case class BillingInfo(
    creditCards: Seq[CreditCard]
)

case class Name(
    firstName: String,
    mi: String,
    lastName: String
)

case class User(
    id: Int,
    name: Name,
    billingInfo: BillingInfo,
    phone: String,
    email: String
)

case class CreditCard(
    name: Name,
    number: String,
    month: Int,
    year: Int,
    cvv: String
```

)

Visually the relationship between these classes looks like Figure 42.1.

```
                        ┌─────────────────────────────────┐
                        │              User               │
                        ├─────────────────────────────────┤
                        │              id: Int            │
                        │         phone: String           │
                        │         email: String           │
                      ▷ │  billingInfo: BillingInfo       │ ◁
                   ┌────│          name: Name             │────┐
                   │    └─────────────────────────────────┘    │
                   │                                           │
                   │                                           │
      ┌────────────────────────────┐       ┌────────────────────────────┐
      │        BillingInfo         │       │            Name            │
      ├────────────────────────────┤       ├────────────────────────────┤
      │ creditCards: Seq[CreditCard]│      │     firstName: String      │
      │              △             │       │            mi: String      │
      └────────────────────────────┘       │      lastName: String      │
                   │                       └────────────────────────────┘
                   │ *
      ┌────────────────────────────┐
      │         CreditCard         │
      ├────────────────────────────┤
      │         name: Name         │ ◁──────────────────────┘
      │      number: String        │
      │        month: Int          │
      │         year: Int          │
      │        cvv: String         │
      └────────────────────────────┘
```

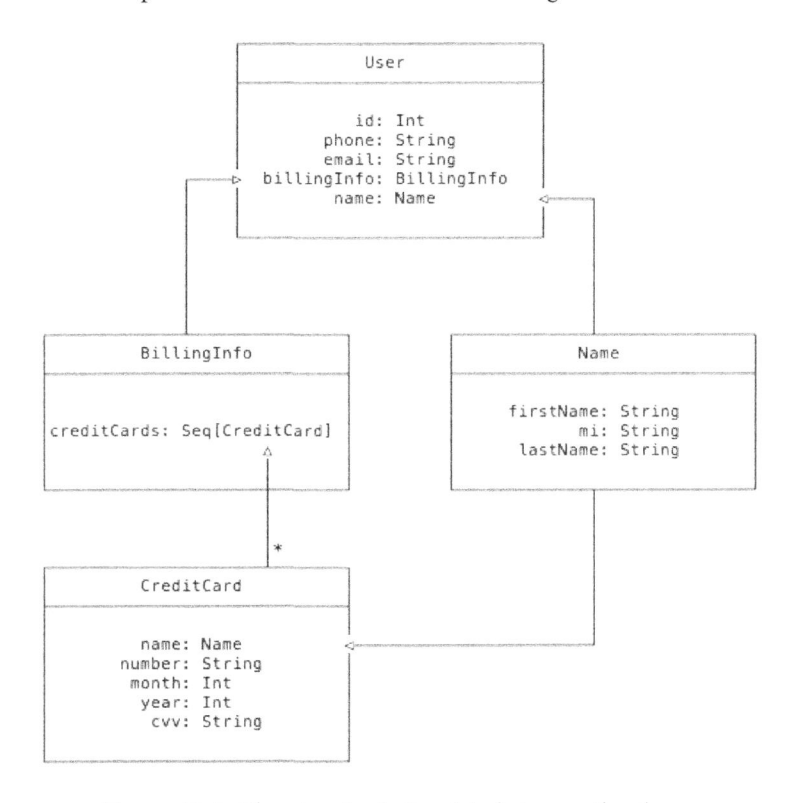

Figure 42.1: The visual relationship between the classes

Notice a few things about this code:

- `User` has fields of type `Name` and `BillingInfo`
- `CreditCard` also has a field of the `Name` type

Despite a little complexity, creating an initial instance of `User` with this hierarchy is straightforward:

```
object NestedCopy1 extends App {

    val hannahsName = Name(
        firstName = "Hannah",
        mi = "C",
        lastName = "Jones"
```

```
        )

        // create a user
        val hannah1 = User(
            id = 1,
            name = hannahsName,
            phone = "907-555-1212",
            email = "hannah@hannahjones.com",
            billingInfo = BillingInfo(
                creditCards = Seq(
                    CreditCard(
                        name = hannahsName,
                        number = "1111111111111111",
                        month = 3,
                        year = 2020,
                        cvv = "123"
                    )
                )
            )
        )

}
```

So far, so good. Now let's take a look at what you have to do when a few of the fields need to be updated.

Updating the phone number

First, let's suppose that Hannah moves. I kept the address out of the model to keep things relatively simple, but let's suppose that her phone number needs to be updated. Because the phone number is stored as a top-level field in User, this is a simple copy operation:

```
// hannah moved, update the phone number
val hannah2 = hannah1.copy(phone = "720-555-1212")
```

Updating the last name

Next, suppose that a little while later Hannah gets married and we need to update her last name. In this case you need to reach down into the Name instance of the User object and update the `lastName` field. I'll do this in a two-step process to keep it clear.

First, create a copy of the `name` field, changing `lastName` during the copy process:

```
// hannah got married, update her last name
val newName = hannah2.name.copy(lastName = "Smith")
```

If you print `newName` at this point, you'll see that it is "Hannah C Smith."

Now that you have this `newName` instance, the second step is to create a new "Hannah" instance with this new `Name`. You do that by (a) calling `copy` on the `hannah2` instance to make a new `hannah3` instance, and (b) within `copy` you bind the `name` field to `newName`:

```
val hannah3 = hannah2.copy(name = newName)
```

Updating the credit card

Suppose you also need to update the "Hannah" instance with new credit card information. To do this you follow the same pattern as before. First, you create a new `CreditCard` instance from the existing instance. Because the `creditCards` field inside the `billingInfo` instance is a `Seq`, you need to reference the first credit card instance while making the copy. That is, you reference `creditCards(0)`:

```
val oldCC = hannah3.billingInfo.creditCards(0)
val newCC = oldCC.copy(name = newName)
```

Because (a) `BillingInfo` takes a `Seq[CreditCard]`, and (b) there's only one credit card, I make a new `Seq[CreditCard]` like this:

```
val newCCs = Seq(newCC)
```

With this new `Seq[CreditCard]` I create a new "Hannah" instance by copying `hannah3` to `hannah4`, updating the `BillingInfo` during the copy process:

```
val hannah4 = hannah3.copy(billingInfo = BillingInfo(newCCs))
```

Put together, those lines of code look like this:

```
val oldCC = hannah3.billingInfo.creditCards(0)
val newCC = oldCC.copy(name = newName)
val newCCs = Seq(newCC)
val hannah4 = hannah3.copy(billingInfo = BillingInfo(newCCs))
```

You can shorten that code if you want, but I show the individual steps so it's easier to read.

These examples show how the "update as you copy" process works with nested objects in Scala/FP. (More on this after the attribution.)

Attribution

The examples I just showed are a simplification of the code and description found at these URLs:

- The "koffio-lenses" example on GitHub[2]
- The KOFF.io "Lens in Scala" tutorial[3]

Lenses

As you saw, the "update as you copy" technique gets more complicated when you deal with real-world, nested objects, and the deeper the nesting gets, the more complicated the problem becomes. But fear not: there are Scala/FP libraries that make this easier. The general idea of these libraries is known as a "lens" (or "lenses"), and they make copying nested objects much simpler. I cover lenses in a lesson later in this book.

Summary

Here's a summary of what I just covered:

- Because functional programmers don't mutate objects, when an object needs to be updated it's necessary to follow a pattern which I describe as "update as you copy".

- The way you do this in Scala is with the copy method, which comes with Scala case classes.

- As you can imagine, from here on out you're going to be using case classes more than you'll use the default Scala class. The copy method is just one reason for this, but it's a good reason. (You'll see even more reasons to use case classes as you go along.)

---

[2]https://github.com/coffius/koffio-lenses
[3]http://koff.io/posts/292173-lens-in-scala/

What's Next

As mentioned, I write about lenses later in the book, when we get to a point where we have to "update as you copy" complicated objects.

But for now the next thing we need to dig into is `for` comprehensions. Once I cover those, you'll be close to being able to write small, simple, functional applications with everything I've covered so far.

43

A Quick Review of for-Expressions

"You must unlearn what you have learned."

— Yoda

Goals

The goal of this lesson is to review at a high level how for loops work in Scala. This is necessary because Scala/FP developers *really* take advantage of advanced Scala for loop features.

As an example of what I mean, the goal of the next few lessons is to explain what's happening in this for loop:

```
def stackManip: State[Stack, Int] = for {
    _ <- push(3)
    a <- pop
    b <- pop
} yield(b)
```

If you already understand what's happening in that code, feel free to skip over these lessons; otherwise, read on.

Introduction

If you're used to using the for loop in Java, Scala's for loop can work similar to it, but it can also be used in a different manner.

A *very* different manner.

And Scala/FP developers use it in this other manner.

A lot.

For instance, some experienced Scala/FP developers say that this is a "simple" use of a `for` loop in a functional style:

```
def stackManip: State[Stack, Int] = for {
    _ <- push(3)
    a <- pop
    b <- pop
} yield(b)
```

If you're used to traditional `for` loops in languages like C and Java, whatever is happening in this "loop" can be quite a surprise.

A peek into what's happening

Let me explain a little of what's happening: This code is working with a stack, and a `push` function is pushing the number 3 onto a pre-existing stack, and then the next two lines pop values off of the stack. But even knowing that, a few questions come to mind:

- If a `push` function pushes a number onto a stack, where exactly is that stack?
- A `push` function normally doesn't return anything meaningful, so how is it being used as a *generator* in a `for` loop? And what is that underscore character doing on the left side of the `push` expression?
- Assuming that those `pop` functions are popping data off of a stack, again I ask, where is that stack?

In this lesson we'll starting digging into how the Scala `for` expression works. Knowing how it works is a prerequisite for understanding how this `stackManip` method works, and how `for` is used in many Scala/FP situations.

New rule: No more "for loop"

Hmmm ... if you go back and look at that code again, is it really a "loop"? No, not really. However that code works, all it seems to do is to perform three operations on a stack. This thought leads us to a new rule:

For a variety of reasons — including the fact that this code isn't really a *loop* but something called a *comprehension* — I will no longer use the term "`for` loop." From now on, I'll refer to this construct as a "`for` comprehension" or "`for` expression."

I can explain this name by once again taking a short look back at history and mathematics.

To be consistent with the historical references I'm about to share, I'll use the term "for comprehension" in this lesson, but in the remainder of this book I'll use the term "for expression," which is more commonly used.

for-comprehension history

As a quick historical tidbit, the name "comprehension" comes from both Haskell and mathematics, with mathematics preceding Haskell by some large number of years. The book, Haskell, the Craft of Functional Programming[1], provides this introduction:

> "One of the features of a functional language is the *list comprehension* notation, which has no parallels in other paradigms."

Learn You a Haskell for Great Good[2] states:

> "List comprehensions are a way to filter, transform, and combine lists. They're very similar to the mathematical concept of set comprehensions[3]. Set comprehensions are normally used for building sets out of other sets."

If you've used the Scala for/yield expression at all, you know that it meets this definition. Indeed, you'll find the for construct described on a page on the official Scala website titled Sequence Comprehensions[4]. There they state:

> "Comprehensions have the form for (enumerators) yield e, where enumerators refers to a semicolon-separated list of enumerators. An enumerator is either a generator which introduces new variables, or it is a filter."

These definitions lead us to the for comprehension concepts of *generators*, *filters*, and *definitions*.

Generators, filters, and definitions

A Scala for comprehension can contain the following three types of expressions:

---

[1] http://amzn.to/1POe1u9
[2] http://amzn.to/1POaUCv
[3] https://en.wikipedia.org/wiki/Set-builder_notation
[4] http://docs.scala-lang.org/tutorials/tour/sequence-comprehensions.html

- Generators
- Filters
- Definitions

These are shown in the following source code snippet from the book, Programming in Scala[5]:

```
for {
    p <- persons            // generator
    n = p.name              // definition
    if (n startsWith "To")  // filter
} yield
```

Let's look at short, formal definitions for each of these elements.

Generators

Generators have this general form:

```
pattern <- expression
```

In simple cases this results in an assignment, like this:

```
p <- persons
```

In this expression the value p iterates over all of the elements contained in persons. Generators can be more complicated than this, but this is their most simple and common use.

There are three more things to know about generators:

- Every for comprehension begins with a generator
- for comprehensions can have multiple generators
- The left side of a generator can also be a pattern:

```
def getTheSquirrel = for {
    (dog, cat, squirrel) <- getAnimalsOutOfLaundryRoom
} yield squirrel
```

---

[5]http://amzn.to/2fiqDBh

Definitions

`for` comprehension *definitions* have this general form:

```
pattern = expression
```

A definition binds the pattern `pattern` on the left to the value of `expression` on the right.

In the original example in this lesson:

```
n = p.name
```

the variable `n` is bound to the value `p.name`. That statement has the same effect as writing this code outside of a `for` comprehension:

```
val n = p.name
```

Filters

`for` comprehension *filters* have this general form:

```
if (expression)
```

In this code `expression` must have the type `Boolean`.

A filter drops all elements from the iteration for which `expression` returns `false`, so in this code:

```
if (n startsWith "To")
```

any value `n` that does not start with the string "To" will be dropped during the iteration process. (Stated the other way, any value `n` that begins with the string "To" will be retained during the iteration process.)

An example

Here's an example of each of these features in a Scala `for` comprehension:

```
case class Person(firstName: String, lastName: String)

val people = List(
    Person("barney", "rubble"),
    Person("fred", "flintstone")
)

val namesStartingWithB = for {
    p <- people                    // generator
    fname = p.firstName            // definition
    if (fname startsWith "b")      // filter
} yield fname.toUpperCase
```

If you put that code in the Scala REPL, you can then run this statement to see the expected result:

```
scala> namesStartingWithB.foreach(println)
BARNEY
```

Summary

What you started to see in this lesson is that Scala `for` loops are much more than "loops." They're based on mathematical set comprehensions, and they are a way to "filter, transform, and combine lists."

You also saw that a Scala `for` comprehension can contain the following three types of expressions:

- Generators
- Filters
- Definitions

What's next

This lesson provides a quick review of the basic features of `for` comprehensions as background for the next lesson, where you'll learn how to write your own custom collection class to work in a `for` comprehension.

See also

- set comprehensions on Wikipedia[6]
- Sequence comprehensions on scala-lang.org[7]
- Haskell, the Craft of Functional Programming[8]
- Learn You a Haskell for Great Good[9] **states:**
- Programming in Scala[10]

---

[6] https://en.wikipedia.org/wiki/Set-builder_notation
[7] http://docs.scala-lang.org/tutorials/tour/sequence-comprehensions.html
[8] http://amzn.to/1POe1u9
[9] http://amzn.to/1POaUCv
[10] http://amzn.to/2fiqDBh

44

How to Write a Class That Can Be Used in a for-Expression

As a reminder, the reason for the next several lessons on for expressions is so that you can get to a point where you can understand the following code:

```
def stackManip: State[Stack, Int] = for {
    _ <- push(3)
    a <- pop
    b <- pop
} yield(b)
```

To make this code easier to understand — or understandable at all, depending on your background — let's start digging into how the Scala for expression works.

How for-expressions work

The book *Programming in Scala* is the definitive reference for the Scala programming language, and Section 23.6 of that book, "Generalizing for," describes the *translation rules* for how the Scala compiler converts (a) the for expressions you write into (b) a series of method calls that may include map, flatMap, foreach, and withFilter.

Very importantly, just as for expressions are compiled into these four methods, the opposite is also true: if you write a class that implements these methods, it can be used inside a for expression.

Rules about how these methods enable 'for'

In the next several lessons I'll show how to write your own custom data types that can be used in for expressions. To do this you need to know the rules that govern how a for expression is enabled by these methods. *Programming in Scala* gives us these translation rules:

1. If a custom data type defines a `foreach` method, it allows `for` *loops* (both with single and multiple generators). (Note the emphasis on the word "loops" in that definition. This refers to the simple Java-style use of a for loop, i.e., `for (i <- ints) println(i)`.)
2. If a data type defines only `map`, it can be used in `for` expressions consisting of a single generator.
3. If it defines `flatMap` as well as `map`, it allows `for` expressions consisting of multiple generators.
4. If it defines `withFilter`, it allows for filter expressions starting with an `if` within the `for` expression.

While a `for` expression technically doesn't require specific signatures for each of these methods, if you want your custom class to work well with a `for` expression it should generally implement those methods with the signatures shown in this example class:

```
abstract class CustomClass[A] {
    def map[B](f: A => B): CustomClass[B]
    def flatMap[B](f: A => CustomClass[B]): CustomClass[B]
    def withFilter(p: A => Boolean): CustomClass[A]
    def foreach(b: A => Unit): Unit
}
```

If those type signatures don't make sense just yet, fear not, I'll cover them in the next few lessons.

And now — because we're at a point where we *really* need to know how `for` expressions work — in the next few lessons I'll demonstrate how to satisfy these rules as we build a custom class that can be used inside a Scala `for` expression.

Creating a Sequence Class to be Used in a for Comprehension

The best way I know to demonstrate how the Scala for expression works is for us to build our own collection class.

To keep things simple I'm going to create a custom class as a "wrapper" around an existing Scala collection class. The reason for this is that I want you to focus on the effects that writing map, flatMap, withFilter, and foreach methods have on how the class works in a for expression — not on writing the gory internals of a collection class.

A Sequence class

I always like to "begin with the end in mind" and picture how I want to use a class *before* I create it — i.e., its API — and to that end, this is how I want to use a custom class that I'm going to name Sequence:

```
val strings = Sequence("one", "two")
val nums = Sequence(1, 2, 3, 4, 5)
val peeps = Sequence(
    Person("Bert"),
    Person("Ernie"),
    Person("Grover")
)
```

From that code you can see that Sequence will be able to work with generic data types: it will be able to contain a series of String, Int, Person, and other data types.

Given those lines of code, you can infer some initial requirements about the Sequence class:

- Sequence either needs to be a case class, or it needs to have a companion object that implements an apply method, because I want to be able to create new Sequence instances without needing the new keyword.
- Because the class will be used as a container for generic elements, I'll define the class to take a generic type.

- Because Sequence instances can be created with a variable number of initial elements, the Sequence class constructor will be defined to accept a "varargs" parameter.

I'll create this class in a series of steps over the next several lessons.

Create a case class named Sequence

The first step is to create a class named Sequence. I'm going to make it a case class so I can write code like this:

```
val strings = Sequence(1, 2, 3)
```

If I didn't use a case class (or an apply method in a companion object) I'd have to write "new Sequence", like this:

```
val strings = new Sequence("one", "two")
```

Therefore, I start by creating a case class named Sequence:

```
case class Sequence ...
```

Sequence will be a container for generic elements

Next, I know that I want Sequence to contain elements of different types, so I expand that definition to say that Sequence will be a container of generic types:

```
case class Sequence[A] ...
```

Sequence's constructor will take a variable number of input parameters

Next, I know that the Sequence constructor will have one parameter, and that parameter can be assigned to a variable number of elements, so I expand the definition to this:

```
case class Sequence[A](initialElems: A*) ...
```

If you're not familiar with using a *varargs* parameter, the * after the A is what lets you pass a variable number of elements into the Sequence constructor:

```
val a = Sequence(1,2)
val b = Sequence(1,2,3)
val c = Sequence('a', 'b', 'c', 'd', 'e')
```

Later in the Sequence class code you'll see how to handle a variable number of input elements.

If you have a hard time with generics

If you have a hard time using generic types, it can help to remove the generic type A and use Int instead:

```
case class Sequence(initialElems: Int*) ...
```

With this code you only have to think about Sequence being a container for integers, so combined with the varargs constructor parameter, new instances of Sequence can be created like this:

```
val a = Sequence(1,2)
val b = Sequence(3,5,7,11,13,17,23)
```

Feel free to write your own code using Int rather than A, though I'll use A in the rest of this lesson:

```
case class Sequence[A](initialElems: A*) ...
```

Sequence will be backed by a Scala collection class

As I mentioned at the beginning of this lesson, to keep this code from getting too complicated I'm going to implement Sequence as a wrapper around a Scala collection class. I originally wrote this lesson using a custom linked list class, but with that approach there was a lot of code that was unrelated to for expressions, so I opted to take this simpler approach.

The following code shows what I have in mind:

```
case class Sequence[A](initialElems: A*) {

    // this is a book, don't do this at home
    private val elems = scala.collection.mutable.ArrayBuffer[A]()

    // initialize
    elems ++= initialElems
```

}

I make `ArrayBuffer` private in this code so no consumers of my class can see how it's implemented.

Scala constructors

If you haven't use a Scala constructor in a while, remember that everything inside the body of a class that isn't a method is executed when a new instance of the class is created. Therefore, this line of code:

```
elems ++= initialElems
```

is executed when a new class instance is created. For example, when you create a new Sequence like this:

```
val ints = Sequence(1, 2, 3)
```

the `int` values 1, 2, and 3 are added to the `elems` variable when the class is first created.

> If you need to brush up on how Scala class constructors work, see Chapter 4 of the Scala Cookbook[1].

About ++=

If you're not used to the ++= method, this line of code:

```
elems ++= initialElems
```

works just like this `for` loop:

```
for {
    e <- initialElems
} elems += e
```

---

[1] http://amzn.to/24ivK4G

Summary

If you want to test this code before moving on to the next lesson, paste it into the Scala REPL and then create new sequences like these:

```
val strings = Sequence("a", "b", "c")
val nums = Sequence(1, 2, 3, 4, 5)
```

you'll see that they're created properly:

```
scala> val strings = Sequence("a", "b", "c")
strings: Sequence[String] = Sequence(WrappedArray(a, b, c))

scala> val nums = Sequence(1, 2, 3, 4, 5)
nums: Sequence[Int] = Sequence(WrappedArray(1, 2, 3, 4, 5))
```

Notice that `strings` has the type `Sequence[String]`, and `nums` has the type `Sequence[Int]`. That's generics at work.

> Don't worry about the data on the right side of the = showing Sequence(WrappedArray(...)). That's just an artifact of taking a varargs constructor parameter.

What's next

Now that I have a simple `Sequence` class to work with, I'll start to make it work with `for` expressions in the next lesson.

See also

- My article, How to create Scala methods that take variable-arguments (varargs) fields[2]
- How to delete Array and ArrayBuffer elements in Scala[3]

---

[2] http://alvinalexander.com/scala/how-to-define-methods-variable-arguments-varargs-fields
[3] http://alvinalexander.com/scala/how-to-delete-array-arraybuffer-elements-scala-cookbook

46

Making Sequence Work
In a Simple for Loop

So far I have this Sequence class:

```
case class Sequence[A](initialElems: A*) {

    private val elems = scala.collection.mutable.ArrayBuffer[A]()

    // initialize
    elems ++= initialElems

}
```

With that code I can create new Sequence instances like this:

```
val strings = Sequence("a", "b", "c")
val nums = Sequence(1, 2, 3, 4, 5)
```

Next, I'll modify Sequence so I can use it as a generator in a for loop.

> Note: I intentionally use the word "loop" in this lesson because all I'm trying to do is to loop over the elements in the Sequence, like a Java for loop. I'm specifically *not* trying to write for/yield expressions.

Trying to use Sequence in a simple for loop

To get started, let's see what happens if I try to use a Sequence in a simple for loop. When I paste these two lines of code into the Scala REPL:

```
val ints = Sequence(1, 2, 3)
for (i <- ints) println(i)
```

I see this error after the for loop:

```
scala> for (i <- ints) println(i)
<console>:14: error: value foreach is not a member of Sequence[Int]
       for (i <- ints) println(i)
                      ^
```

The bad news is that Sequence won't work in a simple for loop. But the good news is that the Scala compiler error tells me what's wrong:

`"value foreach is not a member of Sequence[Int]"`

How to modify Sequence so it can be used as a for loop generator

The error message tells me that this for loop won't work because Sequence doesn't have a foreach method, so I'll go ahead and implement one.

Because (a) Sequence uses an ArrayBuffer behind the scenes, and (b) I'm not concerned with *how* I implement the foreach method, I'll just piggyback on the ArrayBuffer's foreach method:

```
def foreach(block: A => Unit): Unit = {
    elems.foreach(block)
}
```

(As I mentioned in the last lesson, for the purposes of understanding how the for expression works I don't care *how* I implement a foreach method, I just want to create one as simply as possible to see if that lets me use Sequence inside of for.)

Adding foreach makes my complete Sequence class look like this:

```
case class Sequence[A](initialElems: A*) {

    private val elems = scala.collection.mutable.ArrayBuffer[A]()

    // initialize
    elems ++= initialElems

    def foreach(block: A => Unit): Unit = {
        elems.foreach(block)
    }
```

}

When I paste that class into the REPL, and then paste this code in as well:

```
val ints = Sequence(1,2,3)
for (i <- ints) println(i)
```

I see that Sequence now works as a for loop generator:

```
scala> for (i <- ints) println(i)
1
2
3
```

Excellent. Let's move on to the next step.

Exercises

1. If you don't like the way I implemented foreach, go ahead and implement it however you'd like. I recommend using recursion!

47

How To Make Sequence Work as a Single Generator in a for Expression

Getting Sequence to work as a generator in a simple for loop was cool, but does adding foreach let Sequence also work when I add yield? Let's see.

When I paste this code into the REPL:

```
val ints = Sequence(1,2,3)

for {
    i <- ints
} yield i*2
```

I see this error message:

```
scala> for {
     |     i <- ints
     | } yield i*2
<console>:15: error: value map is not a member of Sequence[Int]
         i <- ints
           ^
```

Sadly, Sequence won't currently work with for/yield, but again the REPL tells us why:

```
error: value map is not a member of Sequence[Int]
```

That error tells us that Sequence needs a map method for this to work. Great — let's create one.

Adding a map method to Sequence

Again I'm going to cheat to create a simple solution, this time using ArrayBuffer's map method inside Sequence's map method:

```
def map[B](f: A => B): Sequence[B] = {
    val abMap: ArrayBuffer[B] = elems.map(f)
    Sequence(abMap: _*)
}
```

This map method does the following:

- It takes a function input parameter that transforms a type A to a type B.
- When it's finished, map returns a Sequence[B].
- In the first line of the function I show abMap: ArrayBuffer[B] to be clear that elems.map(f) returns an ArrayBuffer. As usual, showing the type isn't necessary, but I think it helps to make this step clear.
- In the second line inside the function I use the :_* syntax to create a new Sequence and return it.

About the :_* syntax

If you haven't seen the abMap: _* syntax before, the :_* part of the code is a way to adapt a collection to work with a *varargs* parameter. Recall that the Sequence constructor is defined to take a varags parameter, as shown in Figure 47.1.

```
case class Sequence[A](initialElems: A*)
                                      ↑
                                      └─┐
                                        varargs param
```

Figure 47.1: The Sequence constructor takes a varargs input parameter.

For more information on this syntax, see my tutorial, Scala's missing splat operator[1].

The complete Sequence class

This is what the Sequence class looks like when I add the map method to it:

```
case class Sequence[A](initialElems: A*) {

    private val elems = scala.collection.mutable.ArrayBuffer[A]()
```

---

[1]http://alvinalexander.com/bookmarks/scala/scalas-missing-splat-operator

```
    // initialize
    elems ++= initialElems

    def map[B](f: A => B): Sequence[B] = {
        val abMap = elems.map(f)
        new Sequence(abMap: _*)
    }

    def foreach(block: A => Unit): Unit = {
        elems.foreach(block)
    }

}
```

Does for/yield work now?

Now when I go back and try to use the for/yield expression I showed earlier, I find that it compiles and runs just fine:

```
scala> val ints = Sequence(1,2,3)
ints: Sequence[Int] = Sequence(WrappedArray(1, 2, 3))

scala> for {
     |     i <- ints
     | } yield i*2
res0: Sequence[Int] = Sequence(ArrayBuffer(2, 4, 6))
```

An important point

One point I need to make clear is that this for/yield expression works solely because of the map method; it has nothing to do with the foreach method. You can demonstrate this in at least two ways. First, if you remove the foreach method from the Sequence class you'll see that this for expression still works.

Second, if you create a little test class with this code in it, and then compile it with scalac -Xprint:parse, you'll see that the Scala compiler converts this for expression:

```
for {
    i <- ints
} yield i*2
```

into this map expression:

```
ints.map(((i) => i.$times(2)))
```

To be very clear, defining a foreach method in Sequence enables this for loop:

```
for (i <- ints) println(i)
```

and defining a map method in Sequence enables this for expression:

```
for {
    i <- ints
} yield i*2
```

Summary

I can summarize what I accomplished in this lesson and the previous lesson with these lines of code:

```
// (1) works because `foreach` is defined
for (p <- peeps) println(p)

// (2) `yield` works because `map` is defined
val res: Sequence[Int] = for {
    i <- ints
} yield i * 2
res.foreach(println)   // verify the result
```

What's next?

This is a good start. Next up, I'll modify Sequence so I can use it with filtering clauses in for expressions.

48

Enabling Filtering in a for Expression

Next, let's see if we can use a *filtering* clause inside of a for expression with the Sequence code we have so far.

Trying to use a filter

When I paste the current Sequence class and this code into the Scala REPL:

```
val ints = Sequence(1,2,3,4,5)

val res = for {
    i <- ints
    if i > 2
} yield i*2
```

I see the following error message:

```
<console>:14: error: value filter is not a member of Sequence[Int]
          i <- ints
              ^
```

Again the bad news is that I can't use a filtering clause like if i > 2, and the good news is that the REPL tells me why it won't work. So let's fix this problem.

Before we continue ...

One note before we continue: I ran this example with the Scala 2.11.7 REPL, and that error message isn't 100% accurate. As I mentioned a few lessons ago, the current rule for how to get a custom collection class to work in a for expression is this:

- If a class defines withFilter, it allows for filter expressions starting with an if within the for expression

In versions of Scala up to 2.7 the filter error message shown in the REPL was correct, but starting with Scala 2.8 the preferred solution is to implement a `withFilter` method rather than a `filter` method. Therefore, in the following code I'll implement `withFilter`.

> I'll write more about this shortly, but for the purposes of this lesson you can think of `withFilter` as being just like a `filter` method.

Writing `withFilter`'s type signature

At this point a good question is, "How does a `filter` method work?"

Figure 48.1 shows the Scaladoc for the `filter` method of the Scala `List` class.

```
def filter(p: (A) => Boolean): List[A]
```
Selects all elements of this traversable collection which satisfy a predicate.

    p   the predicate used to test elements.
    returns   a new traversable collection consisting of all elements of this traversable collection that satisfy the given predicate p. The order of the elements is preserved.

Figure 48.1: The Scaladoc for the `filter` method of the Scala `List` class.

By looking at that figure — and from your knowledge of the Scala collection methods — you know these things about how a typical `filter` method works:

1) It takes a function input parameter (FIP). That FIP must be able to be applied to the type of elements in the collection, and must return a `Boolean` value.

2) `filter` loops over the elements in its collection, and returns a new collection that contains the elements for which the passed-in function evaluates to `true`.

For instance, you can pass the anonymous function `_ > 2` into a `List[Int]`:

```
scala> val res = List(1,2,3,4,5).filter(_ > 2)
res: List[Int] = List(3, 4, 5)
```

3) Unlike `map`, `filter` doesn't *transform* elements in the collection, it just returns a subset of the elements in the collection. For instance, when `_ > 2` is applied, all elements in the collection that are greater than 2 are returned. This tells us that `filter`'s return type will be the same as the elements `Sequence` contains.

Put together, these bullet points tell us that a `filter` method for `Sequence` will have this type signature:

```
def filter(p: A => Boolean): Sequence[A] = ???
```

In that code, p stands for the predicate that filter takes as an input parameter. Because Sequence contains elements of type A, the predicate transforms that type to a Boolean, and filter returns a Sequence[A].

When that method body is implemented you'll be able to write code like this:

```
val ints = Sequence(1,2,3,4,5).filter(i > 2)
```

Because Scala for expressions prefer withFilter, I'll go ahead and rename filter to with-Filter at this point:

```
def withFilter(p: A => Boolean): Sequence[A] = ???
```

Given this type signature, all I need to do now is implement withFilter's body.

Implementing withFilter's body

As with foreach and map, I'll implement withFilter's body by calling a method on Sequence's private ArrayBuffer. Because in the real world there are differences in how a true withFilter method works, the easiest thing to do here is to call filter, so I'll do that:

```
def withFilter(p: A => Boolean): Sequence[A] = {
    val tmpArrayBuffer = elems.filter(p)
    Sequence(tmpArrayBuffer: _*)
}
```

When I add this code to the existing implementation of the Sequence class I get this:

```
case class Sequence[A](initialElems: A*) {

    private val elems = scala.collection.mutable.ArrayBuffer[A]()

    elems ++= initialElems

    def withFilter(p: A => Boolean): Sequence[A] = {
        val tmpArrayBuffer = elems.filter(p)
        Sequence(tmpArrayBuffer: _*)
    }

    def map[B](f: A => B): Sequence[B] = {
        val abMap = elems.map(f)
```

```
        new Sequence(abMap: _*)
    }

    def foreach(block: A => Unit): Unit = {
        elems.foreach(block)
    }

}
```

Will this let us use a filtering clause in a for expression? Let's see. When I paste the Sequence class source code into the REPL and then paste in this code:

```
val ints = Sequence(1,2,3,4,5)

val res = for {
    i <- ints
    if i > 2
} yield i*2
```

I see the following result:

```
scala> val res = for {
     |     i <- ints
     |     if i > 2
     | } yield i*2
res: Sequence[Int] = Sequence(ArrayBuffer(6, 8, 10))
```

Excellent, it works as desired. I can now use if clauses inside for expressions with the Sequence class.

I'll implement more functionality in the next lesson, but it's worth pausing for a few moments here to learn more about the differences between implementing withFilter or filter in a class that you want to use in a for expression.

filter vs withFilter

You can read more about how for/yield expressions are translated in a post on the official Scala website titled, "How does yield work?[1]," but the short story is this:

- for comprehensions with if filters are translated to withFilter method calls
- If withFilter does not exist on the class being used in the for comprehension, the compiler will fall back and use the class's filter method instead
- If neither method exists, the compilation attempt will fail

If I had implemented filter in this lesson (rather than withFilter), in the next lesson you'd start to see compiler warning messages like this:

```
Warning:(31, 14) `withFilter' method does not yet exist on
Sequence[A],
using `filter' method instead
        p <- peeps
            ^
```

To avoid those warning messages, I implemented withFilter here.

However — and that's a big *however* — it's important to know that my withFilter method is not exactly what the Scala compiler is expecting.

If you're not familiar with the difference between filter and withFilter on the built-in Scala collection classes, I wrote about them in a blog post titled, "An example that shows the differences between strict and lazy evaluation in Scala[2]." What I wrote there can be summarized by what you find in the withFilter Scaladoc on Scala collection classes like List[3]:

> withFilter creates a *non-strict* filter of this traversable collection. Note: the difference between c filter p and c withFilter p is that the former creates a new collection, whereas the latter only restricts the domain of subsequent map, flatMap, foreach, and withFilter operations.

There are probably ways that I could cheat to create a withFilter method that meets that definition, but I think that obscures the main purpose of this lesson:

---

[1]http://docs.scala-lang.org/tutorials/FAQ/yield.html
[2]http://alvinalexander.com/scala/examples-shows-differences-between-strict-lazy-evaluation-in-scala
[3]http://www.scala-lang.org/api/current/#scala.collection.immutable.List

- If you implement a withFilter or filter method in your custom class, you'll be able to use that class with an if clause in a for expression. (This assumes that you also implement other methods like foreach and map.)

Summary

I can summarize what I accomplished in this lesson and the previous lessons with these lines of code:

```
// (1) a single generator works because `foreach` is defined
for (p <- peeps) println(p)

// (2) `yield` works because `map` is defined
val res: Sequence[Int] = for {
    i <- ints
} yield i * 2
res.foreach(println)

// (3) `if` works because `withFilter` is defined
val res = for {
    i <- ints
    if i > 2
} yield i*2
```

What's next

Now that I have Sequence working in all of these ways, there's just one more thing to learn: how to modify it so we can use multiple generators in a for expression. We'll accomplish that in the next lesson.

How to Enable the Use of Multiple Generators in a for Expression

One cool thing about for expressions is that you can use multiple generators inside of them. This lets you do some nice analytics when you have some interesting data relationships.

For instance, suppose you have some data like this:

```
case class Person(name: String)

val myFriends = Sequence(
    Person("Adam"),
    Person("David"),
    Person("Frank")
)

val adamsFriends = Sequence(
    Person("Nick"),
    Person("David"),
    Person("Frank")
)
```

If I want to find out which friends of mine are also friends of Adam, I can write a for expression like this:

```
val mutualFriends = for {
    myFriend    <- myFriends      // generator
    adamsFriend <- adamsFriends   // generator
    if (myFriend.name == adamsFriend.name)
} yield myFriend
mutualFriends.foreach(println)
```

Notice how I use two Sequence instances as generators in that for expression.

345

Sadly, the compiler tells us that this code won't work, but happily it again tells us why:

```
<console>:17: error: value flatMap is not a member of Sequence[Person]
           myFriend <- myFriends
                       ^
```

Since you're used to reading these error messages now, you know the compiler is telling us that we need to implement a flatMap method in the Sequence class for this code to work.

flatMap, a curious creature

The flatMap method is an interesting creature, and experienced functional programmers seem to use it a lot.

As a bit of background, when you think about map's signature for a moment, you'll remember that it looks like this:

```
def map[B](f: A => B): Sequence[B]
```

As shown, map takes a function that transforms a type A to a type B, and returns a Sequence[B] when it finishes, transforming all of the elements in the Sequence.

flatMap's signature is similar to map:

```
def flatMap[B](f: A => Sequence[B]): Sequence[B]
```

As this shows, flatMap is similar to map, but it's also different. The function flatMap takes transforms a type A to a Sequence of type B — Sequence[B] — and then when it's finished it also returns a Sequence[B]. The type signatures tell us that the difference between map and flatMap is the type of functions they take as input parameters.

flatMap background

If you come to Scala from a background like Java, after a while it becomes apparent that the map function is very cool – and you'll use it all the time – but it can be hard to find a use for flatMap.

As I wrote in the Scala Cookbook[1], I like to think of flatMap as "map flat," because on collec-

---

[1] http://amzn.to/24ivK4G

tions classes it works similarly to a) calling map and then b) calling flatten. As an example of what I mean, these lines of code show the difference between calling map and flatMap on a Seq[String]:

```
scala> val fruits = Seq("apple", "banana", "orange")
fruits: Seq[java.lang.String] = List(apple, banana, orange)

scala> fruits.map(_.toUpperCase)
res0: Seq[java.lang.String] = List(APPLE, BANANA, ORANGE)

scala> fruits.flatMap(_.toUpperCase)
res1: Seq[Char] = List(A, P, P, L, E, B, A, N, A, N, A, O, R, A, N, G, E)
```

map applies the function to each element in the input Seq to create a transformed Seq, but flatMap takes the process a step further. In fact, you can show that calling flatMap is just like calling map and then calling flatten:

```
scala> val mapResult = fruits.map(_.toUpperCase)
mapResult: Seq[String] = List(APPLE, BANANA, ORANGE)

scala> val flattenResult = mapResult.flatten
flattenResult: Seq[Char] = List(A, P, P, L, E, B, A, N, A, N, A, O, R, A, N, G, E)
```

I won't show any more examples of flatMap here, but if you want to see more examples of how it works, please see my article, "A collection of Scala flatMap examples[2]." I also demonstrate more ways to use flatMap in lessons later in this book.

Starting to write a flatMap method

Earlier I showed flatMap's signature to be:

```
def flatMap[B](f: A => Sequence[B]): Sequence[B]
```

Given that signature, and knowing that flatMap works like a map call followed by a flatten call, I can implement flatMap's function body by calling map and then flatten:

```
def flatMap[B](f: A => Sequence[B]): Sequence[B] = {
```

---

[2] http://alvinalexander.com/scala/collection-scala-flatmap-examples-map-flatten

```
    val mapRes: Sequence[Sequence[B]] = map(f)    //map
    flatten(mapRes)                               //flatten
}
```

In the first line of the function body I call the map method we developed in the previous lessons, and I also explicitly show the type of mapRes:

```
val mapRes: Sequence[Sequence[B]] = map(f)    //map
```

Because this result is a little complicated, I like to make the return type obvious. That's a great thing about Scala: You don't have to declare variable types, but you can show them when you want to.

In the second line of this function I quickly run into a problem: I haven't defined a flatten method yet! Let's fix that.

Aside: Why I wrote the code as shown

It's important to note that I wrote the function body like this:

```
val mapRes: Sequence[Sequence[B]] = map(f)    //map
flatten(mapRes)                               //flatten
```

I did this because the function input parameter that flatMap takes looks like this:

```
f: A => Sequence[B]
```

Because that function transforms a type A into a Sequence[B], I can't just call map and flatten on elems. For example, this code won't work:

```
// this won't work
def flatMap[B](f: A => Sequence[B]): Sequence[B] = {
    val mapRes = elems.map(f)
    mapRes.flatten
}
```

The reason I can't cheat like this is because elems.map(f) returns an ArrayBuffer[Sequence[B]], and what I really need is a Sequence[Sequence[B]]. Because of this I need to take the approach I showed earlier:

```
def flatMap[B](f: A => Sequence[B]): Sequence[B] = {
    val mapRes: Sequence[Sequence[B]] = map(f)    //map
    flatten(mapRes)                                //flatten
}
```

How flatten works

Getting back to the problem at hand, I need to write a `flatten` method. If you read the Scala Cookbook[3] you know how a `flatten` method should work — it converts a "list of lists" to a single list. A little example demonstrates this. In the REPL you can create a list of lists like this:

```
val a = List( List(1,2), List(3,4) )
```

Now when you call `flatten` on that data structure you get a combined (or flattened) result of `List(1,2,3,4)`. Here's what it looks like in the REPL:

```
scala> val a = List( List(1,2), List(3,4) )
a: List[List[Int]] = List(List(1, 2), List(3, 4))

scala> a.flatten
res0: List[Int] = List(1, 2, 3, 4)
```

Our `flatten` method should do the same thing.

Writing a flatten function

Seeing how `flatten` works, I can write pseudocode for a `flatten` function like this:

```
create an empty list 'xs'
for each list 'a' in the original listOfLists
    for each element 'e' in the list 'a'
        add 'e' to 'xs'
return 'xs'
```

In Scala/OOP you can implement that pseudocode like this:

---

[3] http://amzn.to/24ivK4G

```
var xs = ArrayBuffer[B]()
for (listB: Sequence[B] <- listOfLists) {
    for (e <- listB) {
        xs += e
    }
}
xs
```

Because I'm working with my custom Sequence I need to modify that code slightly, but when I wrap it inside a function named flatten, it still looks similar:

```
def flatten[B](seqOfSeq: Sequence[Sequence[B]]): Sequence[B] = {
    var xs = ArrayBuffer[B]()
    for (listB: Sequence[B] <- seqOfSeq) {
        for (e <- listB) {
            xs += e
        }
    }
    Sequence(xs: _*)
}
```

The biggest difference here is that I convert the temporary ArrayBuffer to a Sequence in the last step, like this:

```
Sequence(xs: _*)
```

From flatten to flattenLike

There's one problem with this function; the type signature for a flatten function on a Scala List looks like this:

```
def flatten[B]: List[B]
```

Because my type signature isn't the same as that, I'm not comfortable naming it flatten. Therefore I'm going to rename it and also make it private, so the new signature looks like this:

```
private def flattenLike[B](seqOfSeq: Sequence[Sequence[B]]): Sequence[B]
```

The short explanation for why the type signatures don't match up is that my cheating ways have finally caught up with me. Creating Sequence as a wrapper around an ArrayBuffer creates a series of problems if I try to define flatten like this:

```
def flatten[B](): Sequence[B] = ...
```

Rather than go into those problems in detail, I'll leave that as an exercise for the reader. Focusing on the problem at hand — getting a flatMap function working — I'm going to move forward using use my flattenLike function to get flatMap working.

Making flatMap work

Now that I have flattenLike written, I can go back and update flatMap to call it:

```
def flatMap[B](f: A => Sequence[B]): Sequence[B] = {
    val mapRes: Sequence[Sequence[B]] = map(f)   //map
    flattenLike(mapRes)                          //flatten
}
```

Testing flatMap

Now that I think I have a working flatMap function, I can add it to the Sequence class. Here's the complete source code for Sequence, including the functions I just wrote:

```
import scala.collection.mutable.ArrayBuffer

case class Sequence[A](private val initialElems: A*) {

    // this is a book, don't do this at home
    private val elems = ArrayBuffer[A]()

    // initialize
    elems ++= initialElems

    def flatMap[B](f: A => Sequence[B]): Sequence[B] = {
        val mapRes: Sequence[Sequence[B]] = map(f)   //map
        flattenLike(mapRes)                          //flatten
    }

    private def flattenLike[B](seqOfSeq: Sequence[Sequence[B]]): Sequence[B] = {
        var xs = ArrayBuffer[B]()
```

```
        for (listB: Sequence[B] <- seqOfSeq) {
            for (e <- listB) {
                xs += e
            }
        }
        Sequence(xs: _*)
    }

    def withFilter(p: A => Boolean): Sequence[A] = {
        val tmpArrayBuffer = elems.filter(p)
        Sequence(tmpArrayBuffer: _*)
    }

    def map[B](f: A => B): Sequence[B] = {
        val abMap = elems.map(f)
        Sequence(abMap: _*)
    }

    def foreach(block: A => Unit): Unit = {
        elems.foreach(block)
    }

}
```

When I paste that code into the REPL, and then paste in the code I showed at the beginning of this lesson:

```
case class Person(name: String)

val myFriends = Sequence(
    Person("Adam"),
    Person("David"),
    Person("Frank")
)

val adamsFriends = Sequence(
    Person("Nick"),
    Person("David"),
    Person("Frank")
```

)

I can confirm that my for expression with multiple generators now works:

```
val mutualFriends = for {
    myFriend <- myFriends         // generator
    adamsFriend <- adamsFriends   // generator
    if (myFriend.name == adamsFriend.name)
} yield myFriend

mutualFriends.foreach(println)
```

The output of that last line looks like this:

```
scala> mutualFriends.foreach(println)
Person(David)
Person(Frank)
```

Admittedly I did some serious cheating in this lesson to get a flatMap function working, but as you see, once flatMap is implemented, you can use multiple generators in a for expression.

Summary

I can summarize what I showed in all of the for expression lessons with these lines of code:

```
// (1) works because `foreach` is defined
for (p <- peeps) println(p)

// (2) `yield` works because `map` is defined
val res: Sequence[Int] = for {
    i <- ints
} yield i * 2
res.foreach(println)

// (3) `if` works because `withFilter` is defined
val res = for {
    i <- ints
    if i > 2
} yield i*2
```

```
// (4) works because `flatMap` is defined
val mutualFriends = for {
    myFriend <- myFriends        // generator
    adamsFriend <- adamsFriends  // generator
    if (myFriend.name == adamsFriend.name)
} yield myFriend
```

50

A Summary of the for Expression Lessons

As I mentioned at the beginning of these for expression lessons, the book, Programming in Scala[1] describes the *translation rules* for how the Scala compiler converts the for comprehensions you write into a series of method calls that can include map, flatMap, foreach, and withFilter. As a reminder, those rules are:

1. If a custom data type defines a foreach method, it allows for *loops* (both with single and multiple generators). (Note the emphasis on the word "loops" in that definition. This refers to the simple Java-style use of a for loop, i.e., for (i <- ints) println(i).)
2. If a data type defines only map, it can be used in for expressions consisting of a single generator. (Where "for expressions" means for/yield expressions.)
3. If it defines flatMap as well as map, it allows for expressions consisting of multiple generators.
4. If it defines withFilter, it allows for filter expressions starting with an if within the for expression.

For a trait named CustomClass, the method signatures should look like this:

```
trait CustomClass[A] {
    def map[B](f: A => B): CustomClass[B]
    def flatMap[B](f: A => CustomClass[B]): CustomClass[B]
    def withFilter(p: A => Boolean): CustomClass[A]
    def foreach(b: A => Unit): Unit
}
```

Through a series of lessons I showed how you can write your own foreach, map, withFilter, and flatMap methods so that your custom data type can be used inside a for expression.

> As I've noted, I "cheated" a lot in these lessons because I'm not concerned at this point with *how* these methods are implemented. In future lessons I'll show how to properly write these methods.

---

[1] http://amzn.to/2fiqDBh

What's next

As I mentioned in the first for expression lesson, the goal of all of this work is to help you understand how FP code like this can possibly work:

```
def stackManip: State[Stack, Int] = for {
    _ <- push(3)
    a <- pop
    b <- pop
} yield(b)
```

Now that you have the background on how to write a class that works in a for expression, you're much closer to being able to understand how this code works. The following lessons will build on what you just learned until the mysteries of this for expression will be completely revealed.

See also

- "Sequence comprehensions" on scala-lang.org[2]
- How to use multiple generators in Scala 'for' expressions (loops)[3]
- An example to show the differences between strict and lazy evaluation in Scala (filter vs withFilter)[4]
- How does yield work?[5] (includes a discussion of withFilter versus filter)

---

[2] http://docs.scala-lang.org/tutorials/tour/sequence-comprehensions.html
[3] http://alvinalexander.com/scala/how-to-use-multiple-generators-scala-for-expressions-loops
[4] http://alvinalexander.com/scala/examples-shows-differences-between-strict-lazy-evaluation-in-scala
[5] http://docs.scala-lang.org/tutorials/FAQ/yield.html

51

Pure Functions Tell No Lies

Introduction

There's an important point about pure functions that I didn't emphasize enough earlier in this book:

> Pure functions never throw exceptions!

This is an important point I need to stress, especially before getting into the following lessons.

Think of it this way: the signature of a pure function is a binding contract with the consumer of that function. If the function signature says it returns an `Int`:

```
def foo(a: String): Int = ...
```

then by golly it *must* return an `Int`.

Importantly, it can't return an `Int` *most* of the time and throw an exception *some* of the time. If a function was to behave like that, its signature would be a lie. This would be bad for your programming career, because other FP developers won't be happy with you.

Beyond that, it's also bad for your code because a key part of functional programming is something called *function composition*, and if your functions throw exceptions, they won't compose well.

Function composition

As you'll see in the coming lessons, the ability to *compose* functions is a BIG feature of functional programming. Composing functions means that you can easily glue them together to form a solution, like links in a chain. For now you can think of composition as being like this:

```
val solution = myData.function1(arg1)
                    .function2(arg2, arg3)
                    .function3(arg4)
                    .function4(arg5)
```

If one of those functions can throw an exception, that function is a weak link in the chain. If it was a real, physical chain, it would mean that you could never rely on the chain because you'd never know when that link might break. In the code shown it would mean that `solution` might never get bound to a value because an exception could short-circuit the code.

Example

To be clear, you should *never* write functions like these:

```
// bad: can throw an exception
@throws(classOf[NumberFormatException])
def makeFloat(s: String): Float = s.trim.toFloat


// worse: can throw an exception without telling you
def makeInt(s: String): Int = s.trim.toInt
```

Inside those functions both `toFloat` and `toInt` can throw exceptions, and whether or not you warn other developers with a `@throws` clause, from an FP standpoint they're both bad. If other people rely on these functions and they short-circuit, their code won't be reliable.

The Scala/FP way

Rather than throwing exceptions, the Scala/FP idiom is to handle exceptions inside your functions and return an `Option`. This function signature tells the truth to consumers of the function:

```
def makeInt(s: String): Option[Int] = {
    try {
        Some(s.trim.toInt)
    } catch {
        case e: Exception => None
    }
}
```

The signature says, "If all goes well, you're going to get a `Some[Int]` — an `Int` wrapped in a

Some wrapper — but if something goes wrong you're going to get a None."

This is great because it means you can write code that uses makeInt like this:

```
makeInt(input) match {
    case Some(i) => println(s"i = $i")
    case None => println("toInt could not parse 'input'")
}
```

> In addition to Option you can also use Try, Either, or third-party approaches. I just say "Option" here to keep things simple. I show all of the approaches in the next lesson.

Using Option with for

As a preview of what you're going to see in the upcoming lessons, this is also a valid (and important) way of using Option values in for expressions:

```
val result = for {
    x <- makeInt("1")
    y <- makeInt("2")
    z <- makeInt("3")
} yield x + y + z
```

The REPL shows what that code yields:

```
scala> val result = for {
     |     x <- makeInt("1")
     |     y <- makeInt("2")
     |     z <- makeInt("3")
     | } yield x + y + z
result: Option[Int] = Some(6)
```

A great way to think about this particular example is that it shows the "Happy Case" of this for expression. This means that makeInt is able to parse each String and you get the desired result in the end, in this case a Some(6).

But note that the world can also give us "Unhappy Cases":

```
val result = for {
    x <- makeInt("1")
    y <- makeInt("hi mom")
    z <- makeInt("hi dad")
} yield x + y + z
```

In this example `makeInt` isn't going to be able to convert those last two strings to `Int` values, so the result isn't going to be as happy as the previous example.

But fear not: because (a) `makeInt` returns `Option` values, (b) the `Option`, `Some`, and `None` classes have `map` and `flatMap` methods, and (c) the `for` expression is built to work with `map` and `flatMap`, `result` simply ends up being bound to `None`:

```
scala> val result = for {
     |     x <- makeInt("1")
     |     y <- makeInt("hi mom")
     |     z <- makeInt("3")
     | } yield x + y + z
result: Option[Int] = None
```

Unlike an exception blowing up your code, this result is great! Your code didn't short-circuit and go flying off in some other direction with an exception; `result` just ended up being `None`. This isn't a problem at all, because the next part of your code also knows how to deal with an `Option`:

```
result match {
    case Some(i) => println(s"result = $result")
    case None => println("could not add the three strings as Int values")
}
```

This is Scala/FP code as it was meant to be written:

- `makeInt` is a pure function
- `makeInt` returns an `Option`
- therefore:
    - `makeInt` can be used with match/case
    - multiple `makeInt` functions can be used in a `for` expression

As a thought exercise, look back at that Unhappy Case again, and consider what would have happened if `makeInt` would have thrown an exception when the `makeInt("hi mom")` call was reached. (That's what I call a "Really Unhappy Case.")

Keys to remember

The key points of this lesson are:

- Pure functions *never* throw exceptions
- Pure function signatures are a contract with its consumers
- Scala/FP developers use `Option` rather than exceptions
- Scala/FP developers use `Option` rather than `null` values (I didn't demonstrate this point in these examples)
- Scala constructs like `match` and `for` work great with `Option`

Visually, the `Option` portion of the summary looks like Figure 51.1.

```
Option


 null


 exception
```

Figure 51.1: Scala/FP developers use `Option`, *and don't use* `null` *values or exceptions.*

See also

- Scala best practice: How to use the Option/Some/None pattern[1]
- Oracle's Unchecked Exceptions: The Controversy[2]
- I think the first time I heard of the Happy and Unhappy Path terms was in an article titled, First steps with monads in Scala[3]

---

[1] http://alvinalexander.com/scala/best-practice-option-some-none-pattern-scala-idioms
[2] https://docs.oracle.com/javase/tutorial/essential/exceptions/runtime.html
[3] https://darrenjw.wordpress.com/2016/04/15/first-steps-with-monads-in-scala/

52

Functional Error Handling (Option, Try, Or, and Either)

Goals

As you saw in the previous lesson, functional programmers *never* write functions that throw exceptions. As I show in that lesson, a main replacement for throwing exceptions is to return an Option.

As I mentioned, that was a bit of a simplification. While you'll use Option a lot, depending on your needs you may also want to use other Scala classes like Try and Either. In addition to those you can also use third-party approaches like the Or construct in the Scalactic library[1].

This lesson shows each of these approaches, along with the pros and cons of each approach.

Option, Some, and None

I covered Option in the previous lesson, so all I'll do here is repeat the code I showed in that lesson:

```
def makeInt(s: String): Option[Int] = {
    try {
        Some(s.trim.toInt)
    } catch {
        case e: Exception => None
    }
}


makeInt(input) match {
    case Some(i) => println(s"i = $i")
```

---
[1] http://www.scalactic.org/

```
        case None => println("toInt could not parse 'input'")
}

val result = makeInt(input).getOrElse(0)

val result = for {
    x <- makeInt("1")
    y <- makeInt("2")
    z <- makeInt("3")
} yield x + y + z
```

A weakness of Option

While those are idiomatic examples of how to use Option, it's important to note that Option has a weakness: it doesn't tell you anything about *why* something failed. For example, a consumer of the makeInt function can't tell *why* a String wasn't converted to an Int, it only knows that it got a None in return.

For the times when this is a problem, Scala/FP developers use constructs that work like Option but also tell them *why* something failed. These constructs include Try and Either in the Scala API, and Or in the Scalactic library. The rest of this lesson shows those other approaches.

Try, Success, and Failure

When you want to let consumers of your code know *why* something failed, use Try instead of Option. Just like Option has Some (the success case) and None (the failure case), Try has Success and Failure subclasses — and Failure contains the reason why something failed.

To demonstrate this, here's the makeInt function rewritten using Try:

```
import scala.util.{Try, Success, Failure}
def makeInt(s: String): Try[Int] = Try(s.trim.toInt)
```

As shown, all you have to do to use Try is to wrap the exception-throwing code in a Try constructor, and then declare that your function returns its success value wrapped in a Try, such as makeInt returning the type Try[Int] in this example. The REPL shows how this version of makeInt works:

```
scala> makeInt("1")
```

```
res0: scala.util.Try[Int] = Success(1)

scala> makeInt("foo")
res1: scala.util.Try[Int] = Failure(java.lang.NumberFormatException:
    For input string: "foo")
```

The benefit of Try over Option is that when the enclosed code throws an exception, Try returns a Failure object that contains the exception information. That can be useful for logging, or to show a user why something failed.

Like Option, Try also works with match expressions:

```
makeInt("hello") match {
    case Success(i) => println(s"Success, value is: $i")
    case Failure(s) => println(s"Failed, message is: $s")
}
```

It can also be used in for expressions:

```
val answer = for {
    a <- makeInt("1")
    b <- makeInt("10")
} yield a + b
```

The REPL shows the output of the for expression:

```
scala> val answer = for {
     |     a <- makeInt("1")
     |     b <- makeInt("10")
     | } yield a + b
answer: scala.util.Try[Int] = Success(11)
```

See the Try class Scaladoc[2] for more information.

---

[2]http://www.scala-lang.org/api/current/scala/util/Try.html

Either, Left, and Right

An approach that's similar to Try is the Scala Either, Left, and Right classes. While Try has well-named subtypes in Success and Failure, Either relies on convention:

- Left holds the error
- Right holds the success value

Unfortunately, prior to Scala 2.12, that was just a convention. But, following that convention, this is what makeInt looks like when using Either:

```
def makeInt(s: String): Either[String,Int] = {
    try {
        Right(s.trim.toInt)
    } catch {
        case e: Exception => Left(e.toString)
    }
}
```

The REPL shows how this works:

```
scala> makeInt("1")
res0: Either[String,Int] = Right(1)

scala> makeInt("foo")
res1: Either[String,Int] = Left(java.lang.NumberFormatException:
    For input string: "foo")
```

Either can be used with match:

```
makeInt("11") match {
    case Left(s) => println("Error message: " + s)
    case Right(i) => println("Desired answer: " + i)
}
```

In Scala 2.12 Either was redesigned, so right is always the success case. This means that it implements map and flatMap, so it can now be used in for expressions. The REPL shows what this looks like:

```
// works with Scala 2.12 and newer
scala> val answer = for {
     |     a <- makeInt("1")
     |     b <- makeInt("10")
     | } yield a + b
answer: scala.util.Either[String,Int] = Right(11)
```

Using Or from Scalactic

The Scalactic project — created by Bill Venners, co-author of Programming in Scala[3], and creator of ScalaTest[4] — includes an Or construct that works like Option, and also gives you access to the failure message.

Because Scalactic is a third-party library you'll have to include it in your *build.sbt* file. See the Scalactic install page[5] for information on how to get it set up.

Once you have Scalactic set up with SBT, you can define makeInt like this:

```
def makeInt(s: String): Int Or ErrorMessage = {
    try {
        Good(s.trim.toInt)
    } catch {
        case e: Exception => Bad(e.toString)
    }
}
```

Notice that makeInt's signature is a little different than the previous examples:

```
def makeInt(s: String): Int Or ErrorMessage
```

The Int Or ErrorMessage makes it clear that this function is either going to return an Int *or* it's going to return an ErrorMessage. While that's implied with Option, Try, and Either, a benefit of Scalactic is that it makes this very clear.

Once you have makeInt defined, you can use it in all of the following ways. This line:

---

[3] http://amzn.to/2fiqDBh
[4] http://www.scalatest.org/
[5] http://www.scalactic.org/install

```
println(makeInt("1"))
```

prints "Good(1)." This line:

```
println(makeInt("boo"))
```

prints:

```
Bad(java.lang.NumberFormatException: For input string: "boo")
```

This *match* expression:

```
makeInt("11") match {
    case Good(i) => println("Answer: " + i)
    case Bad(msg) => println("Error: " + msg)
}
```

prints:

```
Answer: 11
```

And this *for* expression code:

```
val result = for {
    a <- makeInt("1")
    b <- makeInt("10")
} yield a + b
println(result)
```

prints:

```
Good(11)
```

Scalactic has even more features, including the ability to accumulate error messages. See the Scalactic "Or and Every" page[6] for more information.

---

[6]http://www.scalactic.org/user_guide/OrAndEvery

Personal recommendation

These days I generally use `Option` when I don't care about the failure reason, and I use `Try` or `Or` when I need the failure reason.

Don't forget the Null Object Pattern

As a final note on functional error handling, don't forget that it can sometimes make sense to use the Null Object Pattern[7]. A simple example of this is that you may have a function that returns a `List[Int]`:

```
def doSomething(x: List[Int]): List[Int] = ...
```

With a function like this it can make sense to return an empty `List` rather than using `Option`, `Try`, `Either`, or `Or`:

```
def doSomething(list: List[Int]): List[Int] = {
    if (someTestCondition(list)) {
        // return some version of `list`
    } else {
        // return an empty List
        Nil: List[Int]
    }
}
```

One example of where you can see this in real-world code is with the `filter` method of the Scala `List` class. It returns an empty `List` when you filter out all of the `List` elements:

```
scala> List(1,2,3).filter(_ > 10)
res0: List[Int] = List()
```

Handling `null` values

In all of these examples I showed the `makeInt` function, which handles an exception and returns an `Option`, `Try`, `Either`, or `Or` value. It's important to note that you should use the same technique when dealing with `null` values.

---

[7]http://alvinalexander.com/scala/scala-null-object-pattern-example

For example, when using the Apache HttpClient Java library[8] as shown below, the `entity` variable can end up being `null`:

```
val httpGetRequest = new HttpGet(someUrl)
val httpClient = new DefaultHttpClient
val httpResponse = httpClient.execute(httpGetRequest)
val entity = httpResponse.getEntity()   // null?
```

Rather than returning a `null` value, a Scala/FP function that works with code like this should handle the `null` value just like the previous examples handled the exception:

```
if (entity == null) {
    None
} else {
    val inputStream = entity.getContent
    content = io.Source.fromInputStream(inputStream).getLines.mkString
    inputStream.close
    Some(content)
}
```

A technical term: "Biasing"

On the Scalactic Or and Every page[9] you'll find this text:

> "Or differs from Scala's `Either` type in that `Either` treats both its `Left` and `Right` alternatives in an identical manner, whereas `Or` treats its two alternatives differently: it favors `Good` over `Bad`. Because of this, it is more convenient to work with `Or` when you prefer one alternative over the other; for example, if one alternative represents a valid result and another represents an error."

The technical term for this is to say that `Or` is *biased* to the `Good` result. Similarly `Option` is biased to `Some`, and `Try` is biased to `Success`.

As an example of what this means, if `makeInt` returns a `Some` in a `for` expression, the expression continues, but if it returns a `None`, the `for` expression effectively short-circuits at that point.

---

[8] https://hc.apache.org/httpcomponents-client-ga/
[9] http://www.scalactic.org/user_guide/OrAndEvery

Note: The Scalactic quote was true about Either prior to Scala 2.12, but Either is now biased, and Right is always the success case.)

Key points

In summary, when you're working with code where (a) you want to use something like Option, but (b) you also want the "failure reason," you should use the Scala error-handling constructs Try, Or (from the Scalactic library), or Either.

Table 52.1 shows a comparison of these error-handling classes.

Base Type	Success Case	Failure Case
Option	Some	None
Try	Success	Failure
Or	Good	Bad
Either	Right	Left

Table 52.1: Error-handling classes you can use with Scala.

Table 52.2 shows how I use each set of "optional" classes.

Construct	When to use
Option	When you don't need the error message
Try	Particularly good when you want to wrap exceptions
Or	An alternative to Try when you want the "failure reason"
Either	I don't use Either (because of its unbiased history and naming conventions)

Table 52.2: How I recommend using Scala's "optional" classes.

Lastly, remember that the Null Object Pattern can make sense in certain situations.

What's next

Now that you've seen how Scala's `for` expression works, and how to properly implement error-handling in your Scala/FP code, the next lesson takes a few moments to discussion "idiomatic" Scala/FP code.

See also

- Easing Into Functional Error Handling in Scala[10] by Long Cao was the inspiration for this lesson
- I originally wrote about this topic in a lesson titled, Scala best practice: How to use the Option/Some/None pattern[11]
- The Scalactic website[12]
- The Scalactic "Or and Every" page[13]

---
[10] http://longcao.org/2015/06/15/easing-into-functional-error-handling-in-scala
[11] http://alvinalexander.com/scala/best-practice-option-some-none-pattern-scala-idioms
[12] http://www.scalactic.org/
[13] http://www.scalactic.org/user_guide/OrAndEvery

53

Embrace The Idioms!

> *Idiom: The peculiar character or genius of a language.*
> The definition of "idiom" from dictionary.com

Before you proceed any further in this book you need to be completely convinced that the ways I've shown to write Scala/FP code in this book are better than the ways that you've written imperative code in the past. First, you must buy into the Scala/FP "rules" I outlined early in the book:

1. Scala/FP code has no `null` values
2. Only *pure functions* will be used
3. Immutable variables will be used for all fields (`val` fields)
4. Whenever you use an `if`, you must always also use an `else`

Over the last few lessons I showed several more examples of idiomatic Scala/FP code, including:

1. Because pure functions don't throw exceptions, they instead return `Option`, `Try`, and `Or`
2. Because you never use `null`, you instead use `Option`, `Try`, and `Or`

It's important at this point to believe that all of these points represent better ways to write Scala code than the imperative code you've written up until this point in your career. Quite frankly, if you aren't sold that these approaches are better, there really isn't any reason to read any further, because the rest of this book builds on these points.

Idiomatic Scala/FP

Although I haven't covered all of these topics yet, it's worth pointing out at this point what idiomatic Scala/FP code looks like:

- It uses only pure functions

- It uses `val`, not `var`
- Using only `val` requires using recursion and common collections methods like `map`, `filter`, `fold`, `reduce`
- It uses `Option`, `Try`, and `Or` rather than exceptions or `null` values
- It uses `case` classes with *immutable* fields rather than "OOP" classes with *mutable* fields

Those idioms naturally lead to:

- Scala/FP code uses a lot of `for` expressions, which work well with types like `Option`
- Scala/FP code uses a lot of `match` expressions (pattern matching), which work well with `case` classes

Don't try to make your Scala code look like something else

To demonstrate the point of this lesson — to embrace the Scala/FP idioms — let me share a story from my own history, from somewhere around the year 2000. It goes like this ...

At the time I owned a software consulting firm, and we were trying to teach Java and OOP to developers at a Fortune 500 company. One of their programmers had previously used Visual Basic (VB), and when we started working with him he was trying to write Java code by using the VB standards he knew.

I never used VB so I don't know what those standards were, but I do know that his Java code looked like this:

```
public int Get_Some_Int_Value() {
    int SomeValue = 1;
    int AnotherValue = 2;
    return SomeValue + AnotherValue;
}
```

If you know Java, you know that even in this trivial example that code doesn't look right at all. Java standards look like this:

```
public int getSomeIntValue() {
    int someValue = 1;
    int anotherValue = 2;
    return someValue + anotherValue;
}
```

The important point for this lesson — and for your career — is that you shouldn't try to make your Scala code look like Java, VB, or any other programming language. And specifically in the case of this book: embrace the Scala/FP idioms! Only by embracing the idioms will you see that there's a different way to write your applications, and that different way may result in safer code that's generally easier to understand.

54

What to Think When You See That Opening Curly Brace

"My mother had a great deal of trouble with me, but I think she enjoyed it."

Mark Twain

During the process of writing this book I had to get away from Scala for a while, and when I came back to it one of the first things I saw was some code that looked like this:

```
val x = FOO {
    // more code here
}
```

More accurately, the code I saw looked like this:

```
val x = FOO { (s: State) =>
    // more code here
}
```

Right away I had to ask myself, "Okay, Al, what in the world is FOO, and how does this code work?" It turns out that depending on exactly what the code looks like, FOO can be one of several things.

This style of code is used a lot by experienced Scala developers, so if you don't know what FOO is, it's another potential stumbling block to learning Scala/FP. Therefore, this lesson is about what FOO can possibly be when you see code that looks like that.

The short answer

The short answer is that FOO in this example:

```
val x = FOO {
    // more code here
}
```

can be several things:

- An anonymous class
- A function that takes a by-name parameter

If the code is slightly different and looks like this:

```
val f = FOO { (a: String) =>
    // more code here
}
```

it can be:

- A class that takes a function parameter
- A function that takes a by-name parameter

I'll show examples of each of these in this lesson.

1) An anonymous class

In this code:

```
val mary = new Person {
    val name = "mary"
    val age = 22
}
```

I create an instance of `Person` using Scala's "anonymous class" syntax. There's no way for you to know it by looking at this code, but I could have defined `Person` as either a trait or an abstract class (or less likely as a class), but for this example I created it as a trait:

```
trait Person {
    def name: String
    def age: Int
    override def toString = s"name: $name, age: $age"
}
```

When you paste that trait into the Scala REPL, and then also paste in this code:

```
val mary = new Person {
    val name = "mary"
    val age = 22
}
println(mary)
```

you'll see this output:

```
name: mary, age: 22
```

Discussion

One thing you know about Person is that *it's not* a case class. case classes don't allow the use of the new keyword, and they also must have at least one constructor parameter.

It's also unlikely, though possible, that Person is defined as a class. If Person is a class with name and age fields, those fields would require an override qualifier when mary is created. The only way Person can be a class in this example is if name and age are not defined in the class.

2) A function that takes a by-name parameter

A second thing that can look like this F00 example:

```
val x = F00 {
    // more code here
}
```

is a function that takes a by-name parameter.

In the Scala Cookbook[1] I shared a timer function that can be used like this:

```
val (result, time) = timer {
    // some long-running block of code here ...
    Thread.sleep(1000)
```

---
[1] http://amzn.to/24ivK4G

```
        42
}
```

When I run that code I get a result like this:

```
result: 42, time: 1004.819575
```

As that example shows, the `timer` function does three things:

- Accepts a block of code
- Runs the block of code
- Returns the result of that code along with the length of time it took to run

In the Cookbook I showed that `timer` is a function that's defined to accept a *by-name* parameter named `blockOfCode`:

```
def timer[A](blockOfCode: => A) = {
    val startTime = System.nanoTime
    val result = blockOfCode
    val stopTime = System.nanoTime
    val delta = stopTime - startTime
    (result, delta/1000000d)
}
```

Therefore, for the purposes of this lesson, this `timer` code:

```
val (result, time) = timer {
    Thread.sleep(1000)
    42
}
```

demonstrates that a function that takes a by-name parameter is a second way to let people write code that looks like this pattern:

```
val x = FOO {
    // more code here
}
```

3) A class that takes a function parameter

Another code pattern that you'll see that looks similar to the first two examples is this:

```
val f = FOO { (a: String) =>
    // more code here
}
```

In this code, FOO is either:

- A case class that takes a function input parameter (FIP)
- A function that takes a FIP

Furthermore, in this example that FIP must be defined to take one input parameter that is either a String or a generic type. As an example, you can create a case class that meets that criteria like this:

```
case class StringToInt(run: String => Int)
```

In this code, run is declared to be a FIP that transforms a String to an Int.

You can create an instance of that class by giving it an anonymous function, like this:

```
val stringToInt = StringToInt { s: String =>
    // algorithm can be as long as needed ...
    s.length
}
```

Now that you've created the stringToInt variable, you can call the run function on it at any later time:

```
// prints "7"
println(stringToInt.run("bananas"))
```

Note 1: Blurring out some code

One key to understand what's happening with those curly braces is to recognize that the code shown in Figure 54.1 is a function literal that takes a single input parameter (a String), and returns an Int (because the last line of the code block evaluates to an Int).

```
                           { s: String =>
        s.length
    }
```

Figure 54.1: Blurring out code to understand what's happening in the curly braces.

I find that "blurring out" code like that in my mind is a helpful technique to see the function literal when I see curly braces used like this.

Note 2: `run` is just a field in the class

Another important point to understand is that because `run` is a constructor input parameter:

```
case class StringToInt(run: String => Int)
                       ---
```

it also becomes a public field in the `StringToInt` class. It's a field in that class just like `name` is a field in this `Person` class:

```
case class Person(name: String)
```

Because `name` and `run` are both fields of their classes, this code:

```
val p = Person("mary")
println(p.name)
```

is similar to this code:

```
val stringToInt = StringToInt { s: String =>
    s.length
}
println(stringToInt.run("bananas"))
```

Note 3: Passing in a real function

If what's happening in the `StringToInt` code isn't clear, you may find that it's easier to pass in an instance of a *named* function as opposed to using an anonymous function. To demonstrate this, rather than giving `StringToInt` an anonymous function, define a "regular," named function that matches `run`'s signature, i.e., a function that transforms a `String` to an `Int`:

```
def len(s: String) = s.length
```

Now you can create a new instance of `StringToInt` by passing `len` into `StringToInt`'s constructor:

```
val stringToInt = StringToInt(len)
```

This is the same approach as before, except this time I declared `len` as a regular, named function.

Note 4: A more complicated example

Here's a slightly more complicated example of this technique. The following code shows a class that's defined to take a function (a FIP) that has two input parameters of generic type A, and transforms those parameters into a potentially different type B:

```
case class Transform2ParamsTo1Param[A, B](fun: (A, A) => B)
```

To be clear, here's the FIP signature by itself:

```
fun: (A, A) => B
```

Now I can write code like this to create an instance of `Transform2ParamsTo1Param`:

```
val x = Transform2ParamsTo1Param { (a: String, b: String) =>
    a.length + b.length
}
```

Then I can call `fun` on x like this:

```
// prints "6"
println(x.fun("foo", "bar"))
```

Because `Transform2ParamsTo1Param` defines its function input parameter `fun` to take generic types, I can also write code like this to take two `Int` values and return an `Int`:

```
val y = Transform2ParamsTo1Param { (a: Int, b: Int) =>
    a + b
}

// prints "3"
println(y.fun(1, 2))
```

While this might seem a little unusual if you come from an OOP background, this is just another example of a class that takes a function input parameter, i.e., an example of passing functions around.

> If code like this isn't comfortable right now, fear not, it wasn't comfortable to me initially either. In my experience, I never got comfortable with it until I started

using the technique in my own code. (Pro tip: Write a lot of code. As the saying goes, "One learns by doing the thing.")

4) A function that takes a function input parameter

Getting back to my FOO examples ... another code pattern that can look like this:

```
val f = FOO { (a: String) =>
    // more code here
}
```

is when a function takes a FIP. I'll show a variation of that in this section.

The following code looks like the FOO and Transform2ParamsTo1Param examples:

```
val res = s2i("hello") { s: String =>
    s.length
}
```

However, in this case s2i is either a case class, or a function that has two parameter groups. This code tells you that s2i's first parameter group must take a String parameter (hello in this case), and the second parameter group takes a function that transforms a String to an Int (or it may use generic types).

While s2i can be implemented as either a function or as a case class, it's most likely a function. I show both approaches next.

a) Implemented as a function

The function approach will have two parameter groups that look like this:

```
def s2i (s: String)(f: String => Int) = f(s)
```

You can verify this by pasting the following code into the Scala REPL:

```
def s2i (s: String)(f: String => Int) = f(s)

val res = s2i("hello") { s: String =>
    s.length
}
```

```
println(res)
```

That last line will print the number 5. This is a straightforward implementation of s2i.

b) Implemented as a *case* class

While this solution is a little more convoluted, it's *possible* that s2i can be implemented as a case class, like this:

```
case class s2i (s: String)(_fun: String => Int) {
    def fun = _fun(s)
}

val res = s2i("hello") { s: String =>
    s.length
}

println(res.fun)
```

As the code shows, the primary difference to the consumer of s2i is that for the class you must call println(res.fun) to see the result, as opposed to calling println(res) with the function.

Aside: A practical use of multiple parameter groups

In the Scala Cookbook I shared a practical example of the multiple parameter group approach with this using code:

```
using(io.Source.fromFile("example.txt")) { source =>
    for (line <- source.getLines) {
        println(line)
    }
}
```

using is cool because it automatically calls the close method on the resource that's passed into it in the first parameter group. As you'll see in the code that follows, it calls close *after* the function that's passed into the second parameter group is run. This is a smart and useful application of this technique.

In this case, using is defined as a function, like this:

```
def using[A <: { def close(): Unit }, B](resource: A)(f: A => B): B = {
    try {
        f(resource)
    } finally {
        resource.close()
    }
}
```

> Notes: I first learned about the using control structure in the book, Beginning Scala[2]. See the Scala Cookbook[3] for a more thorough discussion of this code. Somewhere in history, someone named this code a "Loan Pattern[4]," and Joshua Suereth implemented the same technique in his Scala ARM Library[5].

5) A non-FP possibility: Reassignable Properties

There's another technique that enables code like this, but a) the technique is rarely used, and b) it would never be used in functional programming. Therefore, I won't write about it here, but if you're interested in a technique that lets you write Scala/OOP code like this:

```
def top = new MainFrame {
    title = "First Swing App"
    contents = new Button {
        text = "Click me"
    }
}
```

see my article, Reassignable variables and properties[6].

Key points

The following code examples provide a summary of the key points of this lesson.

---

[2]http://amzn.to/1MRH8tp
[3]http://amzn.to/24ivK4G
[4]https://wiki.scala-lang.org/display/SYGN/Loan
[5]https://github.com/jsuereth/scala-arm
[6]http://alvinalexander.com/scala/reassignable-variables-properties-def-fields-anonymous-class

Anonymous class

This code shows the creation of a `Person` instance using the "anonymous class" technique:

```
val mary = new Person {
    val name = "mary"
    val age = 22
}
```

In this specific example, `Person` may be defined as a trait or abstract class, or (much less likely) as a class.

A function that has a by-name parameter

In this example, `timer` is implemented as a function that declares a by-name parameter, and therefore takes a block of code:

```
val (result, time) = timer {
    // some long-running block of code here
    // ...
}
```

I implemented `timer` like this:

```
def timer[A](blockOfCode: => A) = {
    val startTime = System.nanoTime
    val result = blockOfCode
    val stopTime = System.nanoTime
    val delta = stopTime - startTime
    (result, delta/1000000d)
}
```

A case class that takes a function parameter

In this code, `StringToInt` is implemented as a `case` class that has a function input parameter (FIP), and that FIP apparently transforms a `String` to an `Int`:

```
val stringToInt = StringToInt { s: String =>
    s.length
}
```

For that code I defined this case class:

```
case class StringToInt(run: String => Int)
```

(It's possible that the FIP also uses generic types.)

A case class that takes a FIP that has multiple input parameters

In this example:

```
val x = Transform2ParamsTo1Param { (a: String, b: String) =>
    a.length + b.length
}
```

Transform2ParamsTo1Param is defined as a case class that has a FIP, and that FIP must take two input parameters itself:

```
case class Transform2ParamsTo1Param[A, B](fun: (A, A) => B)
```

A function or class that has multiple parameter groups

I also showed that when you see code like this:

```
val res = s2i("hello") { s: String =>
    s.length
}
```

s2i will be a function or case class that has two parameter groups. It's much more likely to be a function, which will be implemented like this:

```
def s2i (s: String)(f: String => Int) = f(s)
```

It's possible that it could also be a case class, which will be written like this:

```
case class s2i (s: String)(_fun: String => Int) {
    def fun = _fun(s)
}
```

Pattern recognition

I wrote this lesson because over the last few years I've begun to look at computer programming as a form of pattern recognition. This was first made clear to me when I was reading a book about Lisp titled, The Little Schemer[7], where the authors state:

> "The goal of this book is to teach the reader to think recursively ... It is our belief that writing programs recursively in Scheme is essentially simple pattern recognition."

Some patterns are easy for most programmers to understand, and they're adopted in many programming languages. Other patterns are easy for some programmers to recognize, but not for others. As I noted in this lesson, I stumbled on this pattern when I came back to Scala after a brief absence:

```
val x = FOO {
    // more code here
}
```

As a result, I tried to understand all of the things that FOO could possibly be, and I shared that information here.

A final reason I mention this specific pattern is because Scala/FP developers use it very often. Because you'll see it a lot in the code that follows, I wanted to be sure I covered it here.

---

[7]http://amzn.to/2rk1NTC

55

A Quick Review of How `flatMap` Works

> *"The main use case for `flatMap` is iterating over multiple collections."*
>
> (author unknown)

Overview

This lesson shows how `flatMap` is like using `map` followed by `flatten` on the Scala collections classes. As usual, if you're already comfortable with this topic, skip this lesson.

Why would I ever need `flatMap`?

When I first started working with Scala, I assumed `flatMap` was some obscure method on the collections classes that I'd never use. I thought, "Why would I ever need to transform *one element* into a *list* of different elements?" That is, why would I ever want transform this:

```
"foo"
```

into this:

```
List("f", "o", "o")
```

So I ignored `flatMap` for a long time, but then when I started trying to learn Scala/FP, I found that functional programmers *really* love `flatMap`.

Therefore, before you get into the lessons that follow this one, it will help to take a few moments to quickly review how `flatMap` works. I'll start by showing how `map` works before getting into `flatMap`.

A quick review of map's type signature

The type signature for the map method on the Scala List class looks like this:

```
map[B](f: A => B): List[B]
```

This part of the signature:

```
f: A => B
```

tells us that map takes a function input parameter (FIP), and that FIP must transform an element of type A into an element of type B. In this signature, A is the type held by the current List, so map on a List[Int] will take a FIP that has this signature:

```
f: Int => B
```

Next, this part of map's signature:

```
: List[B]
```

says that when map is finished running it will return a List whose elements are all of type B. This tells us that the function map is given will transform all of the individual List elements from type A to type B, and then map somehow accumulates all of those elements and returns a List[B] when it finishes.

While this type signature is cool because it tells us exactly what can *possibly* happen, it also helps to see a specific example. Here's an example that shows how to transform List[String] into a List[Int] by using a function that transforms a String to an Int:

```
scala> val x = List("hi", "world").map(s => s.length)
x: List[Int] = List(2, 5)
```

In this code map applies the anonymous function s => s.length to each element in the original List[String] to yield a new List[Int].

Note that I could have written that anonymous function using this more concise syntax:

```
List("hi", "world").map(_.length)
```

but I showed the verbose syntax because that's what I'll be using in many of the examples that follow.

At this point a key thing to note is that map uses the function it's given to transform one input list to one output list.

flatMap's type signature

flatMap's type signature is different than map's:

flatMap[B](f: A => GenTraversableOnce[B]): List[B]

For the purposes of a List you can simplify this by changing GenTraversableOnce to List, like this:

flatMap[B](f: A => List[B]): List[B]

Where map takes a function that transforms an A to a B — such as a String to an Int:

f: A => B

flatMap takes a function that transforms an A to a List[B]:

f: A => List[B]

An example of this is a function that takes the string "foo" as input, and returns List["f", "o", "o"] as a result. (More on this shortly.)

Notice that despite the fact that map and flatMap take different types of function input parameters, they both return a List[B] in the end:

: List[B]

This implies that even though flatMap takes a function that transforms one input element "foo" into a List["f", "o", "o"] — and then transforms a second element "bar" into List["b", "a", "r"], etc. — in the end it somehow transforms List["f", "o", "o"] and List["b", "a", "r"] into a single list in the end, in this case returning, List["f", "o", "o", "b", "a", "r"].

Conceptually the way this works is that flatMap first applies the given function to each of its elements. For instance, it applies a function to "Foo" to get List["f", "o", "o"]. As flatMap runs, this creates an intermediate "list of lists," such as List(List("f", "o", "o"), List("b", "a", "r")). Finally, the last thing it does is to *flatten* all of those lists into one final list.

You can see this by comparing the two approaches. First, this example shows how flatMap works on a List[String], given the anonymous function shown:

scala> List("foo", "bar").flatMap(s => s.split(""))
res0: List[String] = List(f, o, o, b, a, r)

You can make sense of this result by breaking `flatMap` into two steps. First, run `map` on the input list to get an intermediate result, i.e., the "list of lists" I mentioned. I'll store this result in a variable named `tmpLol`:

```
scala> val tmpLol = List("foo", "bar").map(s => s.split(""))
tmpLol: List[Array[String]] = List(Array(f, o, o), Array(b, a, r))
```

As that output shows, `tmpLol` now contains `List(Array(f, o, o), Array(b, a, r))`. (Although the intermediate result shows a `List` of `Arrays`, that's just an implementation detail; just think of it as a "list of lists.")

Now, when you apply `flatten` to that intermediate result you get the exact same result that I got when applying `flatMap` to the original list:

```
scala> tmpLol.flatten
res1: List[String] = List(f, o, o, b, a, r)
```

This tells us:

- In the first step, `flatMap` transforms "foo" into `Array(f, o, o)`

- Next, it transforms "bar" into `Array(b, a, r)`

- At this point `flatMap` has applied the given function to all of its input `List` elements, and it has an intermediate result of `List(Array(f, o, o), Array(b, a, r))`

- In its last step, `flatMap` transforms that "list of lists" into one final list, i.e., `List(f, o, o, b, a, r)`

What this means

As I mentioned, when I first started using Scala I thought `flatMap` was a bizarre construct that I would never use. But as you saw in the lessons about creating a custom sequence class to work with the `for` expression, `flatMap` plays a key role in getting your custom class to work with `for`.

In fact, because `flatMap` can be a little hard to understand, we're fortunate that Martin Odersky & Company created the `for` expression as some really sweet syntactic sugar for `flatMap` — as you're about to see.

See also

If you want to see more examples of how `flatMap` works with collections classes, see my article, A collection of Scala 'flatMap' examples[1].

---

[1] http://alvinalexander.com/scala/collection-scala-flatmap-examples-map-flatten

56

Option Naturally Leads to flatMap

In the last few lessons I demonstrated some things about `Option` and `flatMap` without explaining *why* they were important, other than to say, "You'll see why this is important soon."

Now you're at that point: In this lesson you'll begin to see why `Option` and `flatMap` are so important to the functional programming style.

Options on top of Options

In the real world there's a "cause and effect" relationship that happens when you use `Option` as a wrapper for your function return types. If the *cause* is that you use `Option` because it's better than exceptions and `null` values, the *effect* is that all of those `Options` eventually coalesce at some point.

I'll demonstrate what I mean with our old friend, the `makeInt` function, and then I'll show a more real-world example.

makeInt

To begin, here's the `makeInt` function I showed a few lessons ago:

```
def makeInt(s: String): Option[Int] = {
    try {
        Some(s.trim.toInt)
    } catch {
        case e: Exception => None
    }
}
```

This is an awesome function, right? By catching the exception inside the function and returning an `Int` wrapped in an `Option`, the function always returns *something* to its calling function. It doesn't try to throw an exception that will short-circuit the rest of your code. This is good. This is how pure functions work.

Although that's good, can you guess what happens when you have code like this, and then you want to add x and y:

```
val x = makeInt(string1)
val y = makeInt(string2)
```

The REPL shows what you'd expect, that x and y have the type Option[Int]:

```
scala> val x = makeInt("1")
x: Option[Int] = Some(1)

scala> val y = makeInt("2")
y: Option[Int] = Some(2)
```

This means that you can't just add x and y:

```
scala> x + y
<console>:14: error: type mismatch;
 found    : Option[Int]
 required: String
       x + y
         ^
```

In fact, the REPL is confused and doesn't even know that you want to try to add two Ints, because those Ints are wrapped inside of Options.

So, what can you do? Let's think, what are our main tools for working with Option values? So far I've used:

- match expressions, or more rarely,
- getOrElse

Let's see what we can do with those.

Adding x and y with `match` expressions

If you try to add x and y using `match` expressions, you end up with code like this:

```
val sum = x match {
    case None => {
        y match {
            case None => {
                0
            }
            case Some(i) => {
                i
            }
        }
    }
    case Some(i) => {
        y match {
            case None => {
                i
            }
            case Some(j) => {
                i + j
            }
        }
    }
}
```

I have to be honest: that code is so ugly I didn't even both to see if it would compile. I definitely don't want to use this approach.

Adding x and y with `getOrElse`

Here's how you might try to do the same thing with `getOrElse`:

```
val sum = x.getOrElse(0) + y.getOrElse(0)
```

That's a bit cleaner, but fortunately some smart people found that there's a better approach that's much more powerful.

Adding x and y with flatMap and map

Somewhere in programming history, someone saw that if you try to add x and y using map:

```
x map { a =>
    y map { b =>
        a + b
    }
}
```

the result would look like this:

```
scala> x map { a => y map { b => a + b }}
res0: Option[Option[Int]] = Some(Some(3))
```

That's interesting; it almost works. The desired result is wrapped inside two Option values. I suspect that seeing the Option[Option[Int]] made them think, "I can make this situation a little better by flattening at least one of those Options … hmm, the word 'flatten' makes me think of flatMap … what if …"

That thought process led to them using flatMap in place of the first map:

```
scala> x flatMap { a => y map { b => a + b }}
res1: Option[Int] = Some(3)
```

"Whoa," they thought, "this gives me the solution wrapped inside only one Option. Now that's something I can work with!"

And then they remembered the relationship between map, flatMap, and the for expression, and a very cool thing happened … (see the next lesson).

57

flatMap Naturally Leads to for

"Since a type like Option that supports map and flatMap can be used in a for expression," they thought, "What would happen if I do this?":

```
val sum = for {
    x <- makeInt("1")
    y <- makeInt("2")
} yield x + y
```

The REPL shows the answer:

```
scala> val sum = for {
     |     x <- makeInt("1")
     |     y <- makeInt("2")
     | } yield x + y
sum: Option[Int] = Some(3)
```

"Whoa," they thought, "not only does this give me the solution wrapped in only one Option, it's also much easier to read than using map and flatMap."

And then they thought, "Because it supports map and flatMap, it should work with more than two Option values, right?" So they put this code in the REPL:

```
val sum = for {
    a <- makeInt("1")
    b <- makeInt("2")
    c <- makeInt("3")
    d <- makeInt("4")
} yield a + b + c + d
```

and saw this result:

```
scala> val sum = for {
     |     a <- makeInt("1")
     |     b <- makeInt("2")
     |     c <- makeInt("3")
     |     d <- makeInt("4")
     | } yield a + b + c + d
sum: Option[Int] = Some(10)
```

Success!

This is much better than chaining together a whole bunch of `flatMap` and `map` functions, and it's even easier to read than using a bunch of `getOrElse` calls.

> And as you're about to see, it's also more flexible (and safer) than using `getOrElse`.

58

for Expressions are Better Than getOrElse

A great thing about using `for` expressions that might not be immediately obvious is that they're better than using a series of `getOrElse` calls. I'll demonstrate what I mean in this lesson.

The `for` expression "Happy Path"

Imagine asking a user to input four `Int` values as strings. You could then sum those values using this `for` expression:

```
val sum = for {
    a <- makeInt(input1)
    b <- makeInt(input2)
    c <- makeInt(input3)
    d <- makeInt(input4)
} yield a + b + c + d
```

Next, assume that they gave you exactly what you asked for, four strings that properly convert to integers, like this:

```
val sum = for {
    a <- makeInt("1")
    b <- makeInt("2")
    c <- makeInt("3")
    d <- makeInt("4")
} yield a + b + c + d
```

This specific example shows the *Happy Path* for this `for` expression. When I say, "Happy Path," it means that you got the input values you desired – strings that convert to integers – and therefore the `for` expression completes properly, with `sum` ending up as `Option(10)`.

The for expression "Unhappy Path"

But a great thing about the for expression is that it also handles the *Unhappy Path*, i.e., the path that's followed when one or more of the String values don't convert to Int values:

```
val sum = for {
    a <- makeInt("ka-boom!")
    b <- makeInt("2")
    c <- makeInt("3")
    d <- makeInt("4")
} yield a + b + c + d
```

Can you guess what happens with this code?

Does it throw an exception? No, of course not, pure functions don't throw exceptions!

Does sum end up with a value? Yes, it does. sum is bound to None, as the REPL shows:

```
scala> val sum = for {
     |     a <- makeInt("ka-boom!")
     |     b <- makeInt("2")
     |     c <- makeInt("3")
     |     d <- makeInt("4")
     | } yield a + b + c + d
sum: Option[Int] = None
```

What happens is that the for expression short-circuits when this line of code is reached:

```
a <- makeInt("ka-boom!")
```

When makeInt receives a String it can't transform into an Int, these things happen:

- makeInt returns a None
- The for expression short-circuits at that point
- sum is bound to None

The None result tells you that makeInt was given something it couldn't convert to an Int.

> Even though this is an Unhappy Path, the good news is that the bad input doesn't completely blow up your for expression. The expression simply yields None, which is much better than throwing an exception.

Compare that to `getOrElse`

Compare that code to the only thing you can do with `getOrElse`:

```
val sum = makeInt(``ka-boom!'').getOrElse(0) +
        makeInt(``2'').getOrElse(0) +
        makeInt(``3'').getOrElse(0) +
        makeInt(``4'').getOrElse(0)
```

When you paste that code into the REPL, you'll see that `sum` is assigned to 9 — a completely different (and wrong) result!

If you think that's bad, this example just uses `Option[Int]` values; imagine what could happen when you use complex, real world classes like `Option[Person]`, `Option[Pizza]`, or `Option[List[List[Friend]]]`.

This is why experienced Scala/FP developers tell you not to use `getOrElse`. When you first start working with Scala it seems like `getOrElse` could be a good thing, but (a) it can also be an incorrect thing when used in the wrong places, and (b) in the long run it can keep you from seeing a much better solution in the `for` expression.

Remember: Embrace the idioms!

Key points

In the last several lessons I showed a `for` expression like this:

```
val sum = for {
    a <- makeInt(string1)
    b <- makeInt(string2)
    c <- makeInt(string3)
    d <- makeInt(string4)
} yield a + b + c + d
```

I mentioned that the Happy Path is when all of the `String` values can be converted to `Int` values and the expression yields a `Some[Int]`, and the Unhappy Path is what happens when a `String` value can't be converted to an `Int` and the expression yields a `None`.

Also, even though that code can be said to have Happy and Unhappy paths, the great thing about the `for` expression is that it handles both cases. In the Happy case `sum` is bound to an `Option[Int]`, and in the Unhappy case `sum` is bound to `None`.

In this lesson I also demonstrated that this code is better than a `getOrElse` approach because `getOrElse` can give you a wrong (or inappropriate) answer. Beyond that, as you'll see in the rest of this book, it can also keep you from embracing the Scala idioms that will lead you to a new style of coding.

What's next

If what's happening in the `for` expressions I've shown so far isn't clear, I hope to clear up any confusion in the next lesson.

59

Recap: Option → flatMap → for

I showed quite a few things in the previous lessons on for expressions, Option, and flatMap, so in this lesson I want to pause a little bit to review a few important points about what I just covered.

At the end of this lesson I'll share an important conclusion, so if you want to skip the "review" portions of this lesson, please be sure to read the conclusion sections (Parts 1 and 2) before moving on to the next lesson.

Point 1: If something can go wrong, a pure function returns Option, Try, or Or

The first point to reiterate is this: Because pure functions don't throw exceptions, they have to do something else when bad things happen, and in Scala, the correct approach is to return an Option, Try, or Or. For example, in my code, makeInt returns an Option[Int]:

```
def makeInt(s: String): Option[Int] = {
    try {
        Some(s.trim.toInt)
    } catch {
        case e: Exception => None
    }
}
```

Option *is a "wrapper"*

You can think of Option as a wrapper, kind of like receiving a wrapped gift on your birthday. In the case of makeInt, Option is a wrapper around an Int. An important feature of this particular wrapper is that it comes with map and flatMap methods. These enable Option to work in for expressions.

If you don't like to think of Option as a "wrapper," it might be even better to think of it as a box. When dealing with an Option[Int], Figure 59.1 shows the Happy Case, where you get a box that contains what you want, an Int, which the Option delivers to you as a Some[Int].

Figure 59.1: You can think of Option *as a box. This box shows a Happy Case, where a* Some[Int] *contains a* 2.

Conversely, in the Unhappy Case you get an empty box, which Option delivers to you as a None, as shown in Figure 59.2.

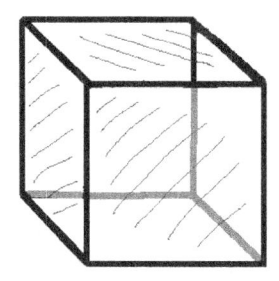

Figure 59.2: A None *can be thought of as an empty box.*

Point 2: How Option's map method works

A second important point is to know how Option's map method works. The key points are:

- It yields a Some[A] for the Happy (success) cases
- It yields a None for all Unhappy (failure) cases

A few REPL examples show this. First, when makeInt can successfully transform a String, it yields a Some[Int]:

```
scala> makeInt("1")
res0: Option[Int] = Some(1)
```

Second, when `makeInt` can't successfully transform a `String`, it yields a `None`:

```
scala> makeInt("foo")
res1: Option[Int] = None
```

As expected, you get a `Some(1)` in the success case and a `None` in the failure case. So far, so good.

Taking this a step further, these examples show how `map` behaves with `Option`'s two possible results:

```
scala> makeInt("1").map(_ * 2)
res2: Option[Int] = Some(2)

scala> makeInt("foo").map(_ * 2)
res3: Option[Int] = None
```

In the first case `makeInt` yields a `Some(1)` and then `map` is called on that result to yield a `Some(2)`. In the second case `makeInt` can't convert `"foo"` into an `Int` so it yields a `None` without even invoking `map`.

The important behavior for your code is that `map` doesn't throw an exception, it just goes down either the Happy Path (yielding a `Some[A]`) or the Unhappy Path (yielding a `None`).

Point 3: `flatMap` works well with multiple `Option`s

The next important point is that while `map` works well with *one* `Option`, `flatMap` shines when it comes to working with *multiple* `Option`s.

As I showed in the previous lessons, given this code:

```
val x = Option(1)
val y = Option(2)
```

if you try to add the two `Option[Int]` values with `map`, you end up with an `Option[Option[Int]]`:

```
scala> x map { a => y map { b => a + b }}
res0: Option[Option[Int]] = Some(Some(3))
```

But because of the way `flatMap` works, you can use it to replace the outer `map` call to yield an `Option[Int]`, which is much easier to work with:

```
scala> x flatMap { a => y map { b => a + b }}
res1: Option[Int] = Some(3)
```

Point 4: Humans prefer for expressions

While that's nice, it can be hard for humans to understand. Fortunately, this is exactly what the much more readable `for` expression does for you; it's a replacement for a series of `flatMap` and `map` calls. You can demonstrate this with the following code:

```
class Test {

    val sum = for {
        a <- makeInt("1")
        b <- makeInt("2")
        c <- makeInt("3")
        d <- makeInt("4")
    } yield a + b + c + d

    def makeInt(s: String): Option[Int] = {
        try {
            Some(s.trim.toInt)
        } catch {
            case e: Exception => None
        }
    }

}
```

When you compile that code with this command:

```
scalac -Xprint:parse Test.scala
```

you'll see this as part of the output:

```
val sum = makeInt("1").flatMap(
  ((a) => makeInt("2").flatMap(
    ((b) => makeInt("3").flatMap(
      ((c) => makeInt("4").map(
        ((d) => a.$plus(b).$plus(c).$plus(d)))))
      )
    )
  )
);
```

Note: You'll have to reformat `scalac`'s output to see it that clearly.

Notice that this is a series of `flatMap` calls followed by a single `map` call. This is how `for` expressions like this are converted by the Scala compiler. While compilers like that code, most humans don't, so we use `for` expressions.

Point 5: `for` isn't always a loop

As a final note, it's important to be clear that this is not a *loop*:

```
val sum = for {
    a <- makeInt("1")
    b <- makeInt("2")
    c <- makeInt("3")
    d <- makeInt("4")
} yield a + b + c + d
```

That is, it doesn't "loop" repeatedly, it just runs once. If you're coming to Scala/FP from languages like C, Java, C#, etc., this behavior can be a surprise.

Conclusion, Part 1

Here's a concise summary of the points I just covered:

- Because pure functions don't (a) return `null` or (b) throw exceptions, they return `Option`, `Try`, or `Or`
- Using `Option` naturally leads your code to look a certain way, a "pattern"

- In the real world that pattern eventually leads to the creation of values of the type Option[Option[A]]
- flatMap works well with Option[Option[A]], but it's hard for humans to read
- The Scala for expression is a human-readable replacement for a series of flatMap and map calls

A more-general observation

When you think about those statements more generally, you'll make this observation:

> *Any* class that implements map and flatMap can be used in a for expression in the same way that I used Option in these examples.

For example, not only does Option work like this, but Try, Or, and Either also work the same way. And they're not the only ones.

Scala collections classes have map and flatMap

The Scala Seq class implements the map and flatMap methods, so it can be used in for expressions, such as this one:

```
val xs = Seq(1,2,3)
val ys = Seq(100,200,300)

for {
    x <- xs
    y <- ys
} yield x + y
```

When that for expression is pasted into the REPL, it yields this result:

```
res0: Seq[Int] = List(101, 201, 301, 102, 202, 302, 103, 203, 303)
```

All of the Scala collections classes have map and flatMap methods and work like this, including List, ArrayBuffer, Vector, etc., even the Map classes.

The Scala Future has map and flatMap

The Scala Future class implements map and flatMap methods, so it can also be used in for expressions, as shown in this example:

```
// (a) create the futures
val f1 = Future { sleep(10*1000); 1 }
val f2 = Future { sleep(2*1000);  2 }
val f3 = Future { sleep(4*1000);  3 }

// (b) run them simultaneously in a for-comprehension
val result = for {
    r1 <- f1
    r2 <- f2
    r3 <- f3
} yield (r1 + r2 + r3)

// (c) do whatever you need to do with the result
result.onComplete {
   case Success(x) => println(s"\nresult = $x")
   case Failure(e) => e.printStackTrace
}
```

This is a particularly interesting example because like `Option`, `Future` is not a *collection* class. However, because it implements `map` and `flatMap`, it can be used in a for expression.

Conclusion, Part 2

Once again, here's the key observation: any class that implements `map` and `flatMap` can be used in a for expression.

Furthermore, while those of us with an OOP background are most comfortable using *collection classes* in for loops, the Scala/FP reality is that *non-collection classes* like `Option`, `Try`, `Future`, and many others can also be used in for expressions. These other classes tend to be "wrappers" of different types, which is why I've been using the term *wrapper*.

As it turns out, the Scala for expression is a sort of glue — a superglue — for getting pure functions to work together. The thing to remember is that for a class to be used with multiple generators in a for expression, that class must implement `map` and `flatMap`.

Similarly, for a function to work well in a for expression, it must return a type that implements `map` and `flatMap`. (I write more on this point in the lessons that follow.)

The m-word

And this is where we get to the fun part.

When speaking casually, some people like to say that any Scala class that implements map and flatMap is a *monad*. While that isn't 100% true, it's in the ballpark of truth.

As Gabriele Petronella wrote in a Stack Overflow post[1]:

> "The only thing monads are relevant for, from a Scala language perspective, is the ability of being used in a for-comprehension."

By this he means that while monads are defined more formally in a language like Haskell, in Scala there is no base Monad trait to extend; all you have to do is implement map and flatMap so your class can be used as a generator in for expressions.

As you'll see as I dig into this more in the coming lessons, classes like List and Option truly are monads, so congratulations — if you thought monads were hard, they aren't; you've already been using them!

See also

The "box" metaphor comes from this adit.io tutorial[2].

---

[1] http://stackoverflow.com/questions/25361203/what-exactly-makes-option-a-monad-in-scala
[2] http://adit.io/posts/2013-04-17-functors,_applicatives,_and_monads_in_pictures.html

60

A Note About Things That Can Be Mapped Over

Goal

The goal of this lesson is to explain a term known in functional programming as a "functor."

Discussion

As I mentioned earlier in this book, at some point in history someone declared that "things that can be mapped-over shall be called *functors*." Therefore, classes like `List`, `Option`, `Future`, and many others are all functors.

As Miran Lipovaca states in his book, Learn You a Haskell for Great Good![1]:

> "Functors are things that can be mapped over."

Think of it as a trait

In his blog post, First steps with monads[2], Darren Wilkinson makes the observation that in pseudocode, you can think of a functor as being a Scala `trait`:

```
trait Functor[A] {
    def map(f: A => B): Functor[B]
}
```

---

[1] http://amzn.to/1POaUCv
[2] https://darrenjw.wordpress.com/2016/04/15/first-steps-with-monads-in-scala/

You can then think of classes like `List`, `Option`, `Future`, and many others as implementing that trait.

Key point

The key point of this lesson: Don't be intimidated when you hear the term "functor"; just think of it like this:

> Functor = map-able

or this:

> Functor = a class that has a `map` method

See also

- The definition of "functor" on Wikipedia[3]
- Darren Wilkinson writes in his article, First steps with monads[4], "Many collection and other container types have a `map` method … any parameterized type that does have a `map` method like this is known as a Functor. Again, the name is due to category theory…"

---

[3] https://en.wikipedia.org/wiki/Functor
[4] https://darrenjw.wordpress.com/2016/04/15/first-steps-with-monads-in-scala/

61

Starting to Glue Functions Together

As I mentioned at the beginning of this book, writing pure functions isn't hard. Just make sure that output depends only on input, and you're in good shape.

The hard part of functional programming involves how you glue together all of your pure functions to make a complete application. Because this process feels like you're writing "glue" code, I refer to this process as "gluing," and as I learned, a more technical term for this is called "binding." This process is what most of the remainder of this book is about.

> As you might have guessed from the emphasis of the previous lessons, in Scala/FP this binding process involves the use of `for` expressions.

Life is good when the output of one function matches the input of another

To set the groundwork for where we're going, let's start with a simplified version of a problem you'll run into in the real world.

Imagine that you have two functions named f and g, and they both a) take an Int as an input parameter, and b) return an Int as their result. Therefore, their function signatures look like this:

```
def f(a: Int): Int = ???
def g(a: Int): Int = ???
```

A nice thing about these functions is that because the output of f is an Int, it perfectly matches the input of g, which takes an Int parameter. This is shown visually in Figure 61.1.

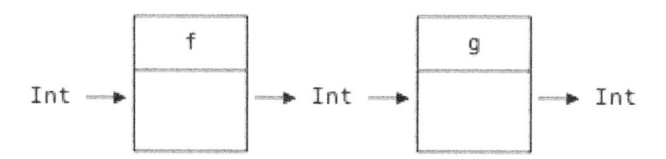

Figure 61.1: The output of f matches the input to g.

Because the output of f is a perfect match to the input of g, you can write this code:

```
val x = g(f(100))
```

Here's a complete example that demonstrates this:

```
def f(a: Int): Int = a * 2
def g(a: Int): Int = a * 3
val x = g(f(100))
println(x)
```

Because f(100) is 200 and g of 200 is 600, this code prints 600. So far, so good.

A new problem

Next, imagine a slightly more complicated set of requirements where f and g still take an Int as input, but now they return a String in addition to an Int. With this change their signatures look like this:

```
def f(a: Int): (Int, String) = ???
def g(a: Int): (Int, String) = ???
```

One possible use case for this situation is to imagine that f and g are functions in an application that uses a rules engine or artificial intelligence (AI). In this situation, not only do you want to know their result (the Int), you also want to know *how* they came up with their answer, i.e., the logical explanation in the form of a String.

> Think of writing an application to determine the shortest route from Point A to Point Z. A function might return a log message like, "I chose B as the next step because it was closer than C or D."

While it's nice to get a log message back from the functions, this also creates a problem: I can no longer use the output of f as the input to g. In this new world, g takes an Int input parameter, but f now returns (Int, String) (a Tuple2[Int, String]). This mismatch is shown visually in Figure 61.2.

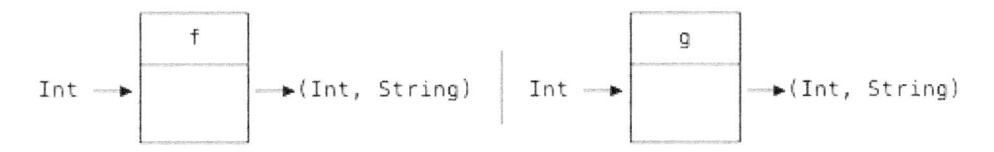

Figure 61.2: The output of f no longer matches the input to g.

When you *really* want to plug the output of f into the input of g, what can you do?

Solving the problem manually

Let's look at how we'd solve this problem manually. First, I'd get the result from f:

val (fInt, fString) = f(100)

Next, I pass fInt into g to get its results:

val (gInt, gString) = g(fInt)

gInt is the final Int result, so now I glue the strings together to get the final String result:

val logMessage = fString + gString

Now I can print the final Int and String results:

println(s"result: $gInt, log: $logMessage")

This code shows a complete example of the manual solution to this problem:

```
object Step2Debug extends App {

    def f(a: Int): (Int, String) = {
        val result = a * 2
        (result, s"\nf result: $result.")
    }

    def g(a: Int): (Int, String) = {
        val result = a * 3
        (result, s"\ng result: $result.")
    }

    // get the output of `f`
    val (fInt, fString) = f(100)

    // plug the Int from `f` as the input to `g`
    val (gInt, gString) = g(fInt)

    // create the total "debug string" by manually merging
    // the strings from f and g
    val debug = fString + " " + gString
    println(s"result: $gInt, debug: $debug")

}
```

That code prints this output:

```
result: 600, debug:
f result: 200.
g result: 600.
```

While this approach works for this simple case, imagine what your code will look like when you need to string many more functions together. That would be an awful lot of manually written (and error-prone) code. We can do better.

62

The "Bind" Concept

Because Scala supports higher-order functions (HOFs), you can improve this situation by writing a `bind` function to glue f and g together a little more easily. For instance, with a properly written `bind` function you can write code like this to glue together f, g, and h (a new function that has the same signature as f and g):

```
val fResult = f(100)
val gResult = bind(g, fResult)
val hResult = bind(h, gResult)
```

While this code might not be beautiful just yet, it's certainly better and less error prone than the code I had at the end of the previous lesson.

In this lesson I'll show how to write a `bind` function to make this work.

The problem statement

Before beginning, let me clearly define the problem. Given three functions with these signatures:

```
def f(a: Int): (Int, String) = ???
def g(a: Int): (Int, String) = ???
def h(a: Int): (Int, String) = ???
```

I want to write a `bind` function that works like this:

```
val fResult = f(100)
val gResult = bind(g, fResult)
val hResult = bind(h, gResult)
```

If you think you know how to do this, step away from the book and start typing in your favorite IDE. Otherwise, read on.

Writing `bind`'s type signature

Let's solve this problem using the function-writing strategy I introduced early in the book: By writing `bind`'s function signature before you do anything else.

`bind`'s input parameters

To understand what `bind`'s signature needs to be, look at this line:

```
val gResult = bind(g, fResult)
```

This tells you that `bind` takes two parameters:

1. The first parameter is the function g. As I just showed, g has the type signature (a: Int): (Int, String) (or, (a: Int) => (Int, String), if you prefer).
2. The second parameter is fResult, which is the output of f. f's signature tells us that fResult's type is (Int, String) (i.e., a Tuple2[Int, String]).

This tells you that `bind`'s input parameters look like this:

```
def bind(fun: (Int) => (Int, String),
        tup: Tuple2[Int, String]) ...
```

Now all you need is `bind`'s return type.

`bind`'s return type

By looking at these two lines of code:

```
val gResult = bind(g, fResult)
val hResult = bind(h, gResult)
```

you can see that gResult will have the type of whatever `bind` returns. Because you know that a) fResult in the first line has the type (Int, String), and b) gResult must have the same type as fResult, you can deduce that c) `bind` must have this same return type: (Int, String).

Therefore, the complete type signature for `bind` must be this:

```
def bind(fun: (Int) => (Int, String),
        tup: (Int, String) ): (Int, String) = ???
```

Now all you have to do is implement the body for bind.

> Note: A Tuple2 can also been written as Tuple2[Int, String].

Writing bind's body

As for writing bind's body, all it does is automate the process I showed at the end of the previous lesson. There I showed this code:

```
val (fInt, fString) = f(100)
```

Imagine that this tuple result will be used as input to bind, so bind will receive:

- The function g as its first parameter
- The tuple (fInt, fString) as its second parameter

Now, where in the previous lesson I had these lines of code:

```
val (gInt, gString) = g(fInt)
val debug = fString + gString
```

you can imagine them being replaced by this bind call:

```
val (gInt, gString) = bind(g, (fInt, fString))
```

By looking at this you can say that bind's algorithm should be:

1. Apply the function you're given (g) to the Int you're given (fInt). This creates an (Int, String) ((gInt, gString) in this example).
2. Append the new string (gString) to the string you were given (fString).
3. Return the new Int (gInt) and the merged String (fString + gString) as the result.

Following that algorithm, a first attempt at bind looks like this:

```
def bind(fun: (Int) => (Int, String),
         tup: Tuple2[Int, String]): (Int, String) =
{
    val givenInt = tup._1
    val givenString = tup._2

    // apply the given function to the given int
```

```
    val (intResult, stringResult) = fun(givenInt)

    // append `stringResult` to the given string
    val newString = givenString + stringResult

    // return the new int and string
    (intResult, newString)
}
```

Once you're comfortable with that code, you can reduce bind until it looks like this:

```
def bind(fun: (Int) => (Int, String),
         tup: Tuple2[Int, String]): (Int, String) =
{
    val (intResult, stringResult) = fun(tup._1)
    (intResult, tup._2 + stringResult)
}
```

(Or you can keep the original version, if you prefer.)

A complete example

Here's the source code for a complete example that shows how f, g, h, and bind work together:

```
object Step3Bind extends App {

    def f(a: Int): (Int, String) = {
        val result = a * 2
        (result, s"\nf result: $result.")
    }

    def g(a: Int): (Int, String) = {
        val result = a * 3
        (result, s"\ng result: $result.")
    }

    def h(a: Int): (Int, String) = {
        val result = a * 4
        (result, s"\nh result: $result.")
```

```
    }

    // bind, a HOF
    def bind(fun: (Int) => (Int, String),
             tup: Tuple2[Int, String]): (Int, String) =
    {
        val (intResult, stringResult) = fun(tup._1)
        (intResult, tup._2 + stringResult)
    }

    val fResult = f(100)
    val gResult = bind(g, fResult)
    val hResult = bind(h, gResult)

    println(s"result: ${hResult._1}, debug: ${hResult._2}")

}
```

Observations

What can we say about bind at this point? First, a few good things:

- It's a useful higher-order function (HOF)
- It gives us a way to bind/glue the functions f, g, and h
- It's simpler and less error-prone than the code at the end of the previous lesson

If there's anything bad to say about bind, it's that it looks like it's dying to be used in a for expression, but because bind doesn't have methods like map and flatMap, it won't work that way.

For example, wouldn't it be cool if you could write code that looked like this:

```
val finalResult = for {
    fResult <- f(100)
    gResult <- g(fResult)
    hResult <- h(gResult)
} yield hResult
```

63

Getting Close to Using bind in for Expressions

Now we're at a point where we see that bind is better than what I started with, but not as good as it can be. That is, I want to use f, g, and h in a for expression, but I can't, because bind is a function, and therefore it has no way to implement map and flatMap so it can work in a for expression.

What to do?

Well, if we're going to succeed we need to figure out how to create a class that does two things:

1. Somehow works like bind
2. Implements map and flatMap methods so it can work inside for expressions

A different way to write map and flatMap methods

I'll do that soon, but first I need to do something else: I need to demonstrate a different way to write map and flatMap methods.

In the previous examples I showed how to write map and flatMap methods for a Sequence class that works like a collection class. Before we solve the bind problem I need to show how to write map and flatMap for classes that are more like a "wrapper" than a "collection." I'll do that next.

64

Using a Wrapper Class in a for Expression

To set the groundwork for solving the problem of using `bind` in a `for` expression, I'm going to create a simple "wrapper" class that you can use in a `for` expression. By the end of this lesson you'll have a class that you can use like this:

```
val result: Wrapper[Int] = for {
    a <- new Wrapper(1)
    b <- new Wrapper(2)
    c <- new Wrapper(3)
} yield a + b + c
```

To keep things simple, the `Wrapper` class won't do much; by the end of this lesson that `for` expression will yield this result:

```
result: Wrapper[Int] = 6
```

But even though it will be simple, this class will demonstrate how to write `map` and `flatMap` methods for these kinds of classes, what I call "wrapper" classes.

> It helps to think of these classes as being different than "collection" classes. As I've mentioned a few times, it's better to think of them as being a wrapper around whatever it is that they wrap.

In this lesson I'll create a wrapper around `Int`. I'll do this because a) `Int` is a simple data type that's easy to understand, and b) it lets us create `map` and `flatMap` methods in a manner that's similar to what `bind` is going to need.

Beginning

Following the concept of "beginning with the end in mind," this is the solution that I'll be able to write by the end of this lesson:

```
val result: Wrapper[Int] = for {
    a <- new Wrapper(1)
    b <- new Wrapper(2)
    c <- new Wrapper(3)
} yield a + b + c
```

This code tells me a few things:

1. `Wrapper` will be a class that takes a single `Int` constructor parameter
2. Because it works with multiple generators in a `for` expression, `Wrapper` must implement `map` and `flatMap` methods
3. Because `result` has the type `Wrapper[Int]`, those `map` and `flatMap` functions must return that same type

Knowing these things, I can begin sketching the `Wrapper` class like this:

```
class Wrapper[Int](value: Int) {
    def map(f: Int => Int): Wrapper[Int] = ???
    def flatMap(f: Int => Wrapper[Int]): Wrapper[Int] = ???
}
```

That's cool, I can sketch quite a bit of the `Wrapper` class just by knowing how it's used in a `for` expression. All that remains now is writing the body of the `map` and `flatMap` methods.

Implementing map

When you look at `map`'s signature:

```
def map(f: Int => Int): Wrapper[Int] = ???
```

you can say these things about `map`:

- It takes a function that transforms an `Int` to an `Int`
- After doing whatever it does, `map` returns a `Wrapper[Int]` (i.e., an `Int` inside a new `Wrapper`)

Writing those statements as comments inside `map`'s body looks like this:

```
def map(f: Int => Int): Wrapper[Int] = {
    // apply `f` to an `Int` to get a new `Int`
    // wrap the new `Int` in a `Wrapper`
}
```

If you're smarter than I was when I first learned about this, you might guess that those comments translate into code that looks like this:

```
def map(f: Int => Int): Wrapper[Int] = {

    // apply `f` to an `Int` to get a new `Int`
    val newInt = f(SOME_INT)

    // wrap the new `Int` in a `Wrapper`
    new Wrapper(newInt)

}
```

As it turns out, map is a very literal interpretation of those two comments. The only question is, what is SOME_INT? Where does it come from?

Where SOME_INT comes from

Remember that when you create a new Wrapper, you create it like this:

```
val x = Wrapper(1)
```

That's where the Int comes from: Wrapper's constructor:

```
class Wrapper[Int](value: Int) { ...
                   ----------
```

This tells me that SOME_INT in map's body should be changed to value, which leads to this code:

```
def map(f: Int => Int): Wrapper[Int] = {

    // apply `f` to an `Int` to get a new `Int`
    val newInt = f(value)
```

```
// wrap the new `Int` in a `Wrapper`
new Wrapper(newInt)
```

}

Figure 64.1 shows how value gets from Wrapper's constructor into the map method.

```
class Wrapper[Int] (value: Int) {

    def map(f: Int => Int): Wrapper[Int] = {
        val newValue = f(value)
        new Wrapper(newValue)
    }

}
```

Figure 64.1: *The* Int *that* map *operates on comes from* Wrapper's *constructor parameter.*

If this feels unusual ...

If this feels unusual at this point — congratulations! Your mind is now at a point where it feels like variables shouldn't just magically appear inside your functions. This is a good thing.

What's happening here is that you're using value just like you would in OOP code. It's a constructor parameter that you're using inside map. This is part of Scala's "functional objects" paradigm.

In another programming language you might write map in a separate WrapperUtils class, where value would be passed in *explicitly*:

```
class WrapperUtils {

    def map(value: Int, f: Int => Int): Wrapper[Int] = {
        val newInt = f(value)
        new Wrapper(newInt)
    }

}
```

But in Scala's "functional objects" approach, you can access value implicitly. Technically this violates my rule that for pure functions, "Output depends only on input," but when you use the functional objects coding style, this is a case where you're allowed to access other fields in your class in a function.

If you've heard the term "closure" before, yes, this is essentially a closure.

Here's the source code for the current Wrapper class:

The current Wrapper class

Getting back to the problem at hand, here's the source code for the Wrapper class with its new map method:

```
class Wrapper[Int](value: Int) {

    def map(f: Int => Int): Wrapper[Int] = {
        // apply `f` to an `Int` to get a new `Int`
        val newInt = f(value)

        // wrap the new `Int` in a `Wrapper`
        new Wrapper(newInt)
    }

    def flatMap(f: Int => Wrapper[Int]): Wrapper[Int] = ???
}
```

If this is confusing ...

If this is confusing, remember that it's the same way that Scala's List class works. It takes some parameters in its constructor:

```
val x = List(1,2,3)
```

and then its map method operates on those parameters:

```
x.map(_ * 2)    // yields `List(2,4,6)`
```

Wrapper works the same way:

```
val x = new Wrapper(1)
x.map(_ * 2)
```

Testing map

If you paste the current Wrapper class into the Scala REPL and then run those last two lines of code, you'll see this output:

```
scala> val x = new Wrapper(1)
x: Wrapper[Int] = 1

scala> x.map(_ * 2)
res0: Wrapper[Int] = 2
```

Very cool.

As a final note, remember that implementing a map method in a class like Wrapper lets you use one generator in a for expression, so this code also works right now:

```
scala> for { i <- x } yield i * 2
res1: Wrapper[Int] = 2
```

So far, so good. Now let's create a flatMap method in Wrapper.

Implementing flatMap

Let's follow the same thought process to see if we can create flatMap's body. First, when you look at flatMap's signature:

```
def flatMap(f: Int => Wrapper[Int]): Wrapper[Int] = {
```

you can say these things about flatMap:

- It takes a function that transforms an Int to a Wrapper[Int]
- After doing whatever it does, flatMap returns a Wrapper[Int]

When I write those statements as comments inside flatMap's signature, I get this:

```
def flatMap(f: Int => Wrapper[Int]): Wrapper[Int] = {
    // apply `f` to an `Int` to get a `Wrapper[Int]`
    // return a new `Wrapper[Int]`
}
```

`flatMap` always seems harder to grok than `map`, but if I'm reading those comments right, the `flatMap` solution is simpler than `map`. Here's what the solution looks like:

```
def flatMap(f: Int => Wrapper[Int]): Wrapper[Int] = {

    // apply `f` to an `Int` to get a `Wrapper[Int]`
    val newValue = f(value)

    // return a new `Wrapper[Int]`
    newValue

}
```

It turns out that `flatMap` is so simple that you can reduce that code to this:

```
def flatMap(f: Int => Wrapper[Int]): Wrapper[Int] = {
    f(value)
}
```

and then this:

```
def flatMap(f: Int => Wrapper[Int]): Wrapper[Int] = f(value)
```

For a "wrapper" class like the `Wrapper`, it turns out that `flatMap` is extremely simple: It just applies the function it's given (`f`) to the value it wraps (`value`).

The complete source code

Here's the complete source code for the `Wrapper` class:

```
class Wrapper[Int](value: Int) {

    def map(f: Int => Int): Wrapper[Int] = {
        val newValue = f(value)
        new Wrapper(newValue)
```

    }

    def flatMap(f: Int => Wrapper[Int]): Wrapper[Int] = f(value)

    override def toString = value.toString
}

If you paste this Wrapper class into the REPL and then run this for expression:

```
val result: Wrapper[Int] = for {
    a <- new Wrapper(1)
    b <- new Wrapper(2)
    c <- new Wrapper(3)
} yield a + b + c
```

you'll see the REPL show this result:

```
result: Wrapper[Int] = 6
```

Kind of a big step

Congratulations, you just implemented map and flatMap methods for a non-collection class, i.e., a type of class that I call a "wrapper."

If this seems like a minor achievement, well, it's actually kind of a big deal. You're about to see that this is an important step that will soon let you use the bind approach in a for expression. (And that's also going to be kind of a big deal.)

65

Making Wrapper More Generic

I created `Wrapper[Int]` in the previous lesson so I wouldn't have to deal with generic types, but now you can convert that class to a more generic class. All you have to do is:

1. Change all the `Int` references to the generic `A`
2. Change the `map` and `flatMap` signatures to return the generic type `B`

With those two changes you can convert this `Int`-specific code:

```
class Wrapper[Int](value: Int) {

    def map(f: Int => Int): Wrapper[Int] = {
        val newValue = f(value)
        new Wrapper(newValue)
    }

    def flatMap(f: Int => Wrapper[Int]): Wrapper[Int] = f(value)

    override def toString = value.toString
}
```

into this more generic code:

```
class Wrapper[A](value: A) {
    def map[B](f: A => B): Wrapper[B] = {
        val newValue = f(value)
        new Wrapper(newValue)
    }
    def flatMap[B](f: A => Wrapper[B]): Wrapper[B] = {
        val newValue = f(value)
        newValue
    }
    override def toString = value.toString
}
```

This new generic class can still be used as a wrapper around Int in a for expression:

```
val intResult: Wrapper[Int] = for {
    a <- new Wrapper(1)
    b <- new Wrapper(2)
    c <- new Wrapper(3)
} yield a + b + c

println(intResult)
```

And now it can also be used as a wrapper around String in a for expression:

```
val stringResult: Wrapper[String] = for {
    a <- new Wrapper("a")
    b <- new Wrapper("b")
    c <- new Wrapper("c")
} yield a + b + c

println(stringResult)
```

There's still one more thing I'd like to do with this code: I'd like to change it so I don't have to use the new keyword when creating each Wrapper instance. I'll do that in the next lesson.

66

Changing "new Wrapper" to "Wrapper"

Now I want to make one last change to the `Wrapper` class: I want to change it so I can just write `Wrapper` to create a new instance, instead of having to write `new Wrapper`. That is, I want to be able to write code like this:

```
val stringResult = for {
    a <- Wrapper("a")
    b <- Wrapper("b")
    c <- Wrapper("c")
} yield a + b + c
```

instead of this:

```
val stringResult = for {
    a <- new Wrapper("a")
    b <- new Wrapper("b")
    c <- new Wrapper("c")
} yield a + b + c
```

This is a small change, but:

- It makes the code more concise
- It will demonstrate a key point about what I'm doing in the larger scheme of things

There are two ways to do this. The first way is to change `Wrapper` from a regular `class` to a `case class`. While that's a good solution, for our purposes it will help to implement this as an `apply` method in a "companion object." (I'll explain why at the end of this lesson.)

Creating an `apply` method in a companion object

Creating an `apply` method in a companion object for `Wrapper` takes just a couple of steps:

1. Modify the `Wrapper` class to make its constructor `private`
2. Create an `object` named `Wrapper` in the same file as the `Wrapper` class
3. Create an `apply` method in the object

1) Make the `Wrapper` class constructor `private`

The first step is to make the `Wrapper` class constructor private. All this requires is to change its class signature from this:

```
class Wrapper[A] (value: A) {
```

to this:

```
class Wrapper[A] private (value: A) {
```

I make it `private` so I can reference it from the companion object, but no outside code can reference it.

2) Create an `object` named `Wrapper` in the same file as the `Wrapper` class

The next step is to create an `object` named `Wrapper` in the same file as the `Wrapper` class:

```
class Wrapper[A] private (value: A) { ...
}

object Wrapper {
}
```

When you do this, you create a *companion object* for the `Wrapper` class.

3) Create an `apply` method in the companion object with the appropriate signature

The last step in the process is to create an `apply` method in the companion object. `apply` is essentially a Factory method[1] that lets us create new `Wrapper` instances without needing the `new` keyword:

```
val a = Wrapper(1)   // 'new' is not needed
```

`apply`'s syntactic sugar

If you know your companion objects, you know that when you write this:

```
val a = Wrapper(1)
```

that code is translated by the Scala compiler into this:

```
val a = Wrapper.apply(1)
```

As shown, that code makes a call to the `apply` method in the companion object. It's an example of Scala's syntactic sugar at work, and I think you'll agree that this code:

```
val a = Wrapper(1)
```

is easier to read than this:

```
val a = Wrapper.apply(1)
```

or even this:

```
val a = new Wrapper(1)
```

Defining `apply`'s signature

We know a few things about the `apply` method. First, from the previous examples we know that it takes an `Int` value, or more generically it takes an `A`. Therefore I can start to write its signature like this:

---

[1] http://alvinalexander.com/java/java-factory-pattern-example

```
def apply[A](value: A)
```

From those examples I also know that `apply` returns a `Wrapper` instance, specifically a `Wrapper` around an `A`, so I can further write this:

```
def apply[A](value: A): Wrapper[A] = ???
```

Now the question is, how does `apply` create a new `Wrapper[A]`?

The answer is that it calls the `Wrapper` class constructor:

```
def apply[A](value: A): Wrapper[A] = new Wrapper(value)
```

The constructor is private to all other code, but because `apply` is created in `Wrapper`'s companion object, `apply` can still see that constructor.

That's the complete `apply` method. Here's what it looks like with the `Wrapper` class from the previous lesson, along with its new companion object:

```
class Wrapper[A] private (value: A) {
    def map[B](f: A => B): Wrapper[B] = {
        val newValue = f(value)
        new Wrapper(newValue)
    }
    def flatMap[B](f: A => Wrapper[B]): Wrapper[B] = {
        val newValue = f(value)
        newValue
    }
    override def toString = value.toString
}

object Wrapper {
    def apply[A](value: A): Wrapper[A] = new Wrapper(value)
}
```

Testing apply

Now you can test the `apply` method with this little `App`:

```
object WrapperExample extends App {

    val intResult = for {
        a <- Wrapper(1)
        b <- Wrapper(2)
        c <- Wrapper(3)
    } yield a + b + c

    println(intResult)

}
```

As shown in the previous lesson, this returns the result 6. The only difference between that lesson and this one is that you can now write `Wrapper(1)` instead of `new Wrapper(1)`. This is solely because of the companion object and its `apply` method.

Why I used `apply`

The reason I wrote an `apply` method in a companion object in this lesson rather than using a `case` class is a technical one: FP developers like to say that a method like `apply` "lifts" an ordinary value into the wrapper. Put another way, an `Int` on its own looks like this:

```
100
```

But when you use `apply` to lift the `Int` into `Wrapper`, the result is a wrapper around the `Int`:

```
Wrapper(100)
```

Key points

On the one hand, the last few lessons have been a series of small steps. You saw how to write a `Wrapper` class that lets you write code like this:

```
val intResult = for {
    a <- Wrapper(1)
    b <- Wrapper(2)
    c <- Wrapper(3)
} yield a + b + c
```

On the other hand, there's been a larger purpose behind all of this: You just wrote your first monad. (At least your first monad in this book.)

As you'll see in the coming lessons, a monad in Scala is simply a class that has `map` and `flatMap` methods (so it can be used with multiple generators in a `for` expression), and also has an `apply` method that's used to "lift" ordinary values like an `Int` into the monad.

That last sentence explains why I used `apply` in this example: I wanted to explain this "lifting" process. Now that you've seen this, in the future I'll use `case` classes for the same purpose.

What's next

While creating our first monad is nice, I'm more interested in solving problems, and I still have a problem to solve: I want to be able to use something like a `bind` function inside a `for` expression so I can use the `f`, `g`, and `h` functions that I introduced a few lessons ago. To do this I'll use everything I just showed about `map`, `flatMap`, and `apply` in the last several `Wrapper` lessons.

67

A Quick Note About Case Classes and Companion Objects

Before you head into the following lessons, I want to note that I'm about to start using `case` classes quite a bit. In general, the reasons I'm about to use `case` classes are:

- I don't want to have to use the `new` keyword to create new instances of classes
- I don't want to have to write companion objects with `apply` methods to achieve this effect

If you know your `case` classes you know that they let you write code like this:

```
for {
    a <- Wrapper(1)
    b <- Wrapper(2)
} yield c
```

rather than this:

```
for {
    a <- new Wrapper(1)
    b <- new Wrapper(2)
} yield c
```

That may seem like a minor difference to some people, but I appreciate that getting rid of the `new` keyword makes the code cleaner and more concise.

As a final note, in real-world Scala/FP code you'll also want to use `case` classes so you can take advantage of the other features they offer, including pattern matching. But in the lessons that follow, I'm really just interested in those two bullet points.

If you're not familiar with writing an `apply` method, see the Scala Cookbook[1] for more information.

---

[1] http://amzn.to/24ivK4G

68

Using bind in a for Expression

A few lessons I asked that if you had three functions with these signatures:

```
def f(a: Int): (Int, String)
def g(a: Int): (Int, String)
def h(a: Int): (Int, String)
```

wouldn't it be cool if you could somehow use those functions in a for expression, like this:

```
val finalResult = for {
    fResult <- f(100)
    gResult <- g(fResult)
    hResult <- h(gResult)
} yield hResult
```

Now that I've covered the "wrapper" concept, in this lesson I'll show exactly how to do that.

A big observation

At some point in the history of Scala, someone made a few observations that made this solution possible. The key insight may have been this:

> For something to be used in a for expression, it doesn't have to be a *class* that implements the map and flatMap methods (like Sequence); it just needs to *return* a type that implements map and flatMap methods.

That's a big observation, or at least it was for me. So far in this book I've shown classes like Sequence and Wrapper that implement map and flatMap so they can be used in for, but the reality is that any function that *returns* such a type can be used in for.

The next conceptual leap

With that observation in hand, it's a small conceptual leap to figure out how to get these functions to work in `for`:

```
def f(a: Int): (Int, String)
def g(a: Int): (Int, String)
def h(a: Int): (Int, String)
```

Can you see the solution?

Instead of these functions returning a tuple, they could return … something else … a type that implements `map` and `flatMap`.

The type these functions return should be something like a `Wrapper`, but where `Wrapper` contained a single value — such as a `Wrapper[Int]` — this type should be a wrapper around two values, an `Int` and a `String`. If such a type existed, `f`, `g`, and `h` could return their `Int` and `String` values wrapped in that type rather than a tuple.

You *could* call it a `TwoElementWrapper`:

```
def f(a: Int): TwoElementWrapper(Int, String)
def g(a: Int): TwoElementWrapper(Int, String)
def h(a: Int): TwoElementWrapper(Int, String)
```

But that's not very elegant. When you think about it, the purpose of `f`, `g`, and `h` is to show how functions can return "debug" information in addition to their primary return value, so a slightly more accurate name is `Debuggable`:

```
def f(a: Int): Debuggable(Int, String)
def g(a: Int): Debuggable(Int, String)
def h(a: Int): Debuggable(Int, String)
```

If `Debuggable` implements `map` and `flatMap`, this design will let `f`, `g`, and `h` be used in a `for` expression. Now all that's left to do is to create `Debuggable`.

Because `Debuggable` is going to work like `Wrapper`, I'm going to try to start with the `Wrapper` code from the previous lesson, and see if I can modify it to work as needed.

Trimming Wrapper down

The first thing I want to do is to convert Wrapper into a case class to simplify it. When I do that, and then rename it to Debuggable, I get this:

```
case class Debuggable[A] (value: A) {
    def map[B](f: A => B): Debuggable[B] = {
        val newValue = f(value)
        new Debuggable(newValue)
    }
    def flatMap[B](f: A => Debuggable[B]): Debuggable[B] = {
        val newValue = f(value)
        newValue
    }
}
```

That's a start, but as this code shows:

```
def f(a: Int): Debuggable(Int, String)
```

Debuggable must take two input parameters. Ignoring generic types for a few moments, this tells me that Debuggable's signature must look like this:

```
case class Debuggable (value: Int, message: String) {
```

When I further remove the generic types and bodies from the map and flatMap methods, Debuggable becomes this:

```
case class Debuggable (value: Int, message: String) {
    def map(f: Int => Int): Debuggable = ???
    def flatMap(f: Int => Debuggable): Debuggable = ???
}
```

Now I just need to think about the logic for the map and flatMap methods.

A reminder of how for translates

An important thing to know at this point is that when you write a for expression like this:

```
val seq = Sequence(1,2,3)
for {
    i <- seq
    j <- seq
    k <- seq
    l <- seq
} yield (i+j+k+l)
```

it will be translated into three `flatMap` calls followed by one `map` call:

```
seq.flatMap { i =>
    seq.flatMap { j =>
        seq.flatMap { k =>
            seq.map { l =>
                i + j + k + l
            }
        }
    }
}
```

For what we're about to do, the most important thing to observe is that `map` is (a) the last function called, and (b) the first one that returns.

You can think of the `flatMap` calls as being a series of recursive calls. `flatMap` keeps calling itself until the final expression is reached, at which point `map` is called. When `map` is called, it executes, returns its result, and then the `flatMap` calls unwind.

With that knowledge in hand, let's implement the `map` and `flatMap` methods for the `Debuggable` class.

Implementing map

When I first created the `IntWrapper` class I showed its `map` signature:

```
def map(f: Int => Int): Wrapper[Int] = ???
```

and then wrote that you could say these things about `map`'s implementation:

- It takes a function that transforms an `Int` to an `Int`
- After doing whatever it does, `map` returns a `Wrapper[Int]`, i.e., an `Int` inside a new `Wrapper`

Similarly, when you look at map's signature in Debuggable:

```
def map(f: Int => Int): Debuggable = ???
```

you can say these things about it:

- It takes a function that transforms an Int to an Int
- After doing whatever it does, map returns a Debuggable instance

As I did with IntWrapper, I write those sentences as comments inside map like this:

```
def map(f: Int => Int): Debuggable = {
    // apply `f` to an `Int` to get a new `Int`
    // wrap that result in a `Debuggable`
}
```

I can implement the first sentence as I did in Wrapper — by applying the function f to the value in Debuggable — to get this:

```
def map(f: Int => Int): Debuggable = {

    // apply `f` to an `Int` to get a new `Int`
    val newValue = f(value)

    // wrap that result in a `Debuggable`
}
```

Now map just needs to return a new Debuggable instance.

The Debuggable constructor takes an Int and a String, which I named value and message. The *value* map should return is the new, transformed value I got by applying f to value, so that part is good.

While it may not be immediately clear *why* I should return the message from the Debuggable constructor, it's the only String message I have, so I'll use it to construct and return a new Debuggable instance:

```
def map(f: Int => Int): Debuggable = {
    val newValue = f(value)
    Debuggable(newValue, message)
}
```

Figure 68.1 shows how the `value` and `message` from the `Debuggable` class relate to how they are used in `map`.

```scala
case class Debuggable(value: Int, message: String) {

    def map(f: Int => Int): Debuggable = {
        val nextValue = f(value)
        Debuggable(nextValue, message)
    }

    def flatMap(f: Int => Debuggable): Debuggable = {
        val nextValue = f(value)
        Debuggable(nextValue.value, message + nextValue.message)
    }
}
```

Figure 68.1: How value *and* message *come into the* map *function.*

When I write Scala/FP functions that use constructor parameters I often like to put a `this` reference in front of those values so I know where they came from. That change leads to this code:

```scala
def map(f: Int => Int): Debuggable = {
    val newValue = f(this.value)
    Debuggable(newValue, this.message)
}
```

That's the complete `map` function.

Why map returns message

The short answer of "why" `message` is returned here is because `map` is the "last function called and the first to return." As you'll see in the details in the next lesson, `map` creates the first message in the stack of messages created in the `for` expression.

flatMap

When I first created the `Wrapper` class I wrote that you could say these things about its `flatMap` implementation:

- It takes a function that transforms an `Int` to a `Wrapper[Int]`
- After doing whatever it does, `flatMap` returns a `Wrapper[Int]`

That led to this code, which was a direct implementation of those statements:

```
def flatMap[B](f: A => Wrapper[B]): Wrapper[B] = {
    val newValue = f(value)
    newValue
}
```

For the debuggable class you can say these things about its flatMap implementation:

- It takes a function that transforms an Int to a Debuggable instance
- After doing whatever it does, flatMap returns a Debuggable instance

Writing flatMap with those statements as comments looks like this:

```
def flatMap(f: Int => Debuggable): Debuggable = {
    // (1) apply the function to an Int to get a new Debuggable
    // (2) return a new Debuggable instance based on the new value
}
```

As with the Wrapper class, for the first comment the question is, "What Int should I apply the function to?" As before, the answer is, "Apply it to the value you hold." This leads to this code:

```
def flatMap(f: Int => Debuggable): Debuggable = {

    // (1) apply the function to an Int to get a new Debuggable
    val newValue: Debuggable = f(value)

    // (2) return a new Debuggable instance based on the new value

}
```

So far this is the same as the Wrapper class. Now let's get the second line working.

The second comment states:

```
// return a new Debuggable instance based on the new value
```

This part was a little tricky for me, and the only way I could understand the solution was by really digging into the code (as shown in the next lesson). The short answer is that you need to create the new Debuggable instance from:

- The Int of the newValue created in the first line
- Appending newValue.message to the message that was passed into the current Debuggable instance

I'll explain this a little more shortly, but the short answer is that this is the solution:

```
Debuggable(nextValue.value, message + nextValue.message)
```

How to think about that

You can think about that solution as follows. Imagine that you have a for expression with a series of Debuggable instances, like this:

```
val finalResult = for {
    fResult <- f(100)
    gResult <- g(fResult)
    hResult <- h(gResult)
} yield hResult
```

Each of those lines — f(100), g(fResult), etc. — are going to add a new message to the overall string of messages. Therefore, at some point you need to string those messages together, and flatMap is the place where that happens. The most recent message is contained in newValue.message, and all of the previous messages are contained in the message that is passed into Debuggable (i.e., this.message).

> I explain this in great detail in the next lesson, so if you want to completely understand how this works, go ahead and look at that lesson at this point.

Finishing flatMap

Finishing up with flatMap, I now know what the second expression looks like, so I add that to flatMap's body:

```
def flatMap(f: Int => Debuggable): Debuggable = {

    // (1) apply the function to an Int to get a new Debuggable
    val newValue: Debuggable = f(value)

    // (2) return a new Debuggable instance based on the new value
    Debuggable(newValue.value, message + newValue.message)
```

}

The completed class

When I add `map` and `flatMap` to the `Debuggable` class definition, I now have this code:

```
case class Debuggable (value: Int, message: String) {
    def map(f: Int => Int): Debuggable = {
        val newValue = f(value)
        Debuggable(newValue, message)
    }
    def flatMap(f: Int => Debuggable): Debuggable = {
        val newValue: Debuggable = f(value)
        Debuggable(newValue.value, message + "\n" + newValue.message)
    }
}
```

Now I just need to figure out how to write the f, g, and h functions so I can write a for expression like this:

```
val finalResult = for {
    fResult <- f(100)
    gResult <- g(fResult)
    hResult <- h(gResult)
} yield hResult
```

Writing f, g, and h

As I mentioned earlier, the solution to getting f, g, and h working in a for expression is that they should return a `Debuggable` instance. More specifically they should:

- Take an `Int` input parameter
- Return a `Debuggable` instance

This tells me that their signatures will look like this:

```
def f(a: Int): Debuggable = ???
def g(a: Int): Debuggable = ???
def h(a: Int): Debuggable = ???
```

In the previous lessons these functions worked like this:

- f multiplied its input value by 2
- g multiplied its input value by 3
- h multiplied its input value by 4

Thinking only about f, I can begin to write it like this:

```
def f(a: Int): Debuggable = {
    val result = a * 2
    val message = s"f: a ($a) * 2 = $result."
    ???
}
```

This gives me a result and message similar to what I had before, but now the function signature tells me that I need to return those values as a Debuggable instance rather than as a tuple. That's a simple step:

```
def f(a: Int): Debuggable = {
    val result = a * 2
    val message = s"f: a ($a) * 2 = $result."
    Debuggable(result, message)
}
```

f now takes an Int input parameter, and yields a Debuggable, as desired.

A test App

g and h are simple variations of f, so when I create them and put all of the functions in a test App along with the original for expression, I get this:

```
object Test extends App {

    val finalResult = for {
        fResult <- f(100)
        gResult <- g(fResult)
```

```
        hResult <- h(gResult)
    } yield hResult

    // added a few "\n" to make the output easier
    // to read
    println(s"value:   ${finalResult.value}\n")
    println(s"message: \n${finalResult.message}")

    def f(a: Int): Debuggable = {
        val result = a * 2
        val message = s"f: a ($a) * 2 = $result."
        Debuggable(result, message)
    }

    def g(a: Int): Debuggable = {
        val result = a * 3
        val message = s"g: a ($a) * 3 = $result."
        Debuggable(result, message)
    }

    def h(a: Int): Debuggable = {
        val result = a * 4
        val message = s"h: a ($a) * 4 = $result."
        Debuggable(result, message)
    }
}
```

Running that App yields this output:

```
value:   2400

message:
f: a (100) * 2 = 200.
g: a (200) * 3 = 600.
h: a (600) * 4 = 2400.
```

While that output may not be beautiful for many people, if this is the first time you've enabled something like this in a for expression it can be a really beautiful thing.

More information

I went through some parts of this lesson a little quicker than usual. My thinking was that if you're comfortable with how `for`, `map`, and `flatMap` work, I didn't want to go too slow. But for people like me who struggle with this concept, I want to cover this topic more deeply. Therefore, the next lesson takes a deep dive into exactly how all of this code works.

69

How Debuggable, f, g, and h Work

If you want to see the nitty-gritty details of how the Debuggable class works with the f, g, and h functions in the previous lesson, this lesson is for you. I won't introduce any new concepts in this lesson, but I'll add a *lot* of debugging statements to that code to show exactly how a for expression like this works.

Source code

The best way to work with this lesson is to check the source code out from my Github project so you can easily refer to the code as you read the lesson. The code is at this URL:

- github.com/alvinj/DebuggableInDetail[1]

The flow of this lesson

The way this lesson works is:

- I'll show the same code as the previous lesson, but with many println statements added for debugging purposes
- After showing the new code, I'll show the output it produces
- After that, I'll explain that output

I hope all of this debug code (and its output) provides a good example of how a for expression works, especially with "wrapper" classes like Debuggable.

The Debuggable class

First, here's the source code for the Debuggable class:

---

[1] https://github.com/alvinj/DebuggableInDetail

```
case class Debuggable(value: Int, msg: String) {

    def map(f: Int => Int): Debuggable = {
        println("\n>>>> entered map   >>>>")
        println(s"map: value: ${value}")
        println(s"map: msg: (${msg})")
        val nextValue = f(value)    //Int
        // there is no `nextValue.msg`
        println(s"map: nextValue: ${nextValue}")
        println("<<<< leaving map   <<<<\n")
        Debuggable(nextValue, msg)
    }

    def flatMap(f: Int => Debuggable): Debuggable = {
        println("\n>>>> entered fmap >>>>")
        println(s"fmap: value: ${value}")
        println(s"fmap: msg: (${msg})")
        val nextValue = f(value)
        println(s"fmap: msg: (${msg})")
        println(s"fmap: next val: ${nextValue.value}")
        println(s"fmap: next msg: \n(${nextValue.msg})")
        println("<<<< leaving fmap <<<<\n")
        Debuggable(nextValue.value, msg + "\n" + nextValue.msg)
    }
}
```

The important notes about this code are:

- I added println statements to show the value and msg that map and flatMap have before they apply their functions
- I added println statements to show the nextValue that map and flatMap have *after* they apply their functions, and also show the new message that's created when flatMap applies its function

The f, g, and h functions

Next, this is how I modified the f, g, and h functions:

```
object DebuggableTestDetails extends App {

    def f(a: Int): Debuggable = {
        println(s"\n[f: a = $a]")
        val result = a * 2
        Debuggable(result, s"f: input: $a, result: $result")
    }

    def g(a: Int): Debuggable = {
        println(s"\n[g: a = $a]")
        val result = a * 3
        Debuggable(result, s"g: input: $a, result: $result")
    }

    def h(a: Int): Debuggable = {
        println(s"\n[h: a = $a]")
        val result = a * 4
        Debuggable(result, s"h: input: $a, result: $result")
    }

    val finalResult = for {
        fRes <- f(100)
        gRes <- g(fRes)
        hRes <- h(gRes)
    } yield hRes

    println("\n----- FINAL RESULT -----")
    println(s"final value: ${finalResult.value}")
    println(s"final msg:   \n${finalResult.msg}")

}
```

As shown, in the f, g, and h functions I show the initial value that each function receives when it's called.

How the for expression is translated

In the output that follows it also helps to understand how the for expression is translated by the Scala compiler. This is what my for expression looks like:

```
val finalResult = for {
    fRes <- f(100)
    gRes <- g(fRes)
    hRes <- h(gRes)
} yield hRes
```

And this is what the code looks like when I compile the for expression with the scalac -Xprint:parse command (and then clean up the output):

```
val finalResult = f(100).flatMap { fResult =>
    g(fResult).flatMap { gResult =>
        h(gResult).map { hResult =>
            hResult
        }
    }
}
```

Notice that there are two flatMap calls followed by one map call.

The output

When I run the test App shown, this is the output I see:

```
[f: a = 100]

>>>> entered fmap >>>>
fmap: value: 200
fmap: msg: (f: input: 100, result: 200)


[g: a = 200]

>>>> entered fmap >>>>
fmap: value: 600
fmap: msg: (g: input: 200, result: 600)


[h: a = 600]

>>>> entered map   >>>>
map: value: 2400
```

```
map: msg: (h: input: 600, result: 2400)
map: nextValue: 2400
<<<< leaving map   <<<<

fmap: msg: (g: input: 200, result: 600)
fmap: next val: 2400
fmap: next msg:
(h: input: 600, result: 2400)
<<<< leaving fmap <<<<

fmap: msg: (f: input: 100, result: 200)
fmap: next val: 2400
fmap: next msg:
(g: input: 200, result: 600
h: input: 600, result: 2400)
<<<< leaving fmap <<<<


----- FINAL RESULT -----
final value: 2400
final msg:
f: input: 100, result: 200
g: input: 200, result: 600
h: input: 600, result: 2400
```

Take a few moments to review that output to see if you understand how it works. One of the most important things to note is that the map method is called last, and it returns before the flatMap method calls return. I'll provide an explanation of all of the output in the sections that follow.

Explaining the output

The first thing that happens is that the f function is called with the value 100:

```
[f: a = 100]
```

You can understand this when you look at the first part of my for expression:

```
val finalResult = for {
    fRes <- f(100)
           ------
```

The desugared for expression shows this even more clearly:

```
val finalResult = f(100).flatMap { fResult =>
                         ------
```

In both of those code snippets, f(100) is the first piece of code that is invoked.

What happens in f

What happens inside of f is that this output is printed:

```
[f: a = 100]
```

After that, the value that's received is doubled, and a new Debuggable instance is created. You can see that in f's body:

```
def f(a: Int): Debuggable = {
    println(s"\n[f: a = $a]")
    val result = a * 2
    Debuggable(result, s"f: input: $a, result: $result")
}
```

The first flatMap is called

The next piece of output looks like this:

```
>>>> entered fmap >>>>
fmap: value: 200
fmap: msg: (f: input: 100, result: 200)
```

This shows that flatMap is invoked. This makes sense when you look at the first line of the desugared for expression:

```
val finalResult = f(100).flatMap { fResult =>
                         --------
```

That code shows that `flatMap` is invoked after `f` is applied to the value `100`.

To understand the debug output, it helps to look at `flatMap`:

```
def flatMap(fip: Int => Debuggable): Debuggable = {
    println("\n>>>> entered fmap >>>>")
    println(s"fmap: value: ${this.value}")
    println(s"fmap: msg: (${this.msg})")
    val nextValue = fip(value)
    println(s"fmap: msg: (${this.msg})")
    println(s"fmap: next val: ${nextValue.value}")
    println(s"fmap: next msg: \n(${nextValue.msg})")
    println("<<<< leaving fmap <<<<\n")
    Debuggable(nextValue.value, msg + "\n" + nextValue.msg)
}
```

The debug output shows that `this.value` in `flatMap` is `200`. This was passed into the new `Debuggable` by `f`. The `this.msg` value is also provided by `f` when it creates the new Debuggable.

At this point there's no more output from `flatMap`. What happens is that this line of code in `flatMap` is invoked:

```
val nextValue = fun(value)
```

That line causes this output to be printed:

```
[g: a = 200]
```

We're now at this point in the desugared `for` expression:

```
val finalResult = f(100).flatMap { fResult =>
    g(fResult)
    ----------
```

What happens in g

The output `[g: a = 200]` shows that the `g` function is entered. Here's `g`'s source code:

```
def g(a: Int): Debuggable = {
    println(s"\n[g: a = $a]")
    val result = a * 3
    Debuggable(result, s"g: input: $a, result: $result")
}
```

As you saw with f, what happens here is:

- g's `println` statement produces the output shown
- a new `result` is calculated
- g creates a new `Debuggable` instance as its last line

The second `flatMap` call is reached

When g returns the new `Debuggable` instance, the second `flatMap` call is invoked, which you can see in the desugared code:

```
val finalResult = f(100).flatMap { fResult =>
    g(fResult).flatMap { gResult => ...
            --------
```

`flatMap` is invoked with values given to it by g, as shown in its output:

```
>>>> entered fmap >>>>
fmap: value: 600
fmap: msg: (g: input: 200, result: 600)
```

g multiplied the value it was given (200) to produce a new value, 600, along with the message shown.

Those lines of debug output are produced by these first three lines of code in `flatMap`:

```
println("\n>>>> entered fmap >>>>")
println(s"fmap: value: ${this.value}")
println(s"fmap: msg: (${this.msg})")
```

After that, `flatMap`'s fourth line of code is reached:

```
val nextValue = fun(value)
```

That line of code causes the next line of output to be produced:

[h: a = 600]

This tells us that the h function was just entered.

Note: The `flatMap` *calls haven't returned yet*

I'll come back to the h function call in a moment, but first, it's important to note that the two `flatMap` function calls haven't returned yet. They both pause when that fourth line of code is reached.

You can understand that by a) looking at `flatMap`'s source code, and b) looking at the desugared `for` expression:

```
val finalResult = f(100).flatMap { fResult =>
    g(fResult).flatMap { gResult =>   // YOU ARE NOW HERE
        h(gResult).map { hResult =>
            hResult
        }
    }
}
```

The `flatMap` calls haven't returned yet because:

- The first `flatMap` function reaches its fourth line, which invokes g
- When g finishes, the second `flatMap` call is invoked
- When that instance of `flatMap` reaches its fourth line, h is invoked
- As you're about to see, when h finishes running, `map` is invoked

h *executes*

Getting back to where I was ... the last line of debug output was this:

[h: a = 600]

This tells you that the h function was just invoked. h prints that output, doubles the value it receives, then creates a new `Debuggable` instance with that new value and new message:

```
def h(a: Int): Debuggable = {
    println(s"\n[h: a = $a]")
    val result = a * 4
```

```
        Debuggable(result, s"h: input: $a, result: $result")
}
```

map is entered

As the desugared for expression shows, after h runs, map is invoked:

```
val finalResult = f(100).flatMap { fResult =>
    g(fResult).flatMap { gResult =>
        h(gResult).map { hResult => ...
```

The map call produces the next debug output you see:

```
>>>> entered map    >>>>
map: value: 2400
map: msg: (h: input: 600, result: 2400)
map: nextValue: 2400
<<<< leaving map    <<<<
```

This shows that map is called, it runs (producing this output), and then it exits. This confirms what I wrote in the previous lesson:

> In a for expression, map is the last function called and the first to exit.

Here's a look at map's source code, followed by its output:

```
def map(f: Int => Int): Debuggable = {
    println("\n>>>> entered map    >>>>")
    println(s"map: value: ${value}")
    println(s"map: msg: (${msg})")
    val nextValue = f(value)    //Int
    // there is no `nextValue.msg`
    println(s"map: nextValue: ${nextValue}")
    println("<<<< leaving map    <<<<\n")
    Debuggable(nextValue, msg)
}
```

```
>>>> entered map    >>>>
map: value: 2400
map: msg: (h: input: 600, result: 2400)
```

```
map: nextValue: 2400
<<<< leaving map  <<<<
```

The flatMap calls unwind

After the map method finishes, the next thing that happens is that the flatMap calls begin to unwind. A look at the de-sugared code reminds you why this unwinding happens now:

```
val finalResult = f(100).flatMap { fResult =>
    g(fResult).flatMap { gResult =>
        h(gResult).map { hResult =>   // map RETURNS
            hResult                    // CONTROL TO flatMap
        }
    }
}
```

What's happened so far is:

- f was called
- When f finished, the first flatMap function was called
- It called g
- When g finished, the second flatMap function was called
- It called h
- When h finished, map was called
- map just finished running

Now that map is finished, flow of control returns to the second flatMap invocation. This is the output from it:

```
fmap: msg: (g: input: 200, result: 600)
fmap: next val: 2400
fmap: next msg:
(h: input: 600, result: 2400)
<<<< leaving fmap <<<<
```

When that flatMap call finishes running, flow of control returns to the first flatMap invocation, which produces this output:

```
fmap: msg: (f: input: 100, result: 200)
fmap: next val: 2400
fmap: next msg:
(g: input: 200, result: 600
h: input: 600, result: 2400)
<<<< leaving fmap <<<<
```

When it finishes, the final output from the application is shown. This is what the `println` statements look like at the end of the `App`:

```
println("\n----- FINAL RESULT -----")
println(s"final value: ${finalResult.value}")
println(s"final msg:   \n${finalResult.msg}")
```

and this is what their output looks like:

```
----- FINAL RESULT -----
final value: 2400
final msg:
f: input: 100, result: 200
g: input: 200, result: 600
h: input: 600, result: 2400
```

Summary

If you had any confusion about how `for` expressions run — especially with wrapper classes like `Debuggable` — I hope this lesson is helpful. I encourage you to work with the source code and modify it until you're completely comfortable with how it works. The lessons that follow will continue to build on this knowledge.

70

A Generic Version of Debuggable

Source code

The source code for this lesson is at this URL:

- github.com/alvinj/FPDebuggable[1]

Using generic types

In this lesson I'll share a version of the `Debuggable` class that uses generic types rather than Ints everywhere.

I'm going to assume that you're used to the process of converting a type-specific class to a class that uses generic types, so rather than explain the conversion process, I'll just show the code:

```
/**
 * The purpose of this class is to show a version of the `Debuggable`
 * class that takes a generic `value` (whereas the previous versions
 * required that `value` be an `Int`).
 */
case class Debuggable[A](value: A, message: String) {

    def map[B](f: A => B): Debuggable[B] = {
        val nextValue = f(value)
        Debuggable(nextValue, message)
    }

    def flatMap[B](f: A => Debuggable[B]): Debuggable[B] = {
        val nextValue = f(value)
```

---

[1] https://github.com/alvinj/FPDebuggable

```
        Debuggable(nextValue.value, message + nextValue.message)
    }
}
```

I used the following code to test this new version of Debuggable:

```
object DebuggableGenericExample extends App {

    def f(a: Int): Debuggable[Int] = {
        val result = a * 2
        Debuggable(result, s"f: multiply $a * 2 = $result\n")
    }

    def g(a: Int): Debuggable[Int] = {
        val result = a * 3
        Debuggable(result, s"g: multiply $a * 3 = $result\n")
    }

    def h(a: Int): Debuggable[Int] = {
        val result = a * 4
        Debuggable(result, s"h: multiply $a * 4 = $result\n")
    }

    val finalResult = for {
        fRes <- f(100)
        gRes <- g(fRes)
        hRes <- h(gRes)
    } yield s"result: $hRes"

    println(finalResult.message)
    println(s"Output is ${finalResult.value}")

}
```

Running that `App` results in this output:

```
f: multiply 100 * 2 = 200
g: multiply 200 * 3 = 600
h: multiply 600 * 4 = 2400

Output is result: 2400
```

This shows that after changing the `Debuggable` class to use generic types, it still works properly with `Int` values.

> If you want to verify that the generics work as advertised, the Github project includes another `App` named `DebuggableGenericsWithFloats` that uses `Floats` rather than `Int` values.

71

One Last Debuggable: Using List Instead of String

Motivation for this lesson

In this lesson I'll (quickly) show a slight variation of the Debuggable class. The motivations for this are:

- It's important to get comfortable writing "wrapper" classes like this
- Many of the lessons that follow show more wrapper classes, and a simple variation now will help get your ready for those later

Source code

The source code for this lesson is at this URL:

- github.com/alvinj/FPDebuggable[1]

From String to List[String]

The change in this lesson is relatively simple: I'll show how to implement Debuggable with a List to store the log messages, rather than using a String as I did in the previous lessons.

Since I want to store the messages as a List[String], the first change is to the Debuggable class signature, which now looks like this:

---

[1]https://github.com/alvinj/FPDebuggable

```
case class Debuggable[A](value: A, log: List[String]) {
                                        ------------
```

Inside the Debuggable class, this change has no effect on map. The log parameter used to be a String, and now it's a List[String], and the code requires no changes:

```
def map[B](f: A => B): Debuggable[B] = {
    val nextValue = f(value)
    Debuggable(nextValue, this.log)
}
```

The change does affect flatMap, which now prepends the old log message before nextValue.log when creating a new Debuggable instance:

```
def flatMap[B](f: A => Debuggable[B]): Debuggable[B] = {
    val nextValue: Debuggable[B] = f(value)
    Debuggable(nextValue.value, this.log ::: nextValue.log)
}
```

The change also affects f (and g and h), which now give Debuggable a List (rather than a String):

```
def f(a: Int): Debuggable[Int] = {
    val result = a * 2
    Debuggable(result, List(s"f: multiply $a * 2 = $result"))
}
```

It also affects the final printing of the log messages:

```
// print a `List` (rather than a `String`)
finalResult.log.foreach(l => println(s"LOG: $l"))
```

The complete source code

With those changes, here's the complete source code for the new version of Debuggable:

```
// `log` is now a list
case class Debuggable[A](value: A, log: List[String]) {

    def map[B](f: A => B): Debuggable[B] = {
        val nextValue = f(value)
```

```scala
        Debuggable(nextValue, this.log)
    }

    // prepend `this.log` before `nextValue.log`
    def flatMap[B](f: A => Debuggable[B]): Debuggable[B] = {
        val nextValue: Debuggable[B] = f(value)
        Debuggable(nextValue.value, this.log ::: nextValue.log)
    }
}

object DebuggableList extends App {

    def f(a: Int): Debuggable[Int] = {
        val result = a * 2
        Debuggable(result, List(s"f: multiply $a * 2 = $result"))
    }

    def g(a: Int): Debuggable[Int] = {
        val result = a * 3
        Debuggable(result, List(s"g: multiply $a * 3 = $result"))
    }

    def h(a: Int): Debuggable[Int] = {
        val result = a * 4
        Debuggable(result, List(s"h: multiply $a * 4 = $result"))
    }

    val finalResult = for {
        fRes <- f(100)
        gRes <- g(fRes)
        hRes <- h(gRes)
    } yield s"result: $hRes"

    finalResult.log.foreach(l => println(s"LOG: $l"))
    println(s"Output is ${finalResult.value}")

}
```

The output of the App looks like this:

```
LOG: f: multiply 100 * 2 = 200
LOG: g: multiply 200 * 3 = 600
LOG: h: multiply 600 * 4 = 2400
Output is result: 2400
```

Discussion

While this was a relatively minor change to the `Debuggable` class, it's helpful to see how that change has a ripple effect throughout the code. I showed this change so you could see that effect, but I also prefer this `List` approach, which is a more "real world" example than the previous `String`-based example.

The Writer monad

If you're interested in where the `Debuggable` class comes from, it's actually an implementation of something known as the Writer monad in Haskell.

As Learn You a Haskell for Great Good![2] states, "the Writer monad is for values that have another value attached that acts as a sort of log value. Writer allows us to do computations while making sure that all the log values are combined into one log value that then gets attached to the result."

Key points

In the last few lessons I showed several different versions of the `Debuggable` class to help you get comfortable with it. Here are a few important points about it:

- A *monad* consists of a class with `map` and `flatMap` methods, along with some form of a "lift" function.

- In Scala, a class built like this is intended to be used in `for` expressions.

- I refer to these as "wrapper" classes. While they're intended to be used in `for` expressions, they're not "containers" like Scala collections classes, they're more a type of "wrapper" or "box." They wrap existing types so they can be used in `for` expressions.

---

[2] http://amzn.to/1POaUCv

See also

When I was struggling to learn what a monad was, the following links were the best resources I found:

- An old Haskell tutorial, You Could Have Invented Monads[3]
- Martin Snyder's YouTube presentation, Monadic Logging and You[4]
- Darren Wilkinson's article, First steps with monads in Scala[5]

You can read more about the Writer monad at these resources:

- The book, Learn You a Haskell for Great Good![6]
- The Writer monad section[7] of the haskell.org wiki

---

[3] http://blog.sigfpe.com/2006/08/you-could-have-invented-monads-and.html
[4] https://www.youtube.com/watch?v=t-YX55ZF4g0
[5] https://darrenjw.wordpress.com/2016/04/15/first-steps-with-monads-in-scala/
[6] http://amzn.to/1POaUCv
[7] https://wiki.haskell.org/All_About_Monads#The_Writer_monad

Key Points About Monads

At this time it's worth taking a moment to pause and make a few observations about monads in Scala:

- Their primary purpose is to let you compose code in `for` expressions (i.e., to glue code together)
- For a Scala class to be a monad, it needs three things:
    - A `map` method
    - A `flatMap` method
    - Some sort of lift function (to "lift" another type into the monad)

As you'll see in the rest of this book, there are different monads for different purposes.

If you ever get confused about monads — such as why in the world they are needed, or why people write about them so much — I encourage you to come back to this section to review those points.

73

Signpost: Where We're Going Next

Now that you've seen what monads are, we're getting closer to being able to write a Scala/FP version of the Coin Flip game that would make an experienced functional programmer smile. That game will make extensive use of composition in a for expression.

However, before I can do that I'm going to have to develop a few new monads, including the IO and State monads. These are two of the most common monads that are used in functional programming.

In the next several lessons I'll demonstrate the IO monad, and then I'll show how to use a State monad. I'll also discuss *composition* a little more when the time is right.

74

Introduction: The IO Monad

"The IO monad does not make a function pure. It just makes it obvious that it's impure."

Martin Odersky

The IO monad is the grandfather of all monads. Wikipedia states[1], "Haskell 1.3 introduced monads as a more flexible way to combine I/O with lazy evaluation."

Before you jump into using the IO monad, let me share a personal warning: Some developers say that the IO monad somehow makes I/O pure. This isn't true — and I wasted a lot of time trying to understand that claim.

As you'll see in the following lessons, if you have a function named getUserInput that returns a type of IO[String], and a user enters the string "bill", getUserInput will return:

IO["bill"]

However, if the user enters the string "zombie", getUserInput will return this:

IO["zombie"]

Clearly those values aren't the same, just like List["bill"] and List["zombie"] aren't the same. This tells you that there's no guarantee that getUserInput will always return the same result when it's called. Whether you want to say that getUserInput isn't idempotent, deterministic, or referentially transparent, clearly it isn't a pure function.

That being said, the IO monad does have at least two potential benefits in Scala:

- When you use it, your I/O function signatures will declare that they return an IO type, such as getUserInput returning IO[String]. This screams to other developers, "Watch out, this function interacts with the outside world!"

---

[1] https://en.wikipedia.org/wiki/Monad_(functional_programming)#History

- It lets you use I/O functions in Scala `for` expressions.

While there's no consensus that the `IO` monad is a huge benefit in Scala, I'll use it in the remainder of this book. After that, you can decide whether those two benefits are useful in your own programming.

See also

If you're interested in the history of monads, see this Wikipedia "monad" article[2].

---

[2] https://en.wikipedia.org/wiki/Monad_(functional_programming)

75

How to Use an IO Monad

"If we want to deal with impure data, we must do it in an impure environment. The taint of impurity spreads around much like the undead scourge..."

From the book,
Learn You a Haskell for Great Good![a]

---

[a] http://amzn.to/1POaUCv

Goal

The goal for this lesson is to show how to use an IO monad. I'm not going to show how to *write* an IO monad right now, I just want to show how to *use* one.

You can think of this lesson like this: If an IO monad was built into the Scala libraries, would you care how it was implemented? Sure, if you ever had a problem with it you'd care how it was written, but if you never had a problem with it, you'd probably just use it, just like you use a String or List without worrying about how they're implemented. So that's the approach I'm going to take in this lesson: I'll assume that an IO monad already exists, and I'll show how to use it.

Background

An IO monad is a wrapper that you can use to wrap around I/O functions. It's not 100% necessary to use an IO monad to handle I/O, but in Scala the benefits of using one are:

- It serves as a "marker" data type. When developers see that a function returns an IO[String], they immediately know that the function reaches out into the outside world to return that String (wrapped in an IO).
- Similarly, if a function signature shows that it returns IO[Unit], developers know that the function writes data to the outside world. (The function presumably takes one or more input parameters that will be written to the outside world.)

- It lets you use I/O functions in for expressions.

I demonstrate these points in this lesson.

Source code

The source code for the next three lessons is available at this URL:

- github.com/alvinj/IOMonad[1]

Three notes about the source code:

- The IO monad code is in the file named *IO.scala*.
- The code in *IO.scala* is a more complex version of a monad than what I've shown this far. I'll discuss it more in future versions of this book, but in these lessons I'm just going to use it without discussing it. As usual, feel free to study the code, and modify it as desired to make it your own. (I will spend a little time discussing a similar State monad in the upcoming lessons.)
- The getLine and putStrLn functions are in the *package.scala* file (i.e., the "package object" for that directory).

Hello, IO World

If an IO monad existed in Scala, you could use it to wrap Scala's existing I/O functions, like this:

```
def getLine: IO[String] = IO(scala.io.StdIn.readLine())
def putStrLn(s: String): IO[Unit] = IO(println(s))
```

In that code, getLine returns a string that's retrieved by scala.io.StdIn.readLine and wraps it in an IO, so its return type is IO[String]. Similarly, putStrLn writes a string to STDOUT using Scala's println function, and because it has nothing meaningful to return, its return type is IO[Unit]. (More on this shortly.)

With those functions in hand you can write a for expression like this to get and then print a person's first and last name:

---

[1] https://github.com/alvinj/IOMonad

```
object IOTest1 extends App {

    for {
        _         <- putStrLn("First name?")
        firstName <- getLine
        _         <- putStrLn(s"Last name?")
        lastName  <- getLine
        _         <- putStrLn(s"First: $firstName, Last: $lastName")
    } yield ()

}
```

A few points about that code:

- When you don't care what's returned by the right-hand side of a line in a for expression, you can use the _ character on the left side of the <- assignment symbol to ignore that value. putStrLn returns IO[Unit], which I don't care about, so I use this approach.

- In the end, this particular for expression doesn't return anything of interest, so I use yield () at the end of it. (Remember that () is a way to return an instance of Unit. You can also write yield Unit, if you prefer.)

When I put that code in an App object, run it, and enter my first and last name, I see the following:

```
First name?
Alvin
Last name?
Alexander
First: Alvin, Last: Alexander
```

Why this works in for

This example shows that these new I/O functions — getLine and putStrLn — can be used inside for expressions. As you can imagine, they work because the IO class implements map and flatMap methods.

Conversely, if you replace getLine and putStrLn with Scala's built-in readLine and println methods, you'll see errors related to println that state, "flatMap is not a member of Unit," and, "map is not a member of Unit."

IO indicates interaction with the outside world

As I mentioned, a great thing about the IO monad is that these signatures clearly tell you that these functions reach out into the outside world:

```
def getLine: IO[String] = ???
def putStrLn(s: String): IO[Unit] = ???
```

When you see signatures like these you know that however getLine works internally, it clearly reaches into the outside world to retrieve a String. Similarly, putStrLn presumably takes the String that it receives and sends it into the outside world.

Monads don't have to be scary

Where "monad" used to be a scary name, now you know that it just means that a data type implements map and flatMap methods so it can be used in for expressions.

I tend to call these things "wrappers," and indeed, the IO monad is just another wrapper data type. For instance, you can imagine that getLine returns a String wrapped inside a box — an IO box — as shown in Figure 75.1.

```
+-------------+
|             |            A String wrapped
|   "alvin"   |  <----+    inside an
|             |            IO box.
+-------------+
```

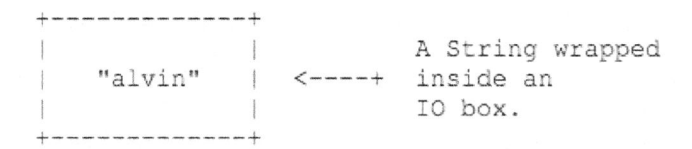

Figure 75.1: The IO monad is just a "wrapper" class. It has map and flatMap methods so it can be used in for expressions.

The great thing about that box is that the for expression knows how to open it, and pull the String out of it.

Just remember that monads in Scala implement map and flatMap so they can be used in for expressions. After that, they're not so scary.

76

Assigning a for Expression to a Function

Once you have an IO monad, you can use it in a `for` expression, and then assign that expression to a function. Notice how `forExpression` in this code is assigned to the large `for` expression. Also notice how the `for` expression ends with `yield ()`, so its return type is `IO[Unit]`:

```
object IOTest2 extends App {

    def forExpression: IO[Unit] = for {
        _          <- putStrLn("First name?")
        firstName  <- getLine
        _          <- putStrLn(s"Last name?")
        lastName   <- getLine
        fNameUC    = firstName.toUpperCase
        lNameUC    = lastName.toUpperCase
        _          <- putStrLn(s"First: $fNameUC, Last: $lNameUC")
    } yield ()

    // run the block of code whenever you want to ...
    forExpression.run

}
```

One thing I didn't mention yet is that an IO monad gives you a way to execute the code at a later time. In this example I execute the `for` expression at a later time by calling the `run` method on the IO monad instance. In fact, no I/O happens until this line is executed:

```
forExpression.run
```

When I run this `App` and then type in my name, the result looks like this:

```
First name?
alvin
Last name?
```

```
alexander
First: ALVIN, Last: ALEXANDER
```

Cool. Now you've seen how to create a function using a `for` expression, where that expression uses a functional approach to I/O. The next lesson takes this one step further by returning to recursion.

A note

On a personal note, I don't particularly like the function name `putStrLn`. However, (a) it comes from Haskell, and therefore (b) you may see experienced Scala/FP developers use it, so I thought I'd show it here so you can get used to it.

77

The IO Monad and a for Expression That Uses Recursion

In the next step of building up our knowledge, I'll add recursion to a for expression. This addition lets you write command-line applications that loop continuously, much like my Coin Flip game did earlier in this book.

Jumping right in, here's the source code for an application that continuously prompts you to input some text. The loop exits when you type in the string, "quit":

```
object FPRecursiveLoop extends App {

    def loop: IO[Unit] = for {
        _     <- putStrLn("Type something: ")
        input <- getLine
        _     <- putStrLn(s"You said '$input'.")
        _     <- if (input == "quit") IO(Unit) else loop   //RECURSE
    } yield ()

    loop.run

}
```

This code is similar to the for expression in the previous lesson, except for this line:

```
_ <- if (input == "quit") IO(Unit) else loop
```

That line can be read as, "If the user types 'quit', return IO(Unit) — thereby ending the recursion — otherwise, recursively call the loop function."

When I run this application and type in a few strings, I see this result:

```
Type something:
foo
You said 'foo'.
```

```
Type something:
bar
You said 'bar'.
Type something:
quit
You said 'quit'.
```

Discussion

If this technique seems simple — that's great! This shows that you're comfortable with the IO monad and recursion.

The cool thing about this loop is that it shows a pattern that you'll soon be able to use to write all sorts of command-line applications. For instance, if you want to write a command-line "To Do List" application, you can write it using this same pattern when you have some IO functions that let you read and write files (or a database).

What's next

Given these examples, this is a good time to take a deeper dive into the IO monad, including:

- Why it was originally created
- The IO monad philosophy

78

Diving Deeper Into the IO Monad

While the IO monad works as I've described — it implements `map` and `flatMap` so it can be used in `for` expressions, and it's intended to wrap I/O functions — there's a little more to it than I've let on so far.

To peel back the IO curtain a little more, I'm going to use a "professional" version of an IO monad. This one comes from the Cats[1] project (which is a play on the name, "category theory"). Cats is a leading library for functional programming in Scala.

Source code

The source code for this project is available at this URL:

- github.com/alvinj/IOMonadHelloWorld

The problem with I/O and FP

If you want to take a deep dive into understanding the need for the IO monad in Haskell, Learn You a Haskell for Great Good![2] is probably the best resource. But to keep things simple in this book, in this lesson I'll reference the first paragraphs from an article titled, An IO monad for Cats[3].

With a few simplifications, that story goes like this:

- In Haskell you only write pure functions.
- That's great, because it means you can compose your functions just like algebraic equations to create software applications.
- But when the Haskell creators got to I/O, they realized they had a problem. I/O functions aren't referentially transparent (RT), so you can't combine them like algebraic

---

[1] https://github.com/typelevel/cats
[2] http://amzn.to/1POaUCv
[3] http://typelevel.org/blog/2017/05/02/io-monad-for-cats.html

expressions. And if you can't compose I/O functions with your pure functions, you can't write an application that interacts with the outside world.

The short story of the problem's solution is that monads were invented in 1991, and in 1998 the IO monad was added to Haskell as a way to deal with I/O. The IO monad contains a bit of a "trick" that lets you use I/O functions as though they are RT.

The IO monad's trick

The trick of the IO monad is that it lets you write I/O functions as *effects*. Philosophically, what happens is that you use IO to *describe* how an I/O function works. Then, instead of dealing with the result of the I/O function at the time when the I/O function appears to be called, you defer the actual *action* until some time later when you really want it to be triggered.

As an example of this, if you run this little Scala app that *doesn't* use the IO monad:

```
object HelloVal extends App {
    val result = println("Hello, world")
}
```

you'll see that it prints "Hello, world" to STDOUT, as expected. Conversely, the IO monad trick looks like this:

```
import cats.effect.IO

object IOMonadAlmostHelloWorld extends App {
    val hello = IO { println("Hello, world") }
}
```

If you run this app, you'll see that no output is produced by this code; the App will run, but it won't produce any output.

What happens here is that instead of hello immediately printing to the outside world, it can be thought of as a *description* of how to print to the outside world. You can pass hello around, and it carries this description of *how* to print to the outside world along with it, but until it's explicitly told to execute, nothing happens.

> Haskell developers refer to this sort of thing as an *effect*, and as a result, the Cats' creators put their IO monad in a package named *cats.effect*.

Continuing the story ... with Cats you trigger the action by calling a method named unsafeRunSync on the IO instance:

```
import cats.effect.IO

object IOMonadHelloWorld extends App {
    val helloEffect = IO { println("Hello, world") }
    // ...
    // some time later ...
    // ...
    helloEffect.unsafeRunSync()
}
```

This is a true "Hello, world" example using the Cats IO monad, because it uses helloEffect.unsafeRunSync() to trigger the action/effect when desired, and Hello, world is printed to STDOUT.

Two notes

I'll make two notes about this code before moving on. First, helloEffect's type is IO[Unit], so I could have declared that type explicitly, like this:

```
val helloEffect: IO[Unit] = IO { println("Hello, world") }
```

Second, every IO monad may have some API differences, and where Cats names their method unsafeRunSync, the Scalaz project names their similar method, unsafePerformIO. Both of these names are intended to show that some "unsafe" I/O is about to happen.

The IO monad philosophy

The IO monad philosophy is described well in the "An IO monad for Cats" article[4], so I'll quote directly from there (with a few minor changes):

> "In Haskell, *effects* are treated as first-class values. The putStrLn function doesn't print to standard out, it returns a value (of type IO ()) which *describes* how to print to standard out, but stops short of actually doing it. These sorts of values can be composed using the monadic operators (think Scala's for expression),

---
[4]http://typelevel.org/blog/2017/05/02/io-monad-for-cats.html

allowing programmers to build up expressions composed of sequences of dependent effects, all of which are merely *descriptions* of the side-effects which will eventually be performed by the runtime. Ultimately, the description which comprises your whole program is the return result from the main function."

A small demonstration of that philosophy

That article includes a demonstration of that philosophy that I've converted into a small but complete application:

```
import cats.effect.IO

object Program extends App {

    val program: IO[Unit] = for {
        _       <- IO { println("Welcome to Scala!  What's your name?") }
        name    <- IO { scala.io.StdIn.readLine }
        nameUC = name.toUpperCase
        _       <- IO { println(s"Well hello, $nameUC!") }
    } yield ()

    // ...
    // ...
    // some time later ...
    // ...
    // ...
    program.unsafeRunSync()
}
```

As this example shows, the IO monad helps you *compose* function calls in a for expression, where those functions can be a combination of a) pure functions, and b) functions with I/O side effects. After composing those function calls and saving the result in a variable, you can then trigger it to be "run" at some point later in your application.

Key point

To be clear, the key point is that the IO monad provides a way for you to write for expressions that use pure functions and I/O functions in a compositional style.

Terminology

Haskell developers use the words "effect" and "action" when talking about the IO monad. I noted the word "effect" above, and with the reminder that `putStrLn` is defined like this:

```
def putStrLn(s: String): IO[Unit] = IO { println(s) }
```

this is how *Learn You a Haskell for Great Good!*[5] uses the term "action" when describing `putStrLn`:

> "We can read the type of `putStrLn` like this: `putStrLn` takes a string and returns an I/O action that has a result type of () (i.e., the empty tuple, also know as unit). An *I/O action* is something that, when performed, will carry out an action with a side-effect (usually either reading input or printing to the screen), and will also contain some kind of return value inside it. Printing a string to the terminal doesn't really have any kind of meaningful return value, so a dummy value of () is used."

Here's another quote from *Learn You a Haskell for Great Good!* that expands on that point:

> "You can think of an I/O action as a box with little feet that goes out into the real world and does something there (like write some graffiti on a wall) and maybe brings back some data. Once it's fetched that data for you, the only way to open the box and get the data inside it is to use the <- construct ... This is how Haskell manages to neatly separate the pure and impure parts of our code."

While that quote is about Haskell, you can see the similarity to Scala/FP when talking about the <- symbol. In fact, this Haskell application is equivalent to the last Scala application I showed in this lesson:

```
import Data.Char

main = do
    _          <- putStrLn "What's your name?"
    name       <- getLine
    let nameUC =  map toUpper name
    putStrLn ("Well hello, " ++ nameUC)
```

---

[5]http://amzn.to/1POaUCv

The Haskell do construct is similar to the Scala for expression, and as this code shows, there are some striking visual similarities between the two constructs.

79

I'll Come Back to the IO Monad

I'll come back to the `IO` monad in a little while when I get to a point where I'll want to write applications using it and the `State` monad at the same time.

Until then, I want to point out one last thing: So far I've only shown how to use the `IO` monad with *console* I/O. Can you guess why that is?

If you've read other Scala `IO` monad tutorials on the internet, you've probably noticed the same thing: Everyone shows how to use "console I/O," but nobody discusses other types of I/O, such as file, network, and database I/O. At some point the curious reporter in you has to wonder, "Why is that?"

I believe the reason for this has to do with *exception-handling*. For example, imagine that you already have a Scala function like this to read a text file into a `List[String]`:

```scala
def readTextFileAsTry(filename: String): Try[List[String]] = {
    Try {
        val lines = using(io.Source.fromFile(filename)) { source =>
            (for (line <- source.getLines) yield line).toList
        }
        lines
    }
}
```

That function uses Scala's `Try`, `Success`, and `Failure` classes to let you write code like this to handle exceptions:

```scala
val passwdFile = readTextFileAsTry("/etc/passwd-foo")
passwdFile match {
    case Success(lines) => lines.foreach(println)
    case Failure(s) => println(s"Failed, message is: $s")
}
```

Good questions at this time are:

- Should I wrap readTextFileAsTry with IO, so the return type becomes IO[Try[List[String]]]
- Am I supposed to do something else?

I'll dig into these questions later, but first I want to dig into the State monad.

Exercises

If you like open-ended exercises, I recommend the following:

1. Try wrapping the readTextFileAsTry function with the IO type to see what benefits and drawbacks that approach offers.
2. Try using a function like the Apache Commons IO[1] project's *org.apache.commons.io.FileUtils::readFileToString* function — which can throw an IOException — with the Cats IO monad. What benefits and drawbacks does that approach offer with real-world code?

---

[1]https://commons.apache.org/proper/commons-io/javadocs/api-release/index.html?org/apache/commons/io/input/package-summary.html

80

Functional Composition

> *"Do not write code that works. Write code such that it is impossible that it does not work."*
>
> Kris Nuttycombe, on Twitter[a]
>
> ---
> [a]https://twitter.com/nuttycom/status/872960182145495041

This is a good time to say that it's impossible to overstate how important *function composition* is to "Pure FP" developers. The desire to compose *everything* — to make all code read like algebraic equations — is immense. The Pure FP mantra can be stated as, "If functions can't be composed like algebraic equations, they're wrong."

Function composition in simple terms

This page on utah.edu[1] offers a simple definition of function composition:

> "*Composition* is a fancy term which means 'combining' ... Function composition is the process of combining two or more functions to produce a new function. Composing functions together is like snapping together a series of pipes for our data to flow through."

Technically there are at least two types of function composition, but for now I'm only interested in the meaning of composition where you turn this code:

```
val y = g(x)
val z = f(y)
```

into this code:

---
[1]http://www.cs.utah.edu/~germain/PPS/Topics/composition.html

```
val z = f(g(x))
```

Wikipedia refers to that last line as a "highly-composed form."

The utah.edu page makes interesting points about these examples:

- You can refer to the first two lines as *non-composed* code.
- Non-composed code explicitly uses extra variables to hold the intermediate state (such as y in this example), while with the highly-composed form of code the compiler implicitly creates temporary, hidden variables behind the scenes.

My key points are:

- Function composition is like combining algebraic equations.
- You can only compose functions when your functions are pure.
- Beware: sometimes when you use *too much* function composition — i.e., the highly-composed form — your code can be hard to read. This isn't always true, but because we programmers spend the majority of our time reading code, this is something to keep an eye out for. (Make sure your code is easy to maintain.)

An example of functional composition using IO

In theory, now that you have the Cats[2] IO monad to make your I/O functions composable, you can compose the CoinFlip game inside a `for` expression:

(The full code listing is shown on the next page.)

---

[2]http://typelevel.org/cats/

```
def mainLoop(gameState: GameState, random: Random): IO[Unit]  = for {
    _              <- IO { showPrompt() }
    userInput <- IO { getUserInput() }
    _              <- if (userInput == "H" || userInput == "T") for {
    // this first line is a hack; a for-expression must begin with a generator
    _                  <- IO { println("you said H or T") }
    coinTossResult =   tossCoin(random)
    newNumFlips    =   gameState.numFlips + 1
    newGameState   =   createNewGameState(
                         userInput, coinTossResult, gameState, random, newNumFlips)
    _                  <- IO { printGameState(
                               printableFlipResult(coinTossResult), newGameState)}
    _                  <- mainLoop(newGameState, random)
} yield Unit
else for {
_ <- IO { println("did not enter H or T") }
_ <- IO { printGameOver() }
_ <- IO { printGameState(gameState) }
} yield Unit
} yield Unit

mainLoop(s, r).unsafeRunSync()
```

While I personally wouldn't want to maintain that particular block of code, I appreciate that it shows that with the addition of the IO monad, all of my code can theoretically be composed into one for expression, with one function call after another, with a few variable assignments mixed in as well.

Source code

You can download the source code shown at this URL:

- github.com/alvinj/CoinFlipGameWithCatsIO[3]

---

[3]https://github.com/alvinj/CoinFlipGameWithCatsIO

See also

- The quotes in the utah.edu article are the same as in this medium.com article[4].
- The Wikipedia definition of function composition[5] states, "function composition is an act or mechanism to combine simple functions to build more complicated ones. Like the usual composition of functions in mathematics, the result of each function is passed as the argument of the next, and the result of the last one is the result of the whole."

---

[4] https://medium.com/javascript-scene/master-the-javascript-interview-what
[5] https://en.wikipedia.org/wiki/Function_composition_(computer_science)

81

An Introduction to Handling State

"State is the root of all evil."

Joe Armstrong, Erlang creator

Keeping in mind that the end goal of these monad lessons is to be able to write my Coin Flip game (and other applications) entirely in a Scala/FP compositional style, the next thing I need to look at is how to handle "state" in an FP manner. (There's no way for you to know that at this time, but I know that.)

Transitioning from IO to State

While the IO monad is a wrapper that makes I/O functions easier to work with in for expressions, the State monad is a wrapper that makes the concept of "state" easier to work with in for expressions. The next few lessons will first demonstrate the problems of trying to work with state without a State monad, and then I'll show how the State monad helps to alleviate those problems.

Handling State Manually

If you don't happen to have a State monad laying around, you can still handle state in Scala/FP. The basic ideas are:

- First, create some sort of construct to model the state of your application at any moment in time. Typically this is a case class, but it doesn't have to be.
- Next, create a "helper" function that takes a) the previous state and b) some sort of increment or "delta" to that state. The function should return a new state based on those two values.

I'll demonstrate this process in this lesson.

Source code

The source code for this lesson is available at:

- github.com/alvinj/HandlingStateManually[1]

Modeling my bad golf game, Part 1

My brother-in-law recently made me play golf, and as I don't play golf, the results were comical. But, the experience makes for a simple example of state, so here we go …

Imagine that you're on the first hole of a golf course, and you swing at a ball three times, with these results:

- The first ball goes 20 yards
- The second ball goes 15 yards
- The third swing is a "swing and a miss," so technically the ball goes 0 yards

One way to model the state after each stroke is with a simple case class that stores the cumu-

---

[1] https://github.com/alvinj/HandlingStateManually

lative distance of all my swings:

```
case class GolfState(distance: Int)
```

Given that model, I can create a "helper" function named nextStroke. It takes the previous GolfState and the distance of the next stroke to return a new GolfState:

```
def nextStroke(
    previousState: GolfState,
    distanceOfNextHit: Int): GolfState = {
    GolfState(previousState.distance + distanceOfNextHit)
}
```

Now I can use those two pieces of code to create an application that models my three swings:

```
object Golfing1 extends App {

    def nextStroke(
        previousState: GolfState,
        distanceOfNextHit: Int): GolfState = {
        GolfState(previousState.distance + distanceOfNextHit)
    }

    val state1 = GolfState(20)
    val state2 = nextStroke(state1, 15)
    val state3 = nextStroke(state2, 0)

    println(state3)   //prints "GolfState(35)"

}
```

In that application, these lines of code simulate my three swings at the ball:

```
val state1 = GolfState(20)
val state2 = nextStroke(state1, 15)
val state3 = nextStroke(state2, 0)
```

The last line of code prints the final golf state as GolfState(35), meaning that the total distance of my swings is 35 yards.

This code won't win any awards — it's repetitive and error-prone — but it does show how you have to model changing state in a Scala/FP application with immutable state variables. (In the following lessons I show how to improve on this situation by handling state in a `for` expression.)

Modeling my bad golf game, Part 2

While that example shows a basic solution to the problem at hand, a more real-world scenario is that you'll want to model the state by keeping a history of all golf strokes. Maintaining a history requires only a small change to the current code.

The following code shows one way to model a series of golf swings by using a state model that stores the series of golf strokes as a `List`:

```scala
object Golfing2 extends App {

    case class GolfState(strokes: List[Int])

    // take the old state, and an increment to that state
    def nextStroke(gs: GolfState,
                   distanceOfNextHit: Int): GolfState = {
        GolfState(distanceOfNextHit :: gs.strokes)
    }

    val state0 = GolfState(Nil)
    val state1 = nextStroke(state0, 20)
    val state2 = nextStroke(state1, 15)
    val state3 = nextStroke(state2, 0)

    println(state3)   //prints "GolfState(List(0, 15, 20))"

}
```

The important part of these examples is getting used to these patterns:

- Creating a `case` class to model the desired state
- Writing a function that takes a) an existing state, and b) an increment to that state, and returns a new state based on those values

Aside: Thinking of state as pushing onto a list

As a brief aside, when you search the internet for State monad examples, you'll often see that people compare it to pushing items onto a list. That's a valid comparison, and in fact, I can rewrite the previous example like this:

```
object Golfing2bPushPop extends App {

    def push[A](xs: List[A], a: A): List[A] = a :: xs

    // model the three swings
    val s0: List[Int] = Nil
    val s1 = push(s0, 20)
    val s2 = push(s1, 15)
    val s3 = push(s2, 0)

    // prints "List(0, 15, 20)"
    println(s3)

}
```

The concept of handling state in FP applications is often similar to pushing items onto a list, so examples like these are valid metaphors (though they're not complete on their own).

A pop function

Note that a pop function isn't required for this example, but I can write one like this:

```
def pop[A](xs: List[A]): (A, List[A]) = (xs.head, xs.tail)
```

At the end of Golfing2bPushPop I can then use pop like this:

```
val (swing3, state2) = pop(s3)
println(s"swing3 = $swing3")   //swing3 = 0
println(s"state2 = $state2")   //state2 = List(15, 20)
```

Recap

All of these examples show how to *manually* handle state in a Scala/FP application. You can significantly improve this situation by handling state in a for expression with a good State monad.

In the next lesson I'll show how to write a simple State monad that lets you *manually* handle state in a for expression. In the lesson after that I'll show how to completely automate state handling in a for expression with a significantly improved State monad.

83

Getting State Working in a for Expression

Knowing that I wanted to get my code working in a `for` expression, I attempted to create my own `State` monad. I modeled my efforts after the `Wrapper` and `Debuggable` classes I shared about 10-20 lessons earlier in this book. Starting with that code, and dealing with only `Int` values, I created the following first attempt at a `State` monad:

```
/**
 * this is a simple (naive) attempt at creating
 * a State monad
 */
case class State(value: Int) {

    def flatMap(f: Int => State): State = {
        val newState = f(value)
        State(newState.value)
    }

    def map(f: Int => Int) = State(f(value))

}
```

This code is very similar to the `Wrapper` and `Debuggable` classes I created earlier in this book, so please see those lessons if you need a review of how this code works.

With this `State` monad in hand, I can write the following `for` expression to model my golf game:

```
object StateTester extends App {
    val res = for {
        a <- State(20)
        b <- State(a + 15)   //manually carry over `a`
        c <- State(b + 0)    //manually carry over `b`
    } yield c

    println(s"res: $res")   //prints "State(35)"
}
```

The good news about this code is:

- It shows another example of a wrapper class that implements `flatMap` and `map`
- As long as I just need `Int` values, this code lets me use a concept of state in a `for` expression

Unfortunately, the bad news is that I have to manually carry over values like a and b (as shown in the comments), and this approach is still cumbersome and error-prone. Frankly, the only improvement I've made over the previous lesson is that I now have "something" working in a `for` expression.

What I need is a better `State` monad.

84

Handling My Golfing State with a State Monad

Fortunately some other people worked on this problem long before me, and they created a better `State` monad that lets me handle the problem of my three golf strokes like this:

```
val stateWithNewDistance: State[GolfState, Int] = for {
    _             <- swing(20)
    _             <- swing(15)
    totalDistance <- swing(0)
} yield totalDistance
```

Unlike the code in the previous lesson, notice that there's no need to manually carry values over from one line in the `for` expression to the next line. A good `State` monad handles that bookkeeping for you.

In this lesson I'll show what you need to do to make this `for` expression work.

Source code

The source code for this lesson is at:

- github.com/alvinj/StateMonadExample

Handling state with a State monad

With a properly-written `State` monad I can write an application to simulate my golf game like this:

```
object Golfing3 extends App {

    case class GolfState(distance: Int)
```

```
    def swing(distance: Int): State[GolfState, Int] = State { (s: GolfState) =>
        val newAmount = s.distance + distance
        (GolfState(newAmount), newAmount)
    }

    val stateWithNewDistance: State[GolfState, Int] = for {
        _              <- swing(20)
        _              <- swing(15)
        totalDistance  <- swing(0)
    } yield totalDistance

    // initialize a `GolfState`
    val beginningState = GolfState(0)

    // run/execute the effect.
    // `run` is like `unsafeRunSync` in the Cats `IO` monad.
    val result: (GolfState, Int) = stateWithNewDistance.run(beginningState)

    println(s"GolfState:       ${result._1}")   //GolfState(35)
    println(s"Total Distance: ${result._2}")    //35

}
```

I'll explain this code in the remainder of this lesson.

GolfState

First, as with the previous lesson, I use a `case` class to model the distance of each stroke:

```
case class GolfState(distance: Int)
```

There may be better names for this class, but I'm trying to emphasize the concept of state, so I use this name.

The `swing` function

Next, assuming that you haven't worked with a `State` monad like this before, the `swing` function will require a little explanation:

```
def swing(distance: Int): State[GolfState, Int] = State { (s: GolfState) =>
    val newDistance = s.distance + distance
    (GolfState(newDistance), newDistance)
}
```

While `swing` is a little more gory than the `nextStroke` and `push` functions from the previous state lessons, it's similar in concept. The idea is that:

- It takes the distance of a golf swing as an input parameter
- It takes an old state as an input parameter (it takes this parameter as an input to the anonymous function)
- The result of the function is a new `State` instance that's created with the anonymous function
- The anonymous function adds a) the distance that's given as a function input parameter to b) the distance from the previous state, yielding a new distance
- The previous state is the `State` that's passed into the anonymous function (I name that variable `s` so the code will fit on one line in this book, but a better name is `previousState`)
- The new distance is used to yield a new tuple of (GolfState(newDistance), newDistance)
- The `State` monad yields that as a `State[GolfState, Int]`

swing *uses an anonymous function*

Notice that the `swing` function uses many techniques that I demonstrated in the lessons leading up to this point. First, the highlighted section of code in Figure 84.1 is an anonymous function.

```
def swing(distance: Int): State[GolfState, Int] = State { (s: GolfState) =>
    val newDistance = s.distance + distance
    (GolfState(newDistance), newDistance)
}
```

Figure 84.1: An anonymous function is passed into `State` *to create the* `swing` *function.*

The anonymous function can be read as, "Given an existing `GolfState` named `s`, calculate a new distance by adding the distance from `s` to the new `distance` that was passed in. Then use that new distance to create a new `GolfState`, and then return that new `GolfState` and the new distance as a `Tuple2`." Because I'm using a `State` monad I have to yield what it wants, so I yield the `Tuple2` as shown.

Next, notice in Figure 84.2 that a new `State` instance is created by passing that anonymous function into `State`'s constructor.

```
def swing(distance: Int): State[GolfState, Int] = State { (s: GolfState) =>
    val newDistance = s.distance + distance
    (GolfState(newDistance), newDistance)
}
```

A new State instance being constructed

Figure 84.2: A new `State` instance is created by giving it an anonymous function.

From the previous lessons you know this means that:

- `State` is either a `case` class, or a regular class with an `apply` method. (It could also be a function, but because `State` is capitalized, convention makes it most likely to be a class.)

- `State`'s constructor takes a function input parameter (FIP) or a by-name parameter (so it can accept an anonymous function as a parameter).

The for expression

The next part of the code is this `for` expression:

```
val stateWithNewDistance: State[GolfState, Int] = for {
    _             <- swing(20)
    _             <- swing(15)
    totalDistance <- swing(0)
} yield totalDistance
```

All of the previous code was created to enable the `for` expression to be written like this. (This is a good time to note that earlier in the book I wrote, "Writing pure functions is easy, gluing them together is hard.")

This expression assigns a block of code to the variable named `stateWithNewDistance`, where the "block of code" is the `for` expression that models my three swings. As usual, it isn't necessary to show the variable's type, but I do so to be clear that it's an instance of `State`, specifically a `State[GolfState, Int]` instance.

An important point to notice in this code is that I don't have to *manually* carry the state over from one line in the `for` expression to the next line. Because I'm working with a well-written `State` monad, its "magic" takes care of that bookkeeping for me.

The action begins

In the final part of the code, the action begins. First I create an initial state:

```
val beginningState = GolfState(0)
```

Next, I kick off the action by invoking a `run` method on the `State` monad instance, giving it my `beginningState` to get it started:

```
val result: (GolfState, Int) = stateWithNewDistance.run(beginningState)
```

This `run` function has the same purpose as the `unsafeRunSync` method on the Cats IO monad, letting you defer the execution until a later time.

That line of code executes the `for` expression, and when it's finished running I print out the final result:

```
println(s"GolfState:      ${result._1}")   //GolfState(35)
println(s"Total Distance: ${result._2}")   //35
```

The advantages of a `State` monad

As you can see from the code in this lesson, the advantages of a `State` monad are:

- It can be used in a `for` expression
- Inside the `for` expression it handles all of the bookkeeping involved in transitioning from one state to another, so you don't have to handle it manually

The disadvantages of a `State` monad

Conversely, the primary disadvantage of a `State` monad is that some of your other code — such as the `swing` function — gets a little more complicated. In the long run this is offset somewhat by the fact that the state-handling pattern is pretty consistent; there's always a function like `swing` that helps automate the dirty work.

85

The State Monad Source Code

Until this point I treated the `State` monad code as a black box: I asked you to use it as though it already existed in the Scala libraries, just like you use `String`, `List`, and hundreds of other classes without thinking about how they're implemented.

My reason for doing this is that the `State` code is a little complicated. You have to be a real master of `for` expressions to be able to write a `State` monad that works like this.

> Note: A "master of `for` expressions" is a goal to shoot for!

In a way, the `State` monad just implements `map` and `flatMap` methods, so it's similar to the `Wrapper` and `Debuggable` classes I created previously. But it also takes those techniques to another level by using generic types, by-name parameters, and anonymous functions in several places.

Source code

The source code for this lesson is at the same URL as the previous lesson:

- github.com/alvinj/StateMonadExample[1]

The `State` source code

Here's the source code for the `State` monad I used in the previous lesson:

```
case class State[S, A](run: S => (S, A)) {

    def flatMap[B](g: A => State[S, B]): State[S, B] = State { (s0: S) =>
        val (s1, a) = run(s0)
        g(a).run(s1)
```

---

[1] https://github.com/alvinj/StateMonadExample

```
    }

    def map[B](f: A => B): State[S, B] = flatMap(a => State.point(f(a)))
}

object State {
    def point[S, A](v: A): State[S, A] = State(run = s => (s, v))
}
```

In this code the generic type S stands for "state," and then A and B are generic type labels, as usual.

In this first version of this book I'm not going to attempt to fully explain that code, but I encourage you to work with it and modify it until you understand how it works.

A few points worth noting

One point I need to mention is that State takes a constructor parameter named run. The anonymous function I highlighted in the previous lesson is what's assigned to run, as shown in Figure 85.1.

```
def swing(distance: Int): State[GolfState, Int] = State { (s: GolfState) =>
    val newDistance = s.distance + distance
    (GolfState(newDistance), newDistance)
}
```

this code block is assigned to the `run` variable

Figure 85.1: The constructor parameter run *is bound to the highlighted block of code.*

In the previous lesson, this line of code passed beginningState into into run:

```
val result: (GolfState, Int) = stateWithNewDistance.run(beginningState)
```

As a result, the parameter s in the anonymous function is bound to beginningState when that line of code is reached. Therefore, you can think of the first line of the anonymous function as using beginningState rather than s:

```
val newDistance = beginningState.distance + distance
                  --------------
```

Don't be intimidated!

I'll also make two other points at this time. First, I doubt that anyone wrote a `State` monad like this on their first try. I'm sure it took several efforts before someone figured out how to get what they wanted in a `for` expression.

Second, while this code can be hard to understand in one sitting, I've looked at some of the source code inside the Scala collections classes, and there's code in there that's also hard to grok. (Take a look at the sorting algorithms and you'll see what I mean.) Personally, the only way I can understand complex code like this is to put it in a Scala IDE and then modify it until I make it my own.

Where `State` comes from

I believe the original version of this `State` code came from this Github URL:

- github.com/jdegoes/lambdaconf-2014-introgame[2]

As the text at that link states, "This repository contains the material for *Introduction to Functional Game Programming with Scala*, held at LambdaConf 2014 in Boulder, Colorado." While I find a lot of that material to be hard to understand without someone to explain it (such as at a conference session), Mr. De Goes created his own `State` monad for that training session, and I believe that was the original source for the `State` monad I just showed.

> Much of the inspiration for this book comes from attending that conference and thinking, "I have no idea what these people are talking about."

Make it your own!

As a final example of what I mean by "working with that code to make it your own," this is what I did with another `State` monad that I found running wild on the internet:

```
case class State[A,S](run: S => (A,S)) {

    // s1 = state1, s2 = state2, s3 = state3
    def flatMap[B](f: A => State[B,S]): State[B,S] = State { s1: S =>
        val (a, s2) = run(s1)
        val stateChangeToB = f(a)
```

---

[2] https://github.com/jdegoes/lambdaconf-2014-introgame

```
            val (b, s3) = stateChangeToB.run(s2)
            (b, s3)
        }

        def map[B](f: A => B): State[B,S] =
            flatMap(a => State.lift(f(a)))

}

object State {
    /**
      * "lifts" a value and a state into a State[S,A]
      */
    def lift[A,S](value: A): State[A,S] = State(state => (value, state))
}
```

Note: Most experienced FP developers seem to prefer the name point for the method in the object, but I prefer the name lift. I like to think that this method "lifts" a normal variable (such as an Int) into the monad. (If you think of a monad as a wrapper, another possible name for this method is wrap.)

I don't remember for sure, but I believe that I found the original version of this State code in some work by James Earl Douglas, possibly on this slide:

- Slide #3 from a presentation on the State Monad[3]

Again, if you want to understand how the State monad works, it's important to work with the code to make it your own. Change the variable names as desired, add debug statements to the code, break the highly-composed lines into non-composed lines — do whatever you need to do to understand how it works.

---

[3]https://earldouglas.com/talks/state-monad/slides.html#(3)

86

Signpost: Getting IO and State Working Together

The next section of this book contains twelve short lessons that show how to get the IO and State monads working together in a for expression.

Source code

The source code for all of the following StateT "monad transformer" lessons is available at this Github URL:

- StateT monad transformer source code[1]

---

[1] https://github.com/alvinj/FPMonadTransformers

87

Trying to Write a for Expression with IO and State

At this point I'd *like* to be able to show you how to use the IO and State monads together in a for expression.

Unfortunately, that's not possible.

As John De Goes writes in his LambdaConf 2014 project notes[1]:

> "It turns out that for theoretical reasons, we can't just take any two monads M1 and M2 and combine them into another monad M3. It's not possible."

If you've ever seen the image shown in Figure 87.1, it pretty much expresses the frustration I felt when I first read that sentence.

---

[1] https://github.com/jdegoes/lambdaconf-2014-introgame

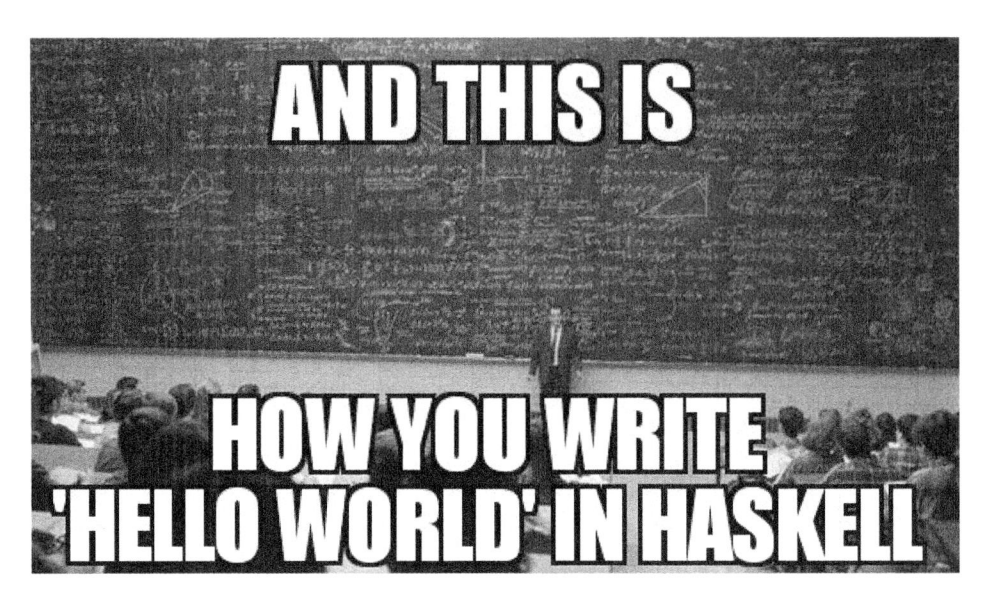

Figure 87.1: How you write "Hello, world" in Haskell. (I don't know the original creator of this image.)

Fortunately, Mr. De Goes goes on to add these statements:

> "However, there are a number of ways to combine monadic effects, ranging from Free monads to monad zippers and views to monad coproducts (and lots more). The particular approach we're going to look at involves *monad transformers*."

I'll follow his approach in this section of the book, culminating with writing for expressions that use the concepts of I/O and State in a way that is pleasing to experienced Scala/FP developers.

88

Seeing the Problem: Trying to Use State and IO Together

If you want to see the problem yourself, you can write a test for expression that uses IO and State. When I put this code in an IDE, it doesn't show any errors:

```
object TryStateAndIoTogether extends App {

    /* State code */
    type Stack = List[String]
    def push(x: String): State[Stack, Unit] = State[Stack, Unit] {
        xs => (x :: xs, ())
    }

    /* IO functions */
    def getLine: IO[String] = IO(scala.io.StdIn.readLine())
    def putStrLn(s: String): IO[Unit] = IO(println(s))

    /**
      * main loop: Prompt a user for some input, then push that input
      * onto a stack
      */
    val res = for {
        _     <- putStrLn("Type anything:")      //IO
        input <- getLine                          //IO
        _     <- push(input)                      //State
        _     <- putStrLn(s"Input: $input")      //IO
    } yield ()

}
```

But when I attempt to run that App, I see the following error output:

```
Error:(31, 15) type mismatch;
 found    : IO[Unit]
 required: State[Stack,?]
    (which expands to)  State[List[String],?]
          _     <- putStrLn(s"Input: $input")

Error:(30, 15) polymorphic expression cannot be instantiated
to expected type;
 found    : [B]State[Stack,B]
    (which expands to)  [B]State[List[String],B]
 required: IO[?]
          _     <- push(input)

Error:(30, 15) type mismatch;
 found    : State[Stack,B]
    (which expands to)  State[List[String],B]
 required: IO[?]
          _     <- push(input)

Error:(28, 15) type mismatch;
 found    : Unit => IO[Nothing]
 required: Unit => IO[B]
          _     <- putStrLn("Type anything:")
```

The short version of those errors messages is that there are "type mismatches," the worst of which is:

```
found    : IO[Unit]
required: State[Stack,?]
```

In this error message the compiler is saying, "I expected State here, but you gave me IO."

If you attempt to translate that for expression into a series of flatMap and map calls, you'll see the type mismatches. In short, because the return type of some method calls doesn't match the expected input parameters of other methods, the code won't compile. What we need is a series of flatMap calls that all return and expect the same wrapper type.

89

Solving the Problem with Monad Transformers

As background for where we're about to go, I want to share one more quote from Mr. De Goes:

> "A *monad transformer* is a special version of a monad that can stack its own effects on those of another monad. If you stack a monad transformer on another monad, the result forms a monad, which combines the effects of both monads together."

> "Not all monads have monad transformers. For example, the IO monad doesn't have a transformer version. Fortunately, we're in luck: while IO doesn't come in a transformer flavor, the State monad does."

The StateT monad transformer

The State monad transformer is named StateT. By convention monad transformers have a T at the end of their name, so in this case StateT is the monad transformer version of State. Similarly, an Option monad transformer is named OptionT.

In the following lessons I'll show everything that's needed to use the StateT monad transformer so you can use the concepts of I/O and State together in a for expression.

90

Beginning the Process of Understanding StateT

"The only way you're going to enjoy these StateT lessons is if you have an intense desire to see all of your code as being like algebra."

~ The author

Source code

As a reminder, the source code for all of the StateT "monad transformer" lessons is available at this Github URL:

- StateT monad transformer source code[1]

Background

In the previous lessons I showed that you can't write a for expression that tries to use an IO monad and a State monad together. If you write out the equivalent map/flatMap calls, you'll see that the data type returned by one method won't match up with the type expected by another method.

As I mentioned, there are a few possible ways to solve this problem, and one common approach is to use something called a *monad transformer*.

---

[1] https://github.com/alvinj/FPMonadTransformers

Goal for the StateT lessons

The main goal for these lessons is to show how to use a monad transformer named StateT that lets us use the concepts of I/O and State together in a for expression. By the end of these StateT lessons I'll show how to create and understand the following code:

```
def sumLoop: StateT[IO, SumState, Unit] = for {
    _     <- putStrAsStateT("\ngive me an int, or 'q' to quit: ")
    input <- getLineAsStateT
    _     <- if (input == "q") {
                liftIoIntoStateT(IO(Unit))
            } else for {
                i <- liftIoIntoStateT(IO(toInt(input)))
                _ <- doSumWithStateT(i)
                _ <- sumLoop
            } yield Unit
} yield Unit

val result = sumLoop.run(SumState(0)).run
println(s"Final SumState: ${result}")
```

In the process of building up to this for expression, I'll show several smaller examples of the individual functions.

What that for expression does

Because that code is a series of functions you haven't seen before, it's hard to tell what that expression does, but the way it works is:

- putStrAsStateT prompts a user to enter an integer value, or q to quit
- getLineAsStateT reads the user input
- If the user enters q, the loop exits
- Otherwise, toInt is called to convert the input to an Int
- That Int is wrapped in an IO and then a StateT
- The game state is updated with the new Int
- The sumLoop function is called recursively

Here's an example of what this code looks like when it's run:

```
give me an int, or 'q' to quit: 1
updateIntState, old sum:    0
updateIntState, new input: 1
updateIntState, new sum:    1

give me an int, or 'q' to quit: 2
updateIntState, old sum:    1
updateIntState, new input: 2
updateIntState, new sum:    3

give me an int, or 'q' to quit: 3
updateIntState, old sum:    3
updateIntState, new input: 3
updateIntState, new sum:    6

give me an int, or 'q' to quit: q
Final SumState: (SumState(6),())
```

To see that output on your system, run the class named `LoopWithQuitLotsOfDebug` in the package *v3_loop_with_quit* in the source code for this lesson.

Motivation

While this may not be the most exciting loop ever created, if you can understand how it works, you'll understand the `StateT` monad transformer, which is probably the most difficult concept in this book. Once you understand it, you'll also understand how monad transformers work in general, meaning that you'll be able to use other transformers, such as `OptionT` in the Cats library.

Furthermore, while this may sound like a bit of hyperbole, I hope you'll also be able to understand every good monad tutorial that has ever been written, and you'll also be able to understand books like Functional Programming in Scala[2], Functional and Reactive Domain Modeling[3], and the monad lessons in Advanced Scala with Cats[4]. More importantly, beyond being able to understand all of those resources, I hope you'll be able to use monads and monad transformers to solve real-world problems.

---

[2]http://amzn.to/2sbY1hE
[3]http://amzn.to/2iOT3Vh
[4]https://underscore.io/training/courses/advanced-scala/

In case I didn't stress that enough, being able to understand monad transformers is a big deal. This topic is basically the "peak of the monad mountain" for FP and this book.

91

Getting Started: We're Going to Need a Monad Trait

One thing that hasn't been important to our Scala/FP lives yet is that the standard Scala library doesn't define a `Monad` trait. Even though I've said that types like `Option`, `List`, and `Future` work like monads, you won't find code like this in the standard library:

```
// this code IS NOT in the Scala standard library
trait Monad
class Option extends Monad
class List extends Monad
class Future extends Monad
```

Until now it didn't matter to us that those types don't extend a base `Monad` trait because we could use all of those types *as if* they were monads because they implement `map` and `flatMap`.

However, because we're now at a point where we need to use the `StateT` monad transformer, and because a transformer can only be stacked on a type that is a known monad — i.e., a type that extends a `Monad` trait — we need to do a little work to let us use classes like `Option`, `List`, and `Future` with `StateT`. Specifically:

- We need to define a `Monad` interface (a `trait`).
- We need to define the types we want to use as monads as instances that extend the `Monad` interface. This will let us use them with `StateT`.

Once we have a `Monad` trait and a `StateT` class, we'll be able to write the loop shown at the beginning of the previous lesson.

> In the real world you won't have to go through this process; you can just use the `Monad` and transformer types from a Scala/FP library like Cats[1]. I'm only taking you through this process so you can understand some of the things that are happening behind the scenes.

---
[1] https://typelevel.org/cats/

A Monad interface

I'm not going to take you all the way through the development of a Monad trait, but I will take you through the initial part of the thought process.

In Scala, you create a Monad interface by defining a trait that declares three methods: the usual map and flatMap methods, and also a lift method that "lifts" a normal value into the monad.

> FP experts prefer to use names like point or pure instead of lift, but because the purpose of the method is to "lift" a normal value into a monad, I prefer the name lift. It's like when you write Some(1); the apply method in Some's companion object essentially "lifts" the regular integer value 1 into the Some wrapper.

Knowing that a Monad interface needs these three methods, I begin sketching the interface like this:

```
trait Monad {
    def flatMap
    def map
    def lift
}
```

Having seen flatMap before, you know that it takes a function that transforms a type A to a type like Wrapper[B]. In this case the wrapper is named Monad, so a first stab at flatMap's signature looks like this:

```
def flatMap[A, B](f: A => Monad[B]): Monad[B]
```

Similarly, you've seen that map is a method that takes a function that transforms a type A to a type B, and then returns a result like Wrapper[B]. Therefore, a first stab at map's type signature looks like this:

```
def map[A, B](f: A => B): Monad[B]
```

Finally, knowing that the purpose of the lift method is to lift a normal type A into a wrapper, a first stab at its signature looks like this:

```
def lift[A](a: A): Monad[A]
```

Putting those together, a first sketch of a Monad interface looks like this:

```
trait Monad {
    def lift[A](a: A): Monad[A]
    def map[A, B](f: A => B): Monad[B]
    def flatMap[A, B](f: A => Monad[B]): Monad[B]
}
```

I'm going to stop at this point because I don't want to get into the gory details, I just want to give you an idea of what the interface looks like. (If you'd like to see the final implementation of the Monad trait, see the source code that comes with this project. But don't get bogged down in that code. Right now it's more important to learn how to *use* a Monad trait, not how to *write* one.)

Creating two Monad instances

As an example of how a Monad trait can be used, if I was in a situation where I needed to use the Scala Option as a real Monad, I'd create an OptionMonad instance like this:

```
implicit val OptionMonad = new Monad[Option] {
    def flatMap[A, B](ma: Option[A])(f: A => Option[B]): Option[B] =
        ma.flatMap(f)
    def lift[A](a: => A): Option[A] = Some(a)
}
```

For the purposes of creating my for expression I don't need an OptionMonad, but because I want to use the IO monad I've been using in this book with StateT, I *do* need an IOMonad instance:

```
implicit val IOMonad = new Monad[IO] {
    def flatMap[A, B](ma: IO[A])(f: A => IO[B]): IO[B] = ma.flatMap(f)
    def lift[A](a: => A): IO[A] = IO(a)
}
```

Notice a few things:

- The flatMap signature is a little more complicated than what I showed in my trait, requiring two input parameter groups. (More on this shortly.)
- I don't define a map method because the map method I inherit from the Monad trait provides the right behavior for them.
- I mark IOMonad as implicit. I do this so it can be "pulled into" some of the code that follows. (More on this shortly.)

Key points

In summary, I created a `Monad` trait so I could create an `IOMonad` instance. Because `IOMonad` extends `Monad`, I'll be able to use it with the `StateT` class that we'll develop next.

92

Now We Can Create StateT

Now that I have a formally-defined Monad trait, I can use it with a StateT class. The guts of the StateT class are pretty gory, so I won't show all of the code here, but I will highlight the important things to know about it.

StateT constructor's run parameter

The first thing to know is that similar to the State monad I showed in previous lessons, the StateT constructor takes a run parameter. run is defined as a function input parameter, so you need to supply it a function when creating a new StateT instance, and it has this type signature:

```
case class StateT(run: S => M[(S, A)]) {
                  -------------------
```

run's signature says that it's a function that transforms a state S to a tuple (S,A) that's wrapped by a monad M. In the previous state lessons, the run parameter in State had the type S => (S,A), so the change here is that the function that's passed in must further wrap (S,A) in a monad. Right away this shows why we needed to formally define a Monad type.

> There's no way for you to know from looking at only this signature that M stands for Monad, S stands for state, and A stands for a base type (something like Int). The only way you could really know that — besides me telling you — is to look at StateT's Scaladoc or its source code.

StateT's flatMap signature

A second thing to know about StateT is that its flatMap signature looks like this:

```
def flatMap[B](g: A => StateT[M, S, B])(implicit M: Monad[M]):
    StateT[M, S, B] = StateT { (s0: S) =>
```

Notice that it has two parameter groups, and the second parameter group takes an implicit Monad input parameter:

```
def flatMap[B](g: A => StateT[M, S, B])(implicit M: Monad[M])
               ------------------------  --------------------
```

This is why I defined the IOMonad to be an implicit variable in the previous lesson:

```
implicit val IOMonad = new Monad[IO] ...
--------
```

In the code in the following lessons, what happens is that when an implicit instance of IOMonad is in scope when flatMap is invoked, the implicit instance is automatically pulled into flatMap's second parameter group.

Another point to notice about StateT's signature is that its return type is StateT[M, S, B]:

```
def flatMap[B](g: A ...)(...): StateT[M, S, B]
                              ---------------
```

This means that flatMap returns a StateT instance, specifically of the type StateT[M, S, B], where M is a monad, S is a state, and B is the transformed version of the base type A.

I know that these details may not be too meaningful yet, but I want to point them out before we continue. If you come back to this lesson after you see the code that follows, I believe they'll be more meaningful then.

> If you want to see all of StateT, see the source code for these lessons. (But again, don't get caught up in it. The current goal is to learn how to *use* StateT, not how to *write* it.)

93

Using StateT in a for Expression

Given a `Monad` and a `StateT` with the attributes described in the previous lessons, we now have enough code to show a few examples of how `StateT` works. In this lesson I'll create the following `for` expression that uses the `add` and `multiply` functions I'm about to build:

```
val forExpression: StateT[IO, IntState, Int] = for {
    _ <- add(2)
    _ <- add(3)
    x <- multiply(10)
} yield x
```

Source code

> The source code for this lesson is in the package named *v1_hard_coded_for*, in the same repository[1] as all of the other `StateT` lessons.

A class to hold the state

The first thing I'll do is create a little `case` class to hold the state of this application, just like I did with the `GolfState` class in the "Handling State Manually" lesson:

```
case class IntState(i: Int)
```

Just as with those `State` lessons, this is a simple container for the "state" in my application.

An "add" function

Next, I'll create an `add` function that works with the `StateT` monad:

---
[1] https://github.com/alvinj/FPMonadTransformers

```
def add(i: Int) = StateT[IO, IntState, Int] { oldState: IntState =>
    val newValue = i + oldState.i
    val newState = oldState.copy(i = newValue)
    IO(newState, newValue)
}
```

Remember that StateT's constructor takes the function input parameter named run, so everything between the curly braces is an anonymous function that I'm passing into run.

You can read add's code like this:

- add takes an input parameter named i, which has the type Int
- add's body creates a new StateT instance, specifically a StateT[IO, IntState, Int]
- The StateT instance is created by passing the anonymous function that's defined in between the curly braces into StateT's constructor
- The anonymous function adds the value i to oldState.i to create newValue
- A newState of type IntState (not shown) is created from oldState, using the usual copy process to update its field i
- In the last line, the newState and newValue are wrapped in an IO

In the end, the result of calling add is a new StateT instance that specifically has the type StateT[IO, IntState, Int].

A "multiply" function

Next, I can do the same thing to create a multiply function:

```
def multiply(i: Int) = StateT[IO, IntState, Int] { oldState: IntState =>
    val newValue = i * oldState.i
    val newState = oldState.copy(i = newValue)
    IO(newState, newValue)
}
```

Because this function is identical to the previous function — with the exception that it multiplies i by oldState.i — I won't describe it again.

Testing add

Before using these functions in a for expression it can help to demonstrate how the add function works outside of a for expression. First, I can call add like this:

```
val a = add(1)    //StateT[IO, IntState, Int]
```

As the comment shows, a has the type StateT[IO, IntState, Int]. Therefore, this code can be read as, "I have a StateT instance named a that's primed to add 1 to something."

The way you use the StateT instance a is that you give an *initial state* to a's run method, like this:

```
val b = a.run(IntState(1))    //IO[(IntState, Int)]
```

Here I've given a the initial state IntState(1) to create the variable b. Intuitively you can guess that somewhere within the final result of this effort you'll find a 2, but at this point that result is wrapped inside the IO type (shown in the comment).

As the comment in that code shows, b has the type IO[(IntState, Int)], meaning that it's an IO wrapped around a tuple. The IO part doesn't make much sense in this little example — I'm not using any form of I/O yet — but I can extract the tuple out of the IO and print the IntState like this:

```
b.map(t => println(s"b state = ${t._1}"))
```

That code results in this output:

```
b state = IntState(2)
```

> IO doesn't have a foreach method, so I use map for the purpose of printing the IntState value.

As a review, here's all of the code again:

```
val a = add(1)                //StateT[IO, IntState, Int]
val b = a.run(IntState(1))    //IO[(IntState, Int)]

b.map(t => println(s"b state = ${t._1}"))
```

Given this overview of how add works, let's create a for expression that uses StateT.

Using StateT in a for expression

Next, let's use the add and multiply functions in a more normal way — in a for expression. I won't use any I/O functions just yet, but this example shows how to use add and multiply in a for expression with a few hard-coded values:

```
val forExpression: StateT[IO, IntState, Int] = for {
    _ <- add(2)
    _ <- add(3)
    x <- multiply(10)
} yield x
```

This creates the variable forExpression as a StateT instance. As you saw in the previous example, you "run" a StateT instance by calling its run method while giving it an initial state:

```
val result: IO[(IntState, Int)] = forExpression.run(IntState(1))
```

Supplied with that initial state, these comments show how the for expression works:

```
val forExpression: StateT[IO, IntState, Int] = for {
    _ <- add(2)            //2+1 = 3 (1 is run's seed value)
    _ <- add(3)            //3+3 = 6
    x <- multiply(10)      //6x10 = 60
} yield x
```

As the comments show, the final result is 60, but we also know that result's type is IO:

```
val result: IO[(IntState, Int)] = forExpression.run(IntState(1))
```

Because result is a tuple wrapped in an IO, I extract the IntState value from result like this:

```
result.map(tuple => println(s"IntState = ${tuple._1}"))
```

That code prints this output:

```
IntState = IntState(60)
```

Key points

While this example uses hard-coded Int values, it shows how to use functions that yield a StateT inside a for expression.

Furthermore, it lays the foundation for what's next: I'll add some I/O functions into a for expression, and that will let us *really* use an IO monad with the StateT monad in a for expression.

94

Trying to Combine IO and StateT in a for Expression

At this point I'm going to try to write my "sum up the integers a user gives me" for expression using IO and StateT. As I try to write it, I'll figure out what parts are missing, and add them in as I go along.

First, a reminder that the intent of this application is to:

- Prompt the user for input, which hopefully will be an Int value
- Sum up those Int values in the loop
- When the user types the letter q, the loop will exit

Source code

> The source code for this lesson is in the package named *v2_loop_without_quit*, in the same repository[1] as all of the StateT lessons. Work with the LoopWithoutQuitLotsOfDebug class to see a lot of debug output, or the LoopWithoutQuitNoDebug class to run the application without debug output.

I/O functions

One of the first things I'll need to solve this problem are some I/O functions to prompt the user and then read their input. I'll start with the IO functions I used in previous lessons:

```
def getLine(): IO[String] = IO(scala.io.StdIn.readLine())
def putStr(s: String): IO[Unit] = IO(print(s))
```

For this lesson I changed the function putStrLn to putStr because I don't want it to print a newline character after printing the string, but otherwise it's the same as before.

---

[1] https://github.com/alvinj/FPMonadTransformers

A toInt function

Next, I need a function to transform a String to an Int. This function will do the trick:

```
def toInt(s: String): Int = {
    try {
        s.toInt
    } catch {
        case e: NumberFormatException => 0
    }
}
```

In this case, toInt returns an Int rather than an Option[Int]. I did that to make my for expression simpler.

A "state" class

Next, I need a little case class to hold the state of the application. In this case I need to track the sum of the integers the user gives me, so I create this class:

```
case class SumState(sum: Int)
```

A state-updating function

Next up, I need a function to update the application's state when a user gives me a new Int. Because this is a "sum" function, all I need to do is re-use the add function I showed in the previous lesson. I'll just give it a new name that makes more sense in the context of this application:

```
def updateAppState(newValue: Int):
    StateT[IO, SumState, Int] = StateT { (oldState: SumState) =>

    // create a new sum from `i` and the previous sum from `s`
    val newSum = newValue + oldState.sum

    // create a new SumState
    val newState: SumState = oldState.copy(sum = newSum)

    // return the new state and the new sum, wrapped in an IO
    IO(newState, newSum)
```

}

I didn't mention it before, but notice that this function's return type gives you a hint of how StateT and IO work together; StateT is a wrapper, and one of the things it wraps is an IO:

```
StateT[IO, SumState, Int]
        --
```

Because StateT encapsulates both concepts — State and IO — in one type, it lets us use both types in a for expression.

Trying to use all of this in a for expression

If I ignore the "type q to quit" part of the application I can write a for expression like this:

```
def sumLoop: StateT[IO, SumState, Unit] = for {
    _     <- putStr("\ngive me an int: ")   //*
    input <- getLine                         //*
    i     <- IO(toInt(input))                //*
    _     <- updateAppStateT(i)
    _     <- sumLoop
} yield Unit
```

Unfortunately this code won't work. The first three lines inside the for expression — the ones tagged with the * comment — return an IO type, and updateAppStateT returns a StateT type.

This is a good time to mention an extremely important point:

- For this process to work, every function call inside the for expression must return a type of StateT[IO, SumState, A]

The type A can vary — it can be a String or Int as needed in this example — but each function must return a StateT[IO, SumState, A].

Therefore, knowing that the problem is (a) those functions return IO, and (b) they need to return StateT[IO, SumState, A], the solution is (c) I need to wrap those IO functions somehow so they'll return the correct type.

95

Fixing the IO Functions with Monadic Lifting

We're at a point where the I/O functions in the previous lesson return an IO type, but they *need* to return a StateT[IO, SumState, A]. Let's fix this problem.

My I/O functions currently look like this:

```
def getLine(): IO[String] = IO(scala.io.StdIn.readLine())
def putStr(s: String): IO[Unit] = IO(print(s))
```

To work in the for expression they need to return the type StateT[IO, SumState, A], so what can I do?

The solution is something called *monadic lifting*. Once again I need to "lift" something, and in this case I need to lift the type IO[A] into the type StateT[IO, SumState, A].

Source code

> You can see the source code for the liftIoIntoStateT function in the package named *v2_loop_without_quit*, in the same repository[1] as all of the StateT lessons.

The "lift" function

Knowing that I need to write a function that lifts an IO[A] into the type StateT[IO, SumState, A], I can sketch the initial function signature like this:

```
def lift(io: IO[A]): StateT[IO, SumState, A] = ???
```

At this point I'll just show the complete function that does the lifting. The function is really just one line long, but I split it into several lines so I can add some comments to it:

---

[1] https://github.com/alvinj/FPMonadTransformers

```
def liftIoIntoStateT[A](io: IO[A]):
    StateT[IO, SumState, A] = StateT { s: SumState =>

        // transform `IO[A]` into `IO(SumState, A)`
        val result: IO[(SumState, A)] = io.map(a => (s, a))

        // use this as a way to see what's going on here.
        // if you enter 1 and then 2 you'll see the output,
        // `(SumState(1), 2)`.
        //result.map(tup => println(s"lift: (${tup._1},
        //${tup._2})"))

        // yield the result of this anonymous function (which
        // will be wrapped by StateT)
        result
}
```

As the function signature shows, this function takes an IO[A] input parameter and yields a StateT[IO, SumState, A] type, which tells you that it "lifts" the given IO value into StateT. The io.map call inside the anonymous function merges the io input parameter and the SumState parameter s into a new type of IO[(SumState, A)]. Then that type is fed into StateT's constructor to yield the final type, StateT[IO, SumState, A].

As I mentioned, the anonymous function body is really only one line long; I just added the extra debug code so you can see the type inside the body. Here's what the function looks like without the intermediate steps:

```
def liftIoIntoStateT[A](io: IO[A]):
    StateT[IO, SumState, A] = StateT { s: SumState =>
        io.map(a => (s, a))  //IO[(SumState, A)]
}
```

The end result is that you can use this function to lift variables of type IO[A] into StateT, specifically the type StateT[IO, SumState, A].

Creating new I/O functions

Now we can use this function to create new I/O functions that yield a StateT so they can be used in the "sum the integers" for expression. First, I use liftIoIntoStateT to transform getLine into a new function I name getLineAsStateT:

```
def getLineAsStateT(): StateT[IO, SumState, String] =
    liftIoIntoStateT(getLine)
```

Then I do the same thing with the putStr function:

```
def putStrAsStateT(s: String): StateT[IO, SumState, Unit] =
    liftIoIntoStateT(putStr(s))
```

Welcome to the top of "Mount Monad"

Okay, admittedly that was a lot of setup work, but even if you don't know it yet, we're now at the top of the monad mountain. Because these functions yield a StateT[IO, SumState, A], they can be used in the for expression I tried to create in the previous lesson. In the next lesson we'll finally get IO and StateT working together!

96

A First IO/StateT for-Expression

Now that we have a collection of functions that all return this type:

```
StateT[IO, SumState, A]
```

we can build a `for` expression to prompt a user to enter integer values, read those values, and then sum them.

To keep things simple, in this lesson I'm going to write a `for` expression that you have to kill manually, such as using CTRL-C at the command line, or pressing a "stop" button in an IDE:

```
def sumLoop: StateT[IO, SumState, Unit] = for {
    _     <- putStrAsStateT("\ngive me an int: ")
    input <- getLineAsStateT
    i     <- liftIoIntoStateT(IO(toInt(input)))
    _     <- doSumWithStateT(i)
    _     <- sumLoop
} yield Unit
```

One thing to notice in this expression is this line:

```
liftIoIntoStateT(IO(toInt(input)))
```

I didn't bother to write a wrapper function around `toInt`, so in that line:

- `toInt` transforms `input` from a `String` to an `Int`
- That value is wrapped in an `IO` (an `IO[Int]`)
- That value is lifted into a `StateT` (a `StateT[IO, SumState, Int]`)

Just like I modified the I/O functions to return `StateT`, these steps are necessary to get `toInt` to work in the `for` expression.

Running the for expression

Now you can run the for expression by giving the run function an initial state, like this:

```
val result: (SumState, Unit) = sumLoop.run(SumState(0)).run
```

Because you have to kill this loop manually you can't see the final result, but with some debug code included in the functions you can see some output. In the source code for this project, if you run the App named *v2_loop_without_quit.LoopWithoutQuitLotsOfDebug*, and enter the numbers 1, 2, and 3 before killing the loop, you'll see this combination of input/output:

```
give me an int: 1
updateIntState, old sum:    0
updateIntState, new input:  1
updateIntState, new sum:    1

give me an int: 2
updateIntState, old sum:    1
updateIntState, new input:  2
updateIntState, new sum:    3

give me an int: 3
updateIntState, old sum:    3
updateIntState, new input:  3
updateIntState, new sum:    6
```

The output comes from the doSumWithStateT function, which looks like this:

```
def doSumWithStateT(newValue: Int):
    StateT[IO, SumState, Int] = StateT { (oldState: SumState) =>

    // create a new sum from `i` and the previous sum from `s`
    val newSum = newValue + oldState.sum
    println(s"updateIntState, old sum:   " + oldState.sum)
    println(s"updateIntState, new input: " + newValue)
    println(s"updateIntState, new sum:   " + newSum)

    // create a new SumState
    val newState: SumState = oldState.copy(sum = newSum)
```

```
    // return the new state and the new sum, wrapped in an IO
    IO(newState, newSum)
}
```

If you also uncomment the map/println statement in liftIoIntoStateT, you'll see this additional SumState output:

```
lift: (SumState(0), 1)
lift: (SumState(1), 2)
lift: (SumState(3), 3)
(SumState(6), ())
```

All of that output shows the internal state of the for expression as you enter the values 1, 2, and 3.

At this point I encourage you to work with the source code in this portion of the project until you understand how it works. As usual, add more comments and debug statements to the code and modify it as desired to make it your own.

97

The Final IO/StateT for Expression

Source code

The source code for this lesson is in the package named *v3_loop_with_quit*, in the same repository[1] as all of the StateT lessons. Work with the LoopWithQuitLotsOfDebug class to see a lot of debug output, or the LoopWithQuitNoDebug class to run the application without debug output.

The final for expression

In the previous lesson I wanted to keep the for expression simple, so I left out the "type q to quit" part of the code, but now it's time to show the complete code that lets the user type q to quit:

```
def sumLoop: StateT[IO, SumState, Unit] = for {
    _     <- putStrAsStateT("\ngive me an int, or 'q' to quit: ")
    input <- getLineAsStateT
    _     <- if (input == "q") {
                liftIoIntoStateT(IO(Unit))
            } else for {
                i <- liftIoIntoStateT(IO(toInt(input)))
                _ <- doSumWithStateT(i)
                _ <- sumLoop
            } yield Unit
} yield Unit

val result = sumLoop.run(SumState(0)).run
println(s"Final SumState: ${result}")
```

The big change to this code begins with this if statement inside the for expression:

```
if (input == "q")
```

---

[1] https://github.com/alvinj/FPMonadTransformers

As the comment after that line shows, if you type q, the expression returns Unit, which is first wrapped in an IO, and then wrapped in a StateT, and the loop/recursion ends. Otherwise, control is passed to the else clause where a second for expression does the work I showed previously, and a recursive call to sumLoop is made, prompting you to enter another integer, or q to quit.

A good thing about this loop is that when you type q you can see the final SumState. Here's the input and output I get when running the LoopWithQuitLotsOfDebug application with the values 1, 2, and 3:

```
give me an int, or 'q' to quit: 1
updateIntState, old sum:    0
updateIntState, new input: 1
updateIntState, new sum:    1

give me an int, or 'q' to quit: 2
updateIntState, old sum:    1
updateIntState, new input: 2
updateIntState, new sum:    3

give me an int, or 'q' to quit: 3
updateIntState, old sum:    3
updateIntState, new input: 3
updateIntState, new sum:    6

give me an int, or 'q' to quit: q
Final SumState: (SumState(6),())
```

As with the for expression in the previous lesson, I encourage you to work with the source code for this portion of the project and add debug statements and modify it until you understand it, making it your own.

You'll probably have to read it more than once

Using and understanding StateT is probably the most difficult topic in this book. But if you can understand it, I believe you'll be able to deeply understand many uses of monads.

Because this topic is difficult, I suspect that you'll have to read these StateT lessons more than once, and I apologize for that. Throughout this book I've tried to make each topic as easy to understand as possible, but "monad transformers" is a deep topic that you may need to review several times to understand.

Focus on how to *use* Monad and StateT

I'd like to add one more thing at this point: Unless you're interested in theory, don't get too caught up in how Monad and StateT are implemented. By that I mean that you should first focus on how to *use* StateT, and after that, if you want to know how to *write* Monad and StateT you can dig into that source code.

> Think of it this way: When you first learned how to sort a list in Scala, did you check the Scala library source code out from Github to see how the sort algorithms were implemented, or did you just try to sort your collection?

98

Summary of the StateT Lessons

As you saw in these StateT lessons, the key to being able to use both the IO and State monads in a for expression is to use a StateT transformer monad that encapsulates both State and IO within the same construct, specifically a StateT[IO, SumState, A] in this examples. StateT works just like State, and it's also a wrapper around IO.

There are other approaches to the problem of using multiple monads in a for expression, but using monad transformers is a common solution. For example, the Cats project[1] includes monad transformers including StateT, OptionT, EitherT, and more.

How about those types!

An interesting thing about everything you've been through in this book is that you're probably used to seeing types like StateT[IO, SumState, A] by now. If you're like me, when you first started this book you probably rarely used anything like that, but by now, seeing types like this is second nature.

Conclusion: Always ask "Why?"

As you saw in these lessons, you have to go through a lot of setup work in FP to be able to use the concepts of State and I/O in the same for expression. Early in this book I encouraged you to always ask "Why?" as you work through the lessons, and this is a good time to do that again:

> Why would anyone go through this much work when it's so much easier to write imperative loops?

---

[1] https://typelevel.org/cats/

I encourage you to answer that question yourself, and I'll provide my own thoughts here.

The first part of my answer is that monads and Scala's `for` expression give FP developers a way to write a sequence of computations using only immutable variables and pure functions. If you want to know how to write a series of computations using only "Pure FP," this is the best way the brightest minds know how to do this today.

The second part of the answer is that you must have a strong — make that *intense* — desire to see *all* of your code as being like math, like algebra. In your mind you can't just settle for writing pure functions, you must also have an intense dislike for mutable variables anywhere in your code. Only when you develop that passion will you be willing to go through this effort, and find the beauty in code like this.

In my own case I can say that going through this process has helped me learn to write better code. In my "Pure OOP" days I never thought much about mutable variables and method signatures, that was the only way I knew how to do things. But these days I use immutable variables and pure functions as much as possible, and I always follow the mantra of "write the function signature first" that I've shown in this book: I first sketch the function signature, and only when I'm confident that the input parameters and return type are correct do I write the function body.

See also

These lessons are heavily based on the code from John De Goes' 2014 LambdaConf presentation, Introduction to Functional Game Programming with Scala[2]. The `Monad` and `StateT` source code comes directly from that project.

---

[2]https://github.com/jdegoes/lambdaconf-2014-introgame

Signpost: Modeling the world with Scala/FP

"Bad programmers worry about the code. Good programmers worry about data structures and their relationships."

Linus Torvalds

As you can imagine, functional programming changes the way you model the world we live in. Where OOP tells us to encapsulate data and behavior in the same class, Scala/FP tells us that *data* should be modeled using `case` classes, and *behavior* — i.e., functions — should be modeled somewhere else. That concept of "somewhere else" is what the next several lessons are about.

Here's an outline of the next nine lessons:

- First, I define the concept of *domain modeling*.
- Next, I provide a short review of domain modeling in OOP. I do this as a means of providing contrast to the FP approaches that follow.
- Then I show how to model FP behavior using a "utilities" class approach, and also do the same thing with companion objects.
- After that I'll show how to put your behaviors in *modules*, an approach that encourages compositionality.
- Finally, I'll show how to write the same application using a hybrid OOP/FP "functional objects" approach.

The next lesson begins with a short discussion of domain modeling.

100

What is a Domain Model?

> *domain: a specified sphere of activity or knowledge; a realm or range of knowledge and responsibility; e.g., "the domain of polymer science"*
>
> ~ definitions from various online dictionaries

Before I get into the process of domain modeling in OOP and FP, it will help to be precise about what a "domain model" is.

Domain

As shown in the introductory quote for this lesson, a *domain* is "a sphere of activity or knowledge." When we build software applications, we work in the domains of the businesses we write applications for. For example, these are some of the businesses I've written software for in my career:

- a pizza company
- a magazine printing company
- a company that creates software for advertising agencies

As you can imagine, each of these businesses has their own sphere of activity or knowledge:

- a pizza company understands pizzas, toppings, customers, orders, stores, drivers, deliveries, etc.
- a printing company understands everything to do with magazines, covers, paper, ink, magazine pages, inserts, etc.
- advertising businesses know about advertisers, print ads, commercials on television and radio, billboards, and terms like "coverage" and "frequency"

As those examples show, each business domain is its own little world, with its own sphere of knowledge.

Domain model

A *domain model* refers to the way we model the objects in a given domain as software engineers. It's a conceptual model where we organize and define the entities we encounter in the domain (pizzas, orders, etc.), the attributes of those entities (toppings, crust size, crust type), the relationships between the entities (a pizza has toppings, an order has one or more pizzas), and the behaviors and interactions of those entities (add topping to pizza, add pizza to order).

A domain model is also a vocabulary or dictionary that represents a shared understanding of the domain. Everyone involved in the project, including the product owner, stakeholders, development team, etc., should understand the vocabulary and be able to use it as a communication tool. When someone says, "A customer calls a store to order a pizza for delivery," all of those terms should be understood by everyone on the project.

The term "domain model" can refer to a visual model, the source code we write, or the written documentation we create, but in any format it is a conceptual model of the domain.

Finally, you can implement a domain model using OOP, FP, any other programming paradigms that may evolve in the future, and in terms of source code, a domain model can be implemented in any programming language.

What's next

In the lessons that follow, I'll first show a Scala/OOP version of a domain model for a pizza store. After that I'll show different ways to implement the domain model using Scala/FP.

A Review of OOP Data Modeling

> *"The problem with object-oriented languages is they've got all this implicit environment that they carry around with them. You wanted a banana but what you got was a gorilla holding the banana and the entire jungle."*
>
> Joe Armstrong

Before I get into the Scala/FP domain modeling lessons, I want to share what a Scala/OOP data model might look like for a Pizza point of sales (POS) system. For the purposes of this lesson I'm going to assume that a pizza store can only sell pizzas; it doesn't sell other things like breadsticks, cheesesticks, salads, beverages, etc.

The source code

The source code for this lesson is at this Github URL:

- github.com/alvinj/PizzaPosOopStyle[1]

A note before we begin

If I was going to model a Pizza POS system using a "100% correct" OOP design, I would make the fields of each class private, and require `get` and `set` method calls on them, like this:

---

[1] https://github.com/alvinj/PizzaPosOopStyle

```
class Pizza {

    type Money = BigDecimal

    // private fields
    private var _crustSize: CrustSize = MediumCrustSize
    private var _crustType: CrustType = RegularCrustType
    private val _toppings = ArrayBuffer[Topping]()

    def getCrustSize = _crustSize
    def setCrustSize(cs: CrustSize) {
        _crustSize = cs
    }

    def getCrustType = _crustType
    def setCrustType(ct: CrustType) {
        _crustType = ct
    }

    def getToppings = _toppings
    def addTopping(t: Topping) {
        _toppings += t
    }

    // more code ...

}
```

However, I'm not going to do that in this lesson because (a) I assume that you understand OOP, (b) this book isn't about OOP, and (c) once I create several classes, that approach requires a lot of boilerplate code that obscures what I want to show. Therefore, in this lesson I'm going to write my OOP classes using public *var* fields without getter and setter methods.

Modeling toppings, crust size, and crust type

To build a pizza you need to define what your toppings, crust size, and crust type look like. In both the OOP and FP worlds, these attributes are best defined as enumerations, as shown here:

```
sealed trait Topping
case object Cheese extends Topping
case object Pepperoni extends Topping
case object Sausage extends Topping
case object Mushrooms extends Topping
case object Onions extends Topping

sealed trait CrustSize
case object SmallCrustSize extends CrustSize
case object MediumCrustSize extends CrustSize
case object LargeCrustSize extends CrustSize

sealed trait CrustType
case object RegularCrustType extends CrustType
case object ThinCrustType extends CrustType
case object ThickCrustType extends CrustType
```

The benefits of enumerations are:

- You can use the types Topping, CrustSize, and CrustType in function signatures
- They work well in other places, such as match expressions
- Type safety in general

Aside: Use enums, not strings

Don't ever use strings where you should use enumerations. That is, don't ever do this:

```
val CHEESE    = "cheese"
val PEPPERONI = "pepperoni"
```

That approach leads to code like this:

```
def addTopping(p: Pizza, t: String)
def getToppings(): Seq[String]
```

Enumerations also work much better with pattern matching.

A Pizza class

Once you have those pizza attributes, you can define the OOP version of a `Pizza` class like this:

```
class Pizza {

    var crustSize: CrustSize = MediumCrustSize
    var crustType: CrustType = RegularCrustType

    // no need for `toppings` to be a `var`; `ArrayBuffer` is mutable
    val toppings = ArrayBuffer[Topping]()

    def addTopping(t: Topping): Unit = { toppings += t }
    def removeTopping(t: Topping): Unit = { toppings -= t }
    def removeAllToppings(): Unit = { toppings.clear() }

    def getPrice(
        toppingsPrices: Map[Topping, Money],
        crustSizePrices: Map[CrustSize, Money],
        crustTypePrices: Map[CrustType, Money]
    ): Money = ???

}
```

Many developers use the `BigDecimal` class to handle currency, so I also create a type alias named `Money` to make those type signatures a little more meaningful:

```
type Money = BigDecimal
```

Here are a few important notes about this non-FP code:

- I use a regular Scala `class` to create `Pizza`, instead of `case class`
- `addTopping`, `removeTopping`, and `removeAllToppings` return `Unit`, and mutate `toppings`

Also, depending on your design beliefs, `getPrice` may or may not be included in this class. (When working on an OOP design, I used to use CRC cards[2] and ask, "What class has the *responsibility* for this behavior?") It's important to note that the actual pizza price depends on the cost of the toppings, crust size, and crust type, so those prices — which are typically stored in a database — would have to be passed into this method.

An OOP `Order` class

Next, here's a Scala/OOP `Order` class that models a customer's order, including how many pizzas they're buying, along with their customer information:

```scala
class Order {

    // an order contains a list of pizzas
    val pizzas = ArrayBuffer[Pizza]()

    // could be a constructor parameter if you always create
    // a customer before creating an order
    var customer: Customer = null

    def addPizzaToOrder(p: Pizza): Unit = {
        pizzas += p
    }

    def removePizzaFromOrder(p: Pizza): Unit = {
        pizzas -= p
    }

    // need to implement these
    def getBasePrice(): Money = ???
    def getTaxes(): Money = ???
    def getTotalPrice(): Money = ???

}
```

---
[2] https://en.wikipedia.org/wiki/Class-responsibility-collaboration_card

Customer-related classes

Next, here are the customer-related classes:

```
class Customer (
    var name: String,
    var phone: String,
    var address: Address
)

class Address (
    var street1: String,
    var street2: String,
    var city: String,
    var state: String,
    var zipCode: String
)
```

In a real-world OOP design those classes would have getter and setter methods, but notice that without them it's easier to see that Customer and Address don't have any behaviors, they're just data structures.

Finally, it's important to note that street2 is actually an optional field; it's not required for all addresses. Depending on your OOP philosophy, you can leave the Address design as shown, and then have street2 be null or an empty String when it isn't present, or you can define it as an optional field:

```
class Address (
    var street1: String,
    var street2: Option[String],   //optional
    var city: String,
    var state: String,
    var zipCode: String
)
```

In OOP this choice is open to debate, but in FP it will *always* be specified as Option[String].

The important points of the OOP design

The important points to note about this design are that the `Pizza` class includes impure methods like these:

```
def addTopping(t: Topping): Unit
def removeTopping(t: Topping): Unit
def removeAllToppings(): Unit
```

The `Order` class also has these impure methods:

```
def addPizzaToOrder(p: Pizza): Unit
def removePizzaFromOrder(p: Pizza): Unit
```

Finally, because `Order` also encapsulates data and behavior, it may also have these built-in methods, which may also end up being impure:

```
def getBasePrice(): Money
def getTaxes(): Money
def getTotalPrice(): Money
```

Recognizing impure method signatures

Remember that when you see a `Unit` return type you should immediately think, "This is not a pure function." In these examples, all of the functions that have `Unit` return types are mutating some internal state.

In addition to those methods, the other methods that take no input parameters are technically not pure functions. These methods presumably make calculations based on the internal state of those classes and therefore might not be mutating any internal state, but you definitely can't use the pure function mantra, "Output depends only on input."

See also

For *much* more information about domain modeling, see these books about *Domain-Driven Design*:

- Domain Driven Design: Tackling Complexity in the Heart of Software[3]

---

[3] http://amzn.to/2vxt1vG

- Implementing Domain-Driven Design[4]

Both of those books are very detailed, and highly-regarded.

---
[4]http://amzn.to/2vy1omg

102

Modeling the "Data" Portion of the Pizza POS System with Scala/FP

"Data structures just are. They don't do anything."

Joe Armstrong, Erlang creator

In FP, the *data* and the *operators on that data* are two separate things; you aren't forced to encapsulate them together like you do with OOP.

The concept is like numerical algebra. When you think about whole numbers whose values are greater than or equal to zero, you have a *set* of possible values that looks like this:

```
0, 1, 2 ... Int.MaxInt
```

Ignoring the division of whole numbers, the possible *operators* on those values are:

```
+, -, *
```

An FP design is implemented in a similar way:

- You have a set of values
- You have a collection of operators that work on those values

In this lesson I'll show how to implement the "data" portion of the Scala/FP model for the Pizza POS system, and in the following lessons I'll show different techniques for modeling the "behaviors" using Scala/FP.

Modeling the data

Modeling the "data" portion of a domain model in Scala/FP is simple:

> Model the data as case classes with immutable fields.

Given that one simple rule, the Scala/FP data model for the Pizza POS system is as follows. First, the toppings, crust size, and crust type are modeled as enumerations, just as they were in the OOP design:

```
sealed trait Topping
case object Cheese extends Topping
case object Pepperoni extends Topping
case object Sausage extends Topping
case object Mushrooms extends Topping
case object Onions extends Topping

sealed trait CrustSize
case object SmallCrustSize extends CrustSize
case object MediumCrustSize extends CrustSize
case object LargeCrustSize extends CrustSize

sealed trait CrustType
case object RegularCrustType extends CrustType
case object ThinCrustType extends CrustType
case object ThickCrustType extends CrustType
```

Next, all of the other classes are modeled as case classes with immutable fields:

```
case class Pizza (
    crustSize: CrustSize,
    crustType: CrustType,
    toppings: Seq[Topping]
)

case class Order (
    pizzas: Seq[Pizza],
    customer: Customer
)

case class Customer (
    name: String,
    phone: String,
    address: Address
)
```

```
case class Address (
    street1: String,
    street2: Option[String],
    city: String,
    state: String,
    zipCode: String
)
```

Notice that this code really is just a simple *data model*; there are no "behaviors" mixed in with the data. Personally, I like this. By separating (a) the data from (b) the operations on that data, the data attributes and relationships are clear. The data model is easy to read, like declaring the design for a relational database.

Skinny domain objects

In his book, Functional and Reactive Domain Modeling[1], Debasish Ghosh states that where OOP practitioners describe their classes as "rich domain models" that encapsulate data and behaviors, FP data models can be thought of as "skinny domain objects." This is because, as this lesson shows, the data models are defined as case classes with attributes, but no behaviors.

What about the operations?

This leads to a very interesting question:

> Because FP separates the data from the operations on that data, how do you implement those operations in Scala/FP?

I'll show several possible approaches in the following lessons.

---

[1] http://amzn.to/2iOT3Vh

103

First Attempts to Organize Pure Functions

"A journey of a thousand miles begins with a single step."

Lao Tzu, in the Tao Te Ching

There are several different ways to implement behaviors (functions) in Scala/FP. I'll begin by showing two possible approaches in this lesson, and then show better in the following lessons.

Introduction

In this lesson I'll show how to put your functions in what I call a "Utils" object. After that, I'll show how to put the same functions in a companion object.

I generally don't recommend using these approaches, but they are what I tried when I first started working with Scala/FP. (I use a style similar to this when writing pure functions in Java for Android applications.)

Source code

Because I don't recommend these approaches in Scala, I haven't created a Github project for this lesson.

Option 1: Handling Scala/FP behavior with a "Utils" class

One option is to implement "behavior" in what I call a standalone "utilities" class. For instance, the `Pizza` case class from the previous lesson can have a corresponding `PizzaUtils` object that contains all of the pure functions that operate on a `Pizza`:

```
object PizzaUtils {

    type Money = BigDecimal

    def addTopping(p: Pizza, t: Topping): Pizza = ???
    def removeTopping(p: Pizza, t: Topping): Pizza = ???
    def removeAllToppings(p: Pizza): Pizza = ???

    def updateCrustSize(p: Pizza, cs: CrustSize): Pizza = ???
    def updateCrustType(p: Pizza, ct: CrustType): Pizza = ???

    def calculatePrice (
        p: Pizza,
        toppingsPrices: Map[Topping, Money],
        crustSizePrices: Map[CrustSize, Money],
        crustTypePrices: Map[CrustType, Money]
    ): Money = ???

}
```

Notice that this is just a collection of pure functions that I put in a standalone `object`. You'd call these functions like this:

```
val pizza2 = PizzaUtils.addTopping(pizza1, Pepperoni)
val pizza3 = PizzaUtils.updateCrustSize(LargeCrustSize)
```

With this approach I find that all of those `PizzaUtils` references clutter up the code, so it's cleaner to import the functions and then use them like this:

```
import PizzaUtils._

val pizza2 = addTopping(pizza1, Pepperoni)
val pizza3 = updateCrustSize(LargeCrustSize)
val price = calculatePrice(
    pizza3,
    toppingsPrices,
    crustSizePrices,
    crustTypePrices
)
```

There are a few things to say about this code. First, all of the functions are pure functions. For instance, `addTopping` and `removeTopping` take a `Pizza` and a `Topping` as inputs, and return a new `Pizza` as a result:

```
def addTopping(p: Pizza, t: Topping): Pizza = ???
def removeTopping(p: Pizza, t: Topping): Pizza = ???
```

The crust size and type functions follow the same pattern:

```
def updateCrustSize(p: Pizza, cs: CrustSize): Pizza = ???
def updateCrustType(p: Pizza, ct: CrustType): Pizza = ???
```

In the OOP design you can mutate the toppings, crust size, and crust type on an existing `Pizza` reference, but in FP you don't do that. Instead, you use functions like these to construct a new, updated pizza from the old pizza and the new toppings, crust size, and crust type. This is the way you update objects in FP, so the pure functions in the following two lessons will look just like these, they'll just be organized differently.

> I wrote about this approach in the earlier, "Update as You Copy" lesson, so I won't belabor this point here. See that lesson for more details.

Notice that a benefit of separating data from behavior is that it forces you to write pure functions. Because (a) the `case` classes contain immutable fields and (b) the behaviors are not encapsulated in the same class, each function must take an instance of the primary data type (such as `Pizza`) as an input parameter, and the function must also evaluate to a result. There's no way for you to "cheat" and mutate a data structure under the covers. The approach itself forces you to write pure functions.

The remainder of the design

If I were to implement more of this approach, I'd eventually create more "utilities" objects, such as an `OrderUtils` object, and possibly one or more objects related to price and tax calculations. But hopefully the `PizzaUtils` object gives you the central idea of this concept: Put all of your pure functions that operate on a domain object in a "Utils" object.

> While I call this a "Utils" object, as you'll see in the next lesson, the preferred name for a collection of functions like this is a "service" class.

Option 2: Handling behavior in FP with a companion object

As a variation of the first approach, rather than putting your functions in a separate Utils object, you can use Scala's concept of a "companion object" for the exact same purpose.

With the companion object approach you put the data model in a case class just as before, but then instead of putting your functions in a separate Utils object, you put them in an object in the same file as the case class, where the object has the same name as the case class. This type of object is known as a companion object[1].

The result looks like this:

```
case class Pizza (
    crustSize: CrustSize,
    crustType: CrustType,
    val toppings: Seq[Topping]
)

object Pizza {
    def addTopping(p: Pizza, t: Topping): Pizza = ???
    def removeTopping(p: Pizza, t: Topping): Pizza = ???
    def removeAllToppings(p: Pizza): Pizza = ???

    def calculatePrice (
        p: Pizza,
        toppingsPrices: Map[Topping, Price],
        crustSizePrices: Map[CrustSize, Price],
        crustTypePrices: Map[CrustType, Price]
    ): Money = ???

    def updateCrustSize(p: Pizza, cs: CrustSize): Pizza = ???
    def updateCrustType(p: Pizza, ct: CrustType): Pizza = ???
}
```

With this approach the functions look just like the PizzaUtils code, but you call them on the Pizza object:

---
[1] https://alvinalexander.com/scala/how-to-create-scala-object

```
val pizza2 = Pizza.addTopping(pizza1, Pepperoni)
val pizza3 = Pizza.updateCrustSize(LargeCrustSize)
```

As before, all of those `Pizza` references tend to create unnecessary noise, so you can eliminate them by importing them like this:

```
import Pizza._

val pizza2 = addTopping(pizza1, Pepperoni)
val pizza3 = updateCrustSize(LargeCrustSize)
```

The end result of these two approaches is nearly identical. The only difference is where you put the functions that operate on `Pizza` instances.

> One thing about companion objects is that a companion object can access the private fields of the case class it's associated with[2]. In OOP this is a helpful attribute, but in FP this feature might encourage you to write impure functions.

What's next

As mentioned, I used these techniques as my first "naive" steps into Scala/FP. In the next lesson I'll show a more advanced technique that shows the concept of "modules" in Scala/FP.

---

[2] https://alvinalexander.com/scala/how-to-static-members-in-scala

104

Implementing FP Behavior with Modules

"A module is a 'smaller program piece' with a well defined interface and a hidden implementation."

From the book, Programming in Scala[a]

---

[a] http://amzn.to/2fiqDBh

The source code

The source code for this lesson is at this Github URL:

- github.com/alvinj/FPModulesIrishSetter[1]

What is a module?

This lesson is about implementing behaviors (functions) in modules, so it begs the question, what is a *module* in Scala?

The book, Programming in Scala[2], describes a *module* like this:

> "A module is a 'smaller program piece' with a well defined interface and a hidden implementation."

The Scala Language Specification provides this hint as to what a module is:

> "The object definition defines a single object (or: module) conforming to the template t."

---

[1] https://github.com/alvinj/FPModulesIrishSetter
[2] http://amzn.to/2fiqDBh

Those quotes provide a start, but they're not too helpful on their own. The slide shown in Figure 104.1 is from a lambdafoo.com presentation[3], and provides the most clear definition of a module that I've seen.

Rewrite Scala to be closer to OCaml

```
trait Ordering {
    type T
    def compare(x: T, y: T): Int
}
```

OCaml

```
module type ORDERING = sig
    type t
    val compare : t -> t -> int
end
```

Figure 104.1: As you'll see in this lesson, a Scala trait is similar to a module in the OCaml language.

As that slide begins to show, the idea of a module in Scala is to use a trait to gather your pure functions into logical units of behavior. In this lesson I'll show how to use Scala traits to create modules, and then how to combine those traits to build larger objects and complete applications.

The essence of the problem

The reasons for adopting a modular programming approach are described in Programming in Scala[4]:

"As a program grows in size, it becomes increasingly important to organize it in a modular way. First, being able to compile different modules that make up the system separately helps different teams work independently. In addition, being able to unplug one implementation of a module and plug in another is useful, because it allows different configurations of a system to be used in different contexts, such as unit testing on a developer's desktop, integration testing, staging, and deployment."

In regards to the first point, in FP it's nice to be able to say, "Hey, Team A, how about if you

---

[3] http://lambdafoo.com/scala-syd-2015-modules/#8
[4] http://amzn.to/2fiqDBh

work on the Order functions, and Team B will work on the Pizza functions?"

In regards to the second point, a good example is that you might use a mock database on your desktop and then use real databases in the Test and Production environments. In this case you'll create traits like these:

```
trait Database { ... }
trait MockDatabase extends Database { ... }
trait TestDatabase extends Database { ... }
trait ProductionDatabase extends Database { ... }
```

One point I'll add to that description is that modularization is a way to help you handle the complexity that comes with building large applications.

The essence of the solution

The essence of the modular solution is also described well in Programming in Scala[5]:

"Any technique that aims to facilitate this kind of modularity needs to provide a few essentials. First, there should be a module construct that provides a good separation of interface and implementation. Second, there should be a way to replace one module with another that has the same interface without changing or recompiling the modules that depend on the replaced one. Lastly, there should be a way to wire modules together. This wiring task can by thought of as *configuring the system*."

The essence of the technique

Given that background, the essence of programming with modules in Scala/FP goes like this:

- You write pure functions, as I did in the previous lesson
- In this case, the pure functions are organized in relatively small, logically-organized traits
- You combine (compose) the traits together as needed to create objects, using the traits as mixins

---

[5]http://amzn.to/2fiqDBh

A simple example

Here's a simple example of this technique. Imagine that you want to define the behaviors for a dog, let's say an Irish Setter. One way to do this is to jump right in and create an `IrishSetter` class:

```
class IrishSetter { ... }
```

This is a bad idea. A better idea is to think about the interfaces for different types of dog behaviors, and then build a specific implementation of an Irish Setter when you're ready.

For example, an initial thought is that a dog is an animal:

```
trait Animal
```

More specifically, a dog is an animal with a tail, and that tail has a color:

```
abstract class AnimalWithTail(tailColor: Color) extends Animal
```

Next, you might think, "Since a dog has a tail, what kind of behaviors can a tail have?" With that thought, you might then sketch a trait like this:

```
trait DogTailServices {
    def wagTail = ???
    def lowerTail = ???
    def raiseTail = ???
    def curlTail = ???
}
```

Next, because you know that you only want this trait to be mixed into classes that extend `AnimalWithTail`, you'll add a self-type to the trait:

```
trait DogTailServices {

    // implementers must be a sub-type of AnimalWithTail
    this: AnimalWithTail =>

    def wagTail = ???
    def lowerTail = ???
    def raiseTail = ???
    def curlTail = ???
}
```

If you read the Scala Cookbook[6], you know that this peculiar looking line declares a *self-type*, which means, "This trait can only be mixed into classes that extend `AnimalWithTail`":

```
this: AnimalWithTail =>
```

Because I want to keep this example simple, I'll go ahead and implement the functions ("services") in the `DogTailServices` class like this:

```
trait DogTailServices {
    this: AnimalWithTail =>
    def wagTail = println("wagging tail")
    def lowerTail = println("lowering tail")
    def raiseTail = println("raising tail")
}
```

Next, as I think more about a dog, I know that it has a mouth, so I sketch another trait like this:

```
trait DogMouthServices {
    this: AnimalWithTail =>
    def bark = println("bark!")
    def lick = println("licking")
}
```

I could keep going on like this, but I hope you see the idea: You think about the *services* (or behaviors) that are associated with a domain object, and then you sketch those services as functions in logically organized traits. (Advice: Just start with your best ideas, then reorganize them as your thinking becomes more clear.)

Since I'm not going to go further and define more dog-related behaviors, I'll stop at this point and create a module as an implementation of an Irish Setter with the services I've defined so far:

```
object IrishSetter
    extends AnimalWithTail(Color.red)
    with DogTailServices
    with DogMouthServices
```

---

[6] http://amzn.to/24ivK4G

If you start the Scala REPL like this:

```
$ scala -Djava.awt.headless=true
Welcome to Scala ...
```

and then import the necessary `Color` class:

```
scala> import java.awt.Color
import java.awt.Color
```

and then import all of those traits into the REPL (not shown here), you'll see that you can call the functions/services on your `IrishSetter`:

```
scala> IrishSetter.bark
bark!
```

```
scala> IrishSetter.wagTail
wagging tail
```

While this is a simple example, it shows the general process of "programming with modules" in Scala.

Aside: headless mode

When I started the Scala REPL, I used this command:

```
scala -Djava.awt.headless=true
```

This starts the JVM in something known as "headless" mode. I did this because creating an instance of an AWT class in the REPL causes the JVM to think, "He's using an AWT class, this must be a GUI application," and the REPL loses input focus. Starting the JVM in headless mode disables that behavior.

If you're using a Mac and want to see what I'm referring to, start the REPL without the `headless` argument:

```
$ scala
Welcome to Scala ...
```

and then run these two commands:

```
scala> import java.awt._
import java.awt._

scala> val c = Color.red
c: java.awt.Color = java.awt.Color[r=255,g=0,b=0]
```

You'll see that the REPL and Terminal lose input focus, and the name `MainGenericRunner` appears in the Mac menu bar. (I assume that a similar thing happens on Windows and Linux systems.) If you use the `headless` argument, this won't happen.

About the name "service"

The name *service* comes from the fact that these functions provide a series of public "services" that are available to external clients. I find that this name makes sense when you imagine that these functions are implemented as a series of web service calls. For instance, when you use Twitter's REST API to write a Twitter client, the functions they make available to you in that API are considered to be a series of web services.

105

Implementing the Pizza POS System Using a Modular Approach

> *"Modular programming is a software design technique that emphasizes separating the functionality of a program into independent, interchangeable modules, such that each contains everything necessary to execute only one aspect of the desired functionality."*
>
> From the Wikipedia entry for modular programming[a]
>
> ---
> [a]https://en.wikipedia.org/wiki/Modular_programming

Now that you've seen how to go through the modular programming process once with some simple traits, I'll go ahead and implement the Pizza Store POS using modules.

The source code

The source code for this lesson is at this Github URL:

- github.com/alvinj/PizzaPosFpModularStyle[1]

The Pizza POS data models

First, although the Pizza POS data model hasn't changed, I'll show it again here as a reminder:

```
case class Pizza (
    crustSize: CrustSize,
```

---
[1]https://github.com/alvinj/PizzaPosFpModularStyle

```scala
    crustType: CrustType,
    toppings: Seq[Topping]
)

case class Order (
    pizzas: Seq[Pizza],
    customer: Customer
)

case class Customer (
    name: String,
    phone: String,
    address: Address
)

case class Address (
    street1: String,
    street2: Option[String],
    city: String,
    state: String,
    zipCode: String
)

sealed trait Topping
case object Cheese extends Topping
case object Pepperoni extends Topping
case object Sausage extends Topping
case object Mushrooms extends Topping
case object Onions extends Topping

sealed trait CrustSize
case object SmallCrustSize extends CrustSize
case object MediumCrustSize extends CrustSize
case object LargeCrustSize extends CrustSize


sealed trait CrustType
case object RegularCrustType extends CrustType
```

```
case object ThinCrustType extends CrustType
case object ThickCrustType extends CrustType
```

The `PizzaService` interface

The next thing I tend to think about are the `Pizza` behaviors, so I initially sketch a `PizzaServiceInterface` trait like this:

```
trait PizzaServiceInterface {

    def addTopping(p: Pizza, t: Topping): Pizza
    def removeTopping(p: Pizza, t: Topping): Pizza
    def removeAllToppings(p: Pizza): Pizza

    def updateCrustSize(p: Pizza, cs: CrustSize): Pizza
    def updateCrustType(p: Pizza, ct: CrustType): Pizza

    def calculatePizzaPrice(
        p: Pizza,
        toppingsPrices: Map[Topping, Money],
        crustSizePrices: Map[CrustSize, Money],
        crustTypePrices: Map[CrustType, Money]
    ): Money

}
```

These are the exact same function signatures I used in the previous lesson; the only difference is that I've put them in a `trait` here, as opposed to a "Utils" class or companion object.

When you write a pure interface like this, you can think of it as a contract, a contract that states, "all non-abstract classes that extend this trait *must* provide an implementation of these services."

In the real world, what I'd do at this point is imagine that I'm the consumer of this API. When I do that, I start sketching some code to make sure I like what this API looks like:

```
val p = Pizza(
    MediumCrustSize,
    RegularCrustType,
    Seq(Cheese)
)

// the functions in PizzaServiceInterface
val p1 = addTopping(p, Pepperoni)
val p2 = addTopping(p1, Mushrooms)
val p3 = updateCrustType(p2, ThickCrustType)
val p4 = updateCrustSize(p3, LargeCrustSize)
```

That code "feels" okay — feels like what I want — so at this point I'd typically start sketching another interface. But since this is a book, I'm going to go ahead and wrap up this module by going through the work of creating a concrete implementation of this interface.

> Notice that this is usually a two-step process. In the first step, you sketch the contract of your API as an *interface*. In the second step you create a concrete *implementation* of that interface. In some cases you'll end up creating multiple concrete implementations of the base interface.

Creating a concrete implementation

Now that I know what the `PizzaServiceInterface` looks like, I can create a concrete implementation of it by writing code for all of the functions I declared:

```
trait PizzaService extends PizzaServiceInterface {

    def addTopping(p: Pizza, t: Topping): Pizza = {
        val newToppings = p.toppings :+ t
        p.copy(toppings = newToppings)
    }

    def removeTopping(p: Pizza, t: Topping): Pizza = {
        val newToppings = ListUtils.dropFirstMatch(p.toppings, t)
        p.copy(toppings = newToppings)
    }


    def removeAllToppings(p: Pizza): Pizza = {
```

```
    val newToppings = Seq[Topping]()
    p.copy(toppings = newToppings)
}

def updateCrustSize(p: Pizza, cs: CrustSize): Pizza = {
    p.copy(crustSize = cs)
}

def updateCrustType(p: Pizza, ct: CrustType): Pizza = {
    p.copy(crustType = ct)
}

def calculatePizzaPrice(
    p: Pizza,
    toppingsPrices: Map[Topping, Money],
    crustSizePrices: Map[CrustSize, Money],
    crustTypePrices: Map[CrustType, Money]
): Money = {
    // TODO implement a real algorithm based on those sequences
    val base = BigDecimal(10)
    val numToppings = p.toppings.size
    val price = base + 1.00 * numToppings
    price
}

}
```

While this two-step process of creating an interface followed by an implementation isn't always necessary, if you want to be an API creator, it's a good discipline to learn.

Database

In the real world, pizza-related prices will be stored in a database, and in this section I want to show the impact that has on a modular design.

Again I'll start with an interface that I'll name `PizzaDaoInterface`. It declares the methods that a "Pizza database access object (DAO)" should have:

```
trait PizzaDaoInterface {
```

```
    def getToppingPrices(): Map[Topping, Money]
    def getCrustSizePrices(): Map[CrustSize, Money]
    def getCrustTypePrices(): Map[CrustType, Money]

}
```

These methods return the pricing data maps that are passed into the `calculatePizzaPrice` function in the `PizzaService` trait.

One way to implement this interface is with a mock object, and that's what I'll do for this lesson. Here's a mock implementation of the `PizzaDaoInterface`:

```
object MockPizzaDao extends PizzaDaoInterface {

    def getToppingPrices(): Map[Topping, Money] = {
        Map(
            Cheese    -> BigDecimal(1),
            Pepperoni -> BigDecimal(1),
            Sausage   -> BigDecimal(1),
            Mushrooms -> BigDecimal(1)
        )
    }

    def getCrustSizePrices(): Map[CrustSize, Money] = {
        Map(
            SmallCrustSize  -> BigDecimal(0),
            MediumCrustSize -> BigDecimal(1),
            LargeCrustSize  -> BigDecimal(2)
        )
    }

    def getCrustTypePrices(): Map[CrustType, Money] = {
        Map(
            RegularCrustType -> BigDecimal(0),
            ThickCrustType   -> BigDecimal(1),
            ThinCrustType    -> BigDecimal(1)
        )
    }
```

}

In the real world you'd also have a `TestPizzaDao` and `ProductionPizzaDao`, but this is enough for our purposes.

The `OrderService` trait

The next thing I'd think about in the Pizza POS system are the behaviors/services related to an `Order`. The main service this trait needs to provide is the ability to calculate the price of an order, so I begin by writing this:

```
trait OrderServiceInterface {

    def calculateOrderPrice(o: Order): Money

}
```

Given an `Order`, `calculateOrderPrice` returns the price of the order as a `Money` type.

To work the database into the application, let's assume that this is where I decide to access the database. I might not do this in the real world, but I don't want to make this example too complicated.

That assumption leads me to add this `database` reference to the interface:

```
trait OrderServiceInterface {

    // implementing classes should provide their own database
    // that is an instance of PizzaDaoInterface, such as
    // MockPizzaDao, TestPizzaDao, or ProductionPizzaDao
    protected def database: PizzaDaoInterface

    def calculateOrderPrice(o: Order): Money

}
```

The implementation of OrderServiceInterface

Now I can put the work in to create an implementation of the `OrderServiceInterface`. I'll share the complete source code for the implementation, and then explain it:

```
trait AbstractOrderService extends OrderServiceInterface {

    // create a concrete implementation of the trait so we
    // can use its `calculatePizzaPrice` function
    object PizzaService extends PizzaService
    import PizzaService.calculatePizzaPrice

    // all implementations of this trait will use these functions,
    // so go ahead and define them here
    private lazy val toppingPricesMap   = database.getToppingPrices()
    private lazy val crustSizePricesMap = database.getCrustSizePrices()
    private lazy val crustTypePricesMap = database.getCrustTypePrices()

    // the publicly-available service
    def calculateOrderPrice(o: Order): Money =
        calculateOrderPriceInternal(
            o,
            toppingPricesMap,
            crustSizePricesMap,
            crustTypePricesMap
        )

    private def calculateOrderPriceInternal(
        o: Order,
        toppingPrices: Map[Topping, Money],
        crustSizePrices: Map[CrustSize, Money],
        crustTypePrices: Map[CrustType, Money]
    ): Money = {
        val pizzaPrices: Seq[Money] = for {
            pizza <- o.pizzas
        } yield {
            calculatePizzaPrice(
                pizza,
                toppingPrices,
```

```
            crustSizePrices,
            crustTypePrices
        )
    }
    pizzaPrices.sum
}

}
```

To understand this code, it helps to look at the `calculateOrderPriceInternal` function first. When you look at its code you'll see:

- It requires the three data maps from the database
- It also requires the `calculatePizzaPrice` function from the `PizzaService` trait

Knowing that, the other lines of code make sense. First, I create a concrete instance of the `PizzaService`:

```
object PizzaService extends PizzaService
```

You can't call functions on a trait, so you need to create a concrete instance of that trait before you do anything else. This technique is common with the modular programming approach, and it's known as "reifying" the trait. (The word *reify* is defined as, "Taking an abstract concept and making it concrete.")

Next, I import the function I need from `PizzaService`:

```
import PizzaService.calculatePizzaPrice
```

After that, I get the data maps I need from the `database` reference:

```
private lazy val toppingPrices = database.getToppingPrices()
private lazy val crustSizePrices = database.getCrustSizePrices()
private lazy val crustTypePrices = database.getCrustTypePrices()
```

I implement these as `private` because nobody else needs to access them.

I further define them as `lazy` for a totally different reason: This trait still isn't completely useful. Because it doesn't have a concrete `database` reference, it's not completely usable as it is (which is why I include the word "Abstract" in the trait name). To make use of this trait I'll have to extend it one more time.

Using the MockPizzaDao

Because the `AbstractOrderService` class is nearly complete, it takes just one more step to create an implementation of it that works with the `MockPizzaDao`. All you have to do is declare an object that extends the trait and state that its `database` reference is the `MockPizzaDao`:

```
object MockDbOrderService extends AbstractOrderService {
    val database = MockPizzaDao
}
```

This is a nice technique, because if you want a `ProductionPizzaDao` you can easily create a similar object to use in Production:

```
object ProductionOrderService extends AbstractOrderService {
    val database = ProductionPizzaDao
}
```

Now that I have the `MockDbOrderService`, I can test all of my code in a "driver" class to show that it all works the way I want it to work.

A driver class to test the design

Here's a driver class I created to test the API I created. I explain what I'm doing in the comments in the code, so please see those comments for the primary discussion of this code:

```
object MainDriver extends App {

    // create a concrete PizzaService instance so i can
    // call its functions
    object PizzaService extends PizzaService

    // import all of its functions
    import PizzaService._

    // create a sample Address
    val address = Address(
        "1 Main Street",
        None,
        "Talkeetna",
        "AK",
```

```scala
        "99676"
    )

    // create a sample Customer
    val customer = Customer(
        "Alvin Alexander",
        "907-555-1212",
        address
    )

    // start to create an Order for the Customer. notice that
    // this brings up a question, should i have used an Option
    // for the Seq[Pizza] parameter?
    val o1 = Order(
        Seq[Pizza](),   //TODO use Option here instead?
        customer
    )

    // create a pizza
    val p1 = Pizza(
        MediumCrustSize,
        RegularCrustType,
        Seq(Cheese)
    )

    // with the current api, this is what you have to do to
    // add a new pizza to an existing order. this tells me
    // that OrderServiceInterface needs an `addPizzaToOrder`
    // function.
    val newPizzas = o1.pizzas :+ p1
    val o2 = o1.copy(pizzas = newPizzas)

    // build another pizza
    val p2 = Pizza(
        MediumCrustSize,
        RegularCrustType,
        Seq(Cheese)
    )
```

```
// test the PizzaService functions
val p2a = addTopping(p2, Pepperoni)
val p2b = addTopping(p2a, Mushrooms)
val p2c = updateCrustType(p2b, ThickCrustType)
val p2Last = updateCrustSize(p2c, LargeCrustSize)

// update the order with the second pizza. again i see
// that i should have create an `addPizzaToOrder` function.
val pizzas3 = o2.pizzas :+ p2Last
val o3 = o2.copy(pizzas = pizzas3)
println(o3)

// note that i could have created the second pizza like this
val p2d = updateCrustSize(
    updateCrustType(
        addTopping(
            addTopping(p2, Pepperoni),
            Mushrooms
        ),
        ThickCrustType
    ),
    LargeCrustSize
)

// calculate the price of the current order (o3) using the
// MockDbOrderService
import com.alspizza.pos.services.MockDbOrderService.calculateOrderPrice
val orderPrice = calculateOrderPrice(o3)
println(s"Order Price = $orderPrice")

// i forgot to test `removeTopping`, give it a spin
val p5 = Pizza(
    MediumCrustSize,
    RegularCrustType,
    Seq(Cheese, Pepperoni, Pepperoni, Sausage)
)
val p5a = removeTopping(p5, Pepperoni)
```

```
    println("\nSHOULD BE Cheese/Pepperoni/Sausage:")
    println(p5a)

}
```

I made two discoveries by writing this driver class, one that you can see, and one that you don't see. The one you can see is that by going through this process I realized that the `OrderServiceInterface` should have had an `addPizzaToOrder` function.

The second thing you can't see is that by going through this process I realized that I didn't like the way I originally implemented the code in the `AbstractOrderService` trait. By working with this driver class I was able to improve my original approach to create the code you currently see in `AbstractOrderService`. (My previous mistakes were in leaving the price maps publicly available, and in requiring `MainDriver` to have those, and pass them into an earlier version of the `calculateOrderPrice` method.)

In summary, the main point of creating a driver `App` like this is that it lets me look at my service API from the perspective of a consumer of the API. Going through that process helps me find my mistakes.

Discussion

There are a few important parts about what I showed that I should briefly note:

1. There are multiple ways to provide the "order services" implementation
2. Different designs of the DAO functions might return `Try`, `DBIO`, or another monad
3. I stressed the "interface" and "asbtract" parts of this by using the names `Interface` and `Abstract` in the trait names
4. If i had taken this further you would see the advantages of combining/stacking/composing traits, like you saw with the Irish Setter example

I'll briefly discuss these points in the sections that follow.

1) There are multiple ways to provide the "order services" implementation

There are different ways that I could have implemented the "order service" traits, but I chose the approach shown because the current code tells me that the `getToppingPrices`, `getCrustSizePrices`, and `getCrustTypePrices` functions can be implemented in `AbstractOrderService`. If and when that situation changes, my design would change to reflect that new knowledge.

In short, the solution I showed may not be perfect; it's just an attempt to show a simple example of how to build a modular design that accesses a database for the current problem.

2) The DAO functions might return Try, DBIO, or another monad

The DAO functions I showed return a Map, but when you work with real databases, your functions may end up returning a monadic type. For instance, a function may return Try in case there's a problem accessing the database. The Scala Slick database library methods return a type of DBIO[2], which appears to be similar to the IO approach I described in this book. (I haven't worked with it yet.)

If the functions work that way, the design would change to reflect that change.

3) I stressed the "interface" name

The more I write code — actually, the more I *maintain* code — the more I prefer code that is obvious. For instance, many times I prefer a "verbose" style instead of a concise style, and that has to do with maintaining the code. I work on many different projects, and I don't like having to take extra time to try to understand code that has been reduced to an extremely condensed form.

The same is true for naming things like traits and classes. I prefer meaningful names, so while my style may go against the grain, I like to see the word "Interface" in a trait name when I truly mean that the trait is intended to be an interface, and I like to use the word "Abstract" when the trait is truly abstract (i.e., when it's not completely ready to be reified). I prefer that style, but if that's too literal for your taste, use whatever style you prefer.

4) If I had taken this further ...

If I had built out a larger version of this example you would have seen many traits for different parts of the domain vocabulary:

- Possibly a separate "price calculator" trait
- Almost certainly there would be a series of traits for calculating taxes (which would be required for selling pizzas in different countries)
- Traits to model different employee roles

---

[2] http://slick.lightbend.com/doc/3.2.0/dbio.html

- A set of traits to model coupons and discounts

As just one example, if we decided to start selling other products besides pizza there would be a series of traits that would look something like this:

```
sealed trait Product

trait Pizza extends Product
trait Breadsticks extends Product
trait Cheesesticks extends Product

trait Beverage extends Product
trait BottledBeverage extends Beverage
trait CannedBeverage extends Beverage
```

The exact implementation of those traits would depend on (a) what their behaviors (services) are, and (b) how you want to organize them, but almost certainly you'll want to be able to add a `Product` to an `Order` like this:

```
trait OrderServicesInterface {
    def addProductToOrder(o: Order, p: Product): Order
    ...
}
```

Benefits of this approach

The benefits of a modular style of programming are described well in the original quote I shared from Programming in Scala[3]:

- As a program grows in size, it's important to organize it in a modular way as a means to handle complexity

- With separate modules, multiple teams can work on different modules independently

- Being able to unplug one implementation and plug in a different one lets you build different configurations, such as using a mock database in development and real databases in Test and Production

---

[3] http://amzn.to/2fiqDBh

Disadvantages of this approach

The main disadvantage of this approach is that you may need to learn a few new Scala programming techniques. (But if you want to be a top Scala developer, that's actually a good thing.)

For instance, if you haven't used traits as mixins, you'll be using that technique a lot, because it's the essence of the modular solution. Along with that you'll also want to use techniques like self-types, which I demonstrated in this lesson.

As another example of learning new techniques, when I first learned the "reify" technique, I had never seen a line of code like this before:

```
object OrderService extends OrderService
```

That line is a real head-scratcher if someone demonstrates it without explaining it.

Finally, it will take time and experience to learn how to properly organize your traits. For example, one thing I intentionally tried to show with the "order services" traits is that there are times that you'll want to avoid hard-coding one trait to another. In my example I intentionally had the `OrderServiceInterface` contain a reference to the `PizzaDaoInterface` so it wouldn't be hardwired to the `MockPizzaDao` (or any other specific DAO implementation):

```
trait OrderServiceInterface {

    protected def database: PizzaDaoInterface

}
```

If you come to Scala/FP from an OOP background, it can take a while to get used to modular programming with traits, but that example shows the pattern of how to avoid tying one trait to a concrete implementation of another trait.

See also

The primary references for this style of programming are:

- The "Modular Programming Using Objects" chapter in the book, *Programming in Scala*[4]
- The book, *Functional and Reactive Domain Modeling*[5], by Debasish Ghosh, shows long, detailed examples of this technique

Other references that may be helpful:

- Class composition with mixins[6] on scala-lang.org
- Using Scala traits as modules[7]
- How to use Scala traits as simple mixins[8]
- Scala: How to limit which classes can use a trait by inheritance[9]
- How to define a Scala trait so it can only be subclassed by a certain type[10]

---

[4]http://amzn.to/2fiqDBh
[5]http://amzn.to/2iOT3Vh
[6]https://docs.scala-lang.org/tour/mixin-class-composition.html
[7]http://www.warski.org/blog/2014/02/using-scala-traits-as-modules-or-the-thin-cake-pattern/
[8]https://alvinalexander.com/scala/how-to-use-scala-traits-as-mixins-mixing-in-traits
[9]https://alvinalexander.com/scala/how-to-limit-which-classes-can-use-traits-inheritance-in-scala
[10]https://alvinalexander.com/scala/how-to-define-scala-trait-subclassed-certain-self-types

The "Functional Objects" Approach

It seems like most Scala/FP developers prefer the modular programming approach shown in the previous lesson, but there's still one more way you can implement behaviors in your code: Follow the same approach used in the Scala collections classes, such as the List class.

Option 4: Handling behavior with functional objects

In Chapter 6 of the book Programming in Scala[1], the authors define the term, "Functional Objects" as "objects that do not have any mutable state." Like the List class, this means that the List methods don't mutate the internal List state; instead, you get a copy of a new List as a result.

I sometimes refer to this approach as a "hybrid FP/OOP design" because you:

- Model the data as immutable fields in case classes.
- Put the behaviors (methods) in the same class as the data.
- Implement the behaviors as pure functions. They don't mutate any internal state; rather, they return a new instance of the class.

This really is a hybrid approach:

- Like an OOP design, the methods are encapsulated in the class with the data, but
- The methods are implemented as pure functions that don't mutate the data

Example

Using this approach, the Pizza class I used in the previous lesson is built like this:

---

[1] http://amzn.to/2fiqDBh

```
case class Pizza (
    crustSize: CrustSize,
    crustType: CrustType,
    val toppings: Seq[Topping]
) {
    def addTopping(t: Topping): Pizza = ???
    def removeTopping(t: Topping): Pizza = ???
    def removeAllToppings(): Pizza = ???

    def updateCrustSize(cs: CrustSize): Pizza = ???
    def updateCrustType(ct: CrustType): Pizza = ???

    def getPrice(
        toppingPrices: Map[Topping, Money],
        crustSizePrices: Map[CrustSize, Money],
        crustTypePrices: Map[CrustType, Money]
    ): Money = ???
}
```

Notice that unlike the previous approaches, these methods no longer take a Pizza reference as an input parameter. They assume that the Pizza to be operated on is the current Pizza reference, i.e., this.

Code that uses this design looks like this:

```
val pizza1 = Pizza(
    LargeCrustSize,
    ThinCrustType,
    Seq(Cheese)
)
val pizza2 = pizza1.addTopping(Pepperoni)
val pizza3 = pizza2.updateCrustType(ThickCrustType)

val price = pizza3.getPrice(
    toppingPrices,
    crustSizePrices,
    crustTypePrices
)
```

Notice that in this line:

```
val pizza2 = pizza1.addTopping(Pepperoni)
```

the Pepperoni topping is added to whatever toppings are in the pizza1 reference to create a new Pizza instance named pizza2. Following the FP model, pizza1 isn't mutated, it's just used to create a new instance with the updated data.

Are the functions pure?

In this example, because getPrice doesn't take any input parameters, by my own definition it's not a strictly pure function. You can't say, "Output depends only on input," because there appears to be no input.

That being said, what's really going on with these method calls is that they receive an implicit this reference, so under the covers they really look like this:

```
val pizza2 = pizza1.addTopping(this, Pepperoni)
val pizza3 = pizza2.updateCrustType(this, ThickCrustType)

val price = pizza3.getPrice(
    this,
    toppingPrices,
    crustSizePrices,
    crustTypePrices
)
```

In that regard, these methods on the Pizza class are as pure as methods like map and filter on the List class.

The same design as the Scala collections classes

As I mentioned, this approach is exactly how the Scala collections classes are designed:

```
val list = List(1,2,3,4,5)
val littleNumbers = list.filter(_ < 3)
```

Just like the Pizza class, you can say these things about the List class:

- It has an immutable internal data model (in this case the list of numbers 1 to 5)
- filter is defined as a method in List
- filter doesn't mutate the List's internal state; it returns a new List based on (a) its

internal model, and (b) the function you supply to `filter`

I provide a complete example of this approach in the next lesson.

107

Demonstrating the "Functional Objects" Approach

To demonstrate the "functional objects" approach I created an example project, which I share in this lesson. To follow along with this discussion, the source code for this lesson is at this Github URL:

- github.com/alvinj/PizzaPosFpFunctionalObjectsStyle[1]

The enumerations

The enumerations are the same as in all previous lessons:

```
sealed trait Topping
case object Cheese extends Topping
case object Pepperoni extends Topping
case object Sausage extends Topping
case object Mushrooms extends Topping
case object Olives extends Topping


sealed trait CrustType
case object RegularCrustType extends CrustType
case object ThinCrustType extends CrustType
case object ThickCrustType extends CrustType


sealed trait CrustSize
case object SmallCrustSize extends CrustSize
case object MediumCrustSize extends CrustSize
case object LargeCrustSize extends CrustSize
```

---

[1] https://github.com/alvinj/PizzaPosFpFunctionalObjectsStyle

Database access object (DAO)

The DAO for this project is the same as the `MockPizzaDao` from the previous lesson, without bothering to extend an interface:

```
object MockPizzaDao {

    def getToppingPrices(): Map[Topping, Money] = {
        Map(
            Cheese    -> BigDecimal(1),
            Pepperoni -> BigDecimal(1),
            Sausage   -> BigDecimal(1),
            Mushrooms -> BigDecimal(1)
        )
    }

    def getCrustSizePrices(): Map[CrustSize, Money] = {
        Map(
            SmallCrustSize  -> BigDecimal(0),
            MediumCrustSize -> BigDecimal(1),
            LargeCrustSize  -> BigDecimal(2)
        )
    }

    def getCrustTypePrices(): Map[CrustType, Money] = {
        Map(
            RegularCrustType -> BigDecimal(0),
            ThickCrustType   -> BigDecimal(1),
            ThinCrustType    -> BigDecimal(1)
        )
    }

}
```

The `Pizza` model

Finally — getting to the purpose of this lesson — I create the `Pizza` model using the same pizza behaviors I used in the previous lesson, with slight modifications so they can be used inside a `Pizza` class:

```scala
// the data model
case class Pizza (
    crustSize: CrustSize,
    crustType: CrustType,
    val toppings: Seq[Topping]
) {

    // the operations on the data model

    def addTopping(t: Topping): Pizza = {
        this.copy(toppings = this.toppings :+ t)
    }

    def removeTopping(t: Topping): Pizza = {
        val newToppings = Utils.dropFirstMatch(this.toppings, t)
        this.copy(toppings = newToppings)
    }

    def removeAllToppings(p: Pizza): Pizza = {
        val newToppings = Seq[Topping]()
        this.copy(toppings = newToppings)
    }

    def updateCrustSize(cs: CrustSize): Pizza = {
        this.copy(crustSize = cs)
    }

    def updateCrustType(ct: CrustType): Pizza = {
        this.copy(crustType = ct)
    }

    def getPrice(
        toppingPrices: Map[Topping, Money],
        crustSizePrices: Map[CrustSize, Money],
        crustTypePrices: Map[CrustType, Money]
    ): Money = {
        // TODO implement a real algorithm based on those sequences
        val base = BigDecimal(10)
```

```
        val numToppings = this.toppings.size
        val price = base + 1.00 * numToppings
        price
    }

}
```

As those functions show, rather than taking an explicit Pizza reference as an input parameter, the functions refer to the current Pizza instance with the this reference. Other than that change, these functions are identical to the pizza-related functions in the previous lesson.

A "driver" application

When I'm writing classes like this I usually create a little test application I can use to test the API that I'm creating. This is the code I wrote to test the "model" code I just showed:

```
object Driver extends App {

    // initialize the data from database
    val toppingPrices = MockPizzaDao.getToppingPrices()
    val crustSizePrices = MockPizzaDao.getCrustSizePrices()
    val crustTypePrices = MockPizzaDao.getCrustTypePrices()

    // create a pizza
    val pizza1 = Pizza(
        MediumCrustSize,
        ThinCrustType,
        Seq(Cheese, Pepperoni)
    )

    // make sure you can create modified versions of
    // the initial pizza
    val pizza2 = pizza1.addTopping(Olives)
    val pizza3 = pizza2.updateCrustSize(LargeCrustSize)
    println(s"pizza3: $pizza3")

    // getPrice looks like this
    val pizzaPrice = pizza3.getPrice(
        toppingPrices,
```

```
        crustSizePrices,
        crustTypePrices
    )
    println(s"price of pizza3: $pizzaPrice")

    // can also do this
    val pizza4 = pizza1.addTopping(Olives)
                      .updateCrustSize(LargeCrustSize)
                      .updateCrustType(ThickCrustType)
    println(s"pizza4: $pizza4")

}
```

Discussion

Visually, I prefer this "functional object" coding style:

```
val pizza2 = pizza1.addTopping(Pepperoni)
```

to this style:

```
val pizza2 = addTopping(pizza1, Pepperoni)
```

Something about seeing a method name attached to a variable name as `variable.method(parameters)` is easier for my brain to read, though that may just be the result of programming in an OOP style for a few decades.

That being said, I'm currently developing applications using the modular programming style, and I've come to enjoy the process of using traits to build modules, and then combining those modules to build applications. At the time of this writing I can't recommend one style 100% over the other style for all situations.

Summary of the Domain Modeling Approaches

In the last several lessons I showed a variety of ways to model data and behaviors (functions) in Scala/FP.

Defining a data model in Scala/FP is simple: Just model the data as *case* classes with immutable fields. This approach is similar to creating a relational database design, and it becomes a blueprint of the classes, their fields, and their relationships.

When it comes to modeling behaviors I showed several different possible approaches:

- Put your functions in "Utils" classes
- Put your functions in companion objects
- Use a modular programming style
- Use a "functional objects" approach

While I like the readability of the "functional objects" approach, the modular programming style may offer advantages related to using modules, such as letting multiple teams work on different modules simultaneously, and the ability to "wire together" modules to create different configurations.

While I'm sure FP experts will say "just use modules," I encourage you to use both the modular approach and the functional objects approach to see which style you prefer. While the modular approach may be preferred by FP experts, it's worth noting that the Scala language designers could have implemented the collections classes in that manner, but they chose to use the functional objects approach, which I find very readable.

> Historically, the modular programming style has its roots in ML[1]-based languages such as OCaml[2], and this style is also used in other FP languages, such as Haskell and F# (which is based on OCaml).

---

[1] https://en.wikipedia.org/wiki/ML_(programming_language)
[2] https://en.wikipedia.org/wiki/OCaml

109

The Problem with the IO Monad

> *"It doesn't matter how beautiful your theory is, it doesn't matter how smart you are. If it doesn't agree with experiment, it's wrong."*
>
> ~ Richard Feynman

When I first learned about the `IO` monad I thought it was extremely cool. The idea that all of my I/O functions could return an `IO` type sounded terrific. Any developer on a project could look at a function signature in the source code or Scaladoc, see that it returned `IO`, and they would immediately know that it interacted with the outside world.

But as I went from theory to reality, I noticed that *every* example of the IO monad only showed how to use *console* I/O. I couldn't find an example of anyone using the IO monad with *network* or *file* I/O.

The reality

As I dug into it, I learned about the reality of the situation. The short version of the story goes like this:

- Your I/O functions are probably already returning `Try` (or maybe `Option`)
- `Try` and `Option` are both monads, so it doesn't make sense to further wrap those results in `IO`

I'll show an example of this situation in the rest of this lesson, and also show two ways to declare the return type of I/O functions.

Note: Prefer Try over Option for I/O functions

I prefer to use `Try` for file and network I/O functions because I usually want to know what the exception was when a function fails. `Try` gives me the exception when there is a problem, but `Option` just returns `None`, which doesn't tell me what the actual problem was.

Source code

The source code for this lesson is available at the following URL:

- github.com/alvinj/FPIOMonadNotReallyUsed[1]

Discussion

To demonstrate this situation, let's look at a short example. First, imagine that you already have this `readTextFileAsString` function, which returns `Try[String]`:

```
def readTextFileAsString(filename: String): Try[String] =
    Try {
        val lines = using(io.Source.fromFile(filename)) { source =>
            (for (line <- source.getLines) yield line).toList
        }
        lines.mkString("\n")
    }
```

As I showed in the "Functional Error Handling lesson," one way to use functions that return `Try` is like this:

```
val passwdFile = readTextFileAsString("/etc/passwdFoo")
passwdFile match {
    case Success(s) => println(s)
    case Failure(e) => println(e)
}
```

Attempt to wrap that in IO

Next, imagine that you want to wrap all of your functions in the IO monad, so you write this code:

---
[1] https://github.com/alvinj/FPIOMonadNotReallyUsed

```
def readTextFileAsStringIO(filename: String): IO[Try[String]] = {
    IO(readTextFileAsString(filename))
}
```

All that function does is wrap the result of the previous function with the IO monad. As shown, the function now returns the type IO[Try[String]], which you can loosely read as, "A monad wrapped around a monad wrapped around a String."

Now imagine trying to use this result. You might attempt to write code like this:

```
val pfile2 = readTextFileAsStringIO("/etc/passwdFoo")
val z = for {
    a <- pfile2   //get Try[String] out of IO
    b <- a        //get String out of Try
} yield b
println(z)
```

But as you can guess from what you saw in the StateT lessons, that will give you a type mismatch error:

```
Error:(16, 11) type mismatch;
 found    : scala.util.Try[String]
 required: io_examples.v1.IO[?]
        b <- a       //get String out of Try
```

Just as bad as that error, all this approach does is make your code more complicated for no good reason. Because the first function (readTextFileAsString) already returns its result as a Try, you can already use it in for and match expressions; IO doesn't add a benefit here.

Once I dug into this code and saw these problems, I understood why IO doesn't seem to be used in the real world, at least not for file and network I/O in Scala: It makes the code more complicated, and adds no value, other than trying to have all of your I/O functions return an IO type.

If you really like the IO idea ...

If you really like the idea of using an IO type as a way to signal to other developers, "This function interacts with the outside world via I/O," one thing you can do is create a type alias that lets you use IO rather than Try in your function signatures:

```
import scala.util.Try
```

```
type IO[A] = Try[A]
```

With this type alias you can declare that your functions return IO rather than Try:

```
def readTextFileAsString(filename: String): IO[String] =
    Try {
        val lines = using(io.Source.fromFile(filename)) { source =>
            (for (line <- source.getLines) yield line).toList
        }
        lines.mkString("\n")
    }
```

Benefits

Assuming that you're not already using an IO monad in your project, I don't think this approach will be confusing, and it will give you the intended benefits of the IO monad:

- It tells all other developers that this function uses I/O
- It lets developers use the function in the usual monadic ways, i.e., such as combining instances in for expressions

Before you run off and use this approach, I should make a few more points:

- I don't know if anyone uses this technique in the real world
- You arguably get the same two benefits by returning Try

Or take it even further

Finally, if you decide that you do like this type alias technique, you can take it a step further and create a type alias named FileIO for file I/O functions, and NetworkIO for network I/O functions.

As an example of this, the Slick database library[2] from Lightbend has functions that return the type alias DBIO for non-streaming database functions, and StreamingDBIO for streaming functions. Both of those are aliases for the DBIOAction type.

---

[2] http://slick.lightbend.com/

Key points

In summary, the benefits of returning an IO type from your I/O functions are:

- It tells all other developers, "this function uses I/O"
- Because it implements map and flatMap, it lets developers use the function in the usual monadic ways, i.e., in for expressions

However, because functions that work with file and network resources already return Try, it doesn't make sense to stack IO onto Try, and in fact, it only makes your code more complicated, at best.

Therefore, the two main options are:

- Define your I/O functions to return Try.
- As an experiment, create a type alias IO and use it as the function return type instead of Try. You can also take that a step further and declare multiple aliases, such as FileIO, NetworkIO, and DatabaseIO.

110

Lenses, to Simplify "Update as You Copy"

> *"A Lens is an abstraction from functional programming which helps to deal with a problem of updating complex immutable nested objects."*
>
> From this koff.io article[a]
>
> ---
> [a] http://koff.io/posts/292173-lens-in-scala/

Goal

In the "Update as You Copy" lesson I showed that when you use the "update as you copy" approach on nested data structures, your code can quickly get ugly and complicated. As this lesson's introductory quote states, a *Lens* is a way of simplifying this problem. Therefore, the goal of this lesson is to show how lenses work.

Source code

If you want to follow along with the code in this lesson, get a copy of the source code from this Github repository:

- github.com/alvinj/FPLenses[1]

---
[1] https://github.com/alvinj/FPLenses

Lens libraries

There are no "lens" libraries built into Scala, but there are several third-party libraries. In the following example I'll show an example of how to use a library named Quicklens[2].

A Scala Quicklens example

To get started, here's the data model I'll use in this lesson:

```
case class User(
    id: Int,
    name: Name,
    billingInfo: BillingInfo,
    phone: String,
    email: String
)

case class Name(
    firstName: String,
    lastName: String
)

case class Address(
    street1: String,
    street2: String,
    city: String,
    state: String,
    zip: String
)

case class CreditCard(
    name: Name,
    number: String,
    month: Int,
    year: Int,
    cvv: String
```

---

[2] https://github.com/adamw/quicklens

)

```
case class BillingInfo(
    creditCards: Seq[CreditCard]
)
```

Given that model, I create this instance of a User:

```
val user = User(
    id = 1,
    name = Name(
        firstName = "Al",
        lastName = "Alexander"
    ),
    billingInfo = BillingInfo(
        creditCards = Seq(
            CreditCard(
                name = Name("Al", "Alexander"),
                number = "1111111111111111",
                month = 3,
                year = 2020,
                cvv = ""
            )
        )
    ),
    phone = "907-555-1212",
    email = "al@al.com"
)
```

To show how a lens works, assume that you need to change both the User.phone and User.email fields. One way to do this using Quicklens is with a step-by-step process, like this:

```
val user1 = user.modify(_.phone).setTo("720-555-1212")
val user2 = user1.modify(_.email).setTo("al@example.com")
```

That's a good start, but with Quicklens I can do even better. This example shows how to modify those fields as well as the firstName field in the Name object, all with one expression:

```
val newUser = user.modify(_.phone).setTo("720-555-1212")
```

```
                    .modify(_.email).setTo("al@example.com")
                    .modify(_.name.firstName).setTo("Alvin")
```

That's pretty cool, and it's much easier than what I showed at the end of the "Update as You Copy" lesson.

Discussion

As mentioned, lenses let you create updated versions of immutable objects. While the "update as you copy" approach is useful for non-nested objects, a good lens library is extremely helpful when you need to update values that are buried deep inside nested objects.

Lenses basically hide the nasty object-copying operations you would have to handle manually, and they make your code look clean in the process.

Lens projects

I showed the Quicklens library in this lesson because it's relatively simple and easy to use:

- github.com/adamw/quicklens[3]

Here's a list of a few other Scala Lens libraries that are available:

- Monocle[4] is under active development
- You can find an example of the Shapeless lens library on this Github page[5]
- Goggles[6] aims to simplify Monocle

See also

- My example in this lesson is a simplification of the examples on this koff.io page[7]

---

[3] https://github.com/adamw/quicklens
[4] http://julien-truffaut.github.io/Monocle/
[5] https://github.com/milessabin/shapeless/wiki/Feature-overview:-shapeless-2.0.0
[6] https://github.com/kenbot/goggles
[7] http://koff.io/posts/292173-lens-in-scala/

111

Signpost: Concurrency

This section of the book covers tools for writing parallel and concurrent applications in Scala. Here's an outline of the next several lessons:

- First, I'll demonstrate the problem of using mutable data structures with multiple threads
- Then I'll show how to use Akka actors to create long-running parallel processes
- Finally, I'll show how to use Scala futures for "one-shot" tasks that run in parallel and return a result when they complete

112

Concurrency and Mutability Don't Mix

> "If you have two good states, it's better to be in one or
> the other, but we can't ever be in both."
>
> From the book, Becoming Functional[a]

[a] http://amzn.to/2wqdf1H

Source code

The source code for this lesson is available at the following URL:

- github.com/alvinj/FPConcurrencyAndMutability

Goals

The goal of this lesson is to show that concurrency and mutability don't work well together. While history has shown us that it is *possible* to write parallel and concurrent applications with mutable data structures, the reality is that it's much easier to write them using immutable data.

The extremely short version of this lesson goes like this:

```
mutable data structures + multiple threads = very complex
```

My background

Historically, I've enjoyed the complexity of writing multi-threaded applications; I took them on as a challenge. Back in the early 2000s I used Java threads a fair amount, and even wrote a "database connection pool" library that was featured in a book. I mention this only to point out that I'm familiar with the problems of writing parallel/concurrent applications using only the Java `Thread` primitive. Knowing those perils — and being more interested in solving problems than challenging the limits of my brain — when I first learned about Scala futures and Akka actors, I quickly switched to using them.

The problem of mutable data structures and multiple threads

If you try to use mutable data structures with multiple threads, you'll find that it's easy to create race and deadlock conditions. In the case of my database connection pool library, I ran tests on it for *days* at a time with different simulated conditions until I had confidence that it worked properly.

You can easily create corrupt, inconsistent data with threads and mutable data structures. Indeed, I can show the problem with just a few lines of Scala code. Given this class with mutable fields:

```
class Person (
    var name: String,
    var town: String,
    var state: String
) {
    override def toString = s"name: $name, town: $town, state: $state"
}
```

The following code with just one thread running in parallel demonstrates the problem:

```
object SimpleBadConcurrency extends App {

    val me = new Person("Alvin", "Talkeetna", "Alaska")

    val t1 = new Thread {
        override def run {
            Thread.sleep(1000)
            me.town = "Boulder"
            Thread.sleep(3000)
            me.state = "Colorado"
        }
    }

    // start the thread
    t1.start

    println(s"1) $me")

    Thread.sleep(2000)
```

```
    println(s"2) $me")

    Thread.sleep(2000)
    println(s"3) $me")

}
```

That code prints the following output:

```
1) name: Alvin, town: Talkeetna, state: Alaska
2) name: Alvin, town: Boulder, state: Alaska
3) name: Alvin, town: Boulder, state: Colorado
```

In case it's not clear, the data in this line is corrupt:

```
2) name: Alvin, town: Boulder, state: Alaska
```

Boulder is in Colorado, not Alaska.

Of course this is a relatively simple "race condition"[1] example that I created with exaggerated delay times, but it illustrates the real problem: If mutable data can be modified by more than one thread, there's *always* a chance for data corruption. Then, once you start trying to fix that problem with synchronization, you enter the world of multi-thread locks[2].

That can't happen with immutable data structures

Conversely, the same problem *can't happen* with immutable data structures, even when using the Thread primitive. The following code shows why. First, I start with the usual Scala/FP case class with immutable fields:

```
case class Person (
    name: String,
    town: String,
    state: String
) {
    override def toString = s"name: $name, town: $town, state: $state"
}
```

---

[1] https://en.wikipedia.org/wiki/Race_condition
[2] https://en.wikipedia.org/wiki/Deadlock

Next, here's an attempt to write the same code as before:

```
object GoodConcurrency extends App {

    val me = Person("Alvin", "Talkeetna", "Alaska")

    val t1 = new Thread {
        override def run {
            Thread.sleep(1000)

            // this code won't compile - Person is immutable
            //me.town = "Boulder"

            Thread.sleep(3000)

            // this code won't compile - Person is immutable
            //me.state = "Colorado"
        }
    }
    t1.start

    // more code here ...

}
```

As I show in the comments, you can't even write code the same way as the first example because you can't mutate the fields inside the Person object. If you use immutable data structures — such as case classes with immutable fields in Scala/FP — you can't possibly run into the same problem.

Quotes from the masters

Rather than writing more about using threads with mutable data structures, I'll conclude this lesson with a few "quotes from the masters." I found this quote by John Carmack in the book, Learning Concurrent Programming in Scala[3]:

---

[3] http://amzn.to/2fWn70c

> "Programming in a functional style makes the state presented to your code explicit, which makes it much easier to reason about, and, in a completely pure system, makes thread race conditions impossible."

Related to that quote, it's important to note that everything I write in this book about Scala/FP shows how to create a "completely pure system."

In relation to parallel/concurrent programming, Joe Armstrong, creator of the Erlang language, writes:

> "*State* is the root of all evil."

In that comment he's referring to "mutable state."

From this fpcomplete.com article[4] by Bartosz Milewski[5]:

> "Did you notice that in the definition of 'data race' there's always talk of mutation?"

Martin Odersky, creator of the Scala language, once shared this simple equation:

> non-determinism = parallel processing + mutable state

(In programming, "non-determinism" is bad.)

One more quote

In the terrific book, Java Concurrency in Practice[6], Brian Goetz writes about mutable objects. He states, "The publication requirements for an object depend on its mutability." By "publication" he means, "how an object can be shared publicly." He follows that statement with these bullet points:

- *Immutable objects* can be published through any mechanism
- *Effectively immutable objects* must be safely published

---

[4]https://www.fpcomplete.com/blog/
[5]https://www.schoolofhaskell.com/user/bartosz
[6]http://amzn.to/2fdFfSK

- *Mutable objects* must be safely published, and must be either thread-safe or guarded by a lock

For this discussion it doesn't matter what the definition of "effectively immutable objects" is; the key point is that when you use anything but immutable objects, things quickly get more complicated.

As he further writes, "Whenever you acquire a reference to an object, you should know what you are allowed to do with it. Do you need to acquire a lock before using it? Are you allowed to modify its state, or only read it? Many concurrency errors stem from failing to understand these 'rules of engagement' for a shared object. When you publish an object, you should document how the object can be accessed."

A great thing about using only immutable objects in Scala/FP is that there's no need to "document how the object can be accessed." Every object is immutable, and can therefore "be published through any mechanism." I'll end this section with one last quote from his book:

> "Immutable objects are always thread-safe."

What's next

While I won't write any more about the Thread primitive, the following lessons cover Scala's main tools for writing parallel and concurrent applications: Scala futures, and Akka actors.

See also

If you're interested in writing parallel/concurrent applications, I can confirm that these books are excellent:

- Java Concurrency in Practice[7], Brian Goetz
- Learning Concurrent Programming in Scala[8], is written by Aleksandar Prokopec, creator of the Scala Parallel Collections framework

Two main solutions for dealing with concurrency in Scala are to use (a) futures and (b) the Akka actors library. While this book is now a little dated, it covers both of the topics very well:

---

[7] http://amzn.to/2fdFfSK
[8] http://amzn.to/2hqMtjY

- Akka Concurrency[9]

---
[9]http://amzn.to/2y0fKwy

113

Scala Concurrency Tools

Now that you've seen an example of the problem with mutable data structures and concurrency, we'll look at some of the tools Scala provides to support parallel and concurrent programming. The two main tools are:

- Akka actors
- Scala futures (which came from Akka)

Scala also comes with a third tool:

- Parallel collections classes

The Scala and Java industries also provide reactive extensions[1], which are libraries for "composing asynchronous and event-based programs using observable sequences":

- RxScala[2]
- RxJava[3]

In addition to these tools, you can also use the Java `Thread` primitive in the (rare) situations where it makes sense.

In the next lessons I'll focus on Akka actors and Scala futures, which have been the two primary tools in my experience.

The differences between Actors and Futures

The book Akka Concurrency[4] provides a good description of the differences between actors and futures:

---

[1] https://en.wikipedia.org/wiki/Reactive_extensions
[2] https://github.com/ReactiveX/RxScala
[3] https://github.com/ReactiveX/RxJava
[4] http://amzn.to/2y0fKwy

"An *actor* is a live object that can interact between itself and any number of other objects, functioning as long-lived message processors with potentially changing state. The *future*, on the other hand, is intended as a one-shot, single-purpose entity that is only addressable by the chunk of code waiting for the future's promise, and the other chunk of code that fulfills that promise."

Actors and futures are deep topics that entire books have been written about. I won't be able to go into the detail those books cover, but I'll provide an overview of them in the next several lessons, focusing on how they relate to the functional programming concepts presented in this book.

Scala's parallel collections classes

A third tool that can help in certain situations are Scala's parallel collections classes. I won't be covering those classes in this book, but they were written by Aleksandar Prokopec, who wrote a terrific book named Learning Concurrent Programming in Scala[5] that covers those classes, and Scala concurrency in general. Please see that book, or these other resources for learning about Scala's parallel collections classes:

- The scala-lang.org Parallel Collections Overview[6]
- My Examples of how to use parallel collections in Scala[7]

The best tool for each job

No tool is right for every job. A nice benefit of Scala is that it offers different tools for different parallel programming needs:

- *Actors* are long running entities that can run on distributed systems, and respond to messages to perform their tasks. They're useful in building event-driven systems, where each actor can serialize concurrent access to its resource(s).
- *Futures* are intended for "one-shot," concurrent tasks. When it returns, a future is expected to produce a single value as a result, such as accessing a REST web service.
- The *parallel collections classes* may be useful for running algorithms (think `map`, `filter`, etc.) on large data sets.

---

[5] http://amzn.to/2hqMtjY
[6] http://docs.scala-lang.org/overviews/parallel-collections/overview.html
[7] https://alvinalexander.com/scala/how-to-use-parallel-collections-in-scala-performance

- *Reactive extensions* are useful when building asynchronous, event-driven applications; streaming data from external sources; and incrementally propagating changes in the data model throughout the application. (Most of this text is from the book, *Learning Concurrent Programming in Scala*.)
- The Java `Thread` is a relatively primitive tool for building low-level tasks, such as building other parallel/concurrent libraries.

In the lessons that follow I'll demonstrate Akka actors and Scala futures.

See also

- I briefly wrote about the Scala parallel collection classes[8]

---

[8] https://alvinalexander.com/scala/how-to-use-parallel-collections-in-scala-performance

114
Akka Actors

> *"Erlang programs are made up from lots of small sequential programs running at the same time ... When we write an Erlang program we do not implement it as a single process that does everything; we implement it as large numbers of small processes that do simple things and communicate with each other."*
>
> From the book, Programming Erlang[a]
>
> ---
> [a]http://amzn.to/2aab4HF

Introduction

This lesson is about the Akka actors library[1]. In the lesson you'll learn about:

- Actors and the actor model
- Akka's benefits

I also share several Akka examples you can work with.

Technically, Akka isn't *directly* related to functional programming, other than a few key concepts:

- Actors are long-running threads that respond to messages sent to them
- The messages sent to actors are typically instances of immutable case classes and case objects
- Actors typically handle messages within pattern-matching statements
- Actors don't share any state with other actors, so by definition there is no mutable, shared state

---
[1]http://akka.io/

Background: Erlang

The original Scala actor library — which was replaced by Akka — was patterned after the Erlang[2] language. In the book, Programming Erlang[3], Joe Armstrong writes:

> "Erlang belongs to the family of *functional programming languages.* Functional programming forbids code with side effects. Side effects and concurrency don't mix. In Erlang it's OK to mutate state within an individual process but not for one process to tinker with the state of another process."

An Erlang *process* is equivalent to an Akka *actor*, so you can say, "In Akka it's OK to mutate state within an individual actor but not for one process to tinker with the state of another actor."

Notice that unlike "Pure FP," Mr. Armstrong states that it's okay to mutate state within an individual process. This is similar to saying, "It's okay to mutate state within a pure function — such as using a var field and for loop rather than recursion — as long as you don't mutate state outside of the pure function."

Akka benefits

While (in my opinion) Akka isn't *directly* related to functional programming, it's a great way to build massively parallel systems using Scala. All of these industry buzzwords are correctly used to describe Akka:

- asynchronous
- event-driven
- message-driven
- reactive
- scalable ("scale up" and "scale out")
- concurrent and parallel
- non-blocking
- location transparency
- resilient and redundant (no single point of failure with distributed servers)
- fault-tolerant

---

[2] https://www.erlang.org/
[3] http://amzn.to/2aab4HF

All of those benefits are great, but the first great benefit is that Akka and the actor model *greatly* simplify the process of working with multiple, long-running threads. In fact, when working with Akka, you never think about threads; you just write actors to respond to messages in a non-blocking manner, and the threads take of themselves.

Actors and the Actor Model

The first thing to know about Akka actors is the *actor model*, which is a mental model of how to think about a system built with actors. In that model the first concept to understand is an *actor*:

- An actor is a long-running process that runs in parallel to the main application thread, and responds to messages that are sent to it.
- An actor is the smallest unit when building an actor-based system, just like a class is the smallest unit in an OOP system.
- Like a class, an actor encapsulates state and behavior.
- You can't peek inside an actor to get its state. You can send an actor a message requesting state information (like texting a person to ask how they're feeling), but you can't reach in and execute one of its methods or access its fields (just like you can't peak inside someone else's brain).
- An actor has a mailbox (an inbox), and the actor's purpose in life is to process the messages in its mailbox.
- You communicate with an actor by sending it an immutable message. These messages go directly into the actor's mailbox.
- When an actor receives a message, it's like taking a letter out of its mailbox. It opens the letter, processes the message using one of its algorithms, then moves on to the next message in the mailbox. If there are no more messages, the actor waits until it receives one.

Akka experts recommend thinking of an actor as being like a person in a business organization:

- You can't know what's going on inside another person. All you can do is send them a message and wait for their response.
- An actor has one parent, known as a *supervisor*. In Akka, that supervisor is the actor that created it.
- An actor may have children. For instance, a President in a business may have a number of Vice Presidents. Those VPs are like children of the President, and they may also have many subordinates. (And those subordinates may have many subordinates, etc.)

- An actor may have siblings — i.e., other actors at the same level. For instance, there may be 10 VPs in an organization, and they're all at the same level in the organization chart.

Actors should delegate their work

There's one more important point to know about actors: As soon as an actor receives a message, it should delegate its work. Actors need to be able to respond to messages in their mailbox as fast as possible, so the actor mantra is, "Delegate, delegate, delegate."

If you think of an actor as being a person, imagine that one message includes a task that's going to take a month to complete. If the actor worked on that task for a month, it wouldn't be able to respond to its mailbox for a month. That's bad. But if the actor delegates that task to one of its children, it can respond to the next message in its mailbox immediately (and delegate that as well).

Akka benefits

Here are some benefits of using Akka actors, mostly coming from Lightbend's Akka Quickstart Guide[4] and the Akka.io website[5]:

- Event-driven model: Actors perform work in response to messages.
- Communication between actors is asynchronous, allowing actors to send messages and continue their own work without blocking to wait for a reply.
- Actors and streams let you build systems that *scale up*, using the resources of a server more efficiently, and *scale out*, using multiple servers.
- Performance: Actors have been shown to process up to 50 million messages/second on a single machine.
- Lightweight: Each instance consumes only a few hundred bytes, which allows millions of concurrent actors to exist in a single application (allowing ~2.5 million actors per GB of heap).
- Distributed systems without single points of failure. Load balancing and adaptive routing across nodes.
- Strong isolation principles: Unlike regular objects in Scala, an actor does not have a public API in terms of methods that you can invoke. Instead, its public API is defined through messages that the actor handles.

---

[4] http://developer.lightbend.com/guides/akka-quickstart-scala/
[5] http://akka.io

- Location transparency: Because the location of actors doesn't matter — they can be running on the current server or some other server — actor instances can start, stop, move, and restart to scale up and down, as well as recover from unexpected failures.

A video example

Back in 2011 I started developing a "personal assistant" named SARAH, which was based on the computer assistant of the same name on the television show Eureka[6]. SARAH is like the Amazon Echo[7] running on your computer, and the entire application was based on Akka actors. You speak to it to access and manage information:

- Get news headlines from different sources
- Get weather reports and stock prices
- Control iTunes with voice commands
- Check your email
- Perform Google searches

Beyond just *responding* to voice commands with spoken and displayed output, SARAH also has long-running background tasks — small pieces of software I call "agents" — so it can do other things:

- Tell me when I receive new email from people I'm interested in
- Report the time at the top of every hour ("The time is 11 a.m.")

For more information on SARAH, see the "Sarah - Version 2" video at alvinalexander.com/sarah[8]. I haven't worked on SARAH in a while, but it gives you can idea of what can be done with Akka actors.

How Akka relates to FP

In my opinion, the main ways Akka relates to functional programming are:

- Sending messages to actors with immutable `case` classes and `case` objects
- Actors respond to messages with pattern-matching statements in their `receive` method

---

[6] http://www.imdb.com/title/tt0796264/
[7] http://amzn.to/2y4bgoJ
[8] https://alvinalexander.com/sarah

- Because actors don't share state, it's often easier to implement actor behaviors with pure functions
- Because actors run on different threads, they give you a relatively simple way to implement concurrency in an application with immutable data

What's next

Given this background, the next lesson shows several examples of how to use Akka actors.

Akka Actor Examples

In this lesson I'll show two examples of applications that use Akka actors, and I'll show where you can find a third Akka application that's more complicated, but hopefully not too complicated for a next step.

Source code

The source code for this lesson is available at the following URL:

- github.com/alvinj/FPAkkaHelloWorld[1]

An Akka Hello, world example

Let's look at an example of how to write a "Hello, world" application using Akka.

Writing a Hello actor

An actor is an instance of the `akka.actor.Actor` class, and once it's created, all it does is respond to messages that are sent to it. For this "Hello, world" example I want an actor that responds to "hello" messages, so I start with code like this:

```
case class Hello(msg: String)

class HelloActor extends Actor {
    def receive = {
        case Hello(s) => {
            println(s"you said '$s'")
            println(s"$s back at you!\n")
        }
```

---

[1] https://github.com/alvinj/FPAkkaHelloWorld

```
            case _ => println("huh?")
    }
}
```

In the first line of code I define a case class named Hello. The preferred way to send messages with Akka is to use instances of case classes and case objects, which support immutability and pattern-matching. Therefore, I define Hello as a simple wrapper around a string.

After that, I define HelloActor as an instance of Actor. The body of HelloActor is just the receive method, which you implement to define the actor's initial behavior, i.e., how the actor responds to the messages it receives.

The way this code works is that when HelloActor receives a new message in its inbox, receive is triggered as a response to that event, and the incoming message is tested against receive's case statements. In this example, if the message is of the type Hello, the first case statement handles the message; if the message is *anything else*, the second case statement is triggered. (The second case statement is a "catch-all" statement that handles all unknown messages.)

Of course actors get more complicated than this, but that's the essence of the actor programming pattern. You create case classes and case objects to define the types of messages you want your actor to receive. Because the only way the rest of your code can interact with the actor is by sending messages to it, those classes and objects become your actor's API. Then inside the receive method you define how you want to respond to each message type. At a high level, that's how you write actor code.

A test program

Now all you need is a little driver program to test the actor. This one will do:

```
object AkkaHelloWorld extends App {

    // an actor needs an ActorSystem
    val system = ActorSystem("HelloSystem")

    // create and start the actor
    val helloActor = system.actorOf(
        Props[HelloActor],
        name = "helloActor"
    )
```

```
    // send the actor two known messages
    helloActor ! Hello("hello")
    helloActor ! Hello("buenos dias")

    // send it an unknown message
    helloActor ! "hi!"

    // shut down the system
    system.terminate()

}
```

Here's how that code works. First, actors need an ActorSystem[2] that they can run in, so you create one like this:

```
val system = ActorSystem("HelloSystem")
```

Just give the `ActorSystem` a unique name, and you're ready to go.

> The `ActorSystem` is the main construct that takes care of the gory thread details behind the scenes. Per the Akka website, "An ActorSystem is a heavyweight structure that will allocate 1...N Threads, so create one per logical application ... It is also the entry point for creating or looking up actors."

Next, as that quote states, you create new actors with the `ActorSystem`, so this is how you create an instance of a `HelloActor`:

```
val helloActor = system.actorOf(
    Props[HelloActor],
    name = "helloActor"
)
```

There are a few variations of that syntax, but the important part is that you create an instance of `HelloActor` by calling `actorOf` on the `ActorSystem` as shown.

Besides the required `import` statements, that's the entire setup process. At this point the `helloActor` instance is up and running (in parallel with the main application thread), and you can send it messages. This is how you send it a message:

---

[2]http://doc.akka.io/api/akka/2.0/akka/actor/ActorSystem.html

```
helloActor ! Hello("hello")
```

This line of code can be read as, "Send the message `Hello("hello")` to the actor named `helloActor`, and don't wait for a reply."

The ! character is how you send a message to an actor. More precisely, it's how you send a message to an actor *without waiting for a reply back from the actor*. This is by far the most common way to send a message to an actor; you don't want to wait for a reply back from the actor, because that would cause your application's thread to block at that point, and *blocking* is bad.

This `case` statement inside the `HelloActor` will handle this message when it's received:

```
// in HelloActor
case Hello(s) => {
    println(s"you said '$s'")
    println(s"$s back at you!\n")
}
```

Inside that `case` statement I print two lines of output, but this is normally where you call other functions to respond to the message. You'll often delegate work to child actors at this point.

Looking back at the code, after I send the two `Hello` messages to the `HelloActor`, I send it this message:

```
helloActor ! "hi!"
```

Because `HelloActor` doesn't know how to handle a `String` message, it will respond to this message with its "catch-all" `case` statement:

```
// in HelloActor
case _ => println("huh?")
```

At this point the `AkkaHelloWorld` application reaches this line of code, which shuts down the `ActorSystem`:

```
system.terminate()
```

That's the entire Akka "Hello, world" application.

I encourage you to work with the source code from the repository for this lesson. In the *HelloWorld.scala* file, add new messages (as `case` classes and objects), and then add new `case` statements to the `receive` method in `HelloActor` to respond to those messages. Keep fooling around with it until you're sure you know how it all works.

A second example

As a slightly more complicated example, *Echo.scala* in this lesson's source code contains an Akka application that responds to whatever you type at the command line. First, the application has a `case` class and a `case` object that are used to send and receive messages:

```
case class Message(msg: String)
case object Bye
```

Next, this is how the `EchoActor` responds to the messages it receives:

```
class EchoActor extends Actor {
    def receive = {
        case Message(s) => println("\nyou said " + s)
        case Bye => println("see ya!")
        case _ => println("huh?")
    }
}
```

That follows the same pattern I showed in the first example.

Finally, here's a driver program you can use to test the `EchoActor`:

```
object EchoMain extends App {

    // an actor needs an ActorSystem
    val system = ActorSystem("EchoSystem")

    // create and start the actor
    val echoActor = system.actorOf(Props[EchoActor], name = "echoActor")

    // prompt the user for input
    var input = ""
    while (input != "q") {
        print("type something (q to quit): ")
        input = StdIn.readLine()
        echoActor ! Message(input)
```

```
    }

    echoActor ! Bye

    // shut down the system
    system.terminate()

}
```

Notice that after the `ActorSystem` and `echoActor` are created, the application sits in a loop prompting you for input, until you enter the character q. Once you type q and the loop terminates, the `echoActor` is sent one last message:

```
echoActor ! Bye
```

After that, the system shuts down.

This is what the output of the application looks like when you run it and type a few things at the command line:

```
type something (q to quit): hello
you said hello

type something (q to quit): hola
you said hola

type something (q to quit): q
you said q

bye!
```

More examples

I could keep showing more examples, but the pattern is the same:

- Create `case` classes and `case` objects for the messages you want your actor to handle. These messages become the API for the actor.

- Program your actor(s) to respond to those messages as desired.

- Send messages to your actors using !.

If you'd like to work with a more-complicated example that isn't *too* complicated, I created an Akka application that works a little like SARAH and the Amazon Echo[3], albeit at your computer's command line. See this page for more details:

- alvinalexander.com/amazon-echo-akka[4]

That web page describes how the application works, but here's a quick example of some command-line input and output with the application:

```
ekko: weather
stand by ...
The current temperature is 78 degrees, and the sky is partly cloudy.

ekko: forecast
stand by ...
Here's the forecast.
For Sunday, a low of 59, a high of 85, and Partly Cloudy skies.
For Monday, a low of 53, a high of 72, and Scattered Thunderstorms skies.

ekko: todo add Wake Up
1. Wake Up
```

Again, please see that web page for more details and the source code. Additionally, see the "See Also" section at the end of this lesson for more Akka examples.

Where Akka fits in

As these examples show, an actor is an instance of `Actor`. Once created, an actor resides in memory, waiting for messages to appear in its inbox. When it receives a new message, it responds to the message with the `case` statements defined in its `receive` method.

An actor runs on its own thread, so when you send it a message from the main thread in your application, it does whatever it does on that other thread. Depending on your needs, this can be a great approach for reactive programming, because it can help to keep the UI for your application responsive. In something like a Swing (or JavaFX) GUI application, the process can look like this:

---

[3]http://amzn.to/2xwmlgM
[4]https://alvinalexander.com/amazon-echo-akka

- The user provides input through the GUI.
- Your application's event-handling code responds to that input event by sending a message to the appropriate actor.
- The Swing "Event Dispatch Thread" (EDT) remains responsive because the work is not being handled on the EDT.
- When the actor receives the message, it immediately delegates that work to a child actor. (I didn't show that process in this book, but you can find examples on my website and in the Scala Cookbook[5].)
- When the actor (and its children) finish processing the message, it sends a message back, and that message results in the UI being updated (eventually being handled by `SwingUtilities.invokeLater()`, in the case of Swing).

This is exactly the way SARAH works.

While the actor model isn't the only way to handle this situation, actors work well when you want to create parallel processes that will live in memory for a long time, and have messages that they know how to respond to.

In the case of SARAH — which works like Amazon Echo or a long-running instance of Siri — it has many actors that know how to do different kinds of work, including:

- Actors to get news headlines, check my email, get stock quotes, search Google, and get Twitter trends, etc.
- Actors to represent a mouth, ears, and brain, where the "ear actor" listens to your computer's microphone, the "mouth actor" speaks through the computer's speakers, and the "brain actor" knows how to process inputs and outputs, and delegate work to all of the other actors.

Key points

While the Akka actor system isn't *directly* tied to functional programming, it's primary mechanisms are:

- Messages are typically sent with `case` classes and `case` objects
- Actors respond to messages with pattern-matching statements in their `receive` method
- Actors don't share any state with other actors, so there is no mutable, shared state

---

[5]http://amzn.to/24ivK4G

- Because actors don't share state, it's often easier to implement actor behaviors with pure functions

Akka is intended for building reactive, responsive, event-driven (message-driven), scalable systems, and the actor model *greatly* simplifies the process of working with many long-running threads.

Actors work well when you want objects that live in RAM for a long time, and respond to one or more messages during their lifetime. (*Futures*, which you'll see in the next lesson, are better for "one shot," short-lived concurrency needs.)

Finally, all of these buzzwords truly apply to Akka actors: scalable (scale up and scale out), reactive, event-driven, message-driven, concurrent, parallel, asynchronous, non-blocking, location transparency, resilient, redundant, fault-tolerant (and more).

See also

- The Akka website[6]
- The Akka documentation[7]
- Akka is based on the "Actor Model[8]"
- I wrote about Akka[9] Actors in depth in the Scala Cookbook[10]
- SARAH, at alvinalexander.com/sarah[11]
- My "Akkazon Ekko" application, which is a simple version of SARAH: alvinalexander.com/amazon-echo-akka[12]
- Akka was inspired by the Erlang language[13], which is used to "build massively scalable soft real-time systems with requirements on high availability"
- Akka Actors: An example video game[14]
- A 'Ping Pong' Scala Akka actors example[15]
- An Akka actors 'remote' example[16]

---

[6] http://akka.io/
[7] http://akka.io/docs/
[8] https://en.wikipedia.org/wiki/Actor_model
[9] http://akka.io/
[10] http://amzn.to/24ivK4G
[11] https://alvinalexander.com/sarah
[12] https://alvinalexander.com/amazon-echo-akka
[13] https://www.erlang.org/
[14] https://alvinalexander.com/scala/akka-actors-video-game
[15] https://alvinalexander.com/scala/scala-akka-actors-ping-pong-simple-example
[16] https://alvinalexander.com/scala/simple-akka-actors-remote-example

- Understanding the methods in the Scala/Akka Actor lifecycle[17]
- How to create a Scala/Akka Actor whose constructor requires arguments[18]

---

[17]https://alvinalexander.com/scala/understand-methods-akka-actors-scala-lifecycle
[18]https://alvinalexander.com/scala/scala-akka-create-actors-constructors-have-arguments

Scala Futures

> *"Just as Try manages exceptions using effects, another abstraction in the Scala library called Future helps you manage latency as an effect."*
>
> Debasish Ghosh, in the book, Functional and Reactive Domain Modeling[a]

---

[a] http://amzn.to/2iOT3Vh

Source code

The source code for this lesson is at this URL:

- github.com/alvinj/FPFutures[1]

Introduction

While an Akka actor runs for a long time and is intended to handle *many* messages over its lifetime, a Scala *future* is intended as a one-shot, "handle this relatively slow and potentially long-running computation, and call me back with a result when you're done" construct.

While I see Akka as only being related to functional programming in the ways I described in the previous lessons, a Future is directly related to the FP concepts described in this book. Indeed, the book Advanced Scala with Cats[2] says this about Scala futures:

> "Future is a monad that allows us to sequence computations without worrying that they are asynchronous."

---

[1] https://github.com/alvinj/FPFutures
[2] https://underscore.io/books/advanced-scala/

As usual, this means that Future is a class that implements map and flatMap, so it can be used in for expressions.

And as this quote from the scala-lang.org "Futures and Promises" page[3] shows, futures support FP buzzwords like 'combinators' and 'compose':

> "By default, futures and promises are non-blocking, making use of callbacks instead of typical blocking operations. To simplify the use of callbacks both syntactically and conceptually, Scala provides combinators such as flatMap, foreach, and filter used to compose futures in a non-blocking way."

In this lesson I'll show how to run several futures in parallel, and then combine their results in a for expression, and a few other useful Future methods.

Goals

Futures are a large topic that I could write a small book about. Since there are already good books about Akka and futures I'm not going to do that, but I do want to cover enough about futures so you can see:

- Their basic use
- How they're used in a monadic programming style
- How some of the Future callback methods work
- A real-world example

An example in the REPL

Let's start with an example of a Future in the Scala REPL. First, paste in these import statements:

```
import scala.concurrent.Future
import scala.concurrent.ExecutionContext.Implicits.global
import scala.util.{Failure, Success}
```

Now, you can create a future that will sleep for one second, and then return the value 42:

```
scala> val a = Future { Thread.sleep(1000); 42 }
```

---

[3] http://docs.scala-lang.org/overviews/core/futures.html

```
a: scala.concurrent.Future[Int] = Future(<not completed>)
```

Because `Future` has a `map` function, you use it as usual:

```
scala> val b = a.map(_ * 2)
b: scala.concurrent.Future[Int] = Future(<not completed>)
```

This shows `Future(<not completed>)` right away, but if you check b's value again, you'll see that it contains the expected result of 84:

```
scala> b
res1: scala.concurrent.Future[Int] = Future(Success(84))
```

Notice that the 84 you expected is wrapped in a `Success`, which is further wrapped in a `Future`. This is a key point to know: The value in a `Future` is always an instance of one of the `Try` types: `Success` or `Failure`. Therefore, when working with the result of a future, use the usual Try-handling techniques, or one of the other `Future` callback methods. One commonly used callback method is `onComplete`, which takes a partial function, in which you should handle the `Success` and `Failure` cases, like this:

```
a.onComplete {
    case Success(value) => println(s"Got the callback, value = $value")
    case Failure(e) => e.printStackTrace
}
```

When you paste that code in the REPL you'll see the result:

```
Got the callback, value = 42
```

There are other ways to process the results from futures, and I'll list the most common methods later in this lesson.

An example application

I like to use the following application to introduce futures because it's simple, and it shows several key points about how to work with futures:

- How to create futures
- How to combine multiple futures in a `for` expression to obtain a single result
- How to work with that result once you have it, in this case using `onComplete` to handle the result as a side effect

Here's the example:

```scala
package futures.v1

import scala.concurrent.Future
import scala.concurrent.ExecutionContext.Implicits.global
import scala.util.{Failure, Success}

object MultipleFutures1 extends App {

    // (a) create three futures
    val f1 = Future { sleep(800); 1 }
    val f2 = Future { sleep(200); 2 }
    val f3 = Future { sleep(400); 3 }

    // (b) get a combined result in a for-comprehension
    val result = for {
        r1 <- f1
        r2 <- f2
        r3 <- f3
    } yield (r1 + r2 + r3)

    // (c) do whatever you need to do with the result
    result.onComplete {
        case Success(x) => println(s"\nresult = $x")
        case Failure(e) => e.printStackTrace
    }

    // important for a little parallel demo: need to keep
    // the jvm's main thread alive
    sleep(3000)

    def sleep(time: Long): Unit = Thread.sleep(time)

}
```

Creating the futures

Let's walk through that code to see how it works. First, I create three futures with these lines of code:

```
val f1 = Future { sleep(800); 1 }
val f2 = Future { sleep(200); 2 }
val f3 = Future { sleep(400); 3 }
```

Those lines of code are equivalent to calling the `apply` method in `Future`'s companion object:

```
val f1 = Future.apply { sleep(800); 1 }
```

An important thing to know about `Future` is that it *immediately* begins running the block of code inside the curly braces. (It isn't like the Java `Thread`, where you create an instance and later call its `start` method.) For example, the `sleep` function call in `f1` begins running immediately after this line of code:

```
val f1 = Future { sleep(800); 1 }
```

The three futures in the example admittedly don't do much. They sleep for their allotted times, and then return `Int` values. For example, after 800 ms, `f1` will eventually contain the value 1. People often use the word *eventually* with futures because the return time is usually indeterminate: you don't know when you'll get a result back, you just hope to get a successful result back "eventually."

Another important point to know is that a `Future` always returns a type of `Future[A]`. In these examples, that type is `Future[Int]`:

```
val f1: Future[Int] = Future { sleep(800); 1 }
```

> You declare the return type like that, but remember that a `Future` always contains an instance of `Try`, so the actual result of `f1` will be `Future(Success(1))`.

The for expression

The `for` expression in the application looks like this:

```
val result = for {
    r1 <- f1
```

```
    r2 <- f2
    r3 <- f3
} yield (r1 + r2 + r3)
```

You can read this as, "Whenever f1, f2, and f3 return with their values, sum them up with yield, and assign that value to the variable result." I didn't show it in the code, but result also has the type Future[Int]:

```
val result: Future[Int] = for { ...
              -----------
```

It's important to know that the main thread in the application doesn't stop at this point. In fact, if you print the result from System.currentTimeMillis() before and after the for expression, you probably won't see a difference of more than a few milliseconds. I demonstrate this in the example in the next lesson.

onComplete

The final part of the application looks like this:

```
result.onComplete {
    case Success(x) => println(s"\nresult = $x")
    case Failure(e) => e.printStackTrace
}
```

As I showed before, onComplete is a method that's available on a Future, and you use it to process the future's result as a side effect. In the same way that the foreach method on collections classes returns Unit and is only used for side effects, onComplete returns Unit and you only use it for side effects like printing the results, updating a GUI, updating a database, etc.

You can read that code as, "Whenever result has a final value — i.e., after all of the futures return and are summed in the for expression — come here. If everything returned successfully, run the println statement shown in the Success case. Otherwise, if an exception was thrown, go to the Failure case and print the exception's stack trace."

As that code implies, it's completely possible that a Future may fail. For example, imagine that you call a web service in a future, but the web service is down. That Future instance will contain an exception, so when you call result.onComplete like this, control will flow to the Failure case.

That sleep call

A final point to note about small examples like this is that you need to have a `sleep` call at the end of your `App`:

```
sleep(3000)
```

That call keeps the main thread of the JVM alive for three seconds. If you don't include a call like this, the JVM's main thread will exit before you get a result from the three futures, which are running on other threads. This isn't usually a problem in the real world, but it's a problem for little demos like this.

Similar to the real world

While that example doesn't do much and you know up front long it takes for each `Future` to complete, it's remarkably similar to code that you'll use in the real world. For example, if you call a function named `Cloud.executeLongRunningTask()` to get an `Int` result that will take an indeterminate amount of time, you'll still construct the future in the same way:

```
val task: Future[Int] = Future {
    Cloud.executeLongRunningTask(a, b, c)
}
```

Then, whenever the future is finished, you'll also use a method like `onComplete` to process the result:

```
task.onComplete {
    case Success(value) => outputTheResult(value)
    case Failure(e) => outputTheError(e)
}
```

So although the code in the curly braces of the f1/f2/f3 example doesn't do much, the use of futures in that example follows the same pattern that you'll use in the real world:

- Construct one or more futures to run tasks off of the main thread
- If you're using multiple futures to yield a single result, combine the futures in a `for` expression
- Use a callback method like `onComplete` to process the final result

117

A Second Futures Example

Source code

The source code for this lesson is at the same URL as the previous lesson:

- github.com/alvinj/FPFutures

A Futures example with debug output

To create the example in this lesson, I modified the delay times of the first example, added calls to get the Thread IDs, and added time checks at various points in the application to show the details of how futures work, especially with `for` expressions and callback methods. Here's the source code for this example:

```
package futures.v1

import scala.concurrent.Future
import scala.concurrent.ExecutionContext.Implicits.global
import scala.util.{Failure, Success}

object MultipleFuturesWithThreadIds extends App {

    val mainThreadId = Thread.currentThread.getId
    var f1ThreadId = 0L
    var f2ThreadId = 0L
    var f3ThreadId = 0L

    val startTime = currentTime

    /**
     * (a) create the futures. as you'll see in the
     * time-related output, they start running immediately.
     */
```

```scala
val f1: Future[Int] = Future {
    println(s"f1 start:         ${deltaTime(startTime)}")
    f1ThreadId = Thread.currentThread.getId
    sleep(1200)
    1
}
val f2: Future[Int] = Future {
    println(s"f2 start:         ${deltaTime(startTime)}")
    f2ThreadId = Thread.currentThread.getId
    sleep(400)
    2
}
val f3: Future[Int] = Future {
    println(s"f3 start:         ${deltaTime(startTime)}")
    f3ThreadId = Thread.currentThread.getId
    sleep(800)
    3
}

// (b) merge the results when they become available
println(s"before for:       ${deltaTime(startTime)}")
val result: Future[(Long, Int)] = for {
    r1 <- f1
    r2 <- f2
    r3 <- f3
} yield (deltaTime(startTime), r1 + r2 + r3)
println(s"after for:        ${deltaTime(startTime)}")

/**
 * the f1/f2/f3 println statements show that those code
 * blocks are started immediately. but because they're
 * on different threads, the time-related println statements
 * in this (main) thread show that the main thread goes
 * flying right through the for-expression.
 */

// (c) handle the result as a side effect
println(s"before onComplete: ${deltaTime(startTime)}")
```

```
result.onComplete {
    case Success(x) => {

        // sleep to show that for's `yield` expression
        // happens just before this point
        sleep(10)

        // the "in success" time should be almost exactly the
        // same as the longest sleep time, plus the 10ms delay
        // above; approximately 1210ms for my sample times.
        val tInSuccessCase = deltaTime(startTime)
        println(s"in Success case:    ${tInSuccessCase}")
        println(s"\nresult = $x")
        println(s"onComplete tid: ${Thread.currentThread.getId}")

    }
    case Failure(e) => e.printStackTrace
}
println(s"after onComplete:   ${deltaTime(startTime)}")

// important for a small parallel demo: keep the main jvm
// thread alive
println(s"start sleep(2000): ${deltaTime(startTime)}")
sleep(2000)

println("")
println("Thread IDs")
println("----------")
println(s"Main Thread ID: ${mainThreadId}")
println(s"F1 Thread ID:   ${f1ThreadId}")
println(s"F2 Thread ID:   ${f2ThreadId}")
println(s"F3 Thread ID:   ${f3ThreadId}")



def sleep(time: Long) = Thread.sleep(time)
def currentTime = System.currentTimeMillis()
def deltaTime(t0: Long) = System.currentTimeMillis() - t0
```

}

I encourage you to view that code in your IDE as I discuss it in the following paragraphs.

When I run that code at the command line with SBT, I see output that looks like this:

```
f1 start:            1
f2 start:            1
f3 start:            2
before for:          1
after for:           2
before onComplete:   2
after onComplete:    2
start sleep(2000):   2

result = (1204,6)
in Success case:     1215

Thread IDs
----------
Main Thread ID: 85
F1 Thread ID:   74
F2 Thread ID:   72
F3 Thread ID:   73
onComplete tid: 74
```

I rearranged that output slightly to highlight the key points:

- The main thread flies through f1, f2, f3, the for expression, and the onComplete expression almost instantly
- The sleep(2000) statement begins after only 2 ms
- The (1204,6) output shows that the yield statement in the for expression returns its value at 1204 ms
- Because of the 10 ms sleep time I added, the "in Success case" statement prints 11 ms later, at 1215 ms
- I'll discuss the thread IDs shortly, but the important point to notice is that F1, F2, and F3 are all different than the Main Thread ID

A key here is the time the yield statement returns (1204 ms): This value is just a few milliseconds more than f1's sleep time. This confirms that f1, f2 and f3 ran in parallel. If they had run serially — one after the other — the `yield` statement would not have returned until 2400 ms had passed (i.e., the combined run times of `f1`, `f2`, and `f3`).

Also note that I added a 10 ms sleep time in the `Success` case. I did this to show that the `yield` statement returns before `onComplete` is called. (On my computer, if I don't add that delay, the `yield` and `Success` times are identical.)

Key points of this example

I added all of the print statements to the code to show how this process works:

- The futures are started immediately
- The main JVM thread flies right through the `for` and `onComplete` expressions
- `yield` in the `for` expression is executed when all of the futures complete
- `onComplete` is executed immediately after that

The thread IDs

Once you're comfortable with how the code works time-wise, another thing to look at is the printout of the Thread IDs at the end of the `App`:

```
Thread IDs
----------
Main Thread ID: 85
F1 Thread ID:   74
F2 Thread ID:   72
F3 Thread ID:   73
onComplete tid: 74
```

The actual numeric values don't matter, they'll be different if you run them in your IDE or in SBT — and they keep getting larger the more times you run the `App` in SBT — but the important point is that `f1`, `f2`, and `f3` all have different values than the main thread. I show this output as another way to demonstrate that all of the futures ran on different threads than the main thread — they were all running in parallel.

I also show the Thread ID from inside `onComplete`. In this case, it's 74, which is `f1`'s Thread ID:

```
F1 Thread ID:   74
onComplete tid: 74
```

Futures will re-use threads where they can, and while there's no guarantee that this will *always* be the case, I've found that in small examples with these sleep times, the onComplete Thread ID is the same as f1's. (This Thread ID will vary if you make f2 or f3 sleep longer than f1.)

The final result

The actual result of this application isn't too important — I really just want to show how futures work — but the final answer is 6, which I returned in the tuple from yield:

```
result = (1204,6)
```

Details to know about Futures

Here are a few more details to know about futures. First, the scala-lang.org "Futures and Promises" page[1] provides this summary:

> "The idea is simple: a Future is a sort of a placeholder object that you can create for a result that does not yet exist. Generally, the result of the Future is computed concurrently and can be later collected. Composing concurrent tasks in this way tends to result in faster, asynchronous, non-blocking parallel code. A Future is an object holding a value which may become available at some point."

Here are some key points about futures:

- A future represents the result of an asynchronous computation, and has a return type, such as Future[Int].
- The value in a future is always an instance of Try, so you always deal with Success and Failure when handling a future's result.
- You typically work with the results of a future using its callback methods, such as onComplete.
- A future is a monad, and can be composed. It has combinator methods like map, flatMap, filter, etc.
- There's no guarantee that your future's callback method will be called on the same thread the future was run on.

In regards to that last point, here's another quote from the "Futures and Promises" page:

---

[1] http://docs.scala-lang.org/overviews/core/futures.html

"We should now comment on when exactly the callback gets called. Since it requires the value in the future to be available, it can only be called after the future is completed. However, there is no guarantee it will be called by the thread that completed the future or the thread which created the callback. Instead, the callback is executed by *some* thread, at some time after the future object is completed. We say that the callback is executed eventually."

Future's callback methods

The scala.concurrent.Future class Scaladoc[2] separates Future methods into three categories:

1) Callbacks:

- onComplete
- andThen
- foreach

2) Polling:

- isCompleted
- value

3) Transformations:

- transform
- transformWith
- failed
- fallbackTo
- mapTo
- recover
- recoverWith
- transform
- familiar methods: collect, filter, flatten, flatMap, map, withFilter, zip, and zipWith

---

[2] https://www.scala-lang.org/api/current/scala/concurrent/Future.html

An example of transform

As an example of the `transform` combinator, if you put these `import` statements into a Scala REPL session:

```
import scala.concurrent.Future
import scala.concurrent.ExecutionContext.Implicits.global
import scala.util.{Failure, Success}
```

and then paste in these lines of code:

```
val f1 = Future { Thread.sleep(500); 1 }
val rez = f1.transform (
    i => i * 42,
    e => new Exception("something bad happened: " + e)
)
rez.value
Thread.sleep(600)
rez.value
```

you'll see these results:

```
scala> val f1 = Future { Thread.sleep(500); 1 }
f1: scala.concurrent.Future[Int] = Future(<not completed>)

scala> val rez = f1.transform (
     |     i => i * 42,
     |     e => new Exception("something bad happened: " + e)
     | )
rez: scala.concurrent.Future[Int] = Future(<not completed>)

scala> rez.value
res0: Option[scala.util.Try[Int]] = None

scala> Thread.sleep(600)

scala> rez.value
res1: Option[scala.util.Try[Int]] = Some(Success(42))
```

Notice how `rez` is initially listed as `Future(<not completed>)`. After that, `rez.value` yields a None initially, but after you wait long enough for the future to complete, it eventually yields a Some(Success(42)).

> In code outside the REPL you should use callback methods like onComplete and transform, and not value. (value is a method that shows the current value of a Future.)

Key points about callback methods

Here are a few key points about Future's callback methods:

- Callback methods are called asynchronously when a future completes.
- A callback method is executed by some thread, some time after the future is completed.
- onComplete takes a callback function of type Try[T] => Unit. As usual, the Unit return type is a great hint that it only lets you handle the result as a side effect.
- The order in which callbacks are executed is not guaranteed.
- From the "Futures and Promises" page, "onComplete, onSuccess, and onFailure have the result type Unit, so they can't be chained. This design was intentional, to avoid any suggestion that callbacks may be executed in a particular order."

If you struggle with the name ...

One more point about Scala futures: If you're struggling with the concept, it might be because of the name "future." In my case that name slowed me down for a while (and I was *used* to writing multi-threaded code). I kept having to ask myself, "Why are they using the name 'future'? What is that name trying to convey?"

One night I was reading the book Akka Concurrency[3] and I got so frustrated that I wrote 35 alternate names for Future in the margins of the book. I knew the name "thread" wasn't right, because that would be confusing with Java threads. I eventually decided that for me, the name "ConcurrentTask" made more sense than "Future."

Fortunately in Scala you can rename types when you import them, so in the following example I rename Future to ConcurrentTask so you can see what I'm talking about:

```
import scala.concurrent.{Future => ConcurrentTask}    //rename
```

---

[3] http://amzn.to/2xhUNd4

```
// start a long-running task
val task = ConcurrentTask {
    Cloud.executeLongRunningTask(a, b, c)
}

// whenever the task completes, execute this code
task.onComplete {
    case Success(value) => println(s"Success, value = $value")
    case Failure(e) => println(s"Failure: ${e.getMessage}")
}
```

Even as I look at this code four years after I wrote in the margin of that book, the name ConcurrentTask is still easier for my brain to understand than Future. So, if you're struggling with the concept, it may just be the name.

About the name ConcurrentTask

If you're wondering how I came up with the name ConcurrentTask, I found it in the scala-lang.org "Futures and Promises" documentation[4]:

> "Composing *concurrent tasks* in this way tends to result in faster, asynchronous, non-blocking parallel code."

As that quote implies, other meaningful, alternate names for a future can be Asynchronous-Task or NonBlockingParallelTask.

A larger example

If you're interested in a larger, real-world example, the source code for this lesson includes a Swing/GUI application that uses futures and onComplete.

The main class of the application is named *FutureBoard*. The intent of the application is to work a little like a text-only version of Flipboard[5] or an RSS reader. When you go to the File menu and click the Update menu item, the application uses three futures as part of the process of reaching out onto the internet to get content from the Chicago Tribune, the Denver Post, and Scala-related tweets from Twitter. Those three news sources are contacted in parallel

---

[4] http://docs.scala-lang.org/overviews/core/futures.html
[5] https://flipboard.com/

using futures, and the windows in the GUI are updated "whenever."

Until all of those websites change their URLs and/or CSS, the application looks like Figure 117.1.

As usual, I encourage you to work with that code and make it your own to learn more about futures.

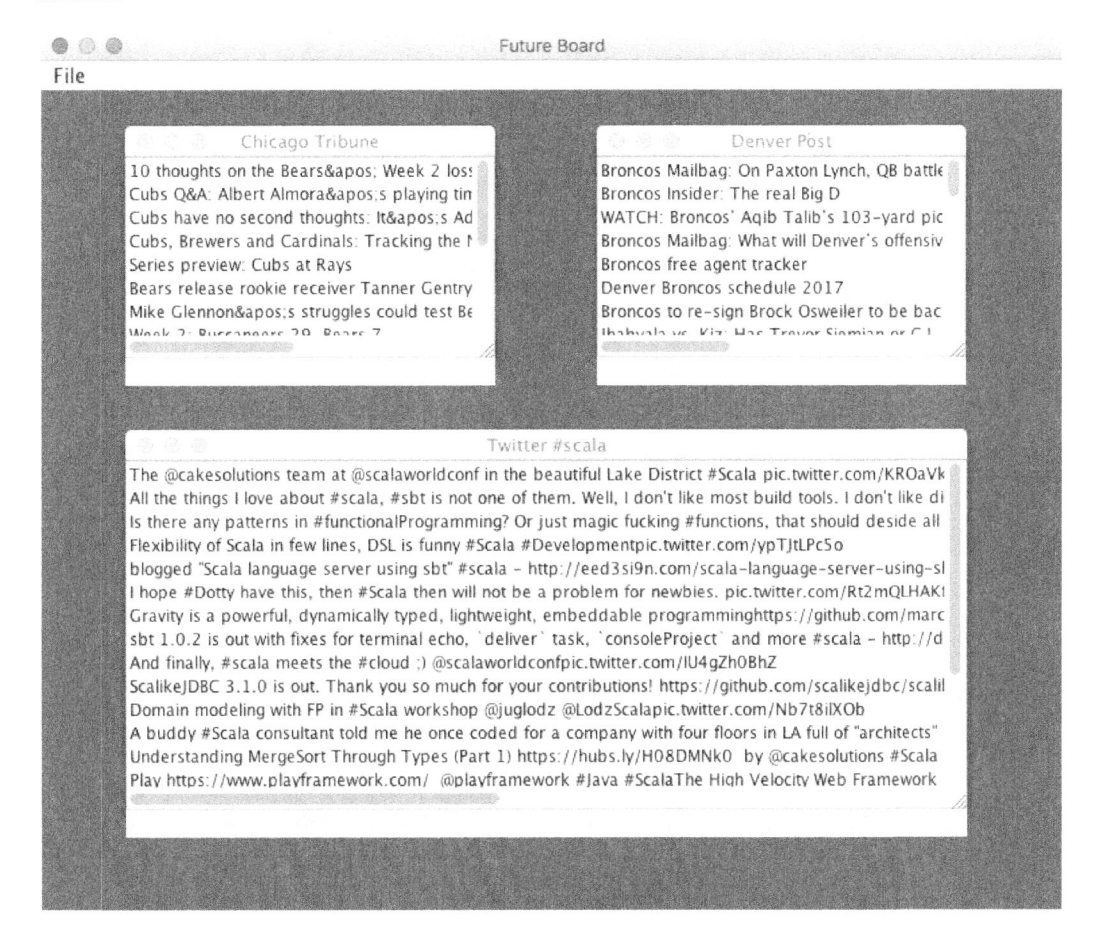

Figure 117.1: What the FutureBoard application looks like after it gets data from its three internet resources.

118

Key Points About Scala Futures

To summarize the last two lessons, here are some key points about working with futures.

First, a few points about Scala futures as they relate to functional programming:

- `Future` implements `map` and `flatMap`, so it works as a monad.
- As Debashish Ghosh wrote in *Functional and Reactive Domain Modeling*[1], "Just as `Try` manages *exceptions* using effects, another abstraction in the Scala library called `Future` helps you manage *latency* as an effect."
- When you need to start several futures and combine their results into one value, merge the results in a `for` expression.
- `Future` has a nice collection of callback methods, and I demonstrated the `map`, `onComplete`, and `transform` methods.
- The value in a future is always an instance of `Try`, so you always work with `Success` and `Failure` when handling a future's result.

Other future keys:

- I think of a future as a one-shot, "handle this relatively slow and potentially long-running computation, and call me back with a result when you're done" construct.
- Personally, I find the name `ConcurrentTask` more meaningful than `Future`.
- A future represents the result of an asynchronous computation, and has a return type of `Future[A]`, which was `Future[Int]` in my examples.
- Futures are started immediately. (Unlike the Java `Thread` class, there is no `run` method to call.)
- The examples show that the main JVM thread flies right through the `for` and `onComplete` expressions. They aren't executed until the future(s) return.
- In the examples I showed, `yield` in the `for` expression is executed when all of the futures complete, and `onComplete` is executed immediately after that.
- You typically work with the results of a future using its callback methods, such as `onComplete` and `transform`.

---

[1] http://amzn.to/2iOT3Vh

- Callback methods are called asynchronously when a future completes.
- There's no guarantee that your future's callback method will be called on the same thread the future was run on.
- There's no guarantee about the order in which callback methods are executed.

Promises

Lastly, I didn't write about the Scala `Promise` class because it's rarely used directly. The book Learning Concurrent Programming in Scala[2] states:

> "A *promise* and a *future* represent two aspects of a single-assignment variable: the promise allows you to assign a value to the future object, whereas the future allows you to read that value."

and then later:

> "We would like to somehow create a bridge between legacy callback-based APIs and futures ... this is where promises come in handy ... Use promises to bridge the gap between callback-based APIs and futures."

See also

- Programming in Scala[3] has an excellent chapter about Scala Futures
- Akka Concurrency[4] is a little out of date now, but it's still an excellent resource about Akka actors and futures
- Learning Concurrent Programming in Scala[5] is an excellent resource about concurrent programming
- My post, A look at how exceptions work with Scala Futures and the onComplete 'Failure' case[6]
- The Future scaladoc[7]
- "Futures and Promises"[8] on scala-lang.org

---

[2] http://amzn.to/2fWn70c
[3] http://amzn.to/2fiqDBh
[4] http://amzn.to/2xhUNd4
[5] http://amzn.to/2ycv1X1
[6] https://alvinalexander.com/scala/how-exceptions-work-scala-futures-oncomplete-failure
[7] http://www.scala-lang.org/api/current/scala/concurrent/Future.html
[8] http://docs.scala-lang.org/overviews/core/futures.html

A Few Notes About Real World Functional Programming

> *"Everything in moderation, including moderation."*
>
> — Benjamin Franklin

At this point you're probably closer to being ready for "real world" functional programming than you think — all you really need now is experience — so in this chapter I want to discuss a few more functional programming topics.

How much do you use "pure" FP?

A great question is, "How often do you use *pure* FP?" To consider the answer, think about a common use of Facebook:

- To upload a new photo of a LOL cat, you type some text, upload the cat photo, and click "Post"

On the server side you can imagine that almost all of Facebook's code involves various types of I/O:

- The server side code receives a POST request with your data in it
- The text portion of your message is stored in a database
- The photo is stored on their filesystem (or possibly in a database)
- Those impure functions return `Try` types, and if all of the functions yield `Success`, the code returns some sort of "success" message back to the JavaScript client-side code

Almost the entire process involves network, database, and file I/O. The same is true when you comment on a friend's post, "like" a friend's post, add a new friend, etc.

If you think about how online stores like Amazon work, you'll find the same thing to be true: I/O dominates the server side of many web applications.

After I finish writing this book I hope to get back to a different type of application that I call "Radio Pi[1]." It's basically a TiVo/DVR time-shifting[2] application for listening to radio stations and podcasts on a Raspberry Pi, and even though I didn't write that initial code in a functional style, I've found the same thing to be true: the server-side application components are dominated by network, database, and file I/O. There are very few pure functions.

I've found that I use pure FP a little more in thick client applications. This is because I tend to maintain state longer inside the application before I commit any changes to I/O. For example, in a thick client version of a Pizza Store POS application I'd probably keep a customer's entire order in memory until the customer pays for the order, at which time I'd save it all to a database. In this regard I'd have intermediate states similar to order1, order2, etc., and as you can guess, when you see variable names like those that represent intermediate states, there's probably going to be a for expression.

> Conversely, with thick client applications you also end up writing a lot of non-FP GUI code, so (a) there's a high percentage of that type of code, and (b) in that code you need to conform to the APIs that frameworks like Swing, JavaFX, and Android require.

I could go on for a while, but the point of these statements is to show that a significant percentage of real world application code involves I/O, including GUI, database, file, and network I/O. My suggestion is what I've shown in this book: have those functions return Try or Option, and then write the rest of your code — the business logic and support libraries — using pure functions.

A monadic style

In all of this discussion, bear in mind that my definition of "pure functions" is, "Output depends *only* on input, and they have no side effects, including I/O." If you think of functions that return an IO type (or Try) as being pure because they return a monadic type, you may think of the percentage of FP code you write as being higher.

As an example of what I mean, imagine that these functions make calls to Twitter to get the latest tweets in each of these categories:

```
def getJavaTweets(): Try[Seq[Tweet]] = ???
def getScalaTweets(): Try[Seq[Tweet]] = ???
def getAlaskaTweets(): Try[Seq[Tweet]] = ???
```

---

[1] https://alvinalexander.com/alradio
[2] https://en.wikipedia.org/wiki/Time_shifting

By definition those are impure functions because they reach out into the outside world, but because they result in a `Try` type they can be used in a `for` expression like this:

```
val interestingTweets = for {
    scalaTweets  <- getScalaTweets()
    javaTweets   <- getJavaTweets()
    alaskaTweets <- getAlaskaTweets()
} yield (scalaTweets, javaTweets, alaskaTweets)
```

The point is that even though this code uses three impure functions, some people consider it to be a functional style. More accurately, I'd certainly say that it's a "monadic style" of programming: The functions return a monadic type, and when you code the `for` expression you only worry about the "happy case," and the unhappy case is handled as well.

> Note that those functions can also return a `Seq` or `Future` and still be used in the same way; they all work because they implement `map` and `flatMap`, and which type you use depends on whether you want access to possible exception information, or not. Just be consistent with the types you use, and they'll all work together in your `for` expressions.

Performance

I'm not an expert about performance in functional programming, so I'll just say a few things about it.

The first point goes like this: If you have a collection with a hundred million people in it, and you only need to change one person's last name, a simple test will show that the "Update as you copy" technique is going to take significantly longer and require a lot more memory than a mutable list. (However, if multiple threads can update that collection, you have to be careful to use synchronization, which can potentially lead you down that rabbit hole.)

Here's a quote from Programming in Scala[3] about this issue:

> "The main disadvantage of immutable objects is that they sometimes require that a large object graph be copied where otherwise an update could be done in place. In some cases this can be awkward to express and might also cause a performance bottleneck. As a result, it is not uncommon for libraries to provide

---
[3] http://amzn.to/2fiqDBh

mutable alternatives to immutable classes. For example, class StringBuilder is a mutable alternative to the immutable String."

The people at typelevel.org — the maintainers of the Cats library — also wrote about potential performance problems[4]:

> "Although unfortunately there are times when programming only with pure functions and writing efficient code in Scala can be at odds, we are attempting to do our best at keeping our library as efficient as we can without making unnecessary sacrifices of purity and usability. Where sacrifices have to be made, we will strive to make these obvious, and will keep them well documented."

Apache Spark

With those comments as background, whether or not performance is going to be a problem depends *a lot* on the complete context of the problem. When you use a framework like Apache Spark[5], "immutability with pure functions" is THE way you work. For example, a few years ago I wrote Spark code like this:

```
val uriCount =
    log.map(p.parseRecord(_).request)
        .filter(req => req != "")   // filter out records that won't parse
        .map(_.split(" ")(1))       // get the uri field
        .map(uri => (uri, 1))       // create a tuple for each record
        .reduceByKey((a, b) => a + b)  // reduce to: (URI, #occurrences)
        .collect                    // convert to Array[(String, Int)]
```

I used that code to read a dataset of one million Apache access log records[6] from one of my websites to get a list of (URI, NumberOfHits) results, which look like this:

```
(/styles/mobile1024.css,  80603)
(/styles/mobile480.css,   80582)
(/styles/mobile768.css,   80375)
(/images/icons/home.png,  79147)
(/images/icons/gear.png,  78993)
```

---

[4] https://typelevel.org/cats/motivations
[5] http://spark.apache.org/
[6] https://alvinalexander.com/scala/analyzing-apache-access-logs-files-spark-scala-part-2

The `log` variable in that example is a list that contains the Apache access log records, and as you can see, I use a series of collections methods — which all act as pure functions — to get the desired result. You can imagine that the process works like this:

- The first `map` call receives 1M records
- One at a time, it transforms each record and passes 1M new records to the first `filter` call
- Whatever records remain are then passed to the next `map` method, etc.

There's a lot of data transforming and copying going on in that process, but Spark works well by spreading the computations across multiple servers.

In summary, when it comes to performance, "context" is everything. I recommend staying with immutable data structures until you know that performance is a problem.

Your style may vary

Just as with other programming paradigms, programming styles in FP vary. For example, even outside of this book I tend to write somewhat verbose code because (a) I think it's easier to read, and (b) I have to maintain it. Some other people write extremely terse code that I find harder to read, but in general, I don't think either approach is wrong.

As an example, I once wrote a Scala shell script that started like this:

```
if (args.length != 2) {
    Console.err.println("Usage: replacer <search> <replace>")
    System.exit(1)
}

val searchPattern = args(0)
val replacePattern = args(1)

// more code here ...
```

In Scala shell scripts, `args` is the name of the variable that holds the arguments to the script, and this was my approach to access them. Until the final output of the script, the rest of the code used pure functions and immutable variables.

One experienced functional programmer commented on my code and wrote that I could begin my script like this instead:

```
val result = args.map { x => ...
```

I don't remember the exact problem I was working on, but using map like this made sense. He then proceeded to put the rest of my code *inside* that map method call as an anonymous function. In the end I don't think either style is wrong; they're just different.

Pure functions with mutable variables inside

Before I write this section, I feel like I need to restate this:

> If you really want to succeed in functional programming, you need to develop a strong desire to see *all* of your code as algebra.

And now, to contradict that statement ... yes, it is possible to write pure functions that use *mutable* variables internally. For instance, if you don't like recursion, you can write code like this:

```
def sum(xs: Seq[Int]): Int = {
    var sum = 0     //OMG, it's a var
    for (x <- xs) sum += x
    sum
}
```

Other FP developers might not be too happy with you, but yes, that's a pure function.

Along this same line of thinking, Erlang[7] is classified as a functional programming language, and in his book, Programming Erlang[8], Joe Armstrong writes, "In Erlang *it's OK to mutate state within an individual process* but not for one process to tinker with the state of another process." (Remember that an Erlang *process* is similar to an Akka *actor*.)

I generally encourage you to use recursion because (a) it's the algebraic way to solve problems like these, (b) you'll want to be comfortable with it when you really need it, and (c) once you break one rule, it becomes easier to break other rules, which will eventually defeat the entire purpose of writing FP code. (Remember the "broken windows" story in The Pragmatic Programmer[9].)

---

[7] https://en.wikipedia.org/wiki/Erlang_(programming_language)
[8] http://amzn.to/2aab4HF
[9] http://amzn.to/2gX483a

As a word of caution about this slippery slope, famed programmer Erik Meijer[10] wrote an article titled, "The Curse of the Excluded Middle," which has the subtitle, " 'Mostly functional' programming does not work." As you can imagine from that subtitle, he writes "mostly functional" code doesn't work any better than "mostly secure" code; that you only get the full benefits of FP by writing *pure* FP code.

---

[10] https://en.wikipedia.org/wiki/Erik_Meijer_(computer_scientist)

120
Signpost: Wrapping Things Up

In this final section of the book, I provide several chapters as a means to wrap up everything I covered in the previous lessons. As I found out when I began writing this section and reviewing the previous chapters, we've come a long way since the beginning of the book.

121

The Learning Path

> *"Unless you try to do something beyond what you have already mastered, you will never grow."*
>
> — Ronald E. Osborn

With the exception of my "programming rules" — which I only understood *after* I learned Haskell — the way I explained functional programming in this book is similar to the way I learned it myself. The learning path went like this:

When I first saw some complex Scala/FP code, I formalized my "Question Everything" philosophy. I decided not to accept FP as a better way of programming unless I could prove it to myself.

Having done that, and having seen people write things like, "A functional language must be lazy," I dug into what "functional programming" really meant. Based on at least ten different resources, I formalized my own definition of FP.

Although pure functions are a simple topic — output must depend *only* on input, and there must be no side effects — I dug into the ramifications of this way of programming.

When I learned that writing pure functions is like writing algebraic expressions, I decided to no longer use mutable variables (because algebra doesn't use mutable variables).

Using only immutable variables naturally led me to write recursive functions. In this new world, I found that recursion is the only way to "loop over this collection to calculate some new value" (other than using built-in Scala collections' methods).

Because pure algebraic functions don't result in `null` values or exceptions, I dug into *functional error handling*, and learned that functions like these should return `Option` and `Try`.

Because combinations of pure functions that return `Option` and `Try` can lead to nested types like `Option[Option[A]]`, I demonstrated how `flatMap` solves this problem.

Because `flatMap` is hard for humans to read, I showed how `for` expressions are a human-friendly replacement for `flatMap`.

At this point I thought I was ready to write complete Scala/FP applications, but then I learned that I still needed to understand how to handle concepts like state and I/O.

State and I/O are handled in FP with the State and IO monads, so I spent a lot of time detailing the problems that lead to the need for monads. During that process I dug deeply into `for` expressions and writing `map` and `flatMap` methods in "wrapper" classes. I then explained that the wrapper classes I created are really monads.

After creating them, I showed how to use the State and IO monads separately, and then showed how this leads to a problem where you can't use them together in `for` expressions. Next, I showed that the solution for this problem is to use monad transformers like StateT.

To help you get ready for using Scala/FP in the real world, I then showed several different techniques you can use to create your domain models, including the "modular" and "functional objects" approaches.

To keep getting you ready for the real world, I demonstrated ScalaCheck[1], type classes (which are used extensively by the Cats library[2]), and lenses. I also demonstrated two main tools for concurrency in Scala: the Akka actors library[3] and Scala futures.

Lastly, I added appendix lessons to the electronic versions of the book to explain several other important concepts, including more details on the `val` function syntax and Scala function signatures; the differences between `val` functions and `def` methods; and how to use collections methods like "fold" and "reduce" in place of writing custom recursion functions. I also demonstrated that Algebraic Data Types are mainly a way of categorizing code that you're already written, as opposed to way of thinking about code that you're going to write.

> Those appendices are not included in the print version of the book, but you can find links to them online at alvinalexander.com/fpbook[4].

In the end, I hope that all of these lessons helped to meet the goals I set out at the beginning of this book.

---

[1] https://www.scalacheck.org/
[2] https://typelevel.org/cats/
[3] https://akka.io/
[4] https://alvinalexander.com/fpbook

Final Summary

> *"Once you're used to programming with pure values and relying on equational reasoning to understand and manipulate programs, it's hard to go back to the side-effecty world where things are much harder to understand."*
>
> Rob Norris (tpolecat), in this Reddit post[a]

---

[a] https://www.reddit.com/r/scala/comments/3zofjl/why_is_future_totally_unusable/

My way to judge the success of this book is to see whether or not it met the goals I established at the beginning of the book. Back then I created two sets of goals, (a) soft goals and (b) concrete goals, and in this lesson I'll provide a review of those goals.

Soft goals

Back in the beginning I wrote that the "soft goals" for this book are:

1. To introduce functional programming in Scala in a simple, thorough way
2. To present the solutions in a systematic way
3. To discuss the motivation and benefits of FP features
4. To share several small-but-complete Scala/FP applications to show how they're organized
5. To save you the time and effort of having to learn another programming language in order to understand Scala/FP
6. In general, to help you "Think in FP"

As a review of those goals, in regards to #1 and #2 I can state that I took the time to explain the main concepts that are needed to understand Scala/FP in both a thorough and systematic way. I presented the concepts in the order in which I learned them, and as a result of taking my time to explain everything in detail, the book is over 1,000 pages long. I can't speak for everyone, but I think this book would have been helpful to the imperative/OOP version of myself back in 2010-2011.

In regards to the motivation and benefits of FP features, I took several lessons to write about the benefits of pure functions and functional programming. I also included "Motivation" sections in several lessons where the motivation might not be immediately obvious, and I also highlighted "Key points" in more than twenty lessons. I always feel like I can do better, but this is a start.

The one part where this book falls a little short of what I wanted to achieve is that I wasn't able to include as many "small but complete" applications as I wanted to include. The book does include early versions of the Coin Flip game, a portion of a Pizza Store application, and the FutureBoard application, but I hoped to include more.

> To help rectify this situation, as I note in the next chapter, I'll make new Scala/FP example projects available at alvinalexander.com/fpbook[1].

In regards to the goal of "saving you the time and effort of having to learn another programming language to understand FP in Scala," I can't be the complete judge of that. What I can tell you is that I covered the main FP topics you'll see with Scala/FP libraries like Cats and Scalaz, including functors, monads, type classes, and domain modeling. I'm confident that the resources I share in the next chapter will be much easier to understand once you've read this book.

Another soft goal of this book is that I want to help you "Think in FP." This means several things:

- Because of their simplicity and easy testability, you should have a strong desire to write only pure functions.
- When you write only pure functions — where output depends only on input, and there are no side effects — you can combine them to create complete solutions, just like you create Linux command pipelines[2] to solve problems.
- Most importantly, you must develop an intense desire to see your code as being like algebra. Each function must be an algebraic expression, and each solution should be a combination of alebraic expressions.
- When you think this way it leads to other ways of "Thinking in FP":
    - Of course you'll only use immutable variables; that's the only type of variable that's used in algebra.

---

[1] https://alvinalexander.com/fpbook
[2] https://alvinalexander.com/blog/post/linux-unix/linux-unix-command-mashups

- Using only immutable variables means that you'll use recursion and built-in Scala collections methods rather than using mutable variables and `for`-loops.
- Pure algebraic functions don't throw exceptions, so your functions result in `Option` and `Try` rather than `null` values and potential exceptions.
- Because you don't use mutable variables — and because you don't want to create temporary, intermediate variables like `pizza1`, `pizza2`, etc. — you use monads in `for` expressions as a way to combine your algebraic expressions.

As a final note about "Thinking in FP," I remember that someone once said, "I'm not smart enough to write OOP methods where I have to keep a large amount of external state in my brain, but I know I can write a pure function." The thought that I can always write a pure function was a big influence on my decision to investigate FP, despite the apparent complexity of monads.

Concrete goals

Back in the beginning I wrote that the concrete goals for the book are:

1. If you have a hard time understanding the book, Functional Programming in Scala[3] ("the red book"), I want to provide the background material that can help make that book easier to understand.
2. To make all of the text and code for the Introduction to Functional Game Programming[4] talk at the 2014 LambdaConf understandable.
3. To make the Cats[5] and Scalaz[6] Scala/FP libraries more understandable. I want you to understand enough Scala/FP concepts so that you can further understand what those libraries are trying to achieve.
4. Provide you with all of the background knowledge you need — anonymous functions, type signatures, `for` expressions, classes that implement `map` and `flatMap`, etc. — so you can better understand the 128,000 *monad* tutorials that Google currently lists in their search results[7].

In regards to the first goal, *Functional Programming in Scala* is a very good book, but as I've mentioned, it covers topics quickly and is therefore a densely-packed book. By taking the time to deeply explore topics like higher-order functions, recursion, `Option` and `Try`, functional

---

[3] http://amzn.to/2sbY1hE
[4] https://github.com/jdegoes/lambdaconf-2014-introgame
[5] https://github.com/typelevel/cats
[6] https://github.com/scalaz/scalaz
[7] https://www.google.com/search?q=monad+tutorial&ie=utf-8&oe=utf-8

state, the IO monad, and more, I hope that this book provides a lot of background to make that book easier to read. (If you look at the table of contents for that book, I think you'll see what I mean.)

I believe I made everything in John De Goes' "Introduction to Functional Game Programming" Github project easier to understand because I modified and shared almost all of the source code from that project in this book's lessons. As a result, if you understand the lessons here, you should be able to understand everything in that project.

> On a personal note, being at that conference was a big influence for me. When I had a hard time understanding some of the concepts in that presentation, I started down a path that eventually led to the creation of this book.

In regards to the Cats/Scalaz goal, because I took so much time explaining how Scala/FP code works under the covers, I didn't spend as much time as I hoped to demonstrate how to use specific elements of the Cats and Scalaz libraries. I did demonstrate *type classes*, which are a major part of understanding the Cats library. I also believe that all of the Cats and Scalaz documentation will make much more sense now that you've read this book. But as a way of coming closer to this goal, I plan to release new Scala/FP tutorials and example projects at alvinalexander.com/fpbook[8], and I'll use Cats and Scalaz in these projects.

Regarding the fourth goal, if you understand the lessons in this book you should have no problem understanding the 128,000+ monad tutorials on the internet. As I demonstrated, a monad in Scala is simply a class that implements `map` and `flatMap`, and also has some sort of "lift" function to lift ordinary values into the monad wrapper. In Scala you create and use classes with these attributes so you can execute a series of function calls in sequence in `for` expressions.

> In Haskell, the use of monads is similar, but slightly different. Because *all* functions are lazily-evaluated in Haskell — meaning that the compiler can optimize your code however it wants to — monads are *really* needed to make sure function calls happen in the desired order. This is especially important if you want to make sure that you prompt a user for input before trying to read their input — something you don't have to worry about in Scala.

---

[8] https://alvinalexander.com/fpbook

What's next

Having provided a summary of the learning path this book provided and an examination of the book's goals, the next chapter provides links to the best Scala/FP learning resources I know.

Where To Go From Here

"Functional programming finds its roots in mathematics — the pursuit of purity and completeness. We functional programmers look to formalize system behaviors in an algebraic and total manner."

A quote from Tim Perrett, Head of Infrastructure Engineering, Verizon

We've come a long way in this book. Way back in the beginning I provided definitions of functional programming and pure functions, and over time I kept adding on more pieces of knowledge until I showed how to use monads and monad transformers to sequence operations, and then I added even more.

As I mentioned early on, one of the goals for this book is to make it easier for you to understand other good FP resources. Therefore, as a way of serving as a launching point for more knowledge, I'll list the best resources I know in the sections that follow.

Scala/FP books

Functional Programming in Scala[1] — "the red book" — is a terrific Scala/FP resource. My only problem with it is that it's a thin, thickly-packed ("dense") book, and as a result, if you don't know some things about Scala or FP, it can be hard to keep with. (Which is one reason I wrote this book.)

If you already know the FP concepts in this book, Functional and Reactive Domain Modeling[2] is another good, densely-packed resource that shares examples from building a real-world business application.

---

[1] http://amzn.to/2sbY1hE
[2] http://amzn.to/2iOT3Vh

There are two main libraries that support FP in Scala, Cats[3] and scalaz[4]. The people at underscore.io have created a good eBook that can help you get started with Cats, titled, Advanced Scala with Cats[5]. (You can pay what you want for the book at that URL.) They also offer several other eBooks at this URL[6].

Functional programming (in general)

These functional programming resources were helpful in developing this book:

- A Practical Introduction to Functional Programming[7] by Mary Rose Cook (code is in Python) was helpful to me early on, and has a few good examples.

- Functional Programming For The Rest of Us[8] was written in 2006 by Slava Akhmechet, but it's still a good resource.

- For a deep dive into FP, search for two PDFs titled "Why Functional Programming Matters." One is the original paper by John Hughes, and the second is a summary of that paper, written by Roger Costello. Amongst other things, the summary paper discusses how modularity leads to more "glue" code.

- If you're interested in the history of Haskell (and FP), search for a PDF titled, "A History of Haskell: Being Lazy with Class."

Functional programming in Scala

These are the best Scala/FP resources I currently know:

- Advanced Scala with Cats[9] is currently the best documentation on using the Cats library

- I was going to include an FP Glossary with this book, but the Scala Glossary on scala-lang.org[10] is a great resource

- Effective Scala[11] by Marius Eriksen of Twitter is a great resource about Scala in general

---

[3] https://typelevel.org/cats/
[4] https://github.com/scalaz/scalaz
[5] https://underscore.io/books/advanced-scala/
[6] https://gumroad.com/underscore#
[7] https://maryrosecook.com/blog/post/a-practical-introduction-to-functional-programming
[8] http://www.defmacro.org/2006/06/19/fp.html
[9] https://underscore.io/books/advanced-scala/
[10] https://docs.scala-lang.org/glossary/
[11] http://twitter.github.io/effectivescala/

- Eugene Yokota's Learning Scalaz[12] is a good learning resource for the Scalaz library
- The Introduction to Functional Game Programming[13] Github repository from the 2014 Lambda Conference
- Daniel Westheide has a good article on type classes in Scala[14], and a nice series about Scala in general
- Chris Taylor's The Algebra of Algebraic Data Types[15] is a great resource on ADTs
- Martin Snyder's video, Monadic Logging and You[16], is a helpful resource about the Writer monad
- Derek Wyatt's post, Here's (one of the reasons) Why Scala is Awesome[17] includes an interesting use of a for expression
- Tim Perrett's Understanding the State Monad[18] shows a "traffic light" example of how to use an older version of the Scalaz State monad
- Darren Wilkinson's First Steps with Monads in Scala[19] explains monads well
- An IO Monad for Cats[20] was written May 2, 2017, and is a good resource on that topic

Math resources

I began this chapter with this quote from Tim Perrett: "Functional programming finds its roots in mathematics — the pursuit of purity and completeness. We functional programmers look to formalize system behaviors in an algebraic and total manner." As that quote implies, if you want to excel in functional programming, you're going to want to learn more about mathematics. I recommend starting with these resources:

- Category theory on Wikipedia[21]
- Functional programming on Wikipedia[22]
- Lambda calculus on Wikipedia[23]
- Mathematical functions on Wikipedia[24]

---

[12] http://eed3si9n.com/learning-scalaz/index.html
[13] https://github.com/jdegoes/lambdaconf-2014-introgame
[14] http://danielwestheide.com/blog/2013/02/06/the-neophytes-guide-to-scala-part-12-type-classes.html
[15] http://chris-taylor.github.io/blog/2013/02/10/the-algebra-of-algebraic-data-types/
[16] https://www.youtube.com/watch?v=t-YX55ZF4g0
[17] http://derekwyatt.org/2011/09/01/heres-one-of-the-reasons-why-monads-are-awesome/
[18] http://timperrett.com/2013/11/25/understanding-state-monad/
[19] https://darrenjw.wordpress.com/2016/04/15/first-steps-with-monads-in-scala/
[20] https://typelevel.org/blog/2017/05/02/io-monad-for-cats.html
[21] https://en.wikipedia.org/wiki/Category_theory
[22] https://en.wikipedia.org/wiki/Functional_programming
[23] https://en.wikipedia.org/wiki/Lambda_calculus
[24] https://en.wikipedia.org/wiki/Function_(mathematics)

- Mathematical logic on Wikipedia[25] (which consists roughly of set theory, model theory, recursion theory, and proof theory)
- I haven't watched them all, but the Catsters videos on YouTube[26] are recommended

At the time of this writing I don't have any favorite books on these subjects, so I recommend starting with those resources and see where they lead you.

Let me share two motivating points here. First, the more you learn about mathematics, the easier and more logical functional programming will be. Second, algorithms like Google's PageRank and other fields like artificial intelligence have their foundations in mathematics. Investing in learning more math is an investment in your future.

>Google has made billions (trillions?) of dollars, all starting with the PageRank algorithm. That algorithm is based on something known as an Eigenvector, which is described well in a PDF titled, The 25-billion dollar Eigenvector[27].

Resources about functors and monads

You'll learn more about functors and monads if you follow those math resources, and in the writing of this book I also found the following non-Scala resources to be helpful in understanding those topics:

- If you don't mind that the source code examples are in Haskell, adit.io has a good, visual article titled, Functors, Applicatives, And Monads In Pictures[28]
- An article titled Understanding Monads[29] had two quotes that I like:
  - "Use the monad abstraction when you need a 'customized sequencing' for operations."
  - "One gentleman once cleverly described monads as something that lets you 'overload semi-colon'" (i.e., the semi-colons that are used in C and Java).

Haskell books

If you're interested in learning about Haskell (now that you've had a thorough introduction to FP), these are the two best Haskell books I know:

---

[25] https://en.wikipedia.org/wiki/Mathematical_logic
[26] https://www.youtube.com/user/TheCatsters
[27] http://www.math.pitt.edu/~annav/1185/google.pdf
[28] http://adit.io/posts/2013-04-17-functors,_applicatives,_and_monads_in_pictures.html
[29] http://missingfaktor.blogspot.com/2013/10/understanding-monads.html

- Learn You a Haskell for Great Good![30]
- Real World Haskell[31]

Video presentations

When they're available, you may want to sign up for the Coursera courses offered by EPFL, including "Functional Programming Principles in Scala" and "Functional Program Design in Scala." You can find more information about those online courses at this URL:

- coursera.org/specializations/scala[32]

Eric Torreborre was a helpful reviewer on the Scala Cookbook[33], and his YouTube video, The Eff monad, one monad to rule them all[34], shows an alternative to monad transformers.

Updates to this book

While this is the end of this book, I plan to create new Scala/FP tutorials and new Scala/FP example projects. As those become available I'll update the following web page, which will be my main, ongoing Scala/FP resource page:

- alvinalexander.com/fpbook[35]

Thank you for reading this book. I hope it's been helpful.

---

[30] http://amzn.to/1POaUCv
[31] http://amzn.to/1TX9olw
[32] https://www.coursera.org/specializations/scala
[33] http://amzn.to/24ivK4G
[34] https://www.youtube.com/watch?v=KGJLeHhsZBo&t=192s
[35] https://alvinalexander.com/fpbook

Index

??? syntax, 24

actor model, 655
actors
    delegate, 656
    differences from futures, 649
ActorSystem, 661
Akka, 206
    and functional programming, 657
    benefits, 654, 656
    EchoActor, 663
    hello, world, 659
    key points, 666
Akka actors library, 653
Akka background
    Erlang, 654
Alan Turing, 41
algebra, 33, 107
    definition, 109
    reason for "Going FP", 108
algorithm, 258
Alonzo Church, 39, 41
always ask why, 17, 567
Amazon Echo, 665
anonymous class, 378
anonymous function, 519
Apache Spark, 694

best idea wins, 18
biasing, 370
BigDecimal, 576
bind, 421
    algorithm, 423
    function signature, 422
    in wrapper class, 429
    observations, 425
    wanting in for, 427
binding functions together, 417
black holes and miracles, 135

book
    audience, 5
    concrete goals, 13, 705
    goals, 9, 12, 703
box metaphor, 414
by-name parameter, 379
by-name parameters, 185
    background, 186
    with multiple parameter groups, 200
by-value parameters, 185

case class, 301, 445
    copy method, 303
    unapply method, 303
Cats, 13
    IO monad, 495
Clojure
    concurrency, 51
closure, 433
Coin Flip game, 287
companion object, 588
composed form, 504
composition, function, 503
concurrency
    and mutability, 641
    best tool for job, 650
    quotes from experts, 644
    Scala tools, 649
conservation of data, 135
control structures
    whilst, 200
    writing your own, 199
critical thinking, 20
curly braces, 377
    keys to remember, 386
curried functions
    creating, 216
Currying, 211
currying

vs partially-applied functions, 220

data flow diagrams, 133
DBIOAction, 632
Debuggable class, 448
    completed, 455
    details, 459
    flatMap, 460
    generic version, 471
    log messages with List, 475
    map, 460
debugging is easier, 46
deterministic algorithms, 53
disclaimer, 15
DogTailServices, 594
domain, 571
domain model, 572
domain modeling
    case classes, 581
    data, 581
    Functional Objects, 617, 621
    OOP, 573
    rich domain model, 583
    skinny domain objects, 583
Domain-Driven Design, 579

Either, Left, and Right, 365
ENIAC, 39
enumerations, 575
Erlang, 22
error handling, 361, 363
error handling, recommendation, 368
Eta-expansion, 154
exceptions
    use Option instead, 358
Expression-Oriented Programming, 119

FIP, function input parameter, 162
flatMap, 391
    background, 346
    Debuggable details, 465
    details, 452
    for expression is easier, 401
    for is easier to read, 394
    in for, 447
    in Wrapper class, 434
    type signature, 392
    with multiple Options, 409
    with Option and map, 400
    writing flatMap method, 347
flatten, 349
for
    translated to map and flatMap, 450
for expression
    filters, 319
    generators, 318
    history, 317
    translated to map, flatMap, 461
    translation rules, 355
for expressions
    easier than flatMap, 410
    review, 315
    Sequence class, 325
    writing a class that works in, 323
FP code
    concise, readable, 49
FP Terminology Barrier, 10
function composition, 357, 503
    Wikipedia, 506
function input parameter, 381
function literal, 139
function signatures, 168
functional error handling, 361, 363
functional error handling, summary, 371
Functional Objects, 617
    example, 621
functional programming, 81
    benefits, 43, 57
    definition, 29, 32
    disadvantages, 59
    like Unix pipelines, 129
    math terminology, 60
    performance, 693
    thought process, 132
functional programming as algebra, 107
functions
    passing around, 144

INDEX

functions are variables, 137
Functor, 77
functor, 415
    thing that can be mapped over, 415
Future, 206
future
    as a monad, 669
    promises, 690
futures, 669
    transform example, 683
    callback methods, 683
    example application, 671
    examples with debug output, 677
    FutureBoard example, 686
    key points, 682, 689
    onComplete, 674
    REPL example, 670

getOrElse, 399, 405
    don't use, 405
getStackTrace, 273
GolfState, 510, 518
    manual states, 511

happy case, 359, 407
happy path, 403
Haskell, 3
headless mode, 596
Higher Order Functions, 161
higher-order function, 31
HOFs
    common control patterns, 164
    designing, 175
hybrid design, 617

I/O
    the problem with FP, 495
I/O functions, 556
I/O wrapper code, 98
idempotent, 92
idiom
    definition, 373
immutable variables
    benefits, 36

    parallel programming, 35
implicit execution context, 206
implicit variable
    multiple parameter groups, 204
impure functions
    signs, 85
interface, 603
IO monad, 495, 501, 629
    and exceptions, 501
    doesn't make a function pure, 485
    doesn't make a function pure, 64
    execute later, 491
    hello, world, 497
    how to use, 487
    in for expression, 493
    philosophy, 497
    professional version, 495
    trying to use with Try, 630
IO monad's trick, 496
IO monad, reality, 629
IOMonad, 541

javap -c, 19
Joe Armstrong, 22
John De Goes, 525, 529
JVM
    stack, 262
    stack frame, 264

koan, 21

lambda, 39
lambda calculus, 39, 40
lambda means anonymous function, 40
lambda symbol, 39
LambdaConf, 13
lazy, 607
Learning Cliff, 10
lens, 635
lifting a value into a wrapper, 443
linked list
    cons cells, 230
Linus Torvalds, 569
list

head, 230
tail, 230
lists
    end with Nil, 241
    visualizing, 229
    ways to create, 233

map, 76
    in for, 447
    in Wrapper class, 430
    type signature, 391
    writing a map function, 179
Martin Odersky, 275
Mary Rose Cook, 32
memoization, 94
method
    convert to function manually, 155
methods
    using like functions, 151
MockPizzaDao, 604, 622
modular programming, 599
    benefits, 613
    disadvantages, 614
module, 591
modules
    programming with, 593
monad, 414
    as a description, 496
    effect, 496
    first monad, 443
    just a wrapper, 490
Monad interface, 540
Monad trait, 539
monad transformer, 533, 535
monadic lifting, 555
monadic style, 692
monads
    action, 499
    action, effect, 496
    can't use together, 529
    effect, 499
    key points, 481
    Writer, 478

Money, 576
Mount Monad, 557
multiple parameter groups, 197

null
    returning from a function, 369
Null Object Pattern, 369

OOP function signatures, 101
Option
    and flatmap, 397
    as a wrapper, 407
    instead of exception, 358
    map method, 408
Option, flatMap, and for, 407
Option, Some, and None, 363
Option, weakness of, 364
OptionMonad, 541
Options, adding multiple, 398
Or, from Scalactic, 367
OrderServiceInterface, 606

parallel collections, 650
parallel programming, 50
parallel vs concurrent, 53
partially-applied function, 212
    example, 213
partially-applied functions
    and the JVM, 218
performance problems, 64
Pizza, 622
PizzaServiceInterface, 602
pop function, 512
promises, 690
proofs, 45
pseudocode, 289
Pure FP, 691
pure function
    definition, 30, 36, 82
    mantra, 82
    signatures, 102
pure function game
    what can this function do?, 102
pure function signatures, 50

INDEX

pure function signatures tell all, 105
pure functions, 44, 357
    and I/O, 97
    benefits, 89
    examples, 83
    never throw exceptions, 357
    return Option, 407
    with mutable variables, 696
pure functions and I/O, 63

question everything, 17
Quicklens, 636

reassignable properties, 386
recursion, 61
    accumulator, 277
    case statements, 237
    conversation, 253
    how unwinding works, 242
    stack and stack frames, 265
    sum function, 235
    thought process, 255
    unwinding, 241, 272
    visualizing, 245
recursion is a by-product, 31
recursion, tail, 275
referential transparency, 92
reify, 607
reifying, 607
reporter metaphor, 15
Richard Feynman, 18, 629
rules for programming, 23

SARAH, 657
Scala/FP, 2
    function signatures, 55
Scala/FP disadvantages
    no standard FP library, 67
Scala/FP idioms, 373
Scalactic, Or, 367
Scalaz, 13
Sequence class, 325
    multiple generators in a for loop, 346
    withFilter, 341

    working as a for loop filter, 339
    working as a for loop generator, 335
    working in a for loop, 331
services, 597
side effects, 33
Slick, 612
stack, 269
state, 283
    GameState, 284
State and IO
    flatMap, 532
    using together, 531
State monad, 515, 517, 523
    like pushing onto a List, 512
    source code, 523
State monad transformer, 533
statements vs expressions, 120
StateT
    add function, 546
    final for expression, 563
    flatMap signature, 543
    multiply function, 546
    simple for expression, 545
    summary, 567
StateT and IO, 551
StateT constructor, 543
Swing
    invokeLater, 191

tail recursion, 275
Terminology Barrier, 75
testing is easier, 45
timer function, 188
transform as you copy, 114
Try
    with match expression, 365
Try, Success, and Failure, 364
type alias, 576
type signatures, 169

unhappy case, 359, 408
unhappy path, 404
Unix pipelines, 124
update as you copy, 61

nested objects, 308
update as you copy, don't mutate, 305
updates to this book, 713
using control structure, 386
utilities class, 585

val function syntax, 140, 174

Walter Isaacson, 11
Wrapper
   apply method, 440
Wrapper class, 429
   making generic, 437
Writer monad, 478

Printed in Great Britain
by Amazon